MATCH
of the MILLENNIUM

MATCH
of the MILLENNIUM

The Saints' 100 Most Memorable Matches

Edited by DAVID BULL and BOB BRUNSKELL

in association with
SOUTHAMPTON FOOTBALL CLUB

&

Southern Daily Echo

Dedicated not only to our many football friends
but to the enemies we have made
by neither including their most memorable games
nor asking them to write about them

First Printed   November   2000
Second Printing   December   2000
Third Printing   November   2001
Fourth Printing   April   2003
Fifth Printing   April   2004

HAGIOLOGY PUBLISHING
170 Westbury Road
Bristol BS9 3AH

ISBN 0-9534474-1-3

Designed and typeset by Perry Associates, Bristol
Printed and bound in Great Britain by The Bath Press

CONTENTS

The front cover illustrates a few of Saints' most memorable moments –

The 'S' side of the late 1940s that just missed out, from Rio to Chesterfield (Matches 36-39)
Terry Paine scoring the 1966 promotion goal at Brisbane Road (Match No. 59)
Ron Davies in one of his four-goal assaults (No. 62)
Mike Channon with the Cup (No. 69)
Matthew Le Tissier bending a Great Escape free-kick in 1994 (No. 94)

The caricature of Ted Bates was kindly drawn by Ron Davies and presented to David Bull, originally for use in *Dell Diamond*. We are grateful to those acknowledged in specific match reports for permission to reproduce other illustrations.

FOREWORD

by Ted Bates

Being in my 64th season with the Saints, I am able to look at the reports that follow, starting at Match No. 30 and going through to No. 100 and say to myself "I played in that one, scored in that one, managed the team that night," – and so on, right through to sitting in the Directors' Box in August 2000, watching the comeback against Liverpool which set everybody asking about previous comebacks, comebacks we have known yet have in many cases forgotten.

Because we inevitably forget, we need books like this one, compiled by a group of Saints' fans with a pride in the Club's history, collaborating with Bob Brunskell of the *Echo* to remind us not just of the ups and downs in my time at The Dell but of what a great side Saints were at the turn of the century, when the sporting press focused on the giants of the Football League and neglected what was being achieved by Southampton. That had not changed a whole lot when I was a manager and some of the London press would rather make up a story than come and talk to my players and me.

Our local media – which mostly meant, day after day, the *Echo* – were always fair, certainly in their criticism of me, in the way they used their superior knowledge of what was what at The Dell and why. I have known their football reporters from the days when they used names like "Commentator" to Graham Hiley today.

Most of the reports in this book are based, to a greater or lesser degree, on the reports filed by those men from the *Echo*.

They bring back such memorable moments or highlight such significant episodes in the Club's 115 years. For me personally, there's the game at White Hart Lane in 1949 when I shot, it hit one post and went across and hit the other post and stayed out – I couldn't believe that!… Scoring against Leicester City from the edge of the box with my head – and there's a photo to prove it… the Reserve team who worked so hard for me to win the Combination Cup in 1954 …the Youth team winning at Old Trafford – that was a bit special… Derek Reeves getting four in that 5-1 Cup win at Maine Road – terrific! …I can still see Brian Clifton's promotion-winning header going in against Reading… those fantastic Cup replays against Notts Forest …beating Wolves 9-3 when they were led astray by Jimmy Melia wearing No. 9… Terry Paine's headed goal at Leyton Orient in our 1966 promotion finale …Ron Davies, holding his ground and then going in to meet those crosses from Paine and Sydenham with his head – four goals for him at Chelsea and another four at Manchester United.

Those are just a few of my memories evoked by matches selected for this book. But, you are bound to ask, why is *your* favourite game missing? Because football is all about opinions, that's why. When it comes to football, assessments of what's good or mediocre, what's crucial or insignificant, are always subjective.

TED BATES.

And always will be, that's for sure

PREFACE

by David Bull

This compendium is a collaborative venture between Hagiology Publishing, Southampton FC and the *Southern Daily Echo.*

Following its first publication, *Dell Diamond,* in 1998, the small group of historically-minded Saints' fans who had formed the Hagiology collective, with a commitment to produce books on the history of Southampton FC, were approached by John O'Sullivan on behalf of the Club: could we bring out more histories than we had planned, starting in 2000?

Assured of support from The Dell for whatever we might need to increase the flow of productions, we were given a similar undertaking by Mike Wright for the *Echo,* with whose Bob Brunskell we had already been collaborating. I had made a guest contribution to Bob's 1998-99 "Where Are They Now?" series in the *Pink* and we now agreed that Dave Juson and I would similarly guest in his 1999-2000 series, "Match of the Century."

Might one of these make a book? The idea of marrying interviews for the former series with some I'd conducted for *Dell Diamond* was attractive, but came second to a book on "Match of the Century." We would take 35 of Bob's games and add 65 written either by members of the Hagiology collective or by some of our fellow-Saints with a bent for recalling our team's past successes – or even, on occasion, failures.

We planned to select 100 games, starting with the 1900 Cup Final, even though some of us felt that 1900 was really the last year of the 19th century. But then, Dave Juson, an authority on Saints' Victorian vanities, put in a word for the halcyon days of 1885-99 and suggested we extend our reach to "Match of the Millennium." That simplified the issue about the status of the year 1900 but leaves unresolved, of course, the question of which millennium the year 2000 falls in. The forgettable football fare of 2000 – not even a "Great Escape" to get the adrenalin rushing – made that an academic question until 26 August when a late comeback against Liverpool settled the issue: our millennium includes 2000 and, if you don't like it, I'm afraid you'll have to exercise your right to ignore Match No. 100.

So now we had to agree on who would write about which 65 memorable games and then find illustrations to match. The original five Hagiologists – Gary Chalk, Duncan Holley, Dave Juson, Norman Gannaway and myself – came up with about 90 "musts", which eventually eroded to 65. And so we have our 100.

Not all of them are games of goals galore: a certain 1-0 victory in 1976 seemed to merit inclusion; and there were other 1-0 wins that just had to be included, from the Wayman-in-agony drama of 1949 to the victory at Middlesbrough in 1982 that took Saints to the very top of the Football League for the first time ever. And not all of our chosen games were wins, or even high-scoring draws: there were some significant 1-1 score-lines, most notably at Brisbane Road in 1966 and again in 1978. There were even defeats. Apart from the losing Cup Finals of 1900 and 1902, three semi-final setbacks (out of the seven Saints have endured) and the League Cup disappointment of 1979, we were inclined to include five especially crushing defeats: in a landmark friendly of 1893, the FA Cup (1939 and 1995), the Football League (1972) and the League Cup (1980). And the select 100 didn't all have to be first team matches: two Reserve, and one Youth, game are there on merit.

If you've stayed with the plot long enough to read that paragraph attempting to justify our selections, you'll have noticed that many a "memorable" match has been chosen less for what it produced on the day than for its special significance in the Club's history – which is why we've even included a dreary Monday in 1936 when The Dell had its lowest attendance. But let me stop there: however earnestly I try to explain the rationale of what's *in,* you will be asking why your most memorable match is *out.* The simplest answer is the one used by Ted Bates, the sage of Southampton himself, in the Foreword: everybody has his or her opinion about what is needed in football. Every fan who cares enough to argue the toss is much better in the transfer market, a far better team-selector and an infinitely superior tactician than anybody who's been paid to manage the show and certainly likely to be a better match-selector than those of us, and me as the final arbiter in particular, who chose these 100 Matches of the Millennium.

If I confess to having felt little need to know the details of the "BT" (Before Ted) period in the life of Southampton FC, that's because I've long been able to rely – on a need-to-know basis – on those two indispensable Chalk and Holley volumes: the encyclopaedic *Saints: a complete record* and their *Alphabet of the Saints,* without constant reference to which this book quite simply could not have been assembled. Those two Official Historians of the Club decided, along with Dave Juson and Norman Gannaway, which pre-1939 games mattered most and which of them should write about which (while leaving a local derby report for me to compile with Clay Aldworth, who is working on a book on Saints v Pompey).

If we weren't going to arrogate all of the postwar games to ourselves, then it was time to phone a friend. Men only, I'm afraid. A pity, that. When previously editing collections of fans' memories, I have found women much more reluctant than men to recollect in print. I successfully prevailed upon a few, but none of them was a Saints fan, alas.

First man in was Chris Newman – the obvious choice for the 1960s and a few later games. Rob Holley chose three matches from the many he might have written, while Ronald Allison, Tom Kelly, Norman Hull, Andy Mercer and Keith Trevis – each had a particular game that had to be included. Three others – Aidan Hamilton, Nick Illingsworth and John Warren – each contributed, in some degree, to a match or two, while Dave Adlem was, as ever, the Bristol resource centre, answering from his attic so many of my editing needs. Who did what in the way of writing and of match-specific research is indicated at the foot of each match report.

And then there were the illustrations. Any book on the local football team is bound to be heavily dependent on the local newspaper whose photographers have enjoyed privileged access to the players and the play. This book has benefited greatly from an understanding with the *Echo* – as part of our three-way Agreement – that it would supply an illustration or two for each report and from Bob Brunskell's willingness to conduct photo searches, with the kind help of his colleagues, Paul Green and Paul Collins.

We had two problems here. First, the *Echo* has sent photographers to away games only in comparatively recent years. Secondly, there are periods – before its library was destroyed in the Blitz and during much of the 1960s and 1970s – when the *Echo* simply does not have available the originals of photos that we've seen in the 'paper – whether in a weekday edition or the *Football Echo*.

We had four fall-back positions. An easy solution was to copy photos from newsprint. But, as you can see, the quality is such that we have been reluctant to do that more than we absolutely had to. Next, we could try photo agencies or the libraries of national newspapers. This took up a lot of time for meagre results: I have used just one agency photo – from Empics, where Jen Little could not have been keener to help. To put it bluntly, so many guardians of football photography do not consider Southampton worth saving. This came across especially strongly as I pursued photos of Ron Davies scoring four at Old Trafford. Even when directed to the main repository of Manchester United illustrations, I was told, ever so courteously, that they didn't "keep games like that."

Which is why our third option was so important. We are most fortunate that Duncan Holley has built up an extensive library of Saints' photos, most of which have come from the collections of ex-players. When the copyright of these is not obviously the *Echo's*, it is invariably not clear whose it is. So, in citing a photo as being from the Holley collection, we have not known whom to credit and hereby invite any unacknowledged copyright-holders to contact us. We fared better in our searches for text, in which we were helped by a number of librarians, archivists and guardians of special collections, acknowledged on page 204. Finally, we have resorted to head-and-shoulder shots, team line-ups and programme covers. These all have their place in illustrating a Football Club's history, but you may feel that we have sometimes used them where you'd have liked to see some action.

With Bob Brunskell having created this compendium's theme and then been its first-line photo editor, we agreed that I should undertake the remaining editorial roles: from commissioning contributions in ways indicated above to writing this introductory explanation of our objectives and approach; and, most important in a collection by 14 writers, editing contributions so as to minimise repetition and then to fit the space available.

A word on that last stage first: we all agreed that each game should fill a two-page spread, with the exception of the 1902 and 1976 FA Cup Finals, each of which gets a double helping; and, two games in the 1930s have been obliged to share a spread – a reflection on a dismal period in the fortunes of the Club. We have always treated a cup tie as one match, even one that went to three replays – save in 1963, when each of the replays with Nottingham Forest was a drama in its own right.

As to avoiding repetition, you don't need four chapters on the trot to trumpet the arrival of Charlie Wayman or Kevin Keegan or whomsoever; and we all agreed that a detailed account of who passed to whom to score would often be less important than putting the game in the context of the season's fortunes generally. That has meant determining whose pen-picture and which progress reports should appear where and has demanded cross-referencing to matches past or upcoming. So, if you're one of those readers who expects each contribution to a compendium to stand alone, you're going to be unhappy with my attempts to locate each report in something resembling a continuously unfolding account (if far from a comprehensive record) of Saints' history.

This continuity is, of course, personified by Ted Bates, who played in Match No. 30 and who was at The Dell, as ever, watching No.100. He was so obviously the person to write a foreword for this book and we are delighted that he agreed to do so.

I have been generously supported in this editorial function by Duncan Holley, as already intimated, as a photo librarian/researcher; by Gary Chalk with his considerable library of *Echo* back copies, scrapbooks and programmes (with Andrew Murray kindly helping him out in the last regard); and by Dave Juson as transcriber, proof-reader and sounding-board-in-general.

Our having agreed that later reports would often include reactions from one or two who had played in the game in question, I was able to interject these by drawing upon three main sources: excerpts from biographies – including those of opponents; interviews conducted by Bob Brunskell for "Where Are They Now?", especially updated by him here and there; and, likewise, interviews for *Dell Diamond,* as recently supplemented when Matthew Le Tissier and Jason Dodd kindly reminisced for me about some of our last few Matches of the Millennium, including the 3-3 draw with Liverpool – in whichever millennium that might be.

Having thus assembled text and illustrations, I am grateful to Mark Perry, of Perry Associates, and to his scanner, David Ball, for bringing this all together in a professional, visually satisfying way.

But I hope this book does more than just look good. I hope that the content will both interest you and inform you – to an extent that rewards all the creativity and sheer hard work that the above-named have put into it

David Bull
Bristol
October 2000

For a note on this reprint, please see over.

Preface to this reprinted edition

We had thought a fourth printing would suffice, but it sold out in November 2003, before we could meet the seasonal demands from the shops. We are persuaded that there continues to be a demand from fans wanting to relive some of Saints' most memorable games of the last millennium.

We have made one change. In researching the illustrations for *In That Number,* Gary Chalk discovered that the photo we had used at page 145, which had been labelled at source as being from the game against Olympique Marseille, was in fact from a match with Napoli. He has kindly come up with the Marseilles newspaper that doubled as a programme for the away leg, to fill that slot.

David Bull
Bristol
March 2004

THE SAINTS' 100 MOST
MEMORABLE MATCHES

1	21/11/85	5-1	v	Freemantle (friendly)
2	24/03/88	2-1	v	Soton Harriers (Hants Junior Cup Final replay)
3	16/03/89	4-1	v	Cowes (Hants Junior Cup semi-final 3rd replay)
4	14/03/91	3-1	v	Royal Engineers (Hants Senior Cup Final)
5	24/10/91	7-0	v	Reading (FA Cup 2nd Qual Rd)
6	26/04/93	0-8	v	Stoke (friendly)
7	06/10/94	3-1	v	Chatham (Southern League)
8	01/02/96	2-3	v	Sheffield Wednesday (FA Cup 1st Rd)
9	23/03/98	0-2	v	Nottingham Forest (FA Cup semi-final replay)
10	03/09/98	4-1	v	Brighton United (Southern League)
11	29/04/99	4-3	v	Bristol City (Southern League)
12	21/04/00	0-4	v	Bury (FA Cup Final)
13	28/12/01	11-0	v	Northampton Town (Southern League)
14	03/02/02	2-1	v	Tottenham Hotspur (FA Cup 1st Rd 2nd replay)
15	26/04/02	1-2	v	Sheffield United (FA Cup Final replay)
16	13/01/06	5-1	v	Portsmouth (FA Cup 1st Rd)
17	11/03/08	3-2	v	Everton (FA Cup 4th Rd)
18	30/08/20	4-0	v	Swindon (Division III)
19	06/05/22	5-0	v	Newport Co (Division III (South))
20	19/03/23	0-1	v	West Ham (FA Cup 4th Rd 2nd replay)
21	28/03/25	0-2	v	Sheffield United (FA Cup semi-final)
22	19/02/27	2-1	v	Newcastle United (FA Cup 5th Rd)
23	26/03/27	1-2	v	Arsenal (FA Cup semi-final)
24	04/05/29	3-0	v	Swansea Town (Division II)
25	26/12/29	1-0	v	Tottenham Hotspur (Division II)
26	14/04/33	6-2	v	Notts County (Division II)
27	30/03/36	0-1	v	Port Vale (Division II)
28	16/01/37	2-3	v	Sunderland (FA Cup 3rd Rd)
29	07/01/39	1-4	v	Chelmsford City (FA Cup 3rd Rd)
30	06/01/40	5-6	v	Reading (League South 'B')
31	04/11/44	3-3	v	Chelsea (League South)
32	03/03/45	12-3	v	Luton Town (League South Cup)
33	25/08/45	5-5	v	Plymouth Argyle (League South)
34	29/12/45	7-0	v	Chelsea (League South)
35	29/04/46	4-2	v	Derby County (League South)
36	24/01/48	3-2	v	Blackburn Rovers (FA Cup 4th Rd)
37	10/06/48	1-2	v	Vasco da Gama (tour match)
38	02/04/49	1-0	v	Tottenham Hotspur (Division II)
39	23/04/49	1-1	v	West Bromwich Albion (Division II)
40	29/04/50	5-3	v	Leicester City (Division II)
41	18/11/50	5-4	v	Coventry City (Division II)
42	01/10/51	0-1	v	Tottenham Hotspur Res (Football Combination)
43	27/12/52	5-3	v	Fulham (Division II)
44	18/02/53	1-2	v	Blackpool (FA Cup 5th Rd)
45	15/11/54	3-1	v	Norwich City Res (Football Comb Cup Final)
46	08/04/57	3-2	v	Man Utd (Youth Cup semi-final, 2nd leg)
47	09/01/60	5-1	v	Manchester City (FA Cup 3rd Rd)
48	18/04/60	1-0	v	Reading (Division III)
49	24/08/60	4-1	v	Liverpool (Division II)
50	05/12/60	5-4	v	Leeds United (League Cup 4th Rd)
51	07/01/61	7-1	v	Ipswich Town (FA Cup 3rd Rd)
52	03/04/63	3-3	v	Nottingham Forest (FA Cup 6th Rd replay)
53	08/04/63	5-0	v	Nottingham Forest (FA Cup 6th Rd 2nd replay)
54	01/04/64	6-4	v	Derby County (Division II)
55	27/04/64	6-1	v	Rotherham United (Division II)
56	18/09/65	9-3	v	Wolverhampton Wanderers (Division II)
57	05/02/66	5-2	v	Portsmouth (Division II)
58	07/05/66	3-2	v	Plymouth Argyle (Division II)
59	09/05/66	1-1	v	Leyton Orient (Division II)
60	04/02/67	6-2	v	West Ham United (Division I)
61	06/05/67	2-1	v	Nottingham Forest (Division I)
62	02/09/67	6-2	v	Chelsea (Division I)
63	14/10/67	1-5	v	Leicester City (Division I)
64	16/08/69	4-1	v	Manchester United (Division I)
65	01/10/69	2-0	v	Rosenborg (Fairs Cup 1st Rd 2nd leg)
66	04/03/72	0-7	v	Leeds United (Division I)
67	18/09/74	3-1	v	Glasgow Rangers (Texaco Cup qtr-final 1st leg)
68	17/02/76	4-0	v	West Bromwich Albion (FA Cup 4th Rd replay)
69	01/05/76	1-0	v	Manchester United (FA Cup Final)
70	03/05/76	2-2	v	Queens Park Rangers (Channon Testimonial)
71	15/09/76	4-0	v	Marseille (Cup-Winners' Cup 1st Rd 1st leg)
72	05/10/76	6-2	v	Wolverhampton Wanderers (Division II)
73	22/01/77	6-0	v	Carlisle United (Division II)
74	16/03/77	2-1	v	Anderlecht (Cup-Winners' Cup 3rd Rd 2nd leg)
75	25/04/78	1-1	v	Orient (Division II)
76	30/01/79	1-0	v	Leeds United (League Cup semi-final 2nd leg)
77	17/03/79	2-3	v	Nottingham Forest (League Cup Final)
78	10/11/79	4-1	v	Nottingham Forest (Division I)
79	02/09/80	1-7	v	Watford (League Cup 2nd Rd 2nd leg)
80	26/12/80	4-4	v	Tottenham Hotspur (Division I)
81	28/11/81	1-0	v	Liverpool (Division I)
82	30/01/82	1-0	v	Middlesbrough (Division I)
83	04/05/82	5-5	v	Coventry City (Division I)
84	28/01/84	1-0	v	Portsmouth (FA Cup 4th Rd)
85	16/03/84	2-0	v	Liverpool (Division I)
86	28/04/84	8-2	v	Coventry City (Division I)
87	17/05/84	3-1	v	Notts County (Division I)
88	04/11/86	4-1	v	Manchester Utd (League Cup 3rd Rd replay)
89	07/03/87	4-0	v	Leicester City (Division I)
90	09/04/88	4-2	v	Arsenal (Division I)
91	21/10/89	4-1	v	Liverpool (Division I)
92	05/02/92	2-2	v	Man Utd: 4-2 on pens (FA Cup 4th Rd replay)
93	09/04/94	5-4	v	Norwich City (Premier League)
94	07/05/94	3-3	v	West Ham United (Premier League)
95	01/03/95	2-6	v	Tottenham Hotspur (FA Cup 5th Rd replay)
96	22/03/95	3-1	v	Newcastle United (Premier League)
97	13/04/96	3-1	v	Manchester United (Premier League)
98	26/10/96	6-3	v	Manchester United (Premier League)
99	08/05/99	2-0	v	Wimbledon (Premier League)
100	26/08/00	3-3	v	Liverpool (Premier League)

St Mary's Young Men's Association 5
Freemantle 1

IN THE BEGINNING: the opponents were Freemantle FC, a side based at the *Waterloo Arms* and, apparently, connected to the neighbouring Christ Church (leastways, one of the curates, Rev. George D'Arcy, was a prominent player); the day was Saturday 21 November 1885; and the place was the "backfield" of the County Cricket Ground, a site later occupied by the Hampshire Bowling Club.

Neither side had any pedigree. Freemantle had reputedly been formed in 1883, but the report featured here appears to be their first mention in the press. It was most certainly the first game for the St Mary's Young Men's Association FC: they had formed only a week or three before the match. And it cannot be stressed too strongly that, despite the heading to the match report, they had absolutely no connection with the YMCA.

Quite why these two clubs had decided to take up Association Football is rather difficult to fathom: Hampshire, in general, and Southampton, in particular, were Rugby hotbeds. True, a South Hants & Dorset Football Association had been formed the previous year; but it had only eleven members and Southampton, with barely two "footer" clubs to knock together, had no affiliates to the new Association, let alone entrants for either of its two cup competitions.

Further north – but, then, almost everywhere in the UK is north of Southampton – the game was exploding, both as a participation and as mass spectator sport, causing all sorts of problems for the Football Association. The old order had been turned upside down as recently as 1883 when a bunch of Lancastrian upstarts by the name of Blackburn Olympic had defeated the Old Etonians in the final of the FA Cup. Not only were Olympic a predominantly working-class side, they radiated a distinct and demonic whiff of professionalism. So not only had the balance of footballing power moved from London to the North and several rungs down the social ladder, but a debate regarding the morality of paid sportsmen was fermenting that would bubble on into the 1990s (when Rugby Union went "open").

The payment of Association footballers had been legalised in July 1885, albeit with severe misgivings and under stringent (though futile) regulations and, in the South especially, was widely regarded as not being cricket – although, strangely, cricket had always employed

L. Ghent, Williams, E. Williamson, Fowle, A. Coles (forwards).

ST. MARY'S Y.M.C.A. v. FREEMANTLE ASSOCIATION FOOTBALL CLUB.—The football club which has just been formed in connection with St. Mary's Young Men's Association, played their first match on Saturday last according to "Association Rules," when they showed that they have among their members the materials with which to form a fairly strong club by practice. During the first half St. Mary's scored four goals rather quickly, three of these being obtained from corner kicks. The game became much faster during the second half, and shortly after the change St. Mary's scored another point. Freemantle then obtained a goal through the ball from a corner kick passing off one of the St. Mary's team and so through the posts. Up to the call of time no further point was scored, so that St. Mary's were the victors by five goals to one. The goals were obtained by Bromley (three) and Fry (2). The Freemantle team showed some good play during the latter part of the game, while the good individual play of each of the St. Mary's team was well sustained throughout.

AVENUE RANGERS v. ARABS—played on the Southampton

professional players. Whatever, an "old boys" club would never win the FA Cup again and not until 1900 would the Final again be contested by a southern club (guess who! Or you may cheat and turn to Match No. 12).

Or you may cheat and turn to Match No. 12).

When the St Mary's Church of England Young Men's Association (to give them their full title) made their historic decision, at the Grove Street Schoolrooms earlier that November, to form a football club, there was no question of their discussing which code it should be; those behind the motion were perversely intent on playing soccer from the start. Perversely, because of the distinct shortage of opponents, and a growing perception that the Association code lacked respectability. Respectability was, however, something the YMA members could take for granted: they were predominantly well-educated, well-connected and drawn from the congregation of Southampton's "mother church"; the less-privileged lads of the parish had separate organisations to cater for their needs. In fact, the church had a multitude of societies to suit all ranks of society and interests, most of which had a strong temperance theme.

The YMA had been formed in, or around, 1881. Its members had athletics and cricket sections, a choral society, attended "ambulance classes" and talks on uplifting subjects, had a "reading room" and their own gymnastics equipment, on which they gave public displays. In return the young men were obliged to perform parochial duties. Options included singing in the choir and teaching in the Sunday schools (according to the *Southampton Times*, in May 1886, St. Mary's had 1,159 Sunday school scholars supervised by 118 teachers). There are also ambiguous references to members "doing large and valuable work among the young men of the town." This possibly refers to helping with the educational activities of the Fo'c'sle and Crow's Nest clubs, which had been established to "improve" the prospects of the disadvantaged youths of the parish, who were ubiquitous

Friendly

in the districts of Chapel, Crosshouse and Kingsland.

It might be argued that the YMA was somewhat elitist. But being part of an exclusive group does wonders for social confidence, which is probably why someone connected with the football club regarded their debut as auspicious enough to justify the circulation of a report to the local newspapers. There were occasional exhortations, in the local football and cricket columns, for club secretaries to heed press deadlines. The report of the

momentous engagement appeared in both the *Hampshire Independent* (opposite) and the *Southampton Times.*

Neither account carries the teams. In the eight match reports placed on record that season, five of them included line-ups, but the personnel are squeezed out of this first report in favour of the players of three local rugby games on the same page. In 1912, when the *Southampton Pictorial* ran a series on the Saints' history, members of the original side were consulted and came up with the side suggested below.

It is an interesting line-up, because four of those named had played for Deanery Association, a side spawned by the Deanery Cricket Club in 1882. The cricket team took their name from the St. Mary's rectory, in the substantial grounds of which they played their home matches. The four players in question were A.A. Fry, A.G. Fry, George McIvor and George Gandy.

We know that A.A. Fry, a schoolteacher, played in that first game because, along with Charles Bromley – the first Saint to score a hat-trick – he is mentioned as a scorer. It is also likely McIvor and Gandy played, as they feature among the five published line-ups. But A.G. Fry, although he would play a couple of games for St. Mary's in 1886-87, isn't mentioned in any of those teams of 1885-86, when he appears to have been giving his undivided attention to Southampton Harriers. Ralph Ruffell also goes without mention, although he would become a fixture between the goalposts the following season and remain one until 1894.

It is unlikely that we will ever know the personnel of that first Saints' team – unless, maybe, someone digs up the original minute books. And we know still less about their opponents: even the name of their scorer has been kept from us, although that was, of course, to protect the St Mary's player whose own goal it was.

But, then, start as you mean to go on. Whoever these eleven pioneers were, it has to be said that they established for their successors down the millennium two cherished and enduring traditions: the propensity to score a lot of goals; and a tendency to concede howlers.

George Muir who played in this first-ever Match, would become a referee in the Southern League and President of the Hampshire FA. And we shall meet him again (notably in Match No.19) as a Director of Southampton FC (1915 – 1936)

St MARY'S YOUNG MEN'S ASSOCIATION:

Ruffell, Muir, McDonnell, A.G. Fry, Deacon, A. Gandy, A.A. Fry, G. Gandy, C. Bromley, McIvor, Varley

No details available of the Freemantle team, the referee or the attendance.

Compiled by **DAVE JUSON** from reports in the *S. Mary's Parish Magazine,* the *Hampshire Independent* and the *Southampton Times;* from Handbooks of the South Hants & Dorset FA and of the Hampshire FA; from records, notably of St Mary's parish, in the Southampton City Archivist's Office; and from local sports histories, especially two 1912 publications – the "History of Southampton Football Club," a series in the *Southampton Pictorial,* and F.J. Montgomery's *History of the Deanery Cricket Club.* Photograph from the *Echo's* collection.

St Mary's 2
Southampton Harriers 1

S. MARY'S Y.M.A. FOOTBALL CLUB – This club (of which Mr. C.E. Bromley is the captain), which entered this season for the Hants Football Cup, have proved very successful, having won 6 matches, losing 3, with 1 drawn – scoring 25 goals in all, against 10. In the last match, v. Petersfield, they won by 10 goals, 5 of which were scored by Mr. A. Fry and 4 by Mr. Bromley.

So the *S. Mary's Parish Magazine,* of January 1888, heralded St Mary's YMA's entry into the sphere of competitive football. The inauguration of the Hampshire FA in April 1887 had provided the catalyst for the Young Men, now in their third season, to tilt for the Holy Grail that was a solid silver cup provided by Mr C.E. Baring, MP for Christchurch: the Hampshire FA Junior Cup.

The cup run had begun at Testwood, where Totton FC, unlike St Mary's, who had to elbow space for themselves on the Common, boasted their own ground. The report in the *Southampton Times* – probably written by F.J. Montgomery, a St Mary's committee man and umpire on the day (we are in the era of an umpire in each half of the field and a referee, to adjudicate, on the touchline) – went on to describe how the visitors dominated, without scoring, until, in the second-half, "A.A. Fry ran the whole length of the field before landing the ball directly in front of his captain, just a few yards out – Bromley simply could not miss." Which opened and concluded the scoring.

Petersfield were the opponents in the next round. Its being a requirement of the competition that matches were played on an enclosed pitch, St Mary's hired the Antelope Cricket Ground, the preserve of Southampton's senior club, Woolston Works. The Antelope stood, appropriately, at the top of St. Mary's Road between Brinton's Terrace and Clovelly Road.

The visitors arrived with only 10 men and without two of their best players, and the 10 goals that resulted were fairly predictable. Drawn at home again in the Third Round, St Mary's settled on a field behind the Anchor Hotel in Redbridge, owned by a Mr. Steadfast. Quite who

Mr. Steadfast was, and how come he had a plot suitable to play cup-tie football on, has never been explained; but he was evidently no fan of St Mary's. So upset was he by the behaviour of their supporters, as the "home" side took Lymington apart 4–0, that he demanded the gate money be donated to the South Hants Hospital. F.J. Montgomery found the antics "hilarious," but Mr. Steadfast was not amused; and although he "reluctantly" accepted an apology from the St Mary's committee, the club never played on his land again. The County Ground became the third "home" ground of their Cup run for the semi-final, which brought Bournemouth Arabs to Southampton.

The Arabs were strongly fancied in Bournemouth to take the cup, and certainly proved tough opponents. Tough enough to take the lead. After that the Arabs were mostly confined to taking long shots, thanks to the stirling defensive combination of Muir and George Carter, "certainly the best on the field," according to the *Southampton Times.* McDonald equalised, after good work by Bromley. And, late in the second-half, "Bromley dribbled in great style down the field, and put the ball through for St. Mary's." The 2-1 win put them into the final against Southampton Harriers.

Primarily an athletics club, the Harriers had started life as the Temperance Amateur Athletic Association, but were now based at the Avenue Hotel, suggesting a dramatic change of philosophy. And quite a change of personnel too, when, earlier that season, several Freemantle players defected to them, upon their club's failing to enter either of the Hampshire FA's cup competitions.

Harriers, who had recently held the mighty Woolston Works to a draw, were favourites. Mid-way through the

The first known photograph of the Saints, with the Hampshire Junior Cup, their first-ever trophy.
Standing (left to right): F.J. Montgomery, Carter, Warn, Sommerville, Fry, G. Candy.
Middle row: Varley, C. Bromley, Muir, A. Gandy. Front: Deacon, Crossley, Ruffell

second-half, all seemed to be going to form, as they led 2-0. Only as the game entered its final stages did the St Mary's forwards begin to play with any co-ordination and suddenly – following a Warn goal – the match, which had appeared dead and buried, was very much alive. The Harriers continued to press forward – perhaps too eagerly for, with just three minutes left, a gap appeared in their defence and Bromley unleashed a "splendid" shot to score. The tie duly ended 2-2, at which point many of the 600 crowd invaded the pitch where Bromley and Noble were debating the possibility of extra-time. Noble, with two of his players carrying knocks, declined to carry on.

The advisability of an extra half-hour may not have been the only item on the captains' agenda, as the *Bournemouth Guardian* noted: St Mary's had been denied a goal by a piece of astute gamesmanship, when, "to the astonishment of both umpires and the referee, the Harriers kicked off from the six yards' mark and no claim was made by St. Mary's for the point. I can't imagine how the Saints, who must be kicking themselves with chagrin at their slip, lost sight of the goal. I don't think they will get the chance again." The fact that goal nets had yet to be introduced was the most likely excuse for the failure of the Saints – as the *Southampton Times* had started calling St. Mary's on the very day of the final – to register the goal.

The replay followed two weeks later. Another estimated crowd of 600 turned out at the County Ground. It included "a generous sprinkling of ladies, who, however, were chivalrously admitted free." This time, St Mary's took the two-goal lead, through McDonald and Warn, the latter after some "pretty passing." Harriers could get only one back, leaving the *Southampton Times* to conclude:

> Soon the final whistle sounded, leaving "Saints" victorious after a magnificent game by two goals to one. Though the Harriers played a great game the St. Mary's played better football.

A Miss Winifred Shute presented the trophy to Bromley who "made a suitable response" – unfortunately unreported – and all the players were "heartily" cheered. "Each of the winning team was presented by a handsome silver medal in commemoration of the match" and, before the crowd dispersed, further rounds of cheers were given, "concluding with three for the ladies."

A trophy at the first time of asking was well worth recording for posterity and a fortnight later the happy players (minus McDonald) posed for a photograph with the Cup prior to a match against Woolston Works at the Antelope. The Works, the Hants' Senior champions, had little trouble in vanquishing the Junior winners 3-0.

The Saints had some way to go to become Southampton's premier side. At least the Harriers would never again be a threat. Many of their players promptly returned to Freemantle, who had acquired an excellent ground off Shirley Road, although "Banquo" Stride joined the Saints.

The April 1888 edition of the *S. Mary's Parish Magazine* noted, somewhat tersely, the achievement of the parish side:

> S. MARY'S FOOTBALL CLUB –We are glad to record a great triumph for the above Club, which has now, by following up its many victories, won the much coveted "Cup" for the year. We cordially congratulate them on their success.

But *was* it the parish side? For the first time in the journal the connection with the YMA goes unacknowledged. In fact, local newspapers had usually dropped "YMA" from reports at the end of the previous year. Apparently, and with no explanation, Saints had severed their links with the St Mary's Young Men's Association.

This disestablishment notwithstanding, they had forever become the "SAINTS."

St MARY'S:
Ruffell, Carter, Muir, Gandy, Varley, Crossley, A.A. Fry, Sommerville, C. Bromley, McDonald, Warn

SOUTHAMPTON HARRIERS:
Walter Newton, Ridges, Bishop, Stride, Bunday, William Newton, Chandler, Noble, Maton, Rogers, Wood
The Harriers were unchanged for the replay, while Deacon replaced Crossley for St Mary's.

Referee: W. Pickford   *Umpires:* Messrs. W. E. Masterman and E.F. Maberley   *Attendance:* 600

Compiled by **DAVE JUSON** and **DUNCAN HOLLEY** from reports in the *S. Mary's Parish Magazine, Southampton Times, Southern Referee* and the *Bournemouth Guardian*. Illustration from Duncan Holley's collection.

St Mary's 4
Cowes 1

**The excitement engendered by this keen and prolonged rivalry
produced a state of excitement that had no parallel in the County.**

That's how F. J. Montgomery – a founding official of St Mary's introduced in the previous report – described, some 40 years later, the penultimate tie in the Saints' attempt to win their second successive Hampshire FA Junior Cup. The semi-final with Cowes went to four games before it produced a finalist.

The first game took place at Northwood Park, Cowes and the cup-holders were accompanied across the water to the Isle of Wight by many of their fans. The team showed five changes from that which had won the Cup in 1888, the newcomers including Stride who had signed, you may recall, from the beaten Harriers. Cowes, whose ranks included five junior county players (to Saints' four), were strongly fancied to lift the cup and started firm favourites. The referee, making his first trip to the Island, was William Pickford, the Hon. Secretary of the Hampshire FA. A journalist on, and later editor of, the *Bournemouth Guardian,* he was the driving force behind the spread of the Association game in Hampshire and Dorset. He would end his distinguished involvement with the winter game dying in harness as President of the Football Association in 1938.

The fancied home side led 1-0 at half-time. Carter's attempted clearance had struck Whiteley and rebounded through the posts. It was hard luck on the Saints' defence, who had all played well, but the "beautiful dribbling" (as Montgomery recalled it) of Staite – a private infantryman stationed at Parkhurst Barracks – was causing a lot of discomfort in the Southampton defence, where it took both Verney and Carter to hold him at times. But St Mary's came back to equalise, with just two minutes remaining, through a "screw shot" from Farwell.

Cowes felt robbed and requested that an extra half-hour be played, but Carter declined: his players had a boat to catch, thank you all the same. It was a satisfied bunch of supporters and fans who disembarked at Southampton Royal Pier that Saturday evening.

Conversely, when the two teams met again a fortnight later, a fair number of Islanders crossed, in specially-run boats, to be among the 2,000 fans at the County Ground. This time, St Mary's scored first, through Fry. But then Staite came into his own and hit the bar with "a brilliant

The Junior Cup winners are joined by referee Pickford and again by F.J. Montgomery, a frequent source in these early reports.
Standing (left to right) Warn, Ruffell, G. Gandy, Pickford, Montgomery, Deacon, Delamotte.
Middle row: Stride, C. Bromley, Carter, Fry. Front: Muir, Verney, Farwell.

shot." And, as in the first game, there were minutes left when the away side equalised, Ballard scoring after "scientific" play between the Cowes wings. Again, the home captain requested extra-time. Again, the visiting captain regretted that his men had a boat waiting.

With honours even on goals scored and boats pleaded, there was now the question of a venue for the third game. When the Hampshire FA met the following Monday, it had before it a letter from the County Cricket Club, offering the use of its ground once more, with the further promise – or inducement? – that the travel expenses of the Cowes team would be met from the gate money. There were those who favoured a neutral venue – Winchester and Portsmouth were suggested – but it was decided to toss a coin. St Mary's won and the game was scheduled for the County Ground the following Wednesday – just three days before the Final was due to take place – with instructions that the match must achieve a finalist.

The off-the-pitch activities having helped to intensify the excitement, the crowd that gathered for the mid-week fixture was considerably larger than on the Saturday. Cowes went in front, courtesy of their centre-forward, Trask, and Bromley equalised. Warn made it 2-1, with a shot that appeared to be "half a yard" behind the line before it was caught by Lieverman, the Cowes goalkeeper, who quickly threw it out. With the home players claiming the goal and the visitors disputing the claim, the referee consulted the linesman and gave the goal. As the *Hampshire Independent* elegantly summarised the fall-out of this incident, "the excitement after this increased both inside and outside the ropes." But, for all that, there were no further goals. St Mary's had at last won the tie 2-1.

Or had they? A written protest from Cowes – that the linesman had not raised his flag to signal a score until after three St Mary's players had claimed the goal – was rejected by the Hants FA. But Cowes ventured a supplementary, oral complaint: that before the referee had actually awarded the goal, the same linesman had stopped the ball with his flag, although technically it was still in play. St Mary's challenged the admissibility of new evidence, but the FA Committee decided to hear it. Cowes produced a fresh witness. The Committee was impressed and reversed its decision. Play It Again, Saints!

At least, St Mary's won the toss. So once more to the County Ground. Thither they came, excited by the acrimonious dispute about Warn's "goal." Cheap railway tickets brought them from the New Forest, while an armada – some 800-strong – crossed from the Island. An unprecedented crowd of 7,000 turned up. Alas, with demand so high, chivalry was pronounced dead: ladies were no longer to be admitted free.

The Saints players were obviously fired up, too. Shot upon shot rained down on Lieverman. Eventually, following a scramble from a Verney corner, Fry poked the ball over the line. Verney made it two when he shot and a team-mate charged the goalkeeper, the ball slipping between the posts unhindered. There were no reports of a Cowes protest and it was 2–0 to St Mary's at half-time.

When the Islanders re-started strongly, Staite scored after a dazzling run. Cowes now enjoyed a purple patch but St Mary's held firm and came back to make it 3-1, when a shot from Fry rolled along the crossbar before dropping obligingly onto Delamotte's head. The same player then added a fourth with a "vigorous" shot.

And that was that. St Mary's fans could feel that justice had been done. The Hants FA at last had its finalists. And the tie had swollen its coffers, William Pickford noted some 46 years later in its *Golden Jubilee Book,* "from embarrassment into affluence." The Final, long postponed, was an anti-climax. St Mary's beat Christchurch 3-0 to win the Cup for the second season running.

It was the semi-final, with all the passion it had aroused locally – and indeed peripherally – that so extended its support as to make St Mary's THE Southampton team and opened the way for the Club to become Southampton St Mary's and, very soon, plain Southampton.

St MARY'S:
Ruffell, Carter, Arter, Deacon, Stride, Verney, Warn, Farwell, C. Bromley, Delamotte, A.A.Fry

COWES:
Lieverman, Watson, Lowe, Matthews, Byng, Norton, Lewis, Staite, Trask, Ballard, Whiteley

Referee: Mr C.S. Wooldridge (Winchester)   *Umpires:* Messrs G.W. Andrews and E.F. Maberley   *Attendance:* 7,000

Compiled by **DUNCAN HOLLEY** from reports in the *Hampshire Independent* and *Southampton Times,* with additional research by **Dave Juson,** drawing upon William Pickford's Hants FA *Golden Jubilee Book,* Norman Gannaway's history of Hampshire's early football and F.J. Montgomery's 1931 account (in the *Hampshire Advertiser*) of the early Saints.

St Mary's 3
Royal Engineers (Aldershot) 1

The Junior Cup exploits of 1887-88 and 1888-89 – as highlighted in the previous two match reports – were followed by a third consecutive win in 1889-90. St Mary's had won the Cup outright without ever losing a game in the competition.

Yet these darlings of the Southampton sporting public were still living, to a degree, in the shadow of Woolston Works. The Works, predominantly made up of Scottish and northern employees of Oswald, Mordaunt & Co. (on what is now the site of Vosper Thorneycroft), had emerged in 1886, won the South Hants & Dorset FA Senior Cup in 1887, the Hants FA Senior Cup in 1888 and then, shortly after, were defunct, consequent upon the financial precariousness of the shipyard. Could Saints step up a grade and succeed the Works at Senior level? The *Hampshire Independent* found opinion divided:

> When the Senior ties commenced there was a very diverse feeling abroad as to [Saints'] chances of getting a look-in at the final; and some whose digestion had interfered with their judgment predicted that, although they had pulled off the junior honours, they would soon go under when pitted against the senior clubs of the county.

If Saints lacked experience at senior level they had continuity in their favour: as the *Southampton Pictorial* would later put it, they were "really a company of old chums imbued with one spirit." The only new faces among the regulars of 1890-91 were two youngsters, Ernie Nicholls and George Marshall, each of whom had joined the Club in 1888. Marshall would remain a fixture in the side until 1896, playing two Southern League seasons. Nicholls, who would record the Saints' first FA Cup goal, would bow out in 1894, but would live to see Saints play in the First Division, dying in 1971, nine months short of his 100th birthday.

Saints' Cup campaign was slow to start: not only was the season severely disrupted by a particularly harsh winter but they got a first round bye. In the Second Round, Geneva Cross, of the Royal Victoria Military Hospital at Netley, were defeated 5-0 (Frank Bromley, Farwell, Kiddle, Nicholls and Verney) in the mud, reckoned to be "ankle deep at the Infirmary goal end" of the Antelope Ground, as frost gave way to rain.

Their semi-final opponents at the County Ground were Banister Court, a school team dominated by teachers. The Courtiers won local approval for their "pretty football" - but the 16 year-old scholar Charles Miller (of whom more later, starting at Match No. 6) who'd been the most eye-catching player for the two previous seasons, seems to have been considered too young and "light" to be pitched in against George Carter and George Marshall.

Saints won 3–0 (Bromley, Farwell & Nicholls), despite a sterling performance between the posts by W.P. Cole who "threw the ball out like an expert labourer, with pints of beer in him, excavating a trench."

And so to a Final against the reigning Senior Cup champions, Royal Engineers, of Aldershot; not the Chatham-based outfit renowned for reaching four FA Cup Finals in the 1870s. The army side were looking to win the trophy outright, having seen off Portsmouth AFC in the 1889 final and the King's Royal Rifles in 1890. It would be their third meeting with Saints that season: they'd lost 4–3 at the Antelope and triumphed 5–1 in Aldershot. Ariel, of the *Southampton Times,* did "not like to say" who might win:

> Although the Saints are naturally warm favourites in many quarters, it is an open secret that the friends of the Engineers look to the final as a fine picking for their men, who have only to come to see to conquer. That famous saying of Julius Caesar, 'Veni, vidi, vici,' has been used and parodied by many hundreds of people under different circumstances since it was first uttered, but it has not always turned up trumps when parodied for use before the event.

Ariel was not the only wordsmith kissed by the classic muse that week. William Pickford drew on Thomas Babington MacAulay's epic poem, *Lays of Ancient Rome,* to produce the team-card opposite.

A record crowd, estimated at 4,000 to 5,000, turned out at the County Ground, which included a large group of "partisans" from Aldershot , not to mention military and civil colleagues from Southampton's Ordnance Survey Offices in London Road.

Royal Engineers (Aldershot)

Sapper R. Hammett
"When my time comes, call me, and I will answer"

Corporal F.C. Kilburn   Sapper D.B. Hamer
"The great Achilles – the sinew and the forehead of our host"

Lieut C.H Versturme   2nd Corporal J. White
Sapper E. A. Jones
"In your straight path a thousand may well be held by three"

Lt. P. Bourne   Sergt Sheldon   Driver Gray
Corporal R. S. Smith   Sapper J. Elson
"Nay, but make haste, the better foot before"

St Mary's

A. Farwell   F. A. Delamotte   E. Nicholls
F.C. Bromley   R.S. Kiddle
"Now tread we a measure, said young Lochinvar"

G. Verney   C. Deacon   W. Stride
"Let him not cross or thwart me"

G. Carter   G. Marshall
"The King is come to marshal us,
All in his armour drest"

R. Ruffell
"Alone stood brave Horatius
But constant still in mind"

"It must be said," the *Southampton Times* commented, "that Saints never played a better game." Nicholls had opened the scoring in the 20th minute with "a stinging shot which no goalkeeper could have saved." And, although a rare slip by Carter had allowed the Engineers to pull level before half-time, two second-half goals brought Saints their first Senior trophy. The crowd's reaction to the first goal – from Frank Bromley, who had inherited his place in the attack from his brother Charles – was demonstrative enough: "a cheer rent the air that might have been heard more than a mile away." But, when Kiddle quickly added another, then "the delight of the Southampton people knew no bounds."

The outcome was appreciated by Ariel:

They have been and gone and done it! Yes, fairly and squarely the Saints went out for the Hants Senior Cup and got it, after a rare old fight, beating the Royal Engineers by three goals to one… once more they had walked smiling through all their opponents.

Teams as per card above

Referee: E.G. Duchesne (Bournemouth)   *Attendance:* 4,000 or more

---

Compiled by **GARY CHALK** and **DAVE JUSON** from the *Echo, Hampshire Independent, Southampton Times* and *Southampton Observer;* from the 1912 series on the Saints' history in the *Southampton Pictorial;* and from William Pickford's Hants FA *Golden Jubilee Book*

St Mary's 7
Reading 0

The *Southampton Times* detected a justifiable air of bonhomie at the annual dinner of the St Mary's Football Club in May 1891, where the president, Dr. Russell Bencraft, announced that

They had 400 members, and strange to say for an athletic club in Hampshire over £100 in the bank (applause). They were going further affield [*sic*] next year and had entered for the English Cup [as the FA Cup then tended to be called]. They had no expectation of doing much, but they would be satisfied if they got through to the first round, and some day he hoped they would do even more (applause).

Saints were on quite a Cup run: three successive wins in the Hampshire Junior Cup, followed by the Senior Cup at the first attempt. So, four winning finals in four seasons of undefeated Hampshire FA Cup football and now they were to go through the 1891-92 season, again winning the Senior Cup and maintaining their record of never having been beaten in an "official" cup competition. And yet, despite not losing in their first attempt at the FA Cup, they would still miss the President's target of reaching the First Round Proper.

An odd story that began well enough at Warmley. Warmley? Precisely. "Very few people in Southampton had heard of Warmley until a short time ago," Ariel suggested in his *Southampton Times* reflections on the First Qualifying Round. "Every little boy in the place knows where it is now, for the Saints, their ideal football players, have beaten the Warmleyites in the first round ties of the national trophy now held by Blackburn Rovers." They had actually won 4-1; and Warmley was, and still is, near Bristol.

The next qualifying round gave them a tie against Reading, who were no strangers, being a fixture in the schedule of friendly matches that, in these pre-Southern League days, made up the bulk of the season. "Reading and Southampton are old friends," observed Ariel, discussing the draw. "It was only a fortnight ago that the clubs fraternised at the tea table after a splendid game [2-2] at the Antelope." The Saints had an admirable reputation for hospitality, usually provided at Dartnell's Grill Room in West Street.

Ariel was referring to the after-match entertainment on 24 September, at which the Reading captain had responded to the speeches and toasts of his hosts by proposing "The health of the Saints" and had "said that the game which they had at Southampton every year was one of the pleasantest engagements of the season, and he prayed it would long continue to be so."

The next side to enjoy Saintly largesse were the 93rd Highland Regiment, when the St. Mary's defence was every bit as munificent as their committee's dinner budget. Ariel waxed lyrical:

The luck of the lucky Saints does not come out on top when they play the 93rd Highlanders. This was the case on Saturday, and the little cherub which usually attends upon the Saints was nowhere to be seen – in fact he was not on the field. Probably it was too wet for him to be in attendance.

Saints lost 2-0. Still, St Mary's were, he noted, quick learners: "I hear Fleming, of the 93rd Highlanders, will make one of the Saints' team against Reading... next Saturday. Fleming has been a 'Saint' for over a year they say." Not only had Jock Fleming been on the books for a year, but, it transpired, so had his team-mate, Sandy McMillan – allegedly!

There were around 4,000 spectators at the Antelope Ground, to watch the first-ever FA Cup-tie in Southampton. A good number at an arena in which the majority of the crowd were obliged to watch from behind a rope around the perimeter of the pitch. The few points of high ground obtainable, in or near the ground, were occupied

The bowler-hatted F.J. Montgomery and J. Hendin (secretary) appear to be making up the eleven for the Saints' first FA Cup-tie in October 1891.
The nine players are (standing, left to right) Nicholls, Delamotte; (seated) Price, Stride, Carter, Ruffell, Kiddle; (on ground) Marshall, Verney.

FA Cup Second Qualifying Round

and the windows of neighbouring houses were crowded. The Saints gave them all, even the legion with obscured views, a rare treat.

Delamotte opened the scoring with what appears to have been Saints' first attack, and thereafter it was almost one-way traffic. "It was manifest to all observers that the Saints were superior to their opponents and outplayed them on every point," Ariel reported. "The Saints were helped by two new members from the 93rd Highlanders, but I honestly believe they would have won easily with their ordinary team." Almost certainly true, even though Fleming netted a hat-trick, but Reading appear to have decided from the start that there was more than one way to skin a full-back.

First, they complained about William Pickford, as Secretary of the Hampshire FA, being selected as referee. Then, the game over, a club official approached the St Mary's secretary and asked for an advance on Reading's share of the gate money. Having been obliged, he proceeded to wire a protest to the FA. The letter of complaint from Reading began: "Dear Sir – In our match Reading v. St. Mary [*sic*] we ask for the tie to be awarded to us, on the ground that two players – Fleming and McMillan – were not qualified to play by Rule 5, which states…" And so on, to the effect that they hadn't signed in time to be eligible under Rule 5 (above).

> ### RULES OF THE CHALLENGE CUP COMPETITION.
>
> 5.—No individual shall be allowed to play for more than one competing Club, but the members of each representative team may be changed during the series of matches, if thought necessary. Except in the first round (and in the second round when played in less than 28 days from the date of first round) of the Qualifying Competition in every season, each individual must have been a recognised playing member for the Club for which he purposes to compete at least 28 days previous to the match. A playing member is one who has either actually played for a Club in the current season, or one who has, in writing, intimated to the Secretary of the Association that he is a playing member of that Club. The Secretary shall, in writing, acknowledge the receipt of every such intimation. In the case of postponed, drawn, or re-played matches, only those players shall be allowed to play who were eligible on the date fixed for the completion of the round in which the match was originally played. A player qualified to play in any round, shall be deemed qualified to play in any subsequent round by virtue of his original qualification.

(margin notes: Qualification of players. See decision of Council (d) page 56)

The following Wednesday, Dr Bencraft and Mr J. Hendin represented St. Mary's at an FA Council meeting in London, where Mr Walker "said he was sorry," according to the *Echo*, "to lay the protest before the Association, and offered to re-play the match if the council gave its permission." This offer was declined and it was explained – fairly apologetically, to judge from the *Echo* account – that while St Mary's "had acted in perfect good faith in the matter," they were out in Reading's favour.

As to "good faith," we will never know if Saints were trying to pull a fast one, but their claims of innocence do echo down the millennium with a somewhat hollow ring. As for Reading, their conduct was churlish, given such an emphatic defeat – although offering a replay was, if sincere, a redeeming gesture.

So that's how Saints came to be out of the Cup without losing a game. Mr Hendin sent a telegram from London to the *Southampton Times*: "Disqualified, poor old Saints."

"Poor old Saints indeed," that paper commented. "A short ending to a long story." Or was it? There is an interesting postscript. Two seasons later Saints would lose 2-1 at Reading in the Second Qualifying Round. This time it would be St. Mary's, now with professionals in their ranks, who would protest. This time the FA would reject it. Reading would go through to the First Round Proper of the Cup, at Preston North End. And lose 18–0.

St MARY'S:

Ruffel, Marshall, Carter, Stride, McMillan, Varney, Kiddle, Nicholls, Fleming, Delamotte, Farwell

READING:

Marrowell, Justins, White, Deane, Lewis, Oliver, Turner, Warburton, Hewitt, Read, Venard

Referee: Mr William Pickford   *Attendance:* 4,000

Compiled by **DAVE JUSON** from reports in the *Echo, Southampton Times* and *Southampton Observer;* and from the 1912 series on the Saints' history in the *Southampton Pictorial,* with additional material from Geoffrey Green's *Official History of the FA Cup.* Team photo from the *Echo* collection. Rule 5 of the FA's Rules reproduced from the earliest available copy in its library.

St Mary's 0
Stoke 8

"Thanks to the enterprise of the Saints," Ariel rejoiced in the *Southampton Times* of 29 April 1893, "Southampton has at last been visited by a first-class English league team."

The Saints' first season with the odd professional had been a sobering one. Only 12 months before, St Mary's had been lords of all they surveyed. True, the vista did not stretch much further than the borders of Hampshire, but neither players nor supporters really knew the meaning of defeat. And now, at the end of a term that had seen the Club's first annual dinner without some impressive silverware on the head table, one would have thought that the last thing Saints needed was a visit from Stoke, original members of the Football League and currently seventh in its First Division.

Ariel was reporting from the County Ground, with spectators "packed round the ropes like peas in a pod, and the grand stand was full to overflowing." Deprived of injured skipper George Carter but re-enforced with Banister Court's precocious Brazilian winger, Charles Miller - destined to be a legend in his native country (see Match No. 39) if not in the town where he had learned his football — Saints got off to a bright start. But Stoke soon took over and scored eight times. Saints were, Ariel concluded, "outplayed fairly and squarely on every point."

As for the spectators, they "thoroughly enjoyed the exhibition, and it is hoped that we shall in future witness more matches of a similar character."

The notion that the spoiled Saints' fans might welcome further 8-0 defeats may seem a little perverse, especially since the result capped a season of set-backs. The previous month Saints had appeared in their third consecutive Hampshire FA Senior Cup Final, with a chance of taking the trophy outright. Their opponents were local rivals, Freemantle. Defeated 5-1, you may recall, in Saints' first-ever game, they had, hitherto, never threatened to eclipse them since. During the summer of

1892, however, the Magpies – as they were known by their adherents – had elected to step up from the junior ranks and there was a lot of excited talk emanating from Shirley and district about their prospects of senior honours. Such talk was sustained by the news that Saints had bid to sign their full-back George Ridges as a professional. Freemantle had persuaded him to stay, although Saints had taken their forward, Jack Dollin, on professional terms (£1 a week and he was found a job).

Yet – curiously, given their open intentions regarding Ridges – they kept his status a secret. Saints had also courted controversy by taking on, as an amateur, Geneva Cross defender "Ginger" Price. Supporters of the Royal Victoria Hospital club were not amused, but St Mary's were old hands at poaching the best local prospects.

No matter that the only instance was clandestine, the development of a policy that admitted paid players into the ranks showed commendable ambition. It also signalled, though, a degree of desperation: two stalwart forwards, Arthur Farwell and F.A. Delamotte, would be unavailable for most of the season, the former's duties at the Edwin Jones department store having ruled out Saturday afternoons and the latter's occupation, as a surveyor, having taken him to Derby.

Saints' aspirations went beyond monopolising the best local players. They were also arranging fixtures with the best and most attractive opponents available to them in the south, including Woolwich Arsenal, who, having gone professional, were pariahs in London and beyond. This certainly pulled in the crowds, but it was, this season, to backfire on the field: their first win wasn't registered until October, when they beat Newbury 4-1 at the Antelope Ground in the First Qualifying Round of

The Brazilian Charles Miller of Banister Court

Friendly

the FA Cup. Again drawn at home in the next round, they lost 4-0 to Maidenhead – their first-ever defeat in an FA-sanctioned competition.

Never shy of learning from negative experiences – recall their pilfering of the 93rd Highlanders, as recorded in the previous report – Saints instantly persuaded the Maidenhead forward F.W. Janes to join them. But he had second thoughts and the episode ended in farce, as both the player and his club were suspended for a week by the FA, following a plea that Janes was in no fit condition to know what he was doing when he signed.

In November, with St Mary's continuing to struggle, the committee took the momentous decision to advertise in the athletic press for fresh blood. This resulted in the arrival of Jack Dorkin, who'd made his reputation with the Royal Engineers – not the Aldershot battalion (of Match No. 4 fame) but the regimental side. Saints had to play their 1892-93 Senior Cup matches without him, however. This was not because he was a professional – according to William Pickford, "Hampshire never subscribed to the 'professional barred' theory" – but because he failed the residential qualifications.

Despite Dorkin's absence Saints cruised to the final, courtesy of a brace of 2-0 wins over Aldershot's Royal Engineers and Portsmouth AFC (a gentlemanly side unconnected with the present Portsmouth FC). The final took place at the familiar surroundings of the County Ground, in front of a 7,000 gate, and Saints were able to count on the services of Delamotte and Farwell, the latter having obtained leave from Mr Edwin Jones. Whether the invitation to Mrs Jones to present the trophy had any bearing on the decision is unknown.

Farwell's presence notwithstanding, Mrs Jones had to present the Cup to Freemantle, 2-1 winners. Saints had now suffered, in this one season, their first two "official" Cup defeats. The Magpies' supporters had something to celebrate – the story goes that, after the pubs closed in Freemantle that night, the Cup was placed in the middle of the street (presumably outside their *Waterloo Arms* HQ) and the fans danced around it – but their vanquished rivals were heading for bigger things at the Antelope.

The Saints' ground was more conveniently located for the bulk of Southampton's population than Freemantle's, situated at what was until recently the Civil Service Club off Malmesbury Road. Moreover, Saints were, as already noted, pitting themselves against more accomplished and reputable opposition; and, while they may have bitten off more than they could chew in the form of Stoke, they had, unquestionably, learned an invaluable lesson.

In a little over a year, three of the Stoke side that had so comprehensively outclassed St Mary's would be on their books. And within two years, the Stoke trainer William Dawson would be at the Club, with another of that 1893 team plus a couple of other Stoke regulars. And the traffic from Stoke continued: in 1898, with three of their former players, Meston, Farrell and Clawley, in their ranks, Saints would reach the FA Cup semi-final (Match No. 9), while Stoke would be relegated to the Second Division.

But the final word, as reported by the *Southampton Times,* must go to the redoubtable George Ridges, replying to the toasts of those assembled at the Waterloo Hall for the Magpies' triumphant Annual Dinner that May. He "did not see why they should not call their club the Southampton Football Club."

St MARY'S:
Ruffell, Taylor, Price, Stride, Marshall, Verney, Nicholls, Nineham, Dorkin, Farwell, Miller

STOKE:
A. Evans, Clare, Thompson, Proctor, Littlehales, Brodie, Dickson, Naughton, Robertson, Baker, J. Evans

Referee's name and attendance not available

Compiled by **DAVE JUSON** from reports in the *Echo, Hampshire Independent, Southampton Observer* and *Southampton Times;* and with reference to William Pickford's Hampshire FA *Golden Jubilee Book* and (with Alfred Gibson) *Association Football and the Men Who Made It.* Both illustrations from **Duncan Holley**'s collection

SOUTHAMPTON ST MARY'S 3
CHATHAM 1

This wasn't just any game. It was the dawn of a new era: SOUTHERN LEAGUE football. Optimism was rampant. Reflecting this mood in his *Southampton Times* column, Ariel predicted that, if the newcomers were "any good at all they should at least go one or two goals better than the men of Kent. Judging from paper form, they ought to be able to do this without killing themselves."

And there were some, he observed, whose forecast extended to the end of the season ahead:

> It is very wonderful to notice the pertinacity with which the prophets continue to prophesy. Southampton St Mary's have not yet played in the competition, but their position at the end of the season has been positively fixed by some people, and I have not heard anybody place them lower than third on the list. Millwall Athletic and Luton only taking precedence.

This faith in Saints was, however, a parochial phenomenon: when Millwall's directors issued invitations to meet them in the Billiter Coffee Rooms in London's Fenchurch Street on 12 January 1894, to discuss setting up the new competition, St Mary's were not at the table. Nor were they invited to a follow-up meeting. And when the Saints committee sent an application to join it was turned down – even though there were but nine clubs lined-up for the 1894–95 season and all bar Millwall and Luton Town were amateur, while Saints had been taking on professionals for as long as, if not longer than, either. As it transpired, an upturn in interest required the creation of a second division, but Saints were spared the trouble of applying for that by the withdrawal of the 2nd Scots Guards and a consequent invitation to take their place.

St Mary's had much to prove to justify their late inclusion. New signing, Alf Littlehales, seemed positive enough when interviewed by "Loiterer" for the local sporting weekly, *Southern Referee*. Although he confessed to knowing little, "from actual experience," about any Southern League opponents, he did not "expect to lose much – not down here, at any rate. I'm certain we shall make them all go."

Littlehales's confidence clearly owed little to his previous experience of playing in Southampton: he had been part of the Stoke side, featured in the previous report. Saints, as noted, had learned from their 8-0 defeat.

The inaugural Southern Leaguers photographed with their honorary officials and the perennial George Muir
Standing (left to right) W. Wheeler (trainer), Marshall, H. Johns (hon. treasurer), Ward, Barrett, Dr Bencraft (President), Hamer, C. Knight (hon. secretary), Muir Middle row: Taylor, Littlehales, Angus, Thompson, Hollands. Front: Nineham, Offer

Southern League

Littlehales was one of three Stoke players signed a year later; Charlie Baker and W.J.G. Thomson were the others, while the Club's other professionals included two – Jack Angus and Henry Offer – with Football League experience. Thus dominated by "mercenaries," Southampton St Mary's would horrify the sensibilities of the strong anti-professional lobby in the South, not least the London FA.

The Club still had four "gentlemen" – half-back George Marshall (to whom you were introduced in Match No. 4) and forward Arthur Nineham, both local lads; and schoolmaster, Herbert Ward, and shipping line cashier, E.J. Taylor – but there was local support for the view that Saints, by fielding professionals, were ahead of the game. As "Old Hand" put it, in the *Southern Referee,* "professionalism is an expensive thing to play with, and the public once educated to it will not be satisfied, but like Oliver Twist, will want more."

That local taste was manifested in the large crowd that assembled at the Antelope Ground – 4,000 to 5,000 according to the *Southampton Times* – to witness the big kick-off, many of them, no doubt, taking advantage of the "cheap fares" advertised by the South Western Railway "from all stations in Hampshire." At 3.15 pm, Mr. C.D. Crisp blew his whistle and Chatham's centre-forward, Gamble, "set the ball in motion up the slope."

While Saints started the stronger side, Chatham threatened first. When Saints 'keeper Jack Barrett missed a cross, "Taffy" Hamer, previously with the Royal Engineers (as in Match No. 4), was on hand to clear. The visitors were not long denied, however, with Barrett again at fault in allowing Gamble to score with "a soft shot." Rallying, he soon made amends with a "brilliant save" from McAucklan and, not long after, Saints equalised when Charlie Baker got down the left and saw his cross converted by Offer.

It was Angus, increasingly dominant, who added Saints' second goal after the interval. The *Southampton Times* description of their third is priceless:

Saints returned to the attack and the whole of the forwards and the half-backs seemed to be making a combined rush at the opposing goal. It was difficult to say who was who, and the ball was not seen again until it had been landed inside the posts with two or three men on top of it. This goal was disputed by the visitors, but the referee allowed it. Gamble made some remarks alleged to be uncomplimentary to the referee, with the result that he was sent off the field.

The goal was eventually credited to the diminutive ex-Millwall winger, Fred Hollands. Ariel acknowledged that Chatham "had some cause for chagrin, for in the rush that took place the ball was in one of these occasions carried right into goal on one of the player's arms." Not a good day for referee Crisp: he also argued with Angus, the Chatham 'keeper and a spectator.

The goal, and the rare event of a dismissal, took some of the sting out of the game. Chatham made several sorties on the Saints' goal, but without profit, and Saints began the first Southern League season with a comfortable victory.

Southern Referee had predicted that the season would be "one of the most interesting we have yet experienced in the South, and it is not too much to say that there is every probability of the class of play so improving that we of the South shall be able to battle with the Northern clubs on more equal terms."

Interesting it certainly was, especially for the seers: Saints did indeed finish third, eight points behind undefeated champions, Millwall, but only two short of Luton. They had certainly confounded those who'd blocked their first attempt at entry.

These were, however, early days. Some indication of the gulf in class between the respective first divisions of the Football League and the Southern League would be available once the FA Cup began to bring the northern professionals to the Antelope – as in our next match of the Millennium.

SOUTHAMPTON St MARY'S:
Barrett, Marshall, Hamer, Taylor, Littlehales, Thomson, Offer, Nineham, Baker, Hollands, Angus

CHATHAM:
Jones, Robertson, Brockwell, Fletcher, Brisley, Lewis, Hall, Enfield, Gamble, Stanford, McAucklan

Referee: Mr C.D. Crisp   *Attendance:* 4,000 or more

Compiled by **GARY CHALK** and **DAVE JUSON** from reports in the *Echo, Southampton Times, Southampton Observer* and *Southern Referee:* and with reference to Paul Harrison's history of the Southern League's first 50 years.

SOUTHAMPTON ST MARY'S 2
SHEFFIELD WEDNESDAY 3

When the First Round Proper of the FA Cup brought Sheffield Wednesday (then often labelled as "The Wednesday") to the Antelope Ground in 1895-96, the *Hampshire Independent* thought it a "momentous" occasion. Yet it was not the first time the humble Southern Leaguers had entertained Football League opposition in this competition. Nottingham Forest had had that distinction the previous season, when they had won 4-1, after overcoming both the spartan state of the changing accommodation – they would have appreciated an oil stove, it seems – and their objections to a frozen surface covered by three inches of snow.

The *Independent* had offered two explanations for this reverse: the more northerly visitors were more accustomed to the Arctic conditions; and the Southampton players had not trained properly. They should accept their responsibilities towards the fans when it came to keeping fit. As if taking that stricture to heart, trainer Dawson spent the week leading up to Wednesday's visit, demanding "self denial and hard work" as he took the team through its paces on Shawford Downs. What was not appreciated at the time – trainer Dawson would reveal it in an *Echo* series almost 30 years later – was that the side even had *tactics:* Hodgkinson, the left-back, had been instructed to stick like glue to Sheffield's star winger, Richards. Hodgkinson, nicknamed "Ironside" by Dawson, was to stick to his task so well that the exasperated Richards would tell him to "go to hell."

Watty Keay, equipped with the boots for a "brilliant shot"

Star players or not, the visitors were not the Football League's greatest – they had, in fact, finished the previous season in mid-table, a place behind Forest – but they had quite a record in the FA Cup, having reached the Final in 1890 and the semi-finals of 1894 and 1895 and, although the coiner of the "momentous" label was not to know it, were on their way to winning the Cup for the first time that very season.

First, though, they had to cope not only with a team that had undergone special training and tactical instruction but with a crowd of "quite 12,000" – the largest yet recorded for a football match in Southampton. Mindful of crowd congestion for the Forest tie the previous season – although this had arisen from the delay in opening the gates while the referee assessed whether the frozen ground was fit to play on – the home committee opened the Antelope gates at the earlier time of 1 o' clock. According to the *Independent,* the masses keenly accepted this invitation to take their places:

> Between that hour and the time announced for the kick off, thousands wended their way to the Antelope Ground. Never have the money changers had such a lively time of it, as for nearly two hours they were literally bombarded. The perpetual cry was 'still they come' and one looked and wondered where they came from. Trains from the outlying districts were literally loaded with human freight. The scene at the ground was a sight for the gods. Thousands lined the ropes and crowded the embankments and hundreds packed the stands. The enclosure was encircled by a dense and perfect sea of faces. Snatches of songs were sung and all was gay. Every coign of vantage had been monopolised, windows and house tops not excepted. Saturday was, in truth, a red letter day in the annals of Hampshire football.

The ground could not take this large crowd. Shortly before the teams ran out, a shed roof collapsed, injuring fans who had been in the shed and some who were perched on top. One George May sustained a broken ankle and a Mr. Brett, who had been inside, suffered serious damage to a knee that prevented him working. His suit against the Club for damages failed, as the shed was

FA Cup First Round

declared out of bounds, although the defendants agreed to help him in his hardship.

While the visitors were at full strength, the Saints fielded a reserve goalkeeper in Walter Cox, whose career with the Club had started as an outfield player. Their first choice, Tom Cain, had recently arrived from Everton cup-tied, while the *Independent* reported that the "military authorities had denied permission for the brilliant [guest] RA keeper, Reilly, to play": ironically, Gunner Reilly would win an FA Amateur Cup Final medal that season, when the Royal Artillery lost 1-0 to Bishop Auckland.

Wednesday won the toss and Cox was immediately called upon to "clear grandly." Play settled down and the home team more than held their own. Indeed, had Farrell not hesitated in front of goal, they might have snatched an early lead. The Saints' centre-forward and captain soon redeemed himself, however, by finding Watty Keay who, "with a brilliant shot, found the net." But "hardly had the shouts subsided," when Brady equalised with a swift, low shot. The same player then gave Wednesday a half-time lead, despite Meston's efforts to clear his lines.

When Davis made it 3-1 soon after the break, the man from the *Independent* observed that "these successive reverses were sufficient to dishearten Saints, but they nevertheless played up pluckily." Thomson thought he had scored, following a foul, but had not realised that the referee, Lieutenant Simpson, had signalled an indirect free-kick. Then, after a "brilliant shot" from Farrell had been tipped over the bar, the ensuing corner led to a "stiff melee", from which Turner "headed through amidst a scene of wild excitement." Encouraged by their unprecedented support, the Saints now "played for all they were worth, but the visitors did not relax their efforts." Try as the home team might, the equaliser would not come and The Wednesday held on to their lead, relieved to hear the final whistle.

The *Hampshire Independent* imagined that "the thousands who witnessed [this] memorable struggle... will in fancy live it o'er again, and its ever changing scenes and incidents will flit kaleidoscopically before their mind's eye."

Amid all the hyperbole, there was no doubt that St Mary's were improving all the time and could compete and hold their own with the famous Football League teams from the north, as they were to prove – momentously so – in the next few seasons.

Standing (left to right)
E.C. Jarvis, Meston,
Marshall, Barrett,
Littlehales, Cox, Wood,
W. Dawson (trainer).

Sitting (left to right)
Baker, Naughton,
Rogers, Farrell,
Thompson, Keay
J. Turner.

SOUTHAMPTON St MARY'S:
Cox, Meston, Thomson, Naughton, Littlehales, Hodgkinson, Baker, Naughton, Farrell, Keay, Turner

SHEFFIELD WEDNESDAY:
Massey, Earp, Brandon, Petrie, Crawshaw, Jamieson, Richards, Brady, Bell, Davis, Spikesley

Referee: Lieut. Simpson   *Attendance:* 12,000

Compiled by **DUNCAN HOLLEY** from the *Hampshire Independent* report and from William Dawson's *Echo* series of 1924

SOUTHAMPTON 0
NOTTINGHAM FOREST 2

Southampton St. Mary's were undefeated Southern League champions in 1896–97, which carried about as much kudos then as it did in 1997.

That summer they became a limited liability company, changed their name to Southampton, made some big-name signings and went on to engrave themselves on the nations' sporting consciousness. Not through winning the Southern League again – which they did – but by undertaking an audacious Cup run which would culminate in one of the most notorious refereeing performances in the annals of the winter game.

Saints swash-buckled through to the First Round of the FA Cup scoring thirteen goals in their three qualifying rounds, earning a home tie with Leicester Fosse of the Football League's Second Division. The 2-1 victory, their first against a Football League club in the Cup, gave them another home match against another Division II club, high-flying Newcastle United, who were evidently dismayed to lose by the only goal of the game. A Geordie scribe, commenting on the draw for the Third Round, somewhat churlishly predicted that: "Southampton are making the trip to Bolton and by next Saturday night we will probably hear the last of the parrot cries concerning the great improvement in the game south of the Thames." An opinion probably shared by footer pundits all over the country. Bolton Wanderers were, after all, one of the elite and Southampton… unknown north of Luton.

So the goalless draw at Burnden Park on 26 February was something of a sensation. The replay, the following Wednesday on the County Ground, a somewhat bigger one. Some 15,000 spectators jostled for a view, as Saints became the first Southern club, in over a dozen years, to reach the semi-finals. Bolton's elimination was a shock. The score, 4–0, was outrageous.

But there was no big secret regarding Saints' overnight rise from obscurity. The directors had assembled an accomplished team – at least nine of whom had First Division experience – and, on paper, if not in the newspapers, it was more than the equal of most Football League sides.

The *Daily Mail,* generally antipathetic to professionalism, felt obliged to explain the ghastly truth to its readers: "While lamenting the methods by which this condition of things has been brought about – that is to say the hiring of aliens – one cannot escape a feeling of gratification that the South is holding its own once more."

Saints continued to hold the South's own in the semi-final. Despite having to trek up to Sheffield United's Bramall Lane (relieved by a week in Matlock Bath) for the tie with Nottingham Forest, and having their best forward, Jack Farrell, reduced to a passenger for most of the game. An equaliser from Harry Haynes earned a 1-1 draw and a replay at the Cup Final venue, Crystal Palace, the following Thursday.

The *Echo* testified that "almost every village in Hampshire contributed its quota to the great gathering at Sydenham this afternoon." This gathering was greeted by "a blinding blizzard, [which] continued to 3 o'clock, when it abated." Saints won the toss, kicked out of a strong wind and dominated, but had nothing to show for their superiority but a penalty, which Joe Turner failed to convert.

Replay action before the blizzard.

Referee Lewis, whose decision to play on in a blizzard led to widespread recriminations and talk of a demonstration

Most reports give Saints the best of the second-half as well, then "so heavy did the snow turn that with less than ten minutes left for play Mr. Lewis [the referee] stopped the game for a time, the players leaving the field." And, "hardly had the players taken up their positions again when the snow recommenced with redoubled fury, and the Forest, assisted by the Blizzard, put on a couple of goals in the last minutes."

Another account attests that Clawley, the Saints 'keeper, had his eyes "choked with snow" and all reports (outside Nottingham at least) agree that the storm was worse when the two goals were scored than when the players had been taken from the pitch. The recriminations started immediately after the final whistle, although one spectator, writing to London's *Morning Leader,* was not swayed by the prevailing indignation: "The demoralising effect of an imported team of mercenaries was evident in the behaviour of the southern partisans at the Crystal Palace on Thursday. Anything more unsportsmanlike it would be difficult to conceive."

The Southampton board promptly protested to the FA, journalists and supporters fulminated, and people who had never previously heard of Southampton were, apparently, outraged, but the FA was intractable. Hardly surprising, as the villain of the piece was an eminent member of their organization. A director of Blackburn Rovers, the referee had, as Simon Inglis points out, "thirty years at the top," and managed to fall out with just about everyone. From Accrington to Antwerp John Lewis was showered with abuse and pelted with bottles, even close friends weren't immune from his often savage temper.

Neither was he the sort of personality that would admit to an error of judgment. Forest went on to win the Cup.

The blizzard was not restricted to Crystal Palace. The *Echo* diligently catalogued the extensive damage to property and "numerous shipwrecks" and attempted to enumerate deaths on land and at sea. Southampton, being a seaport, had concerns related to the gale other than being unfairly denied the Cup.

On Cup Final day our friend Ariel concluded his column by observing that

There can be no doubt that most people in the South, barring the crank who wrote to the papers decrying Southampton, are fully in sympathy with Southampton, and I am not surprised to hear there has been talk about a "demonstration" against Mr. Lewis and the Notts Forest FC. What's the good of that, what's the good of "anyfink," as Chevalier [a famous philosopher of the day] says, now that it is all over.

SOUTHAMPTON:
Clawley, Nicol, Haynes, Petrie, Chadwick, Meston, Brown, Stevens, Buchanan, Keay, Turner

NOTTINGHAM FOREST:
Allsopp, Hitchin, Scott, Forman, McPherson, Wragg, McInnes, Richards, Benbow, Capes, Spouncer

Referee: Mr J. Lewis (Blackburn)   *Attendance:* 15,000

Compiled by **DAVE JUSON** from the *Echo, Southampton Times, Southampton Observer* and the *Daily Mail;* and with reference to the Club Minutes, Geoffrey Green's *Official History of the FA Cup,* Simon Inglis's *League Football And The Men Who Made It* and *Association Football And The Men Who Made It* by Alfred Gibson and William Pickford. Illustrations from **Duncan Holley**'s collection.

SOUTHAMPTON 4
BRIGHTON UNITED 1

Nothing could have been more favourable than the general conditions which attended the opening of the football season at Southampton FC this afternoon. The weather was perfect, there was a large display of bunting on the grand stands, whilst the light and varied coloured costumes of the ladies who graced the opening match by their presence all helped to make up a scene of exceptional brilliancy and charm

"Echoist", *Southern Daily Echo*, 3 September 1898

The weather on Saturday was simply scorching, and made one fancy [the spectators] were off to a cricket match, instead of to the opening of the magnificent new football enclosure "The Dell," which Mr. George Thomas has so liberally provided for the Southampton Football Club. Mr. Thomas is to be congratulated on the success which has crowned his efforts, he has spent month[s] of hard work, working out the various little details and has spared no expense to make the enclosure one of the finest in the country. No wonder the "Daily Mail" representative was so pleased with the ground, it is something to be proud of.

Southampton Amusements, 12 September 1898

The Club's trumpeted move to a new home at The Dell was not all good news for visiting journalists. Echoist felt his readers should be apprised of the arduous conditions he laboured under:

> the accommodation for the press was of a somewhat primitive nature; in fact not nearly so good as that at the County Ground, which was not itself of the best. There was no desk on which to write and the unfortunate scribe had to get his copy out as best he could.

And yet, despite the restricted site, the new ground was, in terms of facilities for players and spectators, among the best-appointed in the country. And its reputed capacity of 24,500 was eight times the average crowd Saints had been attracting to the nearby County Ground.

The Board hadn't the wherewithal to take a share in The Dell – possibly because so much had been spent on assembling a new team for the new ground. Jack Farrell and George Clawley had returned to Stoke during the close season; and Joe Turner, who had ousted Farrell as the season's leading goalscorer, had gone with them. But four

The Mayor kicks off "like an international"

Southern League

internationals had arrived: England's Jack Robinson, the best goalkeeper of his generation, and Harry "Wolf" Wood; and Scotland's Jack Robertson and Peter Meehan. Despite the Saints' reputation for snatching "tip top players" from Football League clubs, the signing of Harry Wood from Wolverhampton Wanderers was still something of a sensation. Trainer, Billy Dawson, had tracked him down in a Walsall pub, after reading that he was out of contract.

Duly appointed skipper to a complement of 23 professionals, Wood led out the chosen XI. Wearing their new, cherry-striped jerseys – as supplied by local sports outfitters, Barton and Dorkin – they were greeted by a special "Yi,Yi,Yi" from the crowd of 6,525, which included members of Southampton Corporation. Their opponents, the recently-created Brighton United, fielded nine Scotsmen, including Roddy McLeod, who would be wearing those cherry stripes by the end of the season.

Then, observed the *Echo*, "Harry Wood was lucky in winning the spin of the coin and [establishing a long tradition] chose to defend the Bedford-Road [Milton] end, with the powerful sun at his back, then the ball was placed in the centre for the Mayor [Alderman G J Tilling], who kicked off like an international."

Saints were soon leading. With "a little finessing," Smith found Keay, who scored The Dell's first goal. McKenzie missed some good chances, while Bullimer saved from Keay, Hartley, Wood, Meston and Chadwick. Then Chadwick, with a high kick, accidentally caught McArthur full on the chin. Bleeding profusely, McArthur was out of the game. Reduced to 10 men, Brighton found themselves confined to their own half and Bullimer needed to be in top form.

The Saints defend the Archers Road End

With half-time approaching, though, McKenzie made a smart run up the left and crossed for Hartley to score.

Debutant McKenzie, who was being dubbed "little Joe Turner" by an appreciative crowd, added a third. McLeod pulled one back with a shot that gave Robinson no "earthly chance," according to the *Southampton Observer*.

The tempo of the game now quickened, tempers had become strained and referee Saywell needed to speak to several players as the fouls became more frequent. The fourth Saints goal, scored by Wood, was considered "just such a goal as there is no doubt about – a shot which beats the goalkeeper almost before it was made."

With a quarter of an hour left to play, both teams were now visibly suffering from the intense heat and the game deteriorated. But it had been a happy start to Saints' long residence at The Dell. George Thomas had less to be happy about. He had been negotiating with his fellow-directors for some months, as to how much the newly-incorporated Southampton Football & Athletic Company Limited would contribute to the development; but when the £5,000 share issue was seriously under-subscribed, he was left with no option other than to lease the stadium for £250 a season, little more than the Saints would expect to pay if they had returned to their landlords at the Hampshire County Cricket Club. Estimates as to how much Thomas – soon to be ousted from the board – was out of pocket vary between £7,000 and £11,000, but it would be nearly 40 years before he could expect to show a profit – a very long-term investment indeed.

As it happened, by the time the directors took the plunge in 1926, it was Mr Thomas's widow from whom they bought what they had referred to, back in 1898, as "our new ground."

SOUTHAMPTON:

Robinson, Nicol, Haynes, Meston, Chadwick, Robertson, Smith, Wood, Hartley, Keay and McKenzie

BRIGHTON UNITED:

Bullimer, Hendry, Caldwell, Farrell, Longair, McAvoy, Clark, McLeod, McArthur, Willock, Mallock

Referee: Mr T W H Saywell   *Attendance:* 6,524

Compiled by **GARY CHALK** and **DAVE JUSON** from the *Echo, Southampton Observer* and *Southampton Times,* with an overture from *Southampton Amusements*

BRISTOL CITY 3
SOUTHAMPTON 4

The climax to the Southern League's fifth season could not have been better stage-managed if Rupert Murdoch and Sir Alex Ferguson had been licensed to decide who played whom when.

As this League increasingly competed for attention with the Football League, sections of the London sporting press (having only an insignificant Second Division Woolwich Arsenal to sustain their readers' interest in the Football League) were agitating for the First Division to be re-organised to accommodate the top Southern League sides. And here were the two top sides of all meeting in Bristol, on the last day of the 1898-99 season, to determine the title.

That title had been Southampton's for the past two seasons. But now these heirs to Millwall's early dominance needed to see off alternative challengers to their supremacy.

Bristol City had finished second to the Saints in 1898 and were now level with them, on this final afternoon of the season, on 33 points. With something of a reputation for "rough play," the City had lost 4-1 away to the "scientific" Saints in early March.

There was mixed news for the Saints. The bad: their hosts were undefeated at St John's Lane throughout 1898–99. The good: with a superior goal average, of 2.43 against 1.79, the Saints needed only to draw to clinch their third successive Championship Shield.

While some 400 Saints' supporters were among the 13,000 at the match, those left at home had the option of following its progress from telegrams posted in the windows of the town's newspaper offices. The drama of the first-half focused principally on Jack Robinson, the Saints 'keeper.

An England international, Robinson had come south from New Brighton for the start of the season. In failing to stop an early shot from the home outside-right, Langham, Robinson so damaged his right hand that he needed to go off for whatever counted as treatment in 1899.

Harry Haynes took his place in goal and the nine outfield players succeeded in preventing any shots at him, pending their 'keeper's return.

Still in pain, he played out the half, admirably protected by his backs, Durber clearing cleverly on several occasions. The defence could not, however, prevent Langham scoring from a free-kick that went into the net off the underside of the crossbar. And that was the news in the half-time wires…

Bristol City 2 Southampton 0

"The Conquering Heroes" of 1898-99 with the Southern League trophy
Standing (left to right) Hamer (trainer), Mr G. Payne (director), Meston, Mr H. Ashton (director), Meehan, Dr. Stancomb (chairman),
Robinson, Durber, Mr A. Wood (director), Chadwick, Haynes, W. Dawson
Sitting: E. Arnfield (secretary), Yates, McLeod, Wood, McLean, Robertson, W. Joyce.

Southern League

The second-half, in which Robinson almost fainted with the pain of his injury, belonged to the visitors.

A half-time shuffle took McLeod to centre-forward and McLean to inside-forward to some effect: within 12 minutes the scores were level.

First, Arthur Chadwick succeeded with a trademark long shot; and then a shot from Jock Robertson took a gentle "hint" off Harry Wood's foot to beat goalkeeper Monteith, who had advanced too far.

With Chadwick and his full-backs successfully protecting Robinson, Saints were now having the better of the game; and a move involving Robertson and Wood ended with McLean making it 3-2. A solemn silence descended over the St John's Lane crowd, an atmosphere of disbelief and resignation to a Saints victory, broken only by the "Southampton whisper" of "Yi! Yi! Yi!" Then, just to make sure, Saints "popped" a fourth, Wood heading in the simplest of chances from a corner.

Bristol finished the game with a spell of pressure; but, despite a goal from Caie, the final telegrams announced that Saints had won 4-3 and were Champions for the third time in a row.

Such was the impact of this news that, when the team's special train steamed into the Docks Station at 10.30. pm, it was greeted by streets filled with enthusiastic supporters.

And before the players transferred to their brakes for a victory procession through the major thoroughfares, the Town Band struck up, not for the first time, a tune appropriate to the undoubted overlords of the south: SEE THE CONQUERING HEROES.

Goalkeeping hero Robinson and the scorers of three of Saints' goals

---

BRISTOL CITY:

Monteith, Davy, Stewart, Jones, McLean, Hamilton, Langham, Finnerhan, Caie, O'Brien, Russell

SOUTHAMPTON:

Robinson, Durber, Meehan, Meston, Chadwick, Haynes, Yates, McLeod, McLean, Wood, Robertson

Referee: Capt. Simpson   *Attendance:* 13,000

Compiled by **GARY CHALK** and **DAVE JUSON** from the *Echo, Southampton Times* and *Southampton Observer;* and from the Saints' history in the *Southampton Pictorial,* 1912

SOUTHAMPTON 0
BURY 4

The Southampton club is the surprise packet of the football world. No team can boast of having fought their way to the front with such lightening-like rapidity as the champions of the South, and if the opinions of experienced judges are worth anything the Southampton men have no superiors.

So readers of *Chums* were informed in October 1899. They were also told that Saints did not play in the Football League because, there being no League clubs in the South, "if Southampton were to enter the competition, about half there time would be spent travelling to the North and back – a proceeding that would soon land them high and dry in bankruptcy court." In fact, there was one League club in the South, but, as intimated in the previous report, *Chums* could be forgiven for forgetting them: Second Division Woolwich Arsenal were struggling to emulate the likes of New Brighton and Glossop in that division let alone to match Saints and Millwall Athletic.

Although Tottenham Hotspur were threatening to become top London dog of the Southern League (of which more, come Match No. 14), Millwall – whose early dominance of the League has already been touched upon – were still the pride of the capital, even more so when they qualified to play Saints in the 1900 FA Cup semi-final by eliminating League Champions, Aston Villa.

Saints had made stately progress to the Crystal Palace semi-final, courtesy of Everton, Newcastle United and West Bromwich Albion. Millwall, a tougher proposition, held Saints to a goalless draw, but league form and the "superior science" of the Southampton side told at Elm Park – by 3-0. "Stirring scenes in Reading later," reported the Football *Echo:*

> Procession of Saints in principle streets.
> Flags, streamers, banners.
> Violins, accordions, rattles,
> Cornets, flutes, harps, sackbuts,
> "Psaltry and all sorts of musick"

There was to be no such jollity after the final. Not among the Saintly hordes at least.

Bury were no Aston Villa. They had joined the Football League's Division Two in 1894, winning promotion at their first attempt, and, one flirtation with relegation apart, had remained anchored in mid-table. They did,

Arthur Chadwick's loser's medal

however, have something of a reputation for pulling off unexpected results. Hence their nickname, "the Shakers."

And shake Saints is precisely what they did. The "favourites" lost the toss and kicked into the sun on a blazing hot day. They fell behind, after 10 minutes, to a goal by McLuckie and, 10 minutes later, they were three goals in arrears. Despite a few impressive runs by outside-left Milward, the Saints never looked in the game.

"A WEAK, WAVERING, PITIABLE AND LAMENTABLE SHOW," concluded "Soton" (the Southampton correspondent of the weekly sporting bible, *Athletic News*):

> I can sadly say, and without doing any injustice to Bury, that from goalkeeper to centre-forward not a man in the Southampton side played up to his reputation.

The Saints were, undoubtedly, the more cultured and talented side. Their Secretary, Mr. Arnfield, was not bluffing when he told *Chums* that the Club "shouldn't dream of engaging a player who wasn't worthy of inclusion in the Aston Villa eleven" - as a weekly wage bill in excess of £60 a week, ludicrously modest as it seems now, testified.

True, Bury had the young Ted Sagar at inside-forward and Plant on the wing, both recently capped by England – although Plant's inclusion was widely regarded as an injustice to Milward, his Southampton counterpart, who was not only in better form, but had already proved himself at international level while with Everton. Moreover, three Saints' players had represented England that season: centre-half Arthur Chadwick; Jack Robinson, the most highly regarded goalkeeper in the country; and young left-winger, Arthur Turner, the only Hampshire man in the Southampton side. And you have already been introduced, also, to Scottish international Meehan at right-back and the inimitable Harry Wood, whose signing in 1898 had been a sensation of Kevin Keegan at the Potter's Heron proportions.

So what had gone wrong? A defeat, perhaps, was excusable – Bury were a modest outfit maybe, but no mugs – but all commentators agreed that the margin of defeat and standard of performance were not. It took 12 rumour-filled years before a serious post mortem was attempted – by "Recorder" of the *Southampton Pictorial*. Reflecting that there had "never been what one could call an official explanation of the team's failure," he revealed that

> the cause of the trouble was some little jealousy between the English and Scottish "schools" in the team. One section wanted McLeod to play at centre forward and the other favoured Farrell. This jealousy, while it disturbed the harmony which was so essential to success, did not develop into disloyalty… but matters went badly for the team from the start, and some players, instead of making special efforts to save the game, attributed their non-success to the deliberate flouting of their wishes.

One player admitted, "I could see that some of the others were not trying, and said to myself. 'Why should I run myself to a stand still'." The *Pictorial* offers scant further enlightenment, but that Jack Farrell, a volatile individual, was the centre of affairs would have surprised few contemporary Sotonians.

The pick of the 1895 exodus from Stoke in the aftermath of Match No. 6, he had returned there for a season, before coming back to Southampton for the 1899-1900 season, earlier in which he had been injured.

Roddy McLeod had deputised successfully and had proved popular, especially with Southampton's football journalists, a member of whom had been physically threatened by Farrell, during his first sojourn at the club, for having the temerity to criticise his game.

If Farrell was the more adroit of the two contenders for the centre-forward place, it would have been natural for some team-mates to prefer the more selfless, and less temperamental, contribution of McLeod. But was that the case? As it transpired both players were transferred at the end of the season and one might reason that McLeod was as culpable for the prevailing lack of spirit as his rival.

Another player on his travels was the Scottish half-back Petrie, who, the *Morning Leader* contended, "would tackle a steam train if called upon." Unfortunately, he also relished tackling the bottle; and being found drunk in The Dell's dressing room that December was probably the penultimate straw, his wretched performance in the final being the last. Both full-backs, Meehan and Peter Durber, were also off to fresh pastures.

The virtual deconstruction of what had been a highly distinguished side – it had, give or take a man or two, won the previous three Southern League championships – hints that the Board was just as dismayed as the supporters about what had transpired.

The directors' actual opinions remain a mystery. There was a board meeting the day after the final at the Bedford Hotel.

The minutes of that gathering contain not one mention of the previous day's game.

A photograph of the Final appears to have captured a rare Saints' attack

---

SOUTHAMPTON:
Robinson, Meehan, Durber, Meston, Chadwick, Petrie, Turner, Yates, Farrell, Wood, Milward

BURY:
Darroch, Thompson, Davidson, Ross, Leeming, Pray, Plant, Sagar, McLuckie, Wood, Richards

Referee: A. Kingscott (Derby)   *Attendance:* 68,945

Compiled by **DAVE JUSON** from the *Times, Athletic News, Echo, Southampton Times, Southampton Observer, Morning Leader, Chums* and the Club minutes; and with reference to Alfred Gibson & William Pickford's *Association Football And The Men Who Made It* and the Hampshire FA's *Golden Jubilee Book* by William Pickford. Illustrations from **Duncan Holley**'s collection

SOUTHAMPTON 11
NORTHAMPTON TOWN 0

The prospect of watching Southern League First Division newcomers, Northampton Town, on their first-ever visit to The Dell was, evidently, not one to galvanise a Southampton public recovering from the excesses of Christmas and which had good reason, by this time, to be somewhat blasé about their team's status.

The Saints were, basically, too good for the Southern League and, as previously noted, too geographically remote to make competing in the Football League financially viable – the moreso if a season had to be wasted winning its Second Division.

Not even the return, in the Northampton forward line, of their former Jekyll and Hyde hero/anti-hero, Jack Farrell (the previous report tells the sad story), coupled with the opportunity to compare him with his eventual replacement, Albert Brown, was enough to stir enthusiasm on a bleak and rainy day that would, predictably, see the pitch reduced to a quagmire.

The attendance was low, then, for a side that had been banging them in at The Dell, where no visitors had scored since Portsmouth (who would add insult to injury by winning the League that season) had won 4-3 there in early November.

For this last match of 1900-01, the reigning champions of the Southern League would be without such stars as C.B. Fry and Joe Turner, but they would include the up-and-coming local, Fred ("Buzzy") Harrison, and winger Arthur Turner from Farnborough.

Recommended to Southampton by a former *Echo* journalist who had moved to the Aldershot area, Turner's uniqueness (until he was joined by Harrison) as the only Hampshireman to play for a side full of northerners and Scots has already been touched upon.

He was also the first professional from the county to be capped by England.

Those who scorned the terraces for the hearth that day would miss not only Saints' highest League score to date – and still unbeaten in "official" peace-time competition – but two notable performances by individual players: one of them on a cornet; the other from the Saints' centre-forward. Albert Brown, a close season capture from Aston Villa, would score seven goals to set an individual scoring record for the Club – unless you count an "unofficial" eight in a war-time game (see Match No. 32). Brown, reputed

to be the fastest forward in the land and known as the "Tamworth Sprinter", would open the scoring "immediately." They didn't put stop watches on goals in 1901, but those familiar with Saints' fastest-ever goal from a kick-off (or who care to read about it in the report of Match No. 34) – scored 44 years later almost to the day and on a similarly-sodden Dell surface – may find the two efforts remarkably similar.

Brown kicked off and made immediate tracks, we are told, over the slippery ground towards the Northampton goal, where, receiving the ball in a good position, he sent a lovely shot past a bemused Cook. And within five minutes, he had a hat-trick. Then Turner, who was tormenting the visiting defenders, added the fourth goal, an excellently-timed shot from close in on the right.

The Saints seemed to revel in the mud whilst their rivals floundered hopelessly – as when one of their defenders turned a long shot from Meston into his own net. Brown thereupon demonstrated how to keep your feet, as he went clean through Northampton's defence to score a brilliant sixth.

And when a shot from him was only partially cleared, Harrison made it seven. With the Saints' attack doing as they pleased, further efforts from Harrison and Chadwick were disallowed for offside. So they had to settle for a half-time score-line that read: Southampton 7, Northampton 0.

Soon after the restart, Meston shot between Cook's legs for goal number eight. Despite the alarming deficit Northampton, at this point, improved their play.

But back came Brown, this time with a shot of such power that it wedged firm between the railings behind the goal and it took a full minute of hauling and pulling before it was retrieved.

The reprieve was short-lived. Brown's next attempt was a "dinking oblique kick" that beat Cook to make it nine. Saints had by now ceased to take the game seriously and the cornet player in the crowd was contributing to the carnival atmosphere.

Brown
Southampton

P 369

OGDEN'S CIGARETTES

A well-known local character by the name of McKeown, he was in sparkling form with renderings of *Break the News to Mother* and *We'll Have One More to Show There's No Ill Feeling.*

A bewildered Northampton side stuck to their guns and Murrell just missed with a low swift shot that beat a cold and wet Robinson.

In the final minutes, Brown once more got through, fed by Wood, to net number ten and then completed the scoring with his seventh, after he had taken the ball from under Murrell's nose, beaten Turner, left Bennett standing and blasted the ball past a hapless Cook.

Some 22 years later, Saints' retired trainer, William Dawson, reminisced, in a *Football Echo* series, on this match and the contribution of the cornet man. Mr McKeown's eccentric support of Southampton had become well-chronicled in local newspaper reports.

"Echoist", the Bob Brunskell or Graham Hiley of this era, had complained of being kept awake by the sound of the cornet for the entire duration of an overnight special to the Bolton Third Round FA Cup tie in 1898.

The up-and-coming "Buzzy" Harrison

Jack Farrell, the returning "hero/anti-hero"

He was, of course, well-known to the Saints' players, not to mention Jack Farrell. McKeown's noted burst into melody on the ninth goal – a private joke, perhaps? – caused the volatile ex-Saint some upset and after the match he sought out the offender, promising that "If I can find him, he won't play the cornet again."

In the same memoir, Bill Dawson further reported how, after the match,

> Mr Jones, who was in charge of the Northampton team, came to me and said,
> "Bill, I have never seen a team stand up better on heavy ground. How can they keep their feet like that?"
> I answered,
> "Oh yes they can stand up pretty well, because they play the game as it should be played, and don't tumble about all over the place."
> Of course, there was a little secret, and I know how the players managed to keep their feet.

But he wasn't saying how. Was it something to do with their studs? That remains a secret.

SOUTHAMPTON:
Robinson, Henderson, Molyneux, Meston, Bowman, Lee, A Turner, Wood, Brown, Chadwick, Harrison

NORTHAMPTON TOWN:
Cook, Bennett, Turner, Pell, Murrell, Howe, Frost, Chapman, Farrell, Coleman, Laurence

Referee: Mr P R Harrower (London)   *Attendance:* "very small"

Compiled by **GARY CHALK** and **DAVE JUSON** from *Echo* reports and William Dawson's 1924 *Echo* series, "A Trainer's Secret"

Southampton 2
Tottenham Hotspur 1

Southampton and Tottenham Hotspur, the giants of the Southern League, had never met before in the FA Cup. The Saints had won this League for four of the last five seasons, missing out only in 1900, when they might have been said – in today's parlance, anyhow – to have been concentrating on reaching their first Cup Final, allowing Spurs to take the League title. In 1901, however, Tottenham had gone one better than the Saints by winning the Cup.

Since their defeat in the 1900 Cup Final (Match No. 12, in case it passed you by), Southampton had acquired new stars. The side that faced Spurs – in the first two of the three games it took the Saints to see off the Cup-holders – included seven players (most of them introduced in earlier reports) who had won or who'd win international caps: Robinson, Fry, Archie Turner, Molyneux, Lee, Chadwick and Wood. The first three of these had all turned out for England when they beat Ireland 3-0 at The Dell (staging an international for the first time) in 1901.

In the first game at White Hart Lane, it was 1-1 at the interval. Then, dominating the early stages of the second-half, the Saints looked, to the *Hampshire Independent*, as if they "were bound to score." But "the home citadel bore a charmed existence and escaped." When the Spurs staged a late rally, the excitement, hitherto "intense," became "painful, and in their state of feverish tension the crowd swayed to and fro as the venue of play changed."

When the swaying stopped, it was still 1-1.

On the following Wednesday, a large contingent of their fans, identifiable by their lilies of the valley and violets, followed the Spurs to The Dell. The home fans, for their part, were egged on by their mascot who was pelted with oranges. When he kicked one into the Milton Road goal, there were huge cheers – although the more superstitious fans may have recalled him performing the same feat before the previous season's First Round tie, when Southampton had gone out to Everton.

The Spurs looked a better side than in the first game and twice led. But the Saints came back, in what C.B. Fry called a "ding-dong" game, with goals from Edgar Chadwick and Joe Turner, the latter after a clearance from Molyneux had burst the original ball. The score remained at 2-2 after 90 minutes. Extra-time was still optional and, on this occasion, with neither side able to plead the need to catch a ferry (a ploy you may recall from Match No. 3), they agreed to play on "in an attempt to achieve a definite result." There would be no further goals, despite a succession of injuries to Southampton players. First, Brown required lengthy treatment after a violent collision with Hughes. Then Bowman was so incapacitated by cramp that Joe Turner had to drop back to cover for him. And finally, Lee received such a nasty kick on the head that he would miss the second replay.

This took place two days later at Elm Park. The pitch was, according to Fry, "like a skating rink," covered in snow and with the touchlines marked out in blue paint, as the game kicked off with snow still falling.

Lee's injury meant a rare first team appearance for a 20 year-old half-back from Bishopstoke, at a time when, as we have already seen, local lads were uncommon in the Saints' line-ups.

Signed from Eastleigh Athletic, Bert Paddington mostly captained the Reserves. Initially needing support from Molyneux against the pace of Cameron and Gilhooley, he survived a goalless first period to have an impressive second-half.

Soon after the interval, though, Fry let in Gilhooley who crossed for Kirwan to "tip" the ball into the net. The Saints retaliated almost immediately when Archie Turner "screwed in a tricky shot." Southampton were finishing the stronger and, at one stage, play remained in the Tottenham half for a full 10 minutes. Griffiths, the Spurs goalkeeper, saved wonderfully from Chadwick and then

A lapel badge produced for the Saints' 1902 Cup run.
It is the earliest-known badge associated with the Club

Joe Turner scored Saints' second goal

Charles Burgess Fry, part of Southampton's growing international set
and yet much more than that: he equalled the world long jump record
while still a student, hit 94 first-class centuries for Hampshire
and played in 26 Tests for England.

Tait turned the ball against one of his own posts. His reprieve was short-lived. With just a few minutes remaining, he attempted a back pass. Brown had read his mind and, beating Griffiths to the ball, he "shot into the net amid a scene of indescribable enthusiasm." The remaining moments were played out "with great energy" but Southampton held on for a memorable victory over the highly-fancied holders.

SOUTHAMPTON:
Robinson, Fry, Molyneux, Meston, Bowman, Lee, A.Turner, Wood, Brown, Chadwick, J.Turner

TOTTENHAM HOTSPUR:
Griffiths, Erentz, Tait, Hughes, McNaught, Jones, Smith, Cameron, Brown, Coupland, Kirwan
*For Southampton, Paddington replaced Lee for the third game,
while Gilhooley replaced Smith for Spurs in the last two games*

Referee: Mr Kingscott   *Attendance:* 6,000

Compiled by **DUNCAN HOLLEY** from reports in the *Hampshire Independent*, with additional material from **David Bull**, drawing upon Iain Wilton's biography of C.B. Fry. Illustrations from **Duncan Holley**'s collection

SOUTHAMPTON 1
SHEFFIELD UNITED 2

For the second time in three seasons, the Saints were in the Cup Final. Sheffield United were on an even more remarkable run, though. This was their third final in four years. Yet Southampton were still the favourites with the London bookmakers. That says something about the prestige of the Southern League. And we have just seen how Spurs, who had chalked up the first Final win – against Sheffield United – the previous season had gone out of this season's competition to their great Southern League rivals.

After eliminating Tottenham, the Saints had entertained Liverpool, the Champions of the Football League. True, the visitors were not having such a great season, but this still promised to be a tough assignment for a side that had completed their triple-play with Spurs only five days earlier. But trainer Dawson had taken them off to the *Clump Inn* at Chilworth, which had replaced the Shawford Downs retreat, of Match No. 8 for instance, as the team's unofficial headquarters for big match warm-ups and they ran out – according to Dawson writing in 1924 – "like a lot of kittens, full of life."

This frolicsome entry may have been for the benefit of the camera: such was the media interest in this game billed as the battle of the Champions of the South against the Champions of the North that the players were "cinematographed" as they ran out onto the pitch.

In what Dawson described as the "finest exhibition of football put up by the Saints," they beat Liverpool 4-1.

Then came two successive revenge wins against the sides who had beaten them in the 1900 Final (Bury) and the 1898 semi-final (Nottingham Forest) and the Saints were back at Crystal Palace for their second Final.

The Clump Inn at Chilworth had become the training camp for the Saints players before big games – like the 1902 Cup Final.
They lined up there, in the week of the game (players only, left to right)
Back row: Bowman, A.Turner, Henderson, Chadwick, Robinson,
Front row: Meston, Brown, Wood, Molyneux, J.Turner, Lee.

The side again prepared at Chilworth. Although goalkeeper Robinson appeared in the photograph taken at the *Clump,* he went down with a chill and his selection was not confirmed until half-an-hour before the Final kicked off, following an interview with the Southampton directors. The directors "and their friends," the *Hampshire Independent* noted, had travelled up that morning in one of the two reserved carriages of the special train that left the Docks Station at 9 o'clock. Harry Wood and his team were in the other reserved saloon, with Moger and Henderson the travelling reserves. C.B. Fry's inclusion at right-back made him the first amateur to appear in a Cup Final since 1893. In an appreciation of his many talents, published just before the semi-final, The *Tatler* judged him to be "the most remarkable cricketer in England,… probably the most popular footballer" and, all in all, "the greatest all-round athlete in the country."

Despite a smallpox scare and the withdrawal of those tickets that combined the railway journey and admission to the ground, the "dense masses of humanity wedged on the slopes" numbered 76,914.

Some of them, having paid admission, sought a superior view, whence they attracted the attention of the man from the *Hampshire Independent* as the teams ran out to such an ovation that

> the surrounding trees shook as though whipped by a gale, denoting the enthusiasm of adventurous individuals who were in their branches.

Sheffield United opened the scoring early in the second-half, through Alf Common, their young inside-right who would achieve lasting fame, three years later, when he became the first player to merit a four-figure fee.

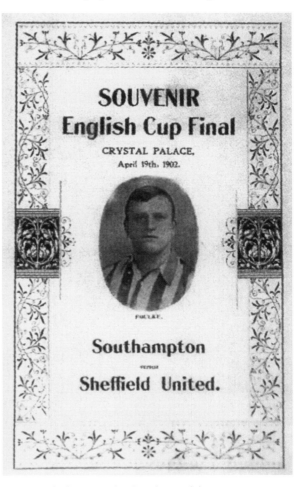

The railway company warns travellers that the combined journey-and-admission tickets have been withdrawn

An artist's depiction of Alf Common's goal in the first game. Fry comes in too late from the left, while Clawley is seemingly too terrified to do more than flap his elbow at the ball. Goodness knows what is going on to the right of the picture

Saints' own star No.8, Harry Wood, left it late to reply. And, even then, the referee consulted his linesman about the possibility of offside before he allowed his equalizer. It seems that Wood was tying his boot-lace in what he himself considered to be an offside position, when the ball reached him. The officials decided, though, that the ball had struck a Sheffield defender and that Wood had been "played on."

Their goalkeeper was not impressed. Described by Fry, in his autobiography, as "the burliest, the heaviest, and the most rubber-like goalkeeper known to history," Billy "Fatty" Foulke weighed more than 20 stone. When he left the dressing room, unclothed, in angry pursuit of the referee, Mr Kirkham took refuge in a broom cupboard. It required a posse of FA officials to dissuade his huge, naked assailant from wrenching the door from its hinges.

So the sides returned to Crystal Palace the following Saturday for what was to prove a better game than the first one - "one of the best finals for some years," according to the *Times*. The Saints were unchanged. The Sheffield outside-right, Bennett, being unfit, Common moved to the wing to accommodate Barnes at inside-right. The attendance was less than half that of the previous Saturday although it did include the Spanish Ambassador.

The Saints' having worn their red-and-white stripes for the first game, it was now Sheffield's turn. So Southampton turned out in white shirts. Within two minutes, they found themselves back in the position from which Wood's disputed effort had rescued then – 1-0 down, courtesy of a Hedley goal. But, undeterred, they ensured that Foulke, a one-cap England international, was the busier of the two

Billy "Fatty" Foulke, who pursued the referee in to a broom cupboard for allowing Southampton's equalizer in the first game

Sheffield United score the winning goal in the replay

'keepers. This pressure continued in the second-half and it would appear, from the match report, that the ball went everywhere but into Foulke's net. It took a "magic" shot from Albert Brown, in the 70th minute, to level matters. "Elated by their success," the *Hampshire Independent* reporter continued, "the Saints again pressed, and Foulke had all his work cut out to stop shots by Chadwick, Wood and Lee." But then, with just two minutes remaining, Barnes, the deputising inside-right, was able to "walk" the ball in after Robinson had failed to cut out a cross. Southampton now made one final push, but Fry blasted a glorious chance high over the bar and they had lost 2-1.

By way of some consolation, Meston "secured" the match ball, just as Bert Lee had done the previous Saturday.

The Saints had failed again at the final hurdle, though, and it would be 74 years before the Club had another chance. But, then, many a reader will already have skipped to Match No. 69.

SOUTHAMPTON:

Robinson, Fry, Molineux, Meston, Bowman, Lee, A.Turner, Wood, Brown, Chadwick, J.Turner

SHEFFIELD UNITED:

Foulke, Thickett, Boyle, Needham, Wilkinson, Johnson, Bennett, Common, Hedley, Priest, Lipsham
Barnes replaced Bennett for the replay

Referee: T.Kirkham (Burslem)   *Attendance:* 33,068

Compiled by **DUNCAN HOLLEY** from the *Hampshire Independent* and William Dawson's 1924 *Echo* series. Additional material by **David Bull,** drawing upon Iain Wilton's biography of C.B. Fry

SOUTHAMPTON 5
PORTSMOUTH 1

The fourteen thousand spectators at the Southampton ground regarded the removal of Harrison from centre to inside right and the substitution of Hedley as pivot was daring; but it was a strategical move of much importance, and not merely a foolish fancy. The arrangement was attended by brilliant results, and was to a considerable extent responsible for the completeness of the victory which the "Saints" gained over their powerful neighbours, Portsmouth.

Thus "Above Bar" opened his report, in the *Athletic News,* on what the headline writer billed as the "THE MATCH OF THE SOUTH." This single paragraph tells us a lot about the way names and tags were used in 1906. A centre-forward could be called a "pivot." But why was "the Southampton ground" not named? Had the Club forgotten to allocate naming rights to its new ground? Seems so. And they'd not even got round to adopting formally the name of "The Dell". So the local correspondent of the Manchester-based *Athletic News* was content to use a simple geographical description for his predominantly northern readership. Likewise, Southampton's nickname (albeit in inverted commas, here) would have made an impact on the north by now. But Portsmouth were plain Portsmouth.

Never mind that, the Rose-is-a-Rose brigade will be saying: what's all this about Portsmouth being "powerful neighbours?" A good question. Since Portsmouth joined

the Southern League in 1899, Saints had had only a slight edge in their encounters, but had won the title, over these six seasons, three times to their neighbour's once. In FA Cup terms, though, this first meeting between the two sides was very much a clash between the southern giants and the novices from down the road. While Saints had recently been to two finals, Portsmouth had yet to venture beyond the Third Round.

That said, Southampton had not themselves got beyond that round since their last Final appearance and were looking, it could be said, to get their FA Cup show back on the road. So it was a setback to have two goalkeepers – first-choice, George Clawley, and his dependable deputy, Tom Burrows, both injured. Bill Stead, the 18 year-old who'd stepped in for the last two League games, came in for his third and last game for the Saints, against his home-town club. If the visitors were reckoning on rattling the rookie 'keeper with what Above Bar described as

This photograph of the 1905-06 squad includes the two injured goalkeepers
– ❶ Burrows and ❷ Clawley – and the 10 outfield members of the side that trounced Portsmouth:
❸ Houlker ❹ Warner ❺ Hartshorne ❻ Lee ❼ Harrison ❽ Hogg ❾ Brown ❿ Tomlinson ⓫ Hedley ⓬ Mouncher

"impetuous rushes calculated to unnerve a youngster," the plan faltered precisely because Stead didn't.

At the other end, Saints' "daring" and "strategical" attacking plan seemed to involve putting pressure on the veteran left-back, George Molyneux, who had joined Portsmouth from the Saints the previous summer, after five seasons at The Dell had brought him three Southern League medals and four England caps. Yet he and his left-half, MacDonald, were made to look "mere novices", as they struggled to contain a home right-wing of Harrison and Tomlinson.

Fred ("Buzzy") Harrison had been spotted on Southampton Common by left-winger Joe Turner, whose place he took for a couple of games. Then he assumed the No. 9 shirt for the final third of the 1902-03 season, hitting 14 goals in a run of five games that included two five-goal hauls in successive home matches. Playing between George Hedley and Harry Wood, he was said by the *Athletic News* to be modelled on the former with the cunning of the latter. Hedley had won two FA Cup medals with Sheffield United, for whom he had scored in the 1902 defeat of Southampton, and would win another with Wolves. In his three seasons at The Dell, he played mainly at inside-forward but, for Portsmouth's visit, he swapped with Harrison, not as some "foolish fancy," we are assured, but as a "strategical move of much importance." In the opinion of Above Bar, it worked because Molyneux had "never played worse," while "so perfectly did Harrison and Tomlinson dovetail that one would have thought their partnership had existed for

England international George Molyneux was made to look a "mere novice" by Saints' right wing

years, particularly as they employed original and ingenious moves and executed them without a hitch."

Although beaten twice in the first-half, goalkeeper Harris kept the visitors in the game by saving "three shots that were apparently certain of reaching their intended destination." Harrison had been "the first to elude his reach" after seven minutes and Brown headed a second from "Tomlinson's perfect centre." Kirby pulled one back for Portsmouth soon after the interval, but Hedley promptly made it 3-1. Saints' fourth by Brown provoked a mixed metaphor from Above Bar, when he suggested it "was the last straw that broke the hearts of Buick... and his confreres" at half-back. So great was their "deterioration [that] play was rarely out of the Portsmouth half." Yet Saints could manage only one more - through Tomlinson, with "the best shot of the afternoon."

The man from the *Athletic News* concluded that Portsmouth had "never given a worse exhibition" against Southampton. Their excuse was that "they did not adapt themselves to the conditions"; but, for Above Bar, the "disaster" of their biggest-ever defeat by their neighbours was a case of

the superiority of youth, backed by skill, over experience trammelled by way of advancing years. From start to finish the visitors were toiling after their fleet footed adversaries, with little prospect of catching them.

And who would want to argue with that testament ?

SOUTHAMPTON:
Stead, Warner, Hartshorne, Hogg, Lee, Houlker, Tomlinson, Harrison, Hedley, Brown, Mouncher.

PORTSMOUTH:
Harris, Walker, Molyneux, Bowman, Buick, MacDonald, Kirby, Cunliffe, Hunter, W. Smith, S. Smith.

Referee: Mr. D.Hammond (Heywood).   *Attendance:* 14,000

Compiled by **CLAY ALDWORTH** and **DAVID BULL** from the *Athletic News* report. Illustrations from **Duncan Holley**'s collection

SOUTHAMPTON 3
EVERTON 2

A goalless Fourth Round draw at Goodison Park on 7 March 1908 brought them swarming to The Dell the following Wednesday afternoon. With local businesses and factories closing for the occasion, there were enough spectators to fill not only the ground – with a record-breaking attendance of 21,690 – but several overlooking trees and rooftops, too.

With the sun "shining brilliantly," the man from the *Hampshire Independent* witnessed this "flow of humanity" entering The Dell, until

> the ground was simply packed everywhere and the gates had to be closed. There were scores on the roofs of the refreshment bars and a crowd of more daring spirits on the roof of the East stand… The scene on the ground was one that baffles description and certainly surpassed anything ever seen locally before, even when Derby County played. The pressure on the terraces at the Archers Rd end was so great that scores of people sought relief by clambering onto the roof of the telegraph office. Banners, umbrellas, rockets and bells were in evidence as excited partisans gave vent to their enthusiasm, but the attention of the crowd was mainly directed to the efforts of those venturesome individuals who risked personal injury in order to reach coigns of vantage. As the police prevented any more roof scaling, a few youths procured a ladder and mounted a tree just outside St Mark's Church.

The mention of the encounter with Derby is a reference to their FA Cup visit in 1899, when they had played in the previous three semi-finals and came to The Dell as beaten finalists. Yet Everton could better that. Their quarter-final win over the Saints in 1905 had taken them into the first of three successive semi-finals, the last two of which they had won – to go on and lift the Cup in 1906 and to lose in 1907. So they, too, came down to Southampton as beaten finalists.

Beaten finalists who had not been good enough, though, to seize their home advantage – thanks largely to the efforts of Herbert Lock in the Southampton goal. The Saints had no changes from the side that had done so well at Goodison, once the funeral of Hodgkinson's brother, who had died on the Saturday, had been postponed for a day. As a mark of respect to the little winger, his team-mates wore black armbands.

Everton soon took the lead with a "speculative" long shot from Young – who had been denied, late in the original game, by the bravery of Lock at what the *Independent* reporter memorably called "the moment of consummation".

Yet the Saints replied with two goals, through "a lovely shot" from Costello and a "neat" conversion by Bainbridge that sent the crowd "frantic." And they still

Bert Lock, hands clasped behind his back, watches as Saints attack

FA Cup Fourth Round (Replay)

led 2-1 at half-time, thanks to further brave goalkeeping by Lock, as Everton mounted four corners in quick succession.

The second-half belonged to Frank Costello, the Saints' inside-left. In this, his first, season at The Dell, he had received plenty of criticism from the local press in previous ties. But now he was featuring in most of Southampton's attacks. And, when Bainbridge swung over a deep cross from the right it appeared to be over hit and passing out of play. Suddenly, and apparently from nowhere, Costello arrived and succeeded not only in meeting the ball with his head but in sending it back over the goalkeeper into the far corner of the net – for a goal described as "magnificent" by one commentator and "brilliant" by another. Many witnesses could not comprehend how he had managed to reach the ball, as a contortionist would have had problems attaining such a position, but the Saints were 3-1 up and a record crowd had experienced a goal that would be talked about for years to come.

Bolton pulled one back for the visitors but - virtually down to 10 men, as Frank Thorpe battled on with a cut head - the defence held

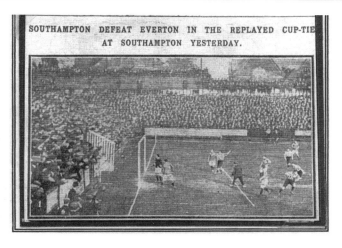

SOUTHAMPTON DEFEAT EVERTON IN THE REPLAYED CUP-TIE AT SOUTHAMPTON YESTERDAY.

firm to secure a famous victory. Thorpe, who had a winners medal with Bury in 1903, would recover in time to play in the semi-final against Second Division Wolves – with every expectation of another final appearance. But Wolves won 2-0 with their second goal coming from George Hedley, who had been a Southampton player when he was introduced to you in the previous report. While he was on his way to his third Cup winners' medal, this would be the last Saints' appearance in a semi-final until 1925.

But the defeat of Everton would not be the last time that a Southampton side would achieve a memorable Cup victory only to succumb in the next round to inferior opponents (fast forward to Matches 47 and 51 for spectacular examples).

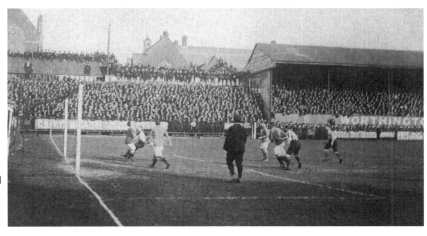

A record crowd of 21,690 is supplemented by others in "coigns of vantage"

SOUTHAMPTON:

Lock, Eastham, Glover, Johnston, Thorpe, Robertson, Bainbridge, Jefferis, Smith, Costello, Hodgkinson

EVERTON:

Scott, W.Balmer, R. Balmer, Makepeace, Taylor, Abbott, Sharp, Bolton, Young, Settle, Hardman

Referee: Mr F.H. Dennis (Middlesbrough) *Attendance:* 21,690

Compiled by **DUNCAN HOLLEY** from reports in the *Hampshire Independent* and with photographs from his collection

Southampton 4
Swindon Town 0

A comprehensive 4-0 win over Swindon Town was the best possible way to mark a major milestone in the Saints' history – the first Football League game ever to be played at The Dell.

Since that purple patch of 1896-1904, when they won the Southern League six times and reached two FA Cup Finals, Southampton had not achieved a lot either in Cup or League.

But now, as a mass exodus from the Southern League joined the newly-formed Third Division of the Football League, Southampton had assembled a team capable of early promotion and more storming Cup runs (as described in the next four reports).

An opening day 1-1 draw at Gillingham – who would finish bottom of the League, just as they had in the Southern League the season before – seems not to have impressed the Southampton public. Only 11,500 came to watch Saints beat a Swindon side that had their tails up after trouncing Luton Town 9-1. But the gates soon improved, as the Saints won seven of their first nine games – to go top of the table – and went into December with 10 wins and only one defeat in their first 16 matches. And The Dell would become their fortress where they would lose only twice all season.

In the first of those home reverses, which started a miserable December, Saints lost 1-0 to Grimsby Town and were left to brood over a missed penalty by their dashing young full-back, Tom Parker.

Parker had blossomed into one of the bright new kids on the block. That's "new" in the sense that he had come into the side towards the end of the First World War and was one of five young players – Allen, Titmuss, Shelley and Rawlings were the others – who would make a solid contribution to Southampton's early post-war successes. On the other hand, there was the loyal older guard – the likes of Arthur Dominy and Alec Campbell – who had seen pre-war service with the Saints.

Campbell, who had won an England amateur cap while still a King Edward's schoolboy, had had a spell with Glossop, but was now installed as captain of his home-town club. He had fought in the First World War and would lose his life in the Second.

Woolston-born Dominy would spend 15 seasons at The Dell – if you count the War, during which he guested

This 1920-21 line-up includes 10 of the players who appeared in Saints' first Football League game at The Dell
Back row (left to right) Parker, Allen, Titmuss. Middle row: Mr Arnfied (Secretary), Mr Wood (director), Shelley, Moorhead, Turner, Mr McIntyre (manager), Mr Muir (director). Front: Barratt, Dominy, Rawlings, Moore, Foxall

several times against them – before moving to Everton, where he occasionally partnered and lastingly befriended the legendary "Dixie" Dean.

He would later manage the Saints (as you can see in the line-up for Match No. 31) – in succession to Tom Parker, whose contribution, as an ex-player, to the Club is ranked, in Chalk and Holley's *Complete Record* of the Saints, as second only to that of Ted Bates.

If Dominy was the pick of the attack against Swindon, capturing the headlines along with Bill Rawlings, Parker and his fellow-defenders had their part to play in laying the foundations of victory. Saints enjoyed vast sweeps of territorial advantage that afternoon, but before they damaged the Wiltshire side, they first had to contain them. The Robins took the field with two highly-rated forwards in Rogers, who had toured South Africa with a Football Association party the previous summer, and a fiery, fast-shooting Scot by the name of Harold Fleming. It was a testament to the effectiveness of the Southampton half-backs, Alec Campbell and Bill Turner, that the deadly duo from Swindon hardly got a kick. Turner was the only player in this home-grown side to have cost a fee.

Even in those days, pace was a precious asset in attack, and Saints had it in abundance. Joe Barratt and Fred Foxall on the flanks, and Dominy and Rawlings inside them, were simply too quick for the Swindon defence.

Saints scored all four goals in the first-half, the first from a corner taken on the left by Foxall. Campbell met

Two of the "bright new kids"
Bill Rawlings (left) and Fred Titmuss (right) join Arthur Dominy

it and drilled it in low. Rawlings, with his back to goal stopped the ball, controlled it then turned to lash it just below the bar.

The second goal, scored by Dominy, was to prove the pick of the bunch. Shelley, a creative presence on the right side of midfield, released winger Barratt on a surging run down the right touchline.

He left his full-back for dead before delivering a precision cross, despatched with great power by the head of Dominy, who had the distinction of having scored the club's first Football League goal at Gillingham.

It proved an uncomfortable afternoon for Macconachie, the Swindon left-back. The former Evertonian was beaten for pace again by Dominy, who accelerated past him and drove powerfully home for the third goal.

A combination of Rawlings's vision and Barratt's pace embarrassed Macconachie again for the fourth. Rawlings guided the ball past him and Barratt nipped in behind him to score.

Swindon were fortunate to escape a heavier beating. Foxall hurtled down the left and set up a sitter for Jimmy Moore which the inside-left scored. Then Rawlings of all people misjudged a cross from Barratt when he was well-placed to score.

But it set up a crowd-pleasing run and that spell at the top. Although they didn't stay there, Saints remained in contention for the championship – only one of this new, 22-strong Division would go up – eventually missing out by five points to Crystal Palace.

SOUTHAMPTON:
Allen, Parker, Titmuss, Shelley, Campbell, Turner, Barratt, Dominy, Rawlings, Moore, Foxall

SWINDON TOWN:
Shiller, Weston, Macconachie, Langford, Hawley, Wareing, Jefferson, Fleming, Rogers, Batty, Davies

Referee: J G A Sharp   *Attendance:* 11,500

Compiled by **BOB BRUNSKELL** from the *Echo* reports. Photographs from **Duncan Holley**'s collection

SOUTHAMPTON 5
NEWPORT COUNTY 0

Their promotion ambitions thwarted by Crystal Palace in their first season in the Football League, the Saints were again in the promotion hunt in 1921-22, this time racing neck-and-neck with Plymouth Argyle for the Championship of what had now become the regionalized Division Three (South).

Argyle had had the advantage in the games between the two runaway contenders, scoring the only goal in two tight encounters. Undefeated since late January and two points ahead of Saints going into the final day of the season, they went to Shepherd's Bush, knowing that a draw with Queens Park Rangers (who would finish fifth) would take them up, whatever Saints might do at The Dell against Newport County (who would finish third from bottom). But wins for the two home sides would take Saints up on superior goal average.

Southampton were undoubtedly promotion material. They had probably their best side since the heady days of Southern League domination. And they certainly had fewer "mercenaries" (a charge you may recall from Match No. 9, in particular). You were introduced to some of this home-grown side in the previous report. Their appearance records speak to their loyalty. Arthur Dominy would complete 369 games for the Saints, a remarkable total for a career interrupted by war, while Bert Shelley's record of 448 appearances would survive until broken by Tommy Traynor in 1964. The 21 goals conceded that season would remain a Football League record until 1979 and, to this day, a record both for the Club and for the Third (South) – an honour for Tom Allen, whose 291 League appearances is still the record for a Southampton goalkeeper. And two of the side – full-back Fred Titmuss, with 237 games, and centre-forward Bill Rawlings (374) - made their England debuts that season. Parker (275 - mostly partnering Titmuss) would have to wait until 1925 for his one cap.

Not bad for the Third Division. Too good, the fans must have hoped, as they came to The Dell, not only to watch Saints win but longing for news of Plymouth's embarrassment at Loftus Road. And to supply the news from London, the Saints' Board sent two of its directors, Messrs Hammock and Muir (who had played in Match No. 1), to Shepherd's Bush, with instructions to phone home.

There was soon plenty to occupy the 9,000 who had come to The Dell, with the Saints taking the lead after just five minutes, when Johnson, fed by Shelley, beat Lowe. Chances for Brown and Campbell followed before the visitors forged their first period of pressure. Lythgoe, a clever inside-forward, tested Allen with several dangerous crosses, which the Newport attack failed to capitalise upon. It was the Saints' attack that dominated the half: Brown, Campbell and Getgood all went close and then Andrews had an effort tipped onto the crossbar by Lowe, the follow-up being hit against the post by Rawlings.

Half-time: Southampton 1, Newport County 0.

And good news relayed from London. Plymouth were two goals down.

So there was a tremendous air of excitement greeting Saints as they came out for the second-half. As in the first-half, it took them but five minutes to score. A corner dropping at the far post was met by Dominy with a fine header into an open goal. A brief spell of Newport pressure followed, with Gittens almost breaching the home defence - only to be foiled by a timely tackle by Titmuss. But the Saints then killed off any chances of a Newport revival with three quick goals. Campbell, moving forward, shot through a crowd of players to score number three. Rawlings then converted a penalty kick, after being fouled, to give him 30 League goals for the season. The fifth goal and the best saw a brilliant forward movement, which enabled Andrews to centre beyond Lowe to the feet of Dominy who, in one swift movement, netted his second goal of the afternoon and 13th of the season. With a five-goal lead after 65 minutes, Saints could afford to settle back. Even with Mr Farrow

Promotion winners
Standing (left to right) A. Lee (trainer), Shelley, Parker, Campbell, Allen, Titmuss, Turner, J. McIntyre (manager).
Seated: Barratt, Dominy, Rawlings, Andrews, Foxall

Division Three (South)

as referee – at Gillingham in September, he had got in the line of a wayward shot and diverted it past Allen – there was no danger. They could allow the visitors to regain some pride and await word from London.

When the word came it was that Plymouth had lost. The cheering drowned out the band that was attempting to entertain those present and Dominy, the skipper, was dragged from the dressing room and carried around the ground shoulder high – Saints were UP!

Poor Plymouth would finish runners-up six seasons in succession. When they eventually won the Third (South) in 1929-30, they would equal another divisional record that the Saints established in that Newport game: they completed a 42-game season with only four defeats.

If you feel you've read enough about records associated with this match, then *look away now*.

It was a game that featured in two record sequences for the Club – both of successive games without conceding a goal AND of games without scoring a goal. If you think that must be a misprint – and who wouldn't at first blush? – then consider the calendar, shown here, for 15 April – 16 September 1922.

From the moment that Gallogley scored Plymouth's bizarre 35th-minute winner at Home Park on 15 April – a ball that swept over Allen on a boisterous wind to hit, in turn, his bar and his neck and then cannon into his net – until the Saints conceded the only goal at home to Leeds United on 28 August, their defence went unbreached for 845 minutes.

But, then, that 65th-minute goal by Dominy against Newport would be the Saints' last for another 500 minutes, when Bert Shelley broke the drought in the 25th minute at home to Barnsley on 16 September.

If you're a record-collector, then this promotion match is truly one for your memory bank.

Whoever said it's only a game?

Calendar of overlapping record sequences – without conceding AND without scoring

1921-22 – Division Three (South)

Apr	15	Plymouth Argyle	(a)	0-1	last goal conceded until 28 Aug
	17	Aberdare	(h)	1-0	
Aug	18	Aberdare	(a)	1-0	
	22	Plymouth Argyle	(h)	0-0	
	24	Northampton Town	(a)	0-0	
	29	Newport County	(a)	1-0	
May	1	Merthyr Town	(a)	1-0	
	6	Newport County	(h)	5-0	last goal scored until 16 Sep

1922-23 – Division Two

Aug	26	South Shields	(a)	0-0	
	28	Leeds United	(h)	0-1	
Sep	2	South Shields	(h)	0-2	
	4	Leeds United	(a)	0-1	
	9	Barnsley	(a)	0-3	
	16	Barnsley	(h)	2-2	

SOUTHAMPTON:
Allen, Hooper, Titmuss, Shelley, Campbell, Getgood, Brown, Dominy, Rawlings, Johnson, Andrews

NEWPORT COUNTY:
Lowe, Arch, Griffin, Groves, E Edwards, Walker, Brittan, Gittens, Skelton, Lythgoe, W Edwards

Referee: Mr P Farrow   *Attendance:* 9,000

Compiled by **GARY CHALK** from the *Echo* and *Daily Mail* reports. Photographs from **Duncan Holley**'s collection

WEST HAM UNITED 1
SOUTHAMPTON 0

As the builders hurried to complete a new stadium for the 1923 Cup Final, the four London sides in the last eight were kept apart in the quarter-final draw. Three of them lost at home, each by 1-0 to northern opponents. The fourth, West Ham United, would eventually go through, by that same score at the expense of Southampton, to their first semi-final – but not until the two sides had played out two 1-1 draws and come to Villa Park for the show-down.

As if rehearsing for Wembley, an excessive number of fans made their way to The Dell – some 5,000 of them as early as 11 o'clock – so that the gates had to be closed a full hour-and-a-quarter before the kick-off, with 21,960 packed inside, not counting a group of soldiers who had climbed onto the East Stand roof. As the teams ran out, the *Hampshire Independent* reporter recorded a "tremendous" roar from this record crowd, but the start was delayed somewhat when the West Ham goalkeeper, Hufton, was twice sent back to the dressing room to change his shirt, the colour of which had clashed with first Southampton's colours and then his own team's.

When the game did eventually get underway, two notable servants of the respective teams were prominent in the early action. First, Arthur Dominy, nearing the 10th anniversary of his Southampton debut, shot just wide as Hufton, now in an acceptable white jersey, went full length. And soon Vic Watson – the England centre-forward who would join the Saints 12 summers later and feature in Match No. 27, after 505 appearances for the Hammers - should have done better with a half-chance. The referee was busy, first having a word with Carter – who not only fouled Rawlings, but then prevented him from getting up – and next rejecting a penalty appeal from the Saints forwards, following an apparent hand-ball by Henderson. Thereupon, play switched to the other end, where Tommy Allen bravely thwarted Watson, injuring himself in the process.

The injured Allen was in the party that travelled to Villa Park for the second replay
Back row (left to right) Christie, Parker, Lock, Allen, Titmuss, Hooper.
Middle row: Brown, Dominy, Rawlings, Elkes, Andrews, Campbell. Front: Shelley, Turner

After the interval, Hufton was tested by a fine shot from Parker. And then Dominy overstepped the ball to waste a "brilliant" passing move that had involved the entire Saints forward line. With the tension rising Hufton went down to save and two Saints players, including Turner, fell over his body as they followed up. The Hammers 'keeper lost his temper, "threatened" the left-half and was duly cautioned by the referee. But then, in the 70th minute "a surprise came" at the other end when Watson scored off the underside off the bar. The Saints replied almost immediately, when Andrews lobbed the ball forward for Elkes to dart in and head past Hufton.

The home side now pushed strongly for the winner and "the closing stages were strenuously fought" – strenuously enough for Hufton to be "laid out" after collecting a Brown cross. The man in the white jersey remained unbeaten, though, and the contest was resumed at the Boleyn Ground four days later. With Allen not recovered from his injury, Herbert Lock, whose heroics of 1908 you may recollect from Match No. 17, was recalled to the first team after an absence of almost 14 years. Telegrams brought him best wishes from his left-back and trainer from that 1908 Cup run, Vic Glover and Billy Dawson, respectively.

For the first five minutes, Southampton swarmed all over their hosts and the ball was "scarcely out of the West Ham half." And, in the eighth minute, the Saints took the lead when a Brown centre was converted by Rawlings. Lock then fisted out from Brown in good style, as the Hammers pressed for an equaliser that soon followed.

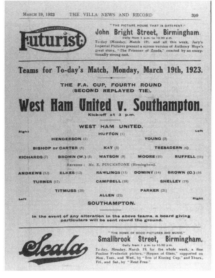

Andrews was caught in possession and Watson ended the resultant move with a flyer from 20 yards. Lock hardly moved as the ball hit the back of his net.

And that's how it stayed, with Turner's "hot dropping drive" and Brown's "rattling shot" against the crossbar the best of the visitors' efforts in the second-half. In extra-time, while Watson was a continuing danger, the Saints made most of the running and looked the fitter side - but to no avail as West ham clung on and as Hufton clung on, with three minutes to go, to a shot from Rawlings, who might have done better from only five yards.

The "Stop Press" news in the *Evening Standard* earmarked Stamford Bridge for the second replay, but it was at Villa Park that hostilities were resumed on Monday 19 March.

The first-half was goalless although the Saints finished it with only 10 men, Dominy having been carried off after a collision with Ruffell. Back at full strength for the second-half, the Saints were going well, with defenders getting forward to join in their attacks. The only goal went, however, to West Ham, who caught the Saints' defence sleeping with a clever free-kick in the 70th minute. As Richards shaped to take the kick a few yards out from the penalty box, Brown suddenly darted into space to receive the ball and tuck it past a startled Lock.

Half-chances came the way of Elkes and Brown but the Saints' big chance had gone. Come Cup Final day, it would not be their fans climbing fences and evading a white horse in the hope of seeing them take on Bolton.

SOUTHAMPTON:
Allen, Parker, Titmuss, Shelley, Campbell, Turner, Brown, Dominy, Rawlings, Elkes, Andrews

WEST HAM UNITED:
Hufton, Henderson, Young, Bishop, Carter, Tresadern, Richards, Brown, Watson, Moore, Ruffell
For Southampton, Lock replaced Allen for both replays,
while Kay replaced Carter, for West Ham, in the second replay

Referee: Mr Pinckstone (Birmingham)   *Attendance:* 22,184

Compiled by **DUNCAN HOLLEY** from the *Hampshire Independent* and with reference to the *Evening Standard*. Photograph from **Duncan Holley**'s collection

SOUTHAMPTON 0
SHEFFIELD UNITED 2

For the first time since 1908, Southampton were in a semi-final – against Sheffield United, the side that had beaten them in the Final of 1902.

Sheffield United were a First Division side, but the Saints, who had had the luck of four home draws, were on a high after seeing off Liverpool in the quarter-final. A free-kick from Bill Rawlings – which he would describe, when visiting The Dell 40 years later, as the best he ever scored – had been enough to earn the Saints a Stamford Bridge semi-final.

On the eve of the game, though, their luck deserted them when Fred Titmuss went down with influenza. And the game itself would be a nightmare for Tom Parker, his regular partner at full-back.

Both teams had to change from their red-and-white stripes – Southampton to white shirts, as in the 1902 replay. Many of their fans in the crowd of 65,754 sported white heather in their lapels.

Bill Rawlings (right) returns to The Dell in 1965,
to talk about his best-ever goal of 1925
and to congratulate George O'Brien on breaking his FA Cup goal-scoring record

Kicking off into a stiff breeze, Southampton started well but it soon struck the *Echo* reporter that the forwards "were out of joint". Fortunately, the Blades too were having trouble finding their rhythm and the only two mentionable chances in the first 40 minutes for either side both fell to Saints. First, Rawlings, fed by Harkus, saw his shot tipped around the post by 'keeper Sutcliffe; and then Harkus himself was a foot wide of the woodwork.

Then came Part One of Tom Parker's nightmare. In his attempt to clear the ball into touch, he succeeded in putting it into his own net.

Tommy Allen was not faultless in the drama, for he had initially lost possession when leaving his goal and had been slow to return to his line.

"Part One of Tom Parker's nightmare" as he (second left) puts the ball past his own goalkeeper.

This misfortune gave Sheffield a 1-0 lead at half-time.

But Southampton launched into them, as soon as play got under way in the second-half and appeared, to the *Echo*, to be "shaking off the devastating moral effect of the first goal." They put United under the "hammer" and, before long, Rawlings was flattened in the area for a clear-cut penalty. Up stepped regular penalty-taker, Tom Parker, for Part Two of his semi-final from Hell. His shot struck Sutcliffe on the shoulder and bounced to safety. To judge from the position of his hands (see the photo below), the Sheffield 'keeper knew nothing about it. And then, before the shock of all this had passed the ball was punted up the field with Tunstall chasing it. Shelley was barring the progress of the winger and Allen

How the Stamford Bridge programme cartoonist saw the contest.

ran out of his goal to collect the ball. That should have ended the matter. But in every vital moment in the game a queer twist of events weighted scales against the Saints. Shelley did not complete the task of covering Tunstall, who was allowed to slip beyond him and touch the ball wide of Allen into the vacant net.

In the space of a couple of minutes Saints had thrown away the chance of levelling matters and then fallen further behind. There was to be no way back and the headlines in Monday's *Echo* summed it up:

**PUPPETS OF FATE – SAINTS' BAD LUCK
AGAINST SHEFFIELD
PARKER'S BITTER EXPERIENCE**

Tom Parker's penalty strikes goalkeeper Sutcliffe to complete "his semi-final from Hell"

SOUTHAMPTON:
Allen, Parker, Hough, Shelley, Campbell, Bradford, Henderson, Dominy, Rawlings, Harkus, Carr.

SHEFFIELD UNITED:
Sutcliffe, Cook, Milton, Pantling, King, Green, Mercer, Sampy, Johnson, Gillespie, Tunstall.

Referee: Mr. W.F.Burrell (Preston)   *Attendance:* 65,754

Compiled by **DUNCAN HOLLEY** from the *Echo* report with action photographs from his collection and an *Echo* photo of O'Brien and Rawlings

SOUTHAMPTON 2
NEWCASTLE UNITED 1

A Dell victory over Newcastle United would not rate these days as one of the Saints' great achievements – witness the sequence of such wins in the 1990s, often coming from behind (as in Match No. 96). But when they beat The Magpies 2-1 at The Dell in the FA Cup Fifth Round of 1927, it was hailed as a major upset and ranked in Southampton at the time as one of their finest results.

To put the performance into perspective, Saints were a middle-of-the-road Second Division side. Newcastle, with the legendary Hughie Gallacher leading the attack, were the best team in the land, destined to be crowned First Division Champions that season. The size of Saints' achievement was clear to the *Echo*:

> In all the triumphs of South teams over their rivals of the North, there was no greater performance than the Saints victory over Newcastle United.
>
> The finest side in the country is Newcastle's second name. Captained by Scotland's attacking leader Hugh Gallacher, they were the North's chief banner bearers. They were beaten in a great fight and one of the most exciting cup ties ever seen at The Dell.

Northern dominance in the FA Cup had been a heavy cross for the South to bear. In between Southampton's two attempts of 1900 and 1902 , Tottenham had become the first club to bring the Cup south. And, since then, the trophy had only once been wrenched – by Spurs again in 1921 – from the grasp of the leading clubs from footballing hotbeds in Yorks, Lancs and Durham.

The Saints, for their part, were into a new cup-running phase, as illustrated in the last two reports, with their quarter-final appearance in 1923 (when they beat Newcastle on the way) and their semi-final of 1925.

Despite their lofty status, Newcastle had an uneasy feeling about their visit to The Dell. Their left-winger, Stan Seymour – who'd scored when they won the Cup in 1924 but who will be familiar to older readers as manager

Presented with ALL SPORTS, October 23rd, 1926.

SOUTHAMPTON FOOTBALL CLUB, 1926-27.

Back row : W. RAYNER (Assistant-Trainer), F. SHELLEY, J. WILKINSON, W. ADAMS, T. ALLEN, E. HOUGH, J. THITCHENER, G. ROBSON, A. KEEPINGS, A. CHADWICK (Manager).
Left to right : Middle row : E. A. LEE (Trainer), J. SWINDEN, E. KING, J. BULLOCK, G. HARKUS, J. BRADFORD, S. WOODHOUSE, R. COOPER, F. MATTHEWS, BISHOP, A. FINDLAY, G. GOSS (Secretary).
Front row : C. COUNDON, W. HENDERSON, S. TAYLOR, W. RAWLINGS, R. ROWLEY, W. MURPHY, S. CRIBB.

of their cup-winning sides of 1951 and 1952 - admitted before the game that "the meeting with Saints is practically the final." He was right in one sense. It was Newcastle's final tie in the 1926-27 competition.

The Magpies would have been quite happy to take Saints back to St James' Park for a replay and after Dick Rowley had scored Saints' second goal with just seven minutes left on the clock, Newcastle threw everything into attack.

The big Dell crowd held their breath as a clearance from George Harkus struck Gallacher on the back of the head and looped inches over the bar.

It was a tie in which Saints could not afford to relax their vigilance for a second. Between scoring their first and second goals, their defence was put under severe pressure but their reluctance to give any ground, and their tight marking of the potentially lethal Gallacher, clearly rattled the little Scot and took the edge off the confidence of his team-mates at the same time.

The key to Saints' success lay in the fact that they succeeded in cutting off the supply line between McKay, the creative genius in the Newcastle midfield, and the normally rampant Gallacher. In that respect, they owed much to Harkus and, if anything by-passed him, to their new pairing at full-back.

During 1925-26, Titmuss had given way to Mike Keeping (and then been sold to Plymouth); and Hough – a late deputy, as we saw, in the 1925 semi-final – had made the right-back slot his when Parker moved to Arsenal (of which more in the next report). Between them, they denied Gallacher time and space to get in a shot on goal.

It was a tribute to the manner in which Saints defended that Newcastle's only goal came from the penalty spot, despatched by Tom McDonald. Yet Saints had dominated the early stages of the cup-tie and Bill Rawlings, their own high-scoring international centre-forward, hit the post from close in. It rattled United and spread unease throughout their own defensive ranks. And it required the aerial dominance of their centre-backs, Gibson and Spence, to bail them out as their full-backs were consistently turned by Saints' wingers, "Spud" Murphy and "Tishy" Henderson (so called because his gait reminded fans of a race horse of that name).

The tie was furiously fought out, so much so that "Commentator", in the *Echo,* felt that "the picturesque part of forward play was lost." In its place, sheer force and strength of purpose provided the only way through. Saints possessed more in that department than Newcastle, with the powerful Rawlings the battering ram which brought down the Magpies' defences.

He forced the corner from which the first Southampton goal came. Murphy hit the flag kick into the middle and Commentator "lost count of the number of Southampton players who were in the goalmouth trying to kick the ball through but, in the end, Rowley succeeded."

Dick Rowley, was a tall, slim Northern Irelander who had moved into The Dell via Andover. He had scored three goals in the previous two rounds and he was to capture the headlines on this day. As the tie hung in the balance, destined it seemed to go back to Tyneside for a replay, Rowley settled it with a moment of pure quality.

Taylor and Murphy began the move in midfield and Taylor picked out Rowley with a pass of stunning accuracy. Young Rowley repaid the compliment by bringing the ball under control with the coolness of a veteran before turning it past the bewildered Newcastle goalkeeper Wilson.

It capped a great afternoon for Rowley and a great afternoon for Taylor, who had worked tirelessly fetching and carrying in midfield. But Rawlings would take over the scoring mantle in the next round, with two goals in a replay victory over Millwall that would take Saints into their second semi-final in three seasons.

But that's the topic of the next report.

SOUTHAMPTON:

Allen, Hough, Keeping, Shelley, Harkus, Woodhouse, Henderson, Rowley, Rawlings, Taylor, Murphy

NEWCASTLE UNITED:

Wilson, Maitland, Hudspeth, Mackenzie, Spencer, Gibson, Urwin, McKay, Gallacher, McDonald, Seymour

Referee: G D Nunnerley (Ellesmere)   *Attendance:* 21,427

Compiled by **BOB BRUNSKELL** from the *Echo* report. Photograph from the *Echo's* collection

ARSENAL 2
SOUTHAMPTON 1

The draw for the FA Cup semi-finals of 1927 paired the two remaining First Division sides – The Arsenal and Cardiff City – with Southampton and Reading, respectively, of the Second Division. Like the Saints, Cardiff were on Cup form in the 1920s, with three semi-final appearances, but there is no denying that the Saints had far more FA Cup pedigree than any of these others.

Yet the Arsenal were the Cup favourites. It is not difficult to see why. In 1925, Herbert Chapman had come from Huddersfield to Highbury and lifted the ailing Arsenal up the First Division - to finish second only to his former club. To that end, he had signed a right-wing pairing of Joe Hulme, reputed to be the fastest winger in the land, and the legendary Charlie Buchan. And, as noted in earlier match reports, he had tempted Tom Parker to leave The Dell for Highbury.

Saints kicked off defending the very goal into which Parker had both steered the ball past his own goalkeeper and then failed to score a penalty in 1925. The first talking point for the crowd of 52,133 – swollen by the decision of Col Wyndham Portal, the Southampton Chairman, to bring along 800 employees from his paper mills – came at the other end, though. When Henderson made a dash into the Arsenal penalty area, Cope charged into his back. The referee gave the foul but insisted it took place outside the area – even though everyone watching witnessed the incident occur a good two yards inside. This would not be the last penalty appeal refused on the day.

Minutes later, Southampton were again unlucky when Lewis pushed Taylor's shot onto a post and out again. It was now Arsenal's turn, though, to mount a prolonged assault on the Saints goal. It resulted in the opening score.

Although it has been credited to Hulme, who had hit a cross shot, the ball was not goal-bound until it struck Hough and deflected past Tommy Allen, trickling over the line at that jinxed end of Stamford Bridge. The rest of the first-half was energetic and absorbing with Arsenal's right-wing pair particularly dangerous, exposing Woodhouse and Keeping on numerous occasions. The latter, with England selectors watching him, chose the wrong time for one of his least impressive appearances in a Saints' shirt. Conversely, Murphy, who was giving Parker a bit of a roasting, was the pick of a Southampton attack that was not functioning as a unit.

In the second-half, Arsenal continued to focus their attacking energies down the vulnerable Southampton left and were rewarded with a second goal, when "quick and clever" play by Hulme on the wing set up Buchan, as the *Echo* put it, "to show a touch of genius in the way he gathered the ball and then scored with a reverse shot." Two goals up and in control, Arsenal's place in the final looked assured. But, with five minutes remaining, Rawlings – until then a shadow of his normal self – rose to head a Murphy corner firmly into the net. There was still time for the game to be saved and Saints knew it. Attacking eagerly, Murphy beat two men as he dribbled into the penalty area pursued by Cope. Perfectly placed,

Bert Shelley watches, with Arsenal's Brain and Hoar, as a shot from Hulme is deflected by Ted Hough past Tommy Allen

he was about to shoot when he was sent sprawling by the Arsenal left-back. With everyone in the ground waiting for his whistle, the referee waved play on.

The London-dominated national press, which had taken so long to give credit to Southampton's achievements, now took their side against the North Londoners (right).

So, if you're given to believing what you read in the nationals, then you may agree with the *Westminster Gazette* that the Saints were "robbed". Although the authors make no mention of penalty decisions, the Arsenal *Official History* admits that the Gunners were lucky to win a game in which "Southampton pressed for much of the game but could only score once."

a penalty should have been given for a palpable foul on Murphy who, had his legs not been swept away from under him, would have probably scored

Daily Telegraph

most referees would have construed the foul as a case for a spot kick

Daily Chronicle

Cope brought down Murphy in the area and there was no option but to award a penalty kick

Daily Sketch

it looked as though the referee might fairly have awarded them a penalty kick

The Times

Robbery or not, Arsenal were on their way to their first Final. While they would allow Cardiff to take the English Cup to Wales on this occasion, it would be a rehearsal for their three finals in the 1930s. The Saints' fortunes would be so different. This would be their last semi-final for 36 years. And – a solitary 1935 flutter apart – they would not even reach the Fourth Round again until 1946.

In the meantime, Parker and Cope, the Arsenal full-backs of 1927, would have come and gone as the Saints' manager and trainer, respectively. There seems to be no evidence that Horace Cope ever taught the players at The Dell how to flatten opponents in the box and get away with it.

How the Stamford Bridge programme cartoonist weighed up the issues

ARSENAL:
Lewis, Parker, Cope, Baker, Butler, John, Hulme, Buchan, Brain, Blyth, Hoar

SOUTHAMPTON:
Allen, Hough, Keeping, Shelley, Harkus, Woodhouse, Henderson, Rowley, Rawlings, Taylor, Murphy

Referee: Mr. Scholey   *Attendance:* 52,133

Compiled by **DUNCAN HOLLEY** from reports in the *Echo* and the various nationals cited; and with reference to the Arsenal *Official History*. Photograph from Duncan Holley's collection

SOUTHAMPTON 3
SWANSEA TOWN 0

Saints had barely started celebrating their highest-ever League finish in 1929 when one side of their ground literally went up in flames. The Dell has witnessed some dramatic scenes over the years, but none so dramatic or frightening as the raging inferno which destroyed the old East Stand in less than two hours.

It was a devastating aftermath to a home match against Swansea, which Saints had won 3-0 to clinch fourth place in the Second Division. The sole consolation was that it occurred at the end of the season.

The only game to suffer was an English Schools Shield Final between Southampton Boys and South Northumberland which had to be switched from The Dell to the nearby Banister Park speedway stadium.

The cause of the fire which reduced the 100-yard long, 1800-seater stand into a heap of twisted metal girders, was a cigarette end, dropped by a spectator. The theory was that it had fallen through a crack in the wooden floor and down into the litter below.

Then it must have smouldered away slowly before bursting into flames and consuming the floor before raging onward and upward through seats and into the top of the stand.

There was no evidence of anything untoward happening as a small Dell crowd left the ground at five o'clock. Even when officials closed up The Dell 30 minutes later everything seemed normal. But within an hour, the East Stand was burning like a torch, the flames fanned into a fury by strong winds.

The first alarm was raised by a youngster who was passing the ground and noticed smoke drifting up from the stand. The fire brigade were called at 6.20 pm, but when their appliances reached The Dell, the blaze had taken such a hold that the stand was beyond salvation. The biggest concern was that the fire would spread to houses close to the stand at the Milton Road end and to the nearby St Mark's School, for the wind was driving the flames in that direction.

But for the heroics of firemen, and one certain firefighter Adams, who risked being overcome by fumes to rip away burning woodwork and sheeting, the consequences would have been much worse. They managed to divert the flames away from the adjoining properties and the worse damage the school suffered was some scorching to outbuildings.

For more than two hours the fireservices were fully stretched with 12 jets of water brought into play from the Archers Road and Milton Road ends of the ground. And the firefighters needed to go beyond Milton Road to hook into a water hydrant at Wilton Avenue, coupling together several hoses and carrying them across gardens and a nearby garage. Meanwhile, the East Stand was crumbling

and crashing down in front of the startled gaze of many on-lookers. The *Echo* described the scene:

> The iron girders carrying the roof of the stand were becoming twisted and distorted; the iron stanchions carrying the girders were becoming warped and grotesquely out of shape in the heat.

> The corrugated iron roof fell upon the burning wooden seats from which just two hours earlier fans had been watching the last match of the season.

It wasn't until just gone ten o'clock that chief officer Hayward withdrew his men, satisfied that the fire was finally out.

Earlier on in that historic day, Saints had cruised to a comfortable victory over Swansea with goals from Willie Haines, "Rigger" Coates and Bert Jepson, each of whom had made his debut earlier in this 1928-29 season, as the thrilling Cup-running side - featured in the last few reports – broke up. Haines took his tally to 16 League goals in 27 games, finishing the season as top scorer. Had he come in sooner than October, Coates, a sailor from Havant, might have overtaken him. His strike was his seventh in his last eight games at inside-forward.

The Saints' FA Cup gloss may have worn off, but George Harkus captained the rebuilt side to fourth in the Second Division, the Club's highest League finish to date – not to be equalled, let alone bettered, until the dramas of the late 1940s, as described in Matches 38 to 40.

The Club had to borrow £10,000 from Norwich Union to rebuild the East Stand and once the site had been cleared of tangled metal, charred wood and ashes, an impressive new structure quickly thrust its way up on to the skyline. Remarkably it took just five weeks to erect over 140 tons of steelwork. Work started on 18 July and, although its roof was not yet in place, the new stand was there to be seen by a crowd of 11,000 when The Dell's 1929-30 season kicked off less than seven weeks later. It was a swift but efficient operation with the suppliers actually assembling everything at their Liverpool plant to ensure accuracy, before taking it all apart and transporting it down to Southampton where a local company, employing a large workforce, re-erected it at The Dell.

It was designed in such a way that several different jobs could be done at once. While the roof members were

being assembled, down below the seating accommodation was installed.

The East Stand may seem like a footballing dinosaur now but how well it has stood the test of time. They built 'em fast in those days, but they built 'em solid.

So, when the bulldozers have flattened The Dell and we are swapping our favourite memories of the ground, there will be those old-timers whose reminiscences will include the fall and rise of the old stand.

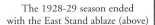

The 1928-29 season ended with the East Stand ablaze (above)

The 1929-30 season started with a new stand in place (left)

SOUTHAMPTON:
White, Hough, Bradford, Luckett, Harkus, Woodhouse, Jepson, Mackie, Haines, Coates, Arnold

SWANSEA TOWN:
Ferguson, Sampy, Milne, Collins, Sykes, McPherson, Hole, Deacon, Cheetham, Gunn, Nicholas

Referee: Mr Gray   *Attendance:* 6,344

Compiled by **BOB BRUNSKELL** from the *Echo* report. Photographs from the collections of **Duncan Holley** (top) and the *Echo* (bottom)

Southampton 1
Tottenham Hotspur 0

The turn of the century rivalry between Saints and Spurs had come to an end in 1908 when Tottenham were elected to the Second Division of the Football League. Nothing to do with topping the Southern League, you understand. Whereas the Saints had won that League six times between 1896-97 and 1903-04, Spurs had won it just the once in 1900. But Tottenham was in the capital, to which the Football League needed to expand, while Southampton remained – for reasons cogently explained at Match No. 12 – off the League's map.

By the time that map had been re-drawn to admit a southern influx and Saints had promptly won their place in the Second Division, Spurs were in Division I. During the run-in to the 1927-28 season, however, they had the shock of their footballing lives.

Having completed their fixtures earlier than most and being seemingly clear of the relegation zone, they went for a short tour of the Netherlands. In their absence, the First Division results went against them to such an extent that they returned to find themselves a point adrift of seven teams who had finished with 39 points, only five points behind fourth-placed Derby. Spurs on 38 and Middlesbrough on 37 were going down with the highest points-tally ever recorded by two relegated sides from a 22-team division.

So Tottenham were back in the Second Division in 1928-29, along with the likes of Millwall and Reading –

and Southampton, of course – who had been with them in the Southern League. They finished in mid-table, while Saints, as noted in the previous report, finished higher than ever before in fourth.

And now, although neither side was setting the division alight in the first half of 1929-30, "Cherry Blossom" predicted in the *Echo* that there would be a record attendance come their Boxing Day meeting at The Dell. He was right.

A crowd of 25,203 – a thousand or so fewer than had watched Spurs beat Saints 3-2 at White Hart Lane on Christmas Day – came to see the "return." And there was room for more, especially in the enclosures under the stands and on the terraces behind the goals.

There were only five seats unfilled of the 2,600 in the new East Stand, but there were almost 200 to spare in the 4,000-capacity West Stand. Even so, some season ticket-

Two weeks after playing before a record-breaking Boxing Day crowd, eight of the side would be Up for The Cup.
Standing (left to right) Mackie, Thompson, Luckett, Rowley, Stoddart, Keeping, Bradford, Wilson.
Kneeling (with mascot): Weale, Cribb, Coates

holders could not reach their seats and, ignoring requests from stewards, sat in the gangways – an invitation to trouble that happily did not occur.

The referee was unchanged from the previous afternoon. So well had Mr Reeve performed at White Hart Lane that Mr Muir – the director previously encountered on crucial telephone duty during Match No. 19 and long before that as a player – accompanied the Tottenham Chairman to the officials' room to congratulate him.

For their part, Saints showed one change from Christmas Day, "Rigger" Coates coming in for Peter Dougall. Continuing to serve on the royal yacht, *Victoria and Albert,* Coates remained an amateur (with eight England Amateur caps to show for it) throughout his six seasons at The Dell.

His stay proved to be less prolific than his initial burst of goal-getting – as recorded in the previous report – had promised. In 1929-30, the goal-scoring was left to Willie Haines and, spectacularly so, to Dick Rowley.

With Stan Cribb – whose two goals at White Hart Lane had included a penalty – missing from the spot at The Dell, it was left to Rowley to score the only goal of the Boxing Day game.

Rowley had recently won three caps for Northern Ireland at inside-right and was about to make it four. In his first two seasons after coming to The Dell in 1926, though, he had been very much in Rawlings's shadow as a goal-scorer. And in 1928-29, Haines had arrived from

Portsmouth to assume the Rawlings mantle, as touched upon in the previous report.

But 1929-30 belonged to Rowley. His Boxing Day goal was his 22nd of the season in this, his, 20th game. Tottenham obviously liked what they saw. After Rowley had brought his League and Cup total for the season to 26 in 26, Spurs bought him for £3,750. With his departure went any chance Saints had of bettering their promising position of 1928-29. In the 1930 half of the season, Saints averaged a point a game to finish seventh.

The Boxing Day crowd had demonstrated the potential support, if only Southampton FC had a side to bring them in. But the sale of Rowley at the start of the 1930s heralded a dreadful decade for Southampton, as a "selling club" struggling to make ends meet.

One of Dick Rowley's three caps – and the shirt – for Northern Ireland

---

SOUTHAMPTON:
White, Bradford, Keeping, Wilson, Stoddart, Luckett, Jepson, Mackie, Rowley, Coates, Cribb

TOTTENHAM HOTSPUR:
Spiers, Illingworth, Herrod, Skitt, Cable, Evans, Bellamy, Thompson, Cook, Meads, Dimmock

Referee: Mr F.W. Reeve (Devonport)   *Attendance:* 25,203

Compiled by **NORMAN GANNAWAY** from the *Echo* report. Illustrations from **Duncan Holley**'s collection

SOUTHAMPTON 6
NOTTS COUNTY 2

During the Easter weekend of 1933, The Dell housed its first Good Friday game. Going back to 1911 in the Southern League, Saints had consistently played home-and-away against the same opponents on Christmas Day and Boxing Day and likewise against another team on Good Friday and Easter Monday.

The FA Council had resolved in 1899, however, that "a Club ought not to be compelled to play any match on Good Friday or Christmas Day." So clubs had a *choice* and Saints had long since exercised theirs in a particular way: they would always be away on the two religious days and play the "return" fixture at The Dell on Boxing Day or Easter Monday, respectively.

In 1933, they broke from that practice, having reached an understanding with neighbouring St Mark's Church that no match would be played while a church service was being held. Despite – or maybe because of – the sunny weather, their Good Friday departure attracted little more than 8,000 spectators to see Notts County. Those who stayed away missed an eight-goal treat, with Saints scoring six of them.

Yet the goal-feast took a while to take off. Southampton were subject to a testing first-half when they faced both sun and wind – conditions that Notts County found equally trying after the interval. The opening 45 minutes ended all-square, Ruddy scoring for the Saints, Fenner for the visitors. County went ahead through Taylor, 13 minutes after the restart. The equaliser came from Bill Luckett, a player with the misfortune to arrive as the side went into decline and to become a durable servant, chalking up over 200 appearances in the dismal 1930s.

For a while, matters remained nicely balanced at 2-2. Then, in contrast to their first-half uncertainty, Saints started to express themselves with impressive authority. Tom Brewis, who'd played mainly at No. 10 on arrival the previous season, seemed happier this season at No. 8. It was he who made it 3-2.

Then, in the last 12 minutes, Southampton really put on the style. Goalkeeper Maidment was given little or no chance with the further three goals that rattled the rigging: from Brewis again, Neal and Bradford from the spot. Six goals had become a rarity for the Saints. They'd not scored

SOUTHAMPTON 0
PORT VALE 1

You will know, if you've been counting carefully, that 1935-36 was the Saints' 50th anniversary season. Initially, the side performed appropriately and went to the top of the Division II table at the end of September, by seeing off Manchester United, the eventual Champions, 2-1 at The Dell. And then, after a poor October, they had celebrated in style on 23 November, by beating Tottenham 2-0 in what was designated the "Golden Jubilee" match, before the season's best home gate of 21,333. The Spurs wrought serious revenge on 28 March, when they inflicted the Saints' heaviest-ever defeat, 8-0 – which may help to explain why the attendance at The Dell, two days later, was the lowest in the Club's Football League history.

On a soaking wet Monday afternoon – an irony as the fixture had been postponed when The Dell was waterlogged the previous month – only 1,875 turned up to watch relegation-bound Port Vale. The Saints made three changes from the Saturday mauling at White Hart Lane, bringing in Albert Roberts and Charlie Sillett at the back and Vic Watson to lead the forward-line.

Watson's arrival was trailered in Match No. 20, when he was playing for the West Ham side that put Saints out of the Cup on their way to the "White Horse" Final. The England international had been brought to The Dell by manager George Kay, who had captained that Hammers' team. In the February, he'd become the oldest player – at 38 years and three months - ever to score a hat-trick for the Club, in a 7-2 demolition of Nottingham Forest that ended a dismal run of 13 games in which only six goals had been scored. But, then, it was that sort of up-and-down season, with just the odd up amid plenty of downs.

In the early stages of the Port Vale game, Stubbs caused a number of problems for the home defenders. At the other end, Southampton's left-wing pair of county cricketers, Arthur Holt (Hampshire) and Laurie Fishlock (Surrey), created several scoring chances spurned by their team-mates. And when Griffiths almost turned the ball

Division Two

that many for four seasons, during which time they'd been on the receiving end of a fair number of fives.

This was, though, a six-point Easter for the Saints, including the completion, on the Monday, of a double over Notts County. Their 20 year-old centre-forward Ted Drake scored both goals in a 2-1 win. He'd been the only forward not to score on Good Friday. You can put that oversight down to a mid-air collision with a County defender: in his first and only fullish season, he scored 20 times in 33 League appearances. The following season, he would be on 22 in 27 when Arsenal came in with enough money to pay off Saints' debts. It is a measure of his contribution that the Southampton-born Drake should be ranked among Saints' legends, even though he played only 74 games for them. But, then, he did score 48 goals.

Despite Drake's emergence, the disappointing Good Friday attendance was typical of a season in which only one in three games attracted a five-figure crowd – can you imagine 7,997 for the visit of Manchester United? – and none brought 12,000 through the turnstiles, even though the break-even target was 14,000.

It had reached a point where the players were asked to wait for their summer wages until the turnstiles started clicking again the following season.

But they were going to click more slowly if the Club continued to sell off the family silver – or gold, if you count Ted Drake.

SOUTHAMPTON:
Scriven, Adams, Tilford, Campbell, Bradford, Woodhouse, Neal, Brewis, Drake, Ruddy, Luckett

NOTTS COUNTY:
Maidment, Stimpson, Mills, Proudfoot, Smith, Grice, Taylor, Fenner, Macartney, Feeney, Haden

Referee: Mr R.G. Rudd (London)   *Attendance:* 8,108

Compiled by **NORMAN GANNAWAY** from the *Echo* report

Division Two

into his own net, Potts just managed to beat it away.

As Port Vale gained an increasing hold on the game, Bert Scriven was kept busy. The Saints' principal goalkeeper in the 1930s, Scriven was especially tested by Roberts and Glidden. Roberts headed against the bar but it was Stabb who scored for the visitors shortly before half-time. Scriven had come out to punch away and was stranded as Stabb returned the ball across his unguarded goal-line. Saints came close to equalising, soon after, when Watson collided with Potts, but Vale survived.

Indeed, they held on to the end, for a 1-0 win. They had kept a clean sheet, despite conceding 106 goals in that relegation season. Never far from the drop-zone themselves, Southampton nevertheless played to bigger home crowds than those recorded in the above report. This time, Manchester United would attract over 17,000 and not until December would gates drop below 10,000. Then came a succession of attendances around the 5,000-mark, before that all-time low against Port Vale.

The faithful few who'd both travelled to Tottenham and spent their Monday afternoon at The Dell would have seen, in that long weekend, the Club's record defeat and its lowest-ever home attendance in the Football League.

Record-seekers sometimes have a morbid streak. There may have been those who took pride in such a "double."

SOUTHAMPTON:
Scriven, Adams, A. Roberts, King, Bradford, Sillett, Neal, Tully, Watson, Holt, Fishlock

PORT VALE:
Potts, Walsh, Vickers, Gunn, Griffiths, Curley, Pinkerton, Glidden, J. Roberts, Stabb, Caldwell

Referee: Mr A.J. Jewell (London)   *Attendance:* 1,875

Compiled by **NORMAN GANNAWAY** from the *Echo* report

SOUTHAMPTON 2
SUNDERLAND 3

In 1937, for the third time in seven seasons, Southampton and Sunderland were drawn together in the Third Round of the FA Cup. It meant a meeting of contrasting significance for the two clubs.

Sunderland were quite a force. First Division runners-up in 1935, they had won the Championship by a handsome margin in 1936. There was little risk of their repeating that success in 1937, so perhaps a Cup run was what their supporters needed. After knocking Saints out in 1931, Sunderland had reached the semi-finals, but they had not gone all the way since 1913.

Southampton, on the other hand, were rooted in the Second Division with a League run of four defeats and three draws behind them and but one win in the last 11 outings. In the close season, George Kay, the manager, had been invited to resign and had headed for Anfield, taking trainer Bert Shelley with him in due course. And there had been a mass resignation of directors. So Southampton came into this 1936-37 season, with a new Board and with secretary, George Goss, adding the job of manager to his duties. One of the players, Johnny McIlwane, became his assistant and coach. The Club was desperate for money. So, if Sunderland needed a Cup run to please their spoiled fans, Saints – who'd won only one cup-tie since their semi-final 10 seasons ago – needed one to please their bank manager.

The £1,062 they received from a record crowd of 30,380 paying £2,741 (shared with Sunderland and the collector of Entertainment Tax) was a start, but this proved to be yet another of those seasons when Saints exited instantly from the Cup. With both teams obliged, as was the custom, to change from their red-and-white stripes, Saints appeared in Cambridge blue, while Sunderland opted for white shirts. But England inside-forward, Raich Carter, did not appear at all. He'd failed a fitness test that morning at Waterloo station.

But his team-mates showed they could manage without him and made the running. On a soft pitch covered in places with sand, they went in at half-time two goals up. A left-wing advance saw Connor provide a short pass from which Gurney scored.

Seeing off a spirited Southampton response, the visitors went further ahead through Hornby, the late replacement for Carter. A changed home formation after the interval did not check Sunderland for long. Within 20 minutes, they were leading 3-0, after Gurney had set up Gallacher, whose "brilliant football" and "unceasing" work made him, in the estimation of the *Sunderland Football Echo,* "the best forward on the field."

To their credit, Saints showed no sign of folding. Far from it: within five minutes, they were back in the game with a move involving three players – John Summers, Jimmy Dunne and Arthur Holt – whose careers exemplify different aspects of the Club's fortunes in the 1930s. The much-travelled Summers was still only 21 when he came to The Dell early in this 1936-37 season in a move funded partly by the Supporters Club. Yet he would retire the following season for 30 years in the Southampton Police.

Dunne was an Irish international who'd lost his place at Highbury when Ted Drake arrived. He joined Southampton in the 1936 close

Having missed his side's opening round at The Dell, Raich Carter would captain them to victory at Wembley

Our Cup competition that year started… against Southampton on their ground. In our previous week's fixture against the Arsenal… I had torn a [leg] muscle… Nevertheless I went away with the rest of the team for special training… and tried frantically to get fit in time… We travelled down to Southampton on the Saturday morning before the match, and I gave my leg a final test by sprinting along the underground platform at Waterloo Station. It was no good. I could still feel the injury and decided not to play. So I watched our first round from the touchline. The boys played well and pulled off a good victory by three goals to two. But that was only the beginning…

Raich Carter

FA Cup Third Round

season to replace one-season wonder, Vic Watson – whereupon he top-scored, won a couple more caps and headed home to Ireland at the end of the season. In stark contrast to all this coming-and-going, Holt – along with Bert Scriven, with whom he was introduced in the previous report – was a stable force of the 1930s, when each of them made over 200 appearances.

And so it was that Dunne passed wide to Summers, who made ground on the right before crossing low for Holt to volley well beyond the reach of Mapson in the Sunderland goal. Then, nine minutes later, Summers himself scored. Receiving from Dick Neal – another signing dependent upon the resources of the Supporters Club – he ran on to beat Mapson as he came out.

Suddenly in the hunt, Saints strove might and main for the equaliser, but no way were Sunderland going to let go of what they had come so far to gain. They were on their way to Wembley and were not going to be moved by a Second Division side. Yet Saints' fight-back compared favourably with their recent Second Division performances, "Cherry Blossom" suggested in the *Echo*. "In nearly every recent match," he complained, "Saints have played as though they had no really clear idea what they intended to do, even with the ball in their possession." He advocated team-talks and mid-week practice matches to develop team-work: any "surprise" moves the team employed had been more likely to surprise themselves than the opposition.

By the time Sunderland won the Cup in May – with eight of the 11 who had gone through at The Dell – Southampton had appointed a new manager, capable, it

Goalkeeper Bert Scriven was one of the "stable forces" in the 1930s

would appear, of carrying out the "Cherry Blossom" plan. He was Tom Parker. Following his career with Saints and Arsenal – as highlighted at Matches 18-23 – he had gone to manage Norwich City. In March, he came home to Southampton. Having come through that month without a win, his new charges then beat his former ones from Carrow Road and, despite taking only one more point from the last four games, Saints had done enough to avoid relegation.

Mr Parker had a busy summer ahead, spending that £1,062-share of a record gate. He started his rebuilding, though, with three free transfers on the first day of the close season. They included two lads released by Norwich City to rejoin him. One of them, Stan Cutting, would stay a couple of seasons. His companion, Eddie Bates, would linger just a little bit longer.

A view of the record 30,380 crowd

SOUTHAMPTON:
Scriven, Sillett, Roberts, King, Henderson, Kingdon, Summers, Neal, Dunne, Holt, Smallwood

SUNDERLAND:
Mapson, Hall, Collins, Thompson, Johnson, McNab, Duns, Hornby, Gurney, Gallacher, Connor

Referee: Mr G.S. Blackhall (Wednesbury)   *Attendance:* 30,380

Compiled by **NORMAN GANNAWAY** from the *Echo* reports, with additional material (and photographs) supplied by **Duncan Holley** including one from the *Sunderland Football Echo* and by **David Bull** from Raich Carter's autobiography. Carter photograph from Brian Leng's collection

CHELMSFORD CITY 4
SOUTHAMPTON 1

In the 20 seasons since the Saints had played in it, the Southern League had become something of an also-ran – except that it was no longer running very much at all, apart from the occasional excitement of a "giant-killing" exploit when one of its members removed a Football League club from the FA Cup.

When the Saints were drawn away in 1939 to Chelmsford City – a club in its first season and lying 20th in the Southern League – the Southampton Directors seemingly could not imagine being on the receiving end of such a feat: had not the Saints been by far the greatest giants that League had ever seen? (if that fact passed you by, then please see Matches 7-15) So they rejected their manager's request to take the team to Clacton-on-Sea for a week of "special training." The Board "considered this unnecessary in view of the financial position" and decided that Mr Parker should reserve such a luxury until the next round.

And so the Saints' party travelled on the day and were met off the train by Mr Thomas, the Chelmsford chairman. A nice gesture, but he had come with a warning: the pitch was covered with water and was frozen underneath. So the big issue for the Southampton players, upon arrival at the ground, was what studs to wear. Fittingly, it was Arthur Holt – whose name survives, in Southampton, as a leading sportsfitter – who became the model for the stud trial. After he had slithered and slipped all over the place, leather studs got the vote over rubber ones.

This footwear research notwithstanding, it was the home side, the *Echo* noted, who were "first to find their feet," as they attacked a Saints' defence that included two occasional deputies in Doug Henderson and Tom Carnaby. Even so, the best early chance fell to Southampton; and how different matters might have been if Briggs had scored. The inside-left, who had arrived on a free transfer from Reading at the start of the season to be the Club's top scorer in 1938-39, had burst through the middle with the home defenders appealing vainly for offside. As he approached the goalkeeper, he steadied himself, only to push the ball the wrong side of the post. Almost immediately, Chelmsford raced up field and Coulter, the left-winger, sent in a cross which Carnaby appeared to have covered. Attempting what he later described as a "hooked overhead clearance", the centre-half instead managed to slice the ball past the startled Warhurst for an own goal.

As Chelmsford tore into the Saints, the "magnificent" play of Jones, their right-half, was exciting both the man from the *Essex Chronicle* and, it would appear, the scout from Plymouth, for whom he who would sign at the end of the season – not to mention the crowd that had been

The 1938-39 squad was allowed a pre-season dip but the Board would not fund a seaside preparation for their cup-tie at Chelmsford. Those taking the water include some of the side humiliated at Chelmsford:
❶ Hill, ❷ Carnaby ❸ Brophy ❹ Bevis ❺ Briggs ❻ Osman ❼ Tomlinson.
Ted Bates ❽ was fortunate to miss this match but would be around for the next 70 or so.
Trainer Horace Cope ❾ was the Arsenal defender who literally wrestled Saints out of the Cup in Match No. 23

FA Cup Third Round

reduced by the weather to 10,741, after Chelmsford had brought in extra seats to raise the capacity of its New Writtle Street ground to 18,000.

Such had been the expectations in Chelmsford of a visit from a Second Division Club. They had come through seven rounds, beating Darlington of the Third North in the Second Round Proper. With 10 Cup goals in those seven ties, Palethorpe, their centre-forward, was enjoying himself against Tom Carnaby and the Chelmsford attack was being held at bay only by Sam Warhurst's inspired goal-keeping. Warhurst was one of those players who had signed for Tom Parker and become established but whose career would be over before the War ended – in his case to become the team's trainer.

By half-time, though, Palethorpe had scored twice, either side of a solitary reply by Holt. In the second-half, Coulter made it 4-1 after the visitors' defence had been "caught napping" by a quick throw-in. Thereupon, as Geoff Tibballs puts it in his compendium of giant-killing feats, "Chelmsford seemed to declare."

Quite why they proved so superior on the day divided the reporters. The *Essex Chronicle* felt that it was a victory for the big boot over a close-passing game that became bogged down in the mud. Yet the *Echo* credited Chelmsford with a better all-round game, both in speed to the ball and in their passing.

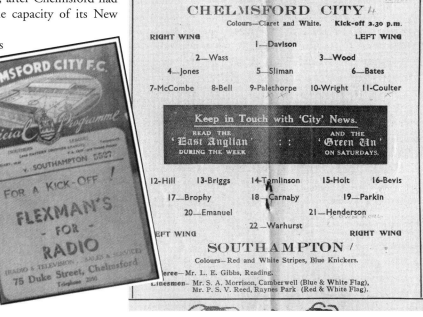

Was there, though, a significant difference in preparation for what remains Southampton's only defeat by non-League opponents in the FA Cup? While the Saints had been denied their breath of sea air, their hosts had relaxed in the brine baths at Southend. And, as for the directors' notion of leaving it until the next round, Southampton would not be playing in the FA Cup at all until 1945-46.

In that first post-war season of the FA Cup, they would achieve what they had managed only once in the 1930s – or, indeed, since those three stirring runs from 1923 to 1927 (as recorded at Matches 20 – 23): they would win a Third Round tie.

In the meantime, football would be rationed by War.

CHELMSFORD CITY:

Davison, Wass, Wood, Jones, Sliman, Bates, Landells, Bell, Palethorpe, Wright, Coulter

SOUTHAMPTON:

Warhurst, Henderson, Emanuel, Parkin, Carnaby, Brophy, Bevis, Holt, Tomlinson, Briggs, Hill

Referee: Mr L.E. Gibbs (Reading)   *Attendance:* 10,741

Compiled by **DAVID BULL** and **DUNCAN HOLLEY** from the *Echo* report and with reference to the Club minutes and Geoff Tibballs's *FA Cup Giant Killers* (compiled, in turn, from the *Essex Chronicle*)

SOUTHAMPTON 5
READING 6

The outbreak of World War Two on Sunday 3 September 1939 meant the immediate cessation of first class football as we had known it and the introduction, come October, of a completely revamped structure.

Southampton Football Club were among the first to be directly affected, in that they were due to travel to White Hart Lane for a Monday evening game against Tottenham in Division Two. We know, from interviews with Saints' players and an account by Spurs' Ronnie Burgess, that players from both teams reported on that fateful Sunday morning to their respective grounds, where they tuned into the Prime Minister's radio announcement that we were at war with Germany.

In their third game of the season, the day before, Saints had secured their first points with a 3-0 home win against Bury. Arthur Holt – of the loyal 1930s record previously touched upon – was playing what would prove to be his last Second Division game for the Club, scoring two of the goals. Both the appearance and the goals would be expunged, however, from the "official" records and Holt, with several team-mates, would join the Southampton War Reserve Police. He'd play 32 war-time games before assuming a player-coach role with the seconds.

These police officers, and others who found work locally for the war effort, would be available, to varying degrees, to participate in the war-time leagues and cups, supplemented with plenty of friendlies. The Dell was not immediately available. Southampton, on account of its armaments centres, was designated an "unsafe area" so far as public assembly was concerned. Not for seven weeks was competitive football permitted at the ground. Meanwhile, away friendlies were arranged with some of the Saints' nearest neighbours.

Then, on 21 October, Saints entertained one of those neighbours, Bournemouth, in the first of 18 games to be played by each of the 10 sides that made up the League South 'B'. Bournemouth won 2-1 and in only one of the 17 remaining games – a 2-0 win over Portsmouth – would the fans see fewer than three goals.

The average tally was 5.77 per match and the last three games of 1939 had produced 25 goals, climaxing in a 9-4 defeat at Brighton.

Police War Reserve 17 Arthur Holt.

It is reasonable to assume, then, that those spectators who came to The Dell for the first match of 1940 may have been expecting a goal or two. They would have been less certain of the line-ups. If you were in the War Reserve, you might hope to play quite regularly, but even Southampton - which earned a reputation during the War for bringing on youngsters, while others courted guest players (often servicemen stationed nearby) – experienced uncertainties about who would be available when.

Those able to make a start for Saints or Reading encountered a pitch slippery underfoot and especially trying for goalkeepers. The wing channels were marginally more sure, a feature that Reading were able to put to good advantage. Even so, their goalkeeper John Mapson – guesting from Sunderland, with whom you met him in Match No. 28 – was soon in action and Southampton were two-up inside a quarter-of-an-hour, one apiece for Jack Bradley – a close-season signing who would have to wait until January 1946 to make his "official" debut – and Tom Hassell, one of the local youngsters who would play plenty of war-time games for the Club (112 in his case), yet never make an "official" appearance, post-war.

Wilf Chitty reduced the deficit before Bradley, combining cleverly with Hassell, added Saints' third. Goals then came thick and fast, four in the last six minutes of the first-half.

The first belonged to Eddie Bates, whose arrival and durability have already been heralded. It's a measure of his stay that, even if not directly mentioned, he'll be associated – as player, coach or manager – with the next 30-odd games and then as somebody present, in some capacity, at pretty well all of the rest, right through to Match No.100.

The next was a leaping header from Fred Briggs, signed by Tom Parker from Reading and another young player in his mid-twenties at the outbreak of war but whose career would be over by the time it ended. So, 5-1 up. But

League South 'B'

Layton and Deverall snatched a couple for Reading to make it 5-3 at the interval.

There were no further goals in the first 25 minutes of the second-half. But Reading were not finished and Fred Smallwood, transferred from Southampton in 1938 as Tom Parker continued to re-build, was a key player in their comeback. In the closing 20 minutes, they struck three times. Henry Sherwood scored twice to level the account and then, in the last minute, Layton beat Sam Warhurst in the slithering mud of the Saints' goalmouth. A 6-5 win for Reading.

Quite a come-back from 5-1 down, although Southampton were handicapped by a second-half injury to Les Hopper, a young amateur who had been linking with Bradley in a manner suggesting a lasting partnership in the making. When "Echoist" praised Tom Parker for his boldness in introducing two young wingers, he was not to know that two games would be the sum of Hopper's Southampton career.

But, as already intimated, this would be the story, initially at least, of the Saints at War – a manager trying to give youth a chance, but so often bringing in young locals who would never graduate to "official" football after a War that lasted so much longer than Mr Parker had anticipated when he counselled his players on 4 September 1939.

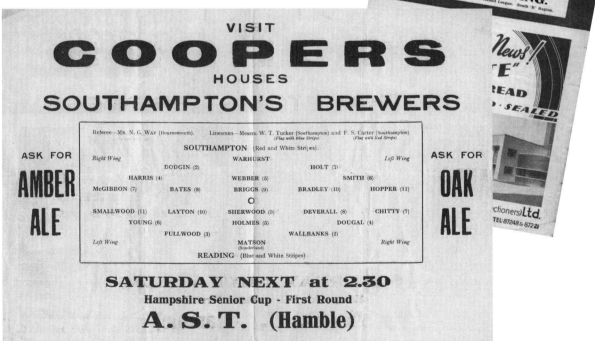

SOUTHAMPTON:

Warhurst, Roles, Holt, Harris, Webber, Smith, Hassell, Bates, Briggs, Bradley, Hopper

READING:

Mapson, Wallbanks, Fullwood, Dougall, Holmes, Young, Chitty, Deverall, Sherwood, Layton, Smallwood

Referee: Mr N.G. Way (Bournemouth)   *Attendance not known*

Compiled by **NORMAN GANNAWAY** from the *Echo* report. Additional material – from interviews with 1939 Saints and Burgess's autobiography – by **David Bull**

SOUTHAMPTON 3
CHELSEA 3

"Talked about and argued about, over factory bench and in factory canteens."

So wrote "Commentator", in the *Echo,* of Southampton's 3-3 draw with Chelsea in the League South in November 1944.

Minor drama – so typical of war-time fixtures, as illustrated in the previous report – preceded the kick-off when Chelsea's left-winger Charlie Mitten failed to arrive, having missed a train it was assumed. He would certainly have had no problem finding the ground. Having served at RAF Beaulieu, Mitten played both football and cricket in the area, including 21 games for the Saints in the 1942-43 season.

In June 1943, though, Mitten was one of three Southampton guests – John Harris and Alf Whittingham were the others – whose proposal to defect to Chelsea was investigated by a Board concerned to ascertain the link with what it called "the temporary retirement" of manager Tom Parker. Other explanations included the Club's refusal to make extra payments, an argument fuelled by the man who would effectively succeed Mr Parker in 1946. At this time, Bill Dodgin was a Southampton player – signed in 1939 and destined to make but four "official" appearances just before he became manager – who was guesting for Clapton Orient in League (South) Cup games for which, he reported, they paid double.

This saga certainly exercised the Board, but Mitten says that extra payments were not on offer at Chelsea: "it was just a bigger club, that was all." For whatever reason, Mitten and Harris were off to Stamford Bridge. Although he would have a few games for Chelsea in 1943-44 (including, as it happens, this one), Alf Whittingham of RAF Christchurch would continue to guest mainly for Southampton - to spectacular effect, as we shall see in the next report. For the moment, though, he needed to take over Mitten's shirt, while Wardle came in at outside-right.

Harris also featured in a strong Chelsea line-up. Their centre-forward, Joe Payne, had joined them in 1938 from Luton Town, the club with whom he'll be forever associated, thanks to his 10 goals for them against Bristol Rovers in 1936. Thereafter, goalscoring feats (like those in the next two reports) tended, it seems, to evoke comparisons with that remarkable achievement. Chelsea's guest players included the England left-back, Eddie

Charlie Mitten, one of the Southampton guests who had defected to Chelsea

Hapgood of Arsenal, partnered at full-back by George Hardwick of Middlesbrough, who would succeed to his international shirt.

Southampton fielded three guests: Tom Eggleston from Derby County; Wilf Grant, the Manchester City winger who would join the Saints after the War; and Dickie Dorsett from Wolves.

Dorsett soon caught the eye with his service to Don Roper. With his speed and shooting ability on the one hand and the war-time need for flexible line-ups on the other, it was Roper's lot to be shunted around the forward-line, as we shall see in the next few reports. This, though, was to be Dorsett's day. After Wardle had opened the scoring for Chelsea – latching onto the rebound as Sam Warhurst parried from Payne – Dorsett equalised from the spot. He almost added another, but Hardwick cleared off the line, while a drive from Roper rebounded from a goalpost.

Chelsea went ahead again early in the second-half, when Payne was fouled following a Harris free-kick and scored from the penalty himself. Another penalty from Dorsett evened the score once more, only for Payne and Whittingham to set up Wardle for Chelsea's third. Dorsett then stepped up to convert the third penalty awarded against Chelsea – each of them for hand-ball.

The thrills were not yet over. In a game in which both goalkeepers earned praise, Warhurst dropped a Payne effort near a post, almost on his goal-line, and was shortly afterwards saved by his crossbar. But the spectators had to be content with six goals, which was below par for these two sides: Chelsea scored 100 and Southampton 96 in their 30 League South games that season.

Yet few of those could have created greater passion for the crowd than this one. Dorsett's hat-trick of penalties has, of course, remained the talking point. Each one was so strongly hit that Anderson, the Chelsea 'keeper, was unable to stop the two he got a hand to.

Still only 25 when the War ended, Dorsett would play on into the fifties. Having scored 32 in 46 League games for Wolves, he would leave them for Aston Villa. He'd get

League South

32 for them, too, but in 257 appearances – a reflection of how much deeper he would often play. Pensioners on the south coast are likely to remember him, though, for scoring in two particular games. He scored Wolves' only goal in their shock 4-1 defeat by Portsmouth in the 1939 Cup Final. And then there were those three penalties – especially memorable if you were there.

As with many footballing feats, fact and fancy over the years become entwined. Recollection from this spectator's eye tells me that two of the successful penalties were taken with the right foot, the third struck with the left.

The available *Echo* account, limited by the demands on space that the next report goes into, neither confirms nor refutes.

Unchallenged recall is of standing on The Dell terraces, behind the Milton Road end goal and of watching entranced as Dorsett, dark hair severely centre-parted, moved up to the penalty spot to whack the ball right-footed hard and true into the Chelsea net. Perhaps the first wholly dramatic moment in my watching career.

Memories are made of this.

The team against Chelsea showed two changes from this line-up of two months earlier.
That's because Saints were fielding as many as seven of their own players – even if Whittingham was guesting for both them and Chelsea
Standing (left to right) Mr Sarjantson (secretary-manager), Evans, Dodgin, Stroud, Taylor, Warhurst, Roles, Gallagher (trainer) Dominy (manager)
Seated: Roper, Bates, Whittingham, Walker, Grant

SOUTHAMPTON:
Warhurst, Eggleston, Roles, Evans, Dodgin, Stroud, Hassell, Bates, Roper, Dorsett, Grant.

CHELSEA:
Anderson, Hardwick, Hapgood, Russell, Harris, Foss, Wardle, Tennant, Payne, Machin, Whittingham.

Referee: Mr W. J. Muller

Attendance not known

Compiled by **NORMAN GANNAWAY** from being there and from the *Echo* report. Additional material – from the Club Minutes and an interview with Charlie Mitten – by **David Bull**. *Echo* photographs

SOUTHAMPTON 12
LUTON TOWN 3

"SOUTHAMPTON'S BIG SCORE"

So said the under-stated *Luton News* headline when the Saints ran up 12 in March 1945.

Saints had beaten Luton Town 12-3. Although this became their second-highest score ever – pipping their three 11-0 wins, dating from the 1901 score-line against Northampton (Match No. 13) to a 1943 victory, also over Luton – this "big score" still fell two short of their record 14-0 defeat of Newbury in the FA Cup of 1894-95.

A war-time shortage of various materials, including paper, meant a shortage of football coverage: match reports were confined to a few column inches, with seldom an action picture in sight. And if you thought the *Luton News* headline was sparing, the *Echo* got by without one at all. There being no Football *Echo* of a war-time Saturday evening, readers craving a local account of the 15 goals scored on Saturday would have to wait until Monday's *Echo* came out. And any Luton fans masochistic enough to want the story of their side's 12-3 defeat would have to wait until the Wednesday, when the *Luton News* next appeared.

Lest you're thinking that war-time scores didn't matter that much, anyhow, the *Echo* noted that a superior goal average could be Southampton's "main hope" of topping their group in the South

Ted Bates was one of four Southampton players to feature in both larrupings of Luton

League Cup and qualifying for the semi-final. Their 29 goals in six games would leave them, though, a point short of Chelsea who went all the way to win at Wembley, with a side that included goalkeeper Ian Black, whom we'll be meeting in Saints' matches of the next few seasons, and inside-forward Joe Payne, introduced in the previous report as a player forever associated with his 10 goals in one game for Luton.

So much so that when the Saints' guest centre-forward scored eight of the 11 against Luton in 1943, his achievement was inevitably compared with Payne's. This guest was Alf Whittingham. However much importance the *Echo* attached to the game, war-time matches have not passed muster with the keepers of "official" records; so, in that sense, Whittingham did not break Albert Brown's record of seven goals in that Northampton game of 1901. But his achievement was remarkable enough for him to be presented, at the next home game, with the match ball signed by his team-mates.

Whittingham was one of four Saints' players to feature in both of these larrupings of Luton. The others were Roles, Bates and Stroud, the Club's top three in war-time appearances. But, such were the vagaries of comings and goings during the war that Luton fielded two completely different elevens, each time including a guest from The Dell – Alf Creecy in 1943 and Jack Bradley in 1945. Whittingham and Tom Eggleston (introduced in the previous report) were the Saints' only guest players for this 1945 game. The rest were their own men. Luton, by comparison, fielded four guests and three players making their only appearance of the season. As the *Luton News* put it, they "again felt the pinch of shortage of class players."

Southampton attacked from the start and it was obvious, from the way Ramsey had settled in at inside-left, that Dorsett – the hero of Match No. 31 who'd so far scored half of the Saints' Cup goals - would not be missed. Sergeant Ramsey of the Duke of Cornwall Light Infantry had arrived the previous season as a centre-half. His transition to right-back, via appearances as a goal-scoring forward, is described in the next report.

This was one of those goal-happy days. He opened the scoring when a shot was blocked and the ball ran loose to him. Luton retaliated but a fine shot from Ramsey soon made it two. The visitors' defence was rocked by the class of the Southampton forwards and Bates, who "played a grand game," duly added a third from close range.

Although Saints "in the end swamped the visitors," the *Echo* acknowledged that there was a time, in the first-half, when Luton were still trying to get on terms and Jack Bradley, their guest-captain, was their inspiration, his "good generalship at inside-left, pull[ing] the side together" for a rally that brought them two quick goals.

Unfortunately for Bradley, when he had a chance, shortly before half-time, to add to those two goals from Woolhead, he shot straight at goalkeeper Len Stansbridge. But soon after the re-start, the game was out of Luton's reach. Ramsey, Whittingham and then Hassell had made it 6-2.

True, the visitors came back with a third goal –

credited to Daniel by the *Luton News* and to Weir by the *Echo*. This served, however, to start another goal rush as Hassell soon scored his second; and, with the Luton defence at sixes and sevens – or, rather, sevens and eights - Ramsey scored his fourth. While Ramsey's work-rate and powerful shooting impressed the *Echo* reporter – "he certainly can 'hammer' a ball" – Roper was unusually quiet on Southampton's right wing, a rarity attributed by the Luton 'paper to a "magnificent" performance by Cooke, his marker, and by the *Echo* to the boil on his left arm. The rest of the home forwards more or less pleased themselves, though, against such a woefully weak defence.

A final flurry of goals came from Whittingham, Stroud and two more inside two minutes from Whittingham.

Alf Whittingham would be demobbed from The Dell with 84 goals in 65 guest appearances, second only, in war-time service, to Don Roper's 86 in 71.

So who cared about weak defences? When the comings and goings of military personnel produced makeshift rear-guards like Luton's, this contributed most excitingly to civilian entertainment.

SOUTHAMPTON:

Stansbridge, Eggleston, Roles; Evans, Dodgin, Stroud; Roper, Bates, Whittingham, Ramsey, Hassell

LUTON TOWN:

Wilkinson; Archer, Cooke; Daniel, Wainwright, Cawdell; Dempsey, Weir, Woolhead, Bradley, Dunkley

Referee: Mr A. Curtis   *Attendance not known*

Compiled by **NORMAN HULL** from reports in the *Echo* and the *Luton News* and with reference to Jack Rollin's *Soccer at War*

SOUTHAMPTON 5
PLYMOUTH ARGYLE 5

It is difficult now to picture how drab everything was in the summer of 1945, the bombsites, the shortages, clothes "on points" and food rationing still in force, and how deprived we all felt of professional sport.

Small wonder that, in the first post-war football season, so many fans crammed through the turnstiles each Saturday despite the fact that there were only two makeshift leagues – the pre-war First and Second Division clubs divided geographically, north and south.

However, it gave Saints the chance to compete against such giants as Arsenal and Chelsea, and they had never met the former in a *real* League match up to that time.

I had just returned from wartime evacuation in rural Wiltshire and knew nothing of football, but as we waited for the season to begin my imagination was stirred by friends' accounts of recent wartime games at The Dell and the exploits of our local heroes. Amongst the latter, one name stood out – "The Don".

Although he has been introduced to you (in Match No. 31) as a goal-scoring forward of considerable versatility, Don Roper was essentially a dashing right-winger with a formidable shot in either foot. And, as he also possessed spectacular skills in the summer game, it seemed entirely appropriate he should share a nickname with the great Australian batsman. He had all the attributes of a schoolboy hero and I awaited the first game that season with eager anticipation, it mattering little it was against one of the less fashionable sides - Plymouth Argyle.

The Dell was undeniably shabby immediately after the war. It had been bombed in 1940 and the Milton Road end was little better than a heap of earth made into rough terracing by wooden battens.

I suppose there must have been crowd barriers but I don't remember them, our having queued for hours so that we could claim a position on the railings (later a wall) just by where our heroes were due to emerge. It had cost me one old penny to bus from my Millbrook home and nine-pence to get in, with a further penny for the programme, a total of 11d, less than a shilling – or 5p, in today's money.

As I remember it, the game was more exciting than skilful with, seemingly, a goal every few minutes – Saints scoring after three, Plymouth in the lead by 14 and the scores level at 2-2 by half-time. Thereafter, it went 3-2, 4-2, 4-3 and then 5-3 before Saints surrendered a point in the last 10 minutes to leave the game at 5-5. Yes, it used to happen even in those days!

The Don performed on cue with electrifying runs down the touch-line, more often than not after through balls provided by his inside-forward. There would be no stopping and playing it back or a hopeful diagonal punt into the middle for him, or for any winger in those days for that matter - it was the goal-line or bust, exhilarating stuff, or at least it seemed so to an impressionable schoolboy. Of course, full-backs were not built for speed in 1945 but most were big and aggressive enough to make going for a ball played inside or outside them distinctly hazardous. The Don was no stranger to the terracing over the touch-line walls.

The game left us breathless and excited and not particularly bothered that we had dropped a point to what was likely to be one of the weakest teams in our division that year. (Plymouth finished bottom, in fact, and could manage only another 32 goals in 41 games). Their centre-forward, Brown, who had once turned out for Saints Reserves in 1935, scored a hat-trick, whereas my hero had been the only Saints forward not to score. Our centre-forward, however, had bagged two.

He was a tearaway sort of player, shirt sleeves flapping, hair all over the place, not particularly skilful as I remember but able to "put himself about" as centre-forwards were expected to do in those days. His name? Ramsey, Alf Ramsey – or "Ramsay", as the programme for this game and, indeed, many thereafter, incorrectly put it. If you didn't recognise him from my description then this is because you missed the clue in the previous report: this phase as an upfront goal-scorer was a transitional one, pending his transformation - as dramatic as that of any caterpillar emerging into a butterfly - into a classic full-back. The inside-right who knew exactly how to bring the best out of The Don that day, and many subsequent days, was a man who, it might fairly be said, would never really change at all in 60-something seasons at The Dell: the unassuming Ted Bates.

Guests would still be allowed in this transitional season – as the next report spectacularly

Transitional striker Alf Ramsey (left) is thwarted by goalkeeper Wright as Ted Bates stalks.

Tea for Two – for "The Don" and his fiancée
A week before their March 1944 wedding, the directors invited Don Roper and his bride to join them for tea at the Polygon
The line-up had an unusually high number of guests, including three in uniform at the front.
Back row (left to right): Bert Head (cashier), Stroud, Bates, Whittingham, Tann, Dodgin,
Mr Prince (director), Arthur Dominy (team manager), Mr Cosgrove (director).
Middle row: Mr Wright (director), Roper, Mr Sarjantson (secretary-manager), Mrs Roper (designate),
Mr Jukes (chairman), Mr Hoskins (director).
Front row: Jimmy Gallagher (trainer), Drinkwater, Jones, Hamilton, Roles.

demonstrates – but the Saints started 1945-46 with 11 of their own. Four of them (Cruickshanks, Stear, Dodgin and Hassell) would never appear in a Football League game proper for the Saints, while two others (Roles and Evans) would play just one game each.

Albie Roles provides an extreme example of a young hopeful who arrived at his club before the War, played umpteen war-time games – in his case, 188, which was more than anybody else for Saints – and then turned out but once for the "official" records. For me, though, the status of their appearances does not matter a jot: their names represent the beginning of a lifetime of obsession and so will ever be remembered.

We walked home that day, kicking a tennis ball around in streets almost devoid of traffic as we went, and I spent the last penny of my shilling on an *Echo* when I got home. It won't have been the *Football Echo*, production of which had yet to be resumed after the war-time restrictions discussed in the previous report. But just think of it, five new pence for an unforgettable afternoon, ½p a goal.

Beat that for footballing value in these inflated times!

SOUTHAMPTON:
Cruikshanks, Stear, Roles, Evans, Dodgin, Stroud, Roper, Bates, Ramsey, Bradley, Hassell

PLYMOUTH ARGYLE:
Wright, Rundle, Silk, Squires, Adams, Gardner, Jones, Prescott, Brown, Thomas, Tinkler

Referee: Mr. G.H. Hann   *Attendance:* 13,000

Compiled by **ROB HOLLEY** from being there and from the *Echo* report. *Echo* photographs

SOUTHAMPTON 7
CHELSEA 0

As the storm clouds of the Second World War were slipping away, Doug McGibbon brought the sun shafting through the dark December skies in 1945 with one of the finest pieces of striking in the history of Southampton Football Club.

A second generation Saints player – his father Charles had played for the Club before the First World War – McGibbon not only collected six goals in a 7-0 thrashing of Chelsea, he also scored the Club's quickest goal from a kick-off. It took him just over four seconds to find the net as the teams restarted the second-half of the League South match at The Dell with Saints already three-up.

It was a sensational way for the Southampton-born centre-forward to complete the first half of a double hat-trick. As Saints kicked off, the ball was played to Ted Bates who, in a rehearsed move he had invented, swept it wide to Bill Stroud who, in turn, crossed it into the path of McGibbon who netted without a Chelsea player having got near the ball.

Salisbury referee George Searle carried a stop-watch and timed the goal at 4.6 seconds. The quickest goal ever recorded in those days had come from a Charlton player in nine seconds. That was at the start of the game; no-one had scored a quicker goal at the re-start and nor does there seem to be any record of anyone doing so since.

It was ironic that the Southampton No. 9 should capture the headlines on that last Saturday of 1945 when so many in the big 23,434 crowd had turned up for a rare close-up of McGibbon's opposite number Tommy Lawton. Supreme among the game's forwards past and present for his awesome power in the air, Lawton was one of the game's true superstars – a huge box-office draw in an age when there was a great mystique about football's giants. Apart from newsreel clips, the game's legion of followers usually had only one chance a year to see the stars. And for Tommy Lawton and the massed ranks of fans on the Solent, this was it.

But Lawton was largely anonymous as McGibbon, who had approached manager Parker at a cricket match to seek a trial, dramatically and spectacularly took centre-stage.

Six-goal Doug McGibbon

Saints' expectations before the game hadn't been high. Goalkeeper Warhurst failed a fitness test after cracking a rib in the previous game against Brentford. Neither Bill Ellerington nor Tom Emanuel was available at full-back. Roles was, as ever, at hand but his partner had to be drafted in from his guest-spot at Cowes: Huddersfield's war-time cap Reg Mountford would have just this one game for Saints. And Jack Bradley simply didn't make it to the ground on time. The inside-left, last seen guesting for Luton, confesses that this was a risk he took when he hitch-hiked and claimed expenses.

It left Saints in the bizarre situation of having to borrow a player from Chelsea. They loaned their reserve winger Buchanan, who had turned out for Saints earlier in the war years. And then to add insult to injury, Buchanan laid on the first of McGibbon's goals. It arrived just four minutes into the game, Buchanan swinging over a corner which a ponderous Chelsea defence failed to clear. McGibbon stole in to score from close range.

The second came from Ted Bates, whose capabilities at inside-forward, as both a taker and maker of chances, have been acclaimed in previous reports. In this case, the man who was destined to become a Dell legend showed great opportunism from another corner, challenging the Chelsea 'keeper Robertson as he grappled to bring the ball under control on the goal-line. Bates forced it out of his hands and over the line.

After 41 minutes, the ever-versatile Don Roper, having been obliged to assume Bradley's inside-left role, curled over the kind of centre which Lawton would have killed for on this day. The man on the end of it was McGibbon with a firm header for his second goal. Within 24 minutes of the restart, McGibbon, incredibly, had put six in the onion bag and Bates had shown the creative side of his nature by cleverly crafting his fourth with a lovely pass. In so far as this "unofficial" League season counts for anything, McGibbon's super effort put him third in the all-time high-scoring performances by Saints players – behind Albert Brown's seven and Alf Whittingham's eight, described in the reports of Matches 13 and 32.

There were a couple of unsung Southampton heroes on the day in the shape of the wing-halves Evans and Stroud, whom the *Echo* reporter found "swift and sure in the tackle and in getting the ball up to the forwards. They played an outstanding part in the success."

To complete a black day for Chelsea, Goulden drove a penalty kick two yards wide. McGibbon went on to score 29 goals in 33 appearances that season, but would leave for Fulham a year later.

6-goal McGibbon scores in $4\frac{3}{5}$ sec. —the fastest-ever

DOUGLAS McGIBBON, the Southampton centre, will remember the match with Chelsea—and not only because he scored six goals.

One of the six was [...] secs. after the start of [...] half—more than halvin[...] held by Iverson, who [...] Villa, scored 9 3-5 sec[...] kick-off in the match v[...] on December 3, 1938.

McGibbon's time wa[...] by the referee. Mr. G[...] Salisbury.

McGibbon is an airc[...] Swindon and the so[...] Southampton centre.

AND BUC[...]

The victory was [...] remarkable because [...] left Bradley did n[...] they borrowed [...] Chelsea. Buchanan [...] game, two of the [...] goals coming fro[...] Lawton had little [...] going against the [...] the Southampton [...] altoge:her had a b[...] missed a penalty [...] injured, spent ha[...] second half in the [...]

Reg Mountford (left), guesting from Huddersfield via Cowes for just one game, managed to get himself photographed with Bill Dodgin and two players – Stansbridge and Veck – returned from overseas

---

SOUTHAMPTON:
Stansbridge, Mountford, Roles, Evans, Dodgin, Stroud, Buchanan, Bates, McGibbon, Roper, Veck

CHELSEA:
Robertson, Winter, Tennant, Russell, Harris, Williams, Spence, Payne, Lawton, Goulden, Bain

Referee: Mr G.V. Searle (Salisbury)   *Attendance:* 23,434

Compiled by **BOB BRUNSKELL** from the *Echo* report, with additional material – from interviews with Ted Bates, Jack Bradley, Doug McGibbon and Bill Stroud; and with reference to several record-book claims for goals from kick-offs – by **David Bull**. Photographs from **Duncan Holley**'s collection

SOUTHAMPTON 4
DERBY COUNTY 2

"Saints beat both FA Cup Finalists" was the proud claim heading the "Sport Day to Day" column by "Commentator" in the *Echo* of Tuesday 30 April 1946. In a different day and age, the achievement might have warranted major space on the back page – or even the front page – but almost a year after the end of the War, the newsprint restrictions discussed in some of our previous war-time reports (especially at Match No. 32) still applied. *The Football Echo* would return, along with real League football, come September.

Meanwhile, for this first peace-time season of 1945-46, the League South had taken on a different meaning: eight clubs from the Midlands were added to the mix of the past six seasons, which is how Derby came to be visiting The Dell as opponents from the "South". More significantly for the purpose of the *Echo*'s headline-writer, though, Derby had won the Cup on the Saturday – that famously entertaining Final in which Bert Turner of Charlton had scored for each side in the last five minutes of ordinary time, before Peter Doherty scored and made two for Jackie Stamps in extra-time.

Without returning to Derby, the Cup-winners came to Southampton for this Monday evening game, bringing the Cup with them. Three of their Final side were missing, most notably Raich Carter. Saints' fans would again be deprived of seeing the England inside-forward. You may recall that he was unfit to play at The Dell in Match No. 28, en route to scoring for Sunderland in the 1937 Final. Now, having collected another winners' medal with his new club, he would miss this game for family reasons, his father-in-law having died while listening to the radio commentary of Saturday's Final. He would not be seen at The Dell until he dropped down to the Second Division with Hull City. It would mean a wait, too, for Southampton's right-back to play against his idol: Bill Ellerington talks with awe of being an apprentice at Sunderland and standing deferentially aside when "Mister Carter" passed along the corridor. Now coming 23 and with almost 60 war-time games behind him, Ellerington was poised to become one of Southampton's enduringly loyal post-war servants.

Elsewhere in the Derby line-up, the injured Dally Duncan and Chick Musson were replaced by Angus Morrison and Tim Ward, respectively. It was a poignant occasion for Ward. The Derby wing-half represents the opposite end of the war-time spectrum to those players who stayed at home in Reserved occupations – the likes of Ted Bates and Albie Roles – and who were able to turn out fairly regularly for their own club. Ward was one of those who had been abroad for the duration, being demobbed to England the Wednesday before the Cup Final. As his son has movingly expressed it in his biography of his father, Tim Ward was putting on boots stored by his club for seven years and his "season was just beginning." Southampton fielded three such players in Billy Bevis, Bob Veck and George Ephgrave. The two wingers had each been demobbed before Christmas, while Ephgrave had arrived earlier in the month after spending four years as a prisoner-of-war in Odessa. "Commentator" delighted in the appearance of Bevis who, he pointed out, had been torpedoed three times and mined once.

Veck put Southampton into a 7th-minute lead, direct from a free-kick past Vic Woodley who had been England's undisputed goalkeeper at the outbreak of war. Then Bates added a second to put Saints well on their way. A McCulloch header pulled something back for Derby before half-time and, immediately after an interval in which the Cup had been paraded, Stamps levelled the scores. Stamps was well-known to the Dell crowd, having scored eight times in 14 guest appearances for the Saints in 1942-43. He retained happy memories of his brief stay, regarding Southampton as a good club with a marvellous atmosphere. Further goals by Bevis and Don Roper spoiled Stamps's return visit, however, and completed the feat captured in the headline.

That is to say that Saints had twice met Charlton Athletic, the beaten finalists, over Easter – the weekend before the Final, winning 3-1 at The Dell on Good Friday and drawing 1-1 at the Valley on Easter Monday. They had the added satisfaction of a good performance against a Derby side that "Commentator" complimented for fluency and endeavour that would have graced the Final itself. There was praise, too, for the Saints' full-backs, Albie Roles and Bill Ellerington, for containing the pace

Thwarted by his hero's bereavement in 1946,
Bill Ellerington would eventually play against "Mister Carter"
when he came to The Dell with Hull City in 1949.
Left to right: Ellerington, Webber, Carter.

League South

of Derby's attacks on a slippery surface and with a sodden match-ball, and also for the interceptions and tenacity of wing-halves George Smith and Bill Stroud.

Moreover, beating Derby was some recompense for Saints' 8-1 setback at the Baseball Ground in the February, their heaviest defeat of 1945-46 – this transitional 42-match season in which they finished in the bottom third with the remarkable goal aggregate of 97-105. Derby finished fourth in a

…in the away-team dressing room at The Dell [Tim Ward] pulled on the white shirt of Derby County…
His boots had been kept for seven years, stored [by] the club… He was back doing what he wanted to do all his life. Playing professional football. Playing for Derby County.

Yet something didn't seem right. Eight of his colleagues had Cup-winners medals, won two days previously. Tim did not … His colleagues' celebratory season was almost over, his own English season just beginning. While he was in the dressing-room at half-time, the Cup was paraded around the Southampton ground.
It seemed appropriate that he was distanced from it.

After the game… the Cup was taken to a Southampton hotel. He knew that the next day the whole of Derby would turn out to welcome them. But it was the Cup-winning players they would want to see, not the soldier who was home from the war. He felt like a spectator who had strayed into the penalty area while a penalty kick was being taken.

Andrew Ward, on his father, Tim

League dominated by the small Midlands contingent. Third-placed Charlton were the only southerners in the top six.

Alex James and Harry Ditton regarded the April 1946 Cup Final as "glorious" and "worth going miles to see."

Southampton supporters had reason to feel something similar about two matches that month at The Dell when the two finalists were beaten in the space of 11 days.

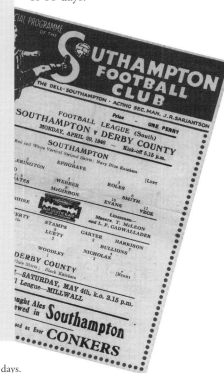

The advertised line-ups for the two games when Saints beat both of the season's Cup Finalists in 11 days.

SOUTHAMPTON:
Ephgrave, Ellerington, Roles, Stroud, Webber, Smith, Bevis, Bates, McGibbon, Roper, Veck

DERBY COUNTY:
Woodley, Nicholas, Rowe, Bullions, Leuty, Ward, Harrison, Stamps, McCulloch, Doherty, Morrison

Referee: Mr J.M. Wiltshire (Dorset)   *Attendance:* 19,000

Compiled by **NORMAN GANNAWAY** from being there, from the *Echo* report and with reference to Martin Tyler's *Cup Final Extra!* Additional material – from Andrew Ward's biography of his father and from an interview with Bill Ellerington – by **David Bull**

SOUTHAMPTON 3
BLACKBURN ROVERS 2

They called it Day's Match, the occasion Round Four of the FA Cup when one of the quickest, most exciting wingers ever to wear the red-and-white stripes of Southampton starred in a famous victory over Blackburn Rovers.

Eric Day took centre-stage on that grey, brooding day in January 1948. On a gluepot of a Dell pitch the footballer who had switched from rugby only while serving in the RAF ran Rovers ragged, capping a superb display with two of the goals in a 3-2 victory.

Saints had already beaten one of England's footballing giants Sunderland in the Third Round, the first time since that memorable Cup run of 1927 (as highlighted in Matches 22-23) that they had seen off First Division opponents. And now they faced another top flight side, with a considerable Cup pedigree. Blackburn Rovers had won the trophy six times and as such were one of the renowned aristocrats of the competition.

But records counted for little on an afternoon when Day sprang on Rovers like an apparition out of the gloom. The *Echo* reporter wrote:

> I doubt if there is a winger faster than Day when he jumps into his stride from a standing start. It was his great acceleration which won the tie against Blackburn Rovers. I have never seen anything more perfect in pace and precision than the way Day took his first goal. He sped into the goalmouth to pick up a crossfield pass from Ted Bates and swept the ball across the front of Blackburn keeper George Marks before scoring with a shot at a reverse angle.

It was a move which not only put the Blackburn backs out of the game but also put an experienced goalkeeper behind him.

The goal was perfectly timed, coming just a minute after Blackburn had taken the lead through Campbell. Charlie Wayman put Saints in front just before half-time courtesy of another assist from Bates, but it was very much nip and tuck going into the second-half when the Rovers No. 9 Charlie McClelland levelled the scores again.

It set the game up for a tense, thrilling finale and it was Saints and, to be precise, Day who had the decisive last say. There were just five minutes left when Day enacted a two-part thriller. Initially he had looked set to score as he sped clear of the blue-and-white shirted Rovers defence. But he carried the ball a little too far and Marks, spreading himself at the winger's feet, gathered the ball safely in his arms. Day never checked his pace and at full tilt had no option but to leap over the goalkeeper's body.

But when he broke through again, the story had a different ending. Again Marks came courageously to meet

him but this time he didn't get the ball. Day was able to put his foot back on it and propel it forward, driving on to sweep it into the empty net.

The feeling of exhilaration it injected into the huge gathering of home fans was enormous. When the whistle sounded they streamed out of the ground all of a buzz having enjoyed one of the club's finest hours. Day was the hero of the hour, but every man Jack in a Southampton shirt had done his bit. George Curtis was superb ploughing through the muddy morass of midfield and stretching out the Rovers defence with his perceptive passing.

Day, Curtis, Wayman... In the two years since Bill Dodgin had taken over as manager, he had been assembling an exciting side. Wayman had again looked a class act against Blackburn. Having put Saints out of the Cup a year before with a hat-trick for Newcastle, he had signed for Southampton in October. In 14 games since then, he had scored nine times and was well on his way to demonstrating the indispensability that will become apparent in the next few reports. Apart from scoring the second goal, he was the one who set up Day for the decider. Bob Pryde, Rovers' uncompromising centre-half and captain, gave Wayman a hard time but the diminutive north-easterner most certainly had the last laugh.

Bates was solid and effective in linking up the attack, playing a vital part in two of the goals. Eric Webber, who'd established himself as Dodgin's centre-half, was caught out of position when McClelland scored his goal, but was otherwise defensively sound and Joe Mallett, although troubled from the early stages by a groin strain, showed why his conversion to left-half would prove so lasting.

One of Blackburn's top players was England international winger Bobby Langton who was generally eclipsed by a certain Alf Ramsey, who had converted to right-back so successfully that he would be capped for England before the year was out.

So good was the cover that Ian Black, in only his fourth game for the Saints but settling in well enough to win a Scottish cap by the end of the season, was not overworked in the Saints goal, although he needed to be on his mettle to save from Campbell and dealt well with a rising drive from McClelland.

The receipts of £3,006 were a Saints record from a 24,274 crowd and Jack Bruton, the Rovers manager, was magnanimous in defeat, saying: "It was a splendid match. Now I hope you go on to Wembley."

FA Cup Fourth Round

Sadly they didn't. After goals by Wayman and Curtis had helped them win 3-0 at home to Swindon in the Fifth Round, they went out 1-0 to Spurs in a quarter-final at The Dell watched by 28,425. And this Cup run, by far their best for 21 years, was matched by a third-place finish in Division Two, the highest position they had ever achieved.

'S' is for success: the emblem of the 1948 FA Cup run. The 'S' men, from the top, are Bill Dodgin, Rochford, Black, Ellerington, Ramsey, Smith, Webber, Mallett, Day, Curtis, Wayman, Bates, Wrigglesworth and Sam Warhurst.

Having rounded goalkeeper Marks, Eric Day (left) has an empty net for his first goal, as Charlie Wayman hovers lest the ball stick in the mud.

SOUTHAMPTON:
Black, Ramsey, Rochford, Smith, Webber, Mallett, Day, Curtis, Wayman, Bates, Wrigglesworth

BLACKBURN ROVERS:
Marks, Cook, Tomlinson, Baldwin, Pryde, Horton, Campbell, Graham, McClelland, Murphy, Langton

Referee: Mr F.J. Lowe   *Attendance:* 24,274

Compiled by **BOB BRUNSKELL** from the *Echo* report. *Echo* photographs

VASCO DA GAMA 2
SOUTHAMPTON 1

When Vasco da Gama entertained English opposition in June 1948, there was rather less hype – this side of the ocean, anyhow – than there was when Manchester United played the Copa Libertadores winners in January 2000.

Club de Regatas Vasco da Gama were taking on not the champions of Europe but a Southampton side that had just finished third in the Second Division. And any claim the visitors had to be of international calibre lay with their goalkeeper, Ian Black, whose one Scottish cap had been won against England at Hampden two months previously, and with right-back Alf Ramsey, who had just won an England 'B' cap in Switzerland.

Participation in the FA tour of Italy and Switzerland had caused Ramsey to miss the first half of the Saints' tour of Brazil. That had the advantage of bringing him across the Atlantic by 'plane, compared with his team-mates who had spent 12 days and nights at sea. That had meant repeated opportunities to over-eat, even when they stuck to the seven-course menu, especially when the crew – "football daft" Saints fans almost to a man, Bill Ellerington recalls – were forcing extra helpings upon them. And that for men liberated from rationbook Britain.

Ian Black gathers while Len Wilkins covers Ismael

But who cared that these athletes would disembark in Rio overfed and under-trained (unless you count the exhibitions of head-tennis with which they'd entertained their fellow-passengers on the *Andes*)? What did the Brazilians know about football? A lot more than their under-prepared guests knew about Brazilian football or the Rio climate, it seems. "It was a mystery tour," Bill Ellerington confesses. "We hadn't a clue what to expect."

Which is why Ramsey arrived to find his team-mates having lost weight – the oppressive heat having more than compensated for further force-feeding by their lavish hosts – and having lost four games out of four.

The third of those had been a 4-2 defeat by São Paulo, the town to which Charles Miller had brought home the Beautiful Game that he had long ago learned in Southampton – as a pupil at Banister Court and as a player for St Mary's (as seen in Match No. 6). How appropriate it was, then, that the 73 year-old Miller kicked off this 1948 exchange in his home-town.

By now, though, the Saints were adjusting. So much so that they won their next game against Corinthians – the São Paulo side that would beat Vasco in the Final of FIFA's latest contrivance for armchair fans.

Then it was back to Rio, first to beat Flamengo and next to face the formidable Vasco da Gama.

Aidan Hamilton points out that seven of the team that faced Southampton would be in Brazil's squad for the 1950 World Cup and six of them would play in the Final itself in Rio, including Ademir, the tournament's Golden Boot.

News of how well Southampton played to hold this star side to 2-1 was relayed not by satellite and Gary Lineker but by messages from the match referee. This official was George Reader, the Southampton school teacher, who had travelled out with the side in order to confer with local

Tour Match

referees. He so impressed his hosts that he was invited to officiate for the tour. It was from that vantage point that he compiled his match reports for the *Echo*.

Mr Reader reported on the fireworks that welcomed the teams onto the pitch and upon the refusal of the commentators and the photographers to leave it:

> The radio and press seem to be deciding factors in this country about the time when a match shall commence.

Rupert Murdoch didn't think of it first, then.

Djalma, who was "very fast and very tricky" and who was cutting in from the right wing "at every opportunity," soon scored. But Charlie Wayman duly

The 73 year-old Charles Miller (last seen as a teenager in Match No 6) kicks off in his home town, watched by Ted Bates (left), Charlie Wayman, George Reader and George Curtis.

equalised with what the match-reporting referee considered "a fine goal." Another fireworks display at half-time created the impression of a November fog for Mr Reader, peering through it to restart the game. But Chico, on Vasco's left flank, immediately found enough daylight to score.

That goal was enough to decide the game, given the strength of a home defence that Mr Reader felt "would compare favourably with Arsenal's." That comparison is not without its irony, since the Brazilians had been hoping to receive the 1948 Champions of the Football League. They would do so a year later, but meanwhile Southampton had adjusted impressively – well enough to

hold the mighty Vasco to 2-1 in what Alf Ramsey considered to be "one of the best matches in which I'd ever played."

Indeed, the game confirmed the "extraordinary capacity" of the under-prepared visitors, as the Flamengo coach generously put it, to assimilate new ideas – both tactical and technical.

There were tactical adjustments at both ends of the field: exploiting Bill Rochford's offside mastery, which the *Gazeta Esportiva* described as "a tactical resource used with perfection and art"; and playing diagonal balls that could release Charlie Wayman, whose usual game – so crucial to the team, as we shall see in the next two reports – was being stifled by the *libero*. The technical lessons included how to play under floodlights, an innovation that Saints would bring home to effect in Match No. 42.

The learning wasn't all one way, though. Southampton had demonstrated "qualities," the Flamengo coach suggested, that the Brazilians could beneficially adopt. It is not clear what they were, but they were not enough to beat Uruguay in the 1950 World Cup.

That final was refereed by George Reader, the undoubted star of that 1948 tour who would eventually become the Chairman of the Club that had discovered, in that torrid summer of 1948, the trials of being a substitute for Arsenal.

VASCO da GAMA:
Barbosa, Augusto, Wilson, Eli, Danilo, Jorge, Djalma (Nestor 45), Maneca, Friaça, Ademir (Ismael 45), Chico.

SOUTHAMPTON:
Black, Ramsey, Rochford, Wilkins, Clements, Mallett (Ballard 45), Day, Scott, Wayman, Curtis, Grant.

Referee: Mr George Reader
Attendances are often not given in Brazil, but "good gate receipts" of $501.000,000 were reported.

Compiled by **DAVID BULL**, from Brazilian match reports, as translated by **Aidan Hamilton**; and drawing upon Alf Ramsey's autobiography and upon research (including interviews with players, one of whom supplied the Miller photograph), as conducted for two chapters on the tour - his own for *Dell Diamond* and Aidan Hamilton's for *An Entirely Different Game*, the story of the Brazilian development of Miller's import from Southampton. Further material and illustration subsequently forwarded from Rio by Aidan Hamilton.

TOTTENHAM HOTSPUR 0
SOUTHAMPTON 1

When the lamed Charlie Wayman courageously scored the match-winning goal for Saints at Tottenham on 2 April 1949, the 15,000 travelling fans among a huge, heaving 69,000 throng at White Hart Lane were convinced they had witnessed a momentous event in the Club's history.

Wayman's goal had lifted Saints eight points clear in Division II and they had just seven matches left to play. Even though their nearest rivals, Fulham and West Bromwich, had games in hand, promotion to the top flight for the first time seemed inevitable. When ecstatic fans squeezed out of the ground after this 1-0 win over fourth-placed Spurs, the talk was not just of promotion, but of winning the Second Division championship.

THE SOUTHAMPTON TUSSLE

King's Lynn, and Clacton Town.

The League side are at home this afternoon to Southampton. We congratulate them that a series of brilliant performances in the League have taken them into what appears to be an unassailable position. They are No. 1 in the table with 49 points from 34 games, and Fulham, their nearest rivals, have six points less. West Bromwich Albion are third with one point fewer, and the Spurs are next with a gap of eight points between them and Southampton. The outlook for our visitors is of roseate hue. They have not yet had First Division football at The Dell, but only a series of unlikely disasters will deprive them of it in 1949-50. Southampton have our best wishes for their success, and may we still hope that a fortuitous run of events will enable us to be runners-up to them? Well, while congratulating the Hampshire club on its outlook we admit to a tinge of envy on their prospects as compared with our own. The Spurs have slipped. We all regret it. Southampton kept pegging away, and they are to-day where they are on merit. They carry with them for the rest of the season our hearty good wishes. What a triumph for Hants if two of its leading clubs carry off the two plums of the Football League.

VARIA

One of the greatest surprises in F.A. Cup history was the

ROOM FOR 60,000 UNDER COVER

Football League—Division II.   April 2nd, 1949   Kick-off 3.15

TOTTENHAM HOTSPUR 0
White Shirts, Blue Knickers

RIGHT WING   GOAL   LEFT WING
DITCHBURN
1
BACKS
TICKRIDGE   LUDFORD
2   3
HALF-BACKS
NICHOLSON   CLARKE   BURGESS (Capt.)
4   5   6
FORWARDS
COX   BAILY   DUQUEMIN   BENNETT   JONES
7   8   9   10   11

Referee: Mr. P. C. ANNETTE (Hants.)
Linesmen: Mr. L. S. Brunsdon, Berks. (Blue and White Flag)
Mr. L. G. Aylott, Surrey (Red and White Flag)

11   10   9   8   7
HEATON   BATES   WAYMAN   CURTIS   DAY
FORWARDS
6   5   4
MALLETT   WEBBER   WILKINS
HALF-BACKS
3   2
ROCHFORD (Capt.)   ELLERINGTON
BACKS
BLACK
GOAL
LEFT WING   RIGHT WING

SOUTHAMPTON 1
Red and White Striped Shirts, Blue Knickers

ANY ALTERATION WILL BE NOTED ON THE BOARD

The Tottenham programme of 2 April 1949
failed to allow for 'unlikely disasters'

But little did Southampton followers realise that, by staying on the pitch after pulling a thigh muscle and heroically going through the pain barrier to score the winning goal, Wayman had done his own chances of finishing the season irreparable damage.

More significantly, he had unwittingly put Southampton's promotion prospects in jeopardy. In truth, the injury didn't clear up until after the season had already run its ill-fated course.

The cruel impact of losing the man who had scored 32 goals in 35 games – to make him the Football League's top scorer that season – will become apparent in the next report. It would mean that Saints would to have to wait another 17 years before bringing top-flight football to the city, that's all.

After a mild early spring, the Tottenham pitch was dry and bumpy for what had been billed as a crucial promotion contest – even though the home programme seems to have already written off Spurs' chances of promotion and had decided that, barring "unlikely disasters", Southampton were as good as up.

The ball, light and mischievous, proved difficult to bring under control and the game, after a drama or two, was taking on all the hallmarks of an uneventful goalless draw.

Today Wayman would have disappeared down the tunnel to have his injury tended. But in 1948-49 the introduction of substitutes was still a long way off. He had treatment off the park and then returned seemingly only as a passenger, hugging the touchline.

There were just 12 minutes left when Ted Bates gathered the ball and ran boldly at the heart of the Tottenham defence. With a mixture of skill, determination and courage he kept the pack of white shirts at bay. But he needed support and found it in the unlikely shape of Wayman.

He had ignored the vice-like pain in his left thigh to keep pace with Bates's surge into the box, and Bates picked him out with a pass across goal.

Wayman valiantly swung out his injured leg and got enough purchase on the ball to restrict the options of Ted Ditchburn.

The goalkeeper could only parry the shot and, as the ball ran loose, Wayman shifted his weight on to his bad leg and connected with his "good" right peg and in it went to the thunderous acclaim of the travelling army from Southampton.

Wayman fell under the press of elated team-mates. It was an unforgettable moment in more ways than one. The wear and tear on his thigh had been profound and, although the first bulletin from Saints trainer Sid Cann

Division Two

I don't know how I got to the ball, to put it into the back of the net... Teddy [Bates] had it and he pushed it to me and I put it on this foot and I hit it and it came back off the goalkeeper and I hit it with my other foot – the one that worked (laughs). Then they carried me off... We went to the Palladium on the night and, oh dear me, talk about in pain!

Charlie Wayman

Back row (left to right): Ellerington, Wilkins, Ramsey, Dodgin, Black, Rochford, Mallett, Warhurst.
Front row: Day, Curtis, Wayman, Bates, Grant, Webber.
Photographed at The Hawthorns in November 1948, most of this eleven would stay together for Saints' storming run – except that Ellerington and Heaton would come in for Ramsey and Grant. And Wayman would by definition be missing for the anti-climax.

DIVISION II	P.	W.	L.	D.	Goals F.	A.	P.
Southampton	35	22	6	7	67	30	51
Fulham	34	18	9	7	61	33	43
West Bromwich A.	33	18	8	7	53	35	43
Tottenham	35	14	8	13	55	34	41
Cardiff	34	15	9	10	50	41	40
West Ham	34	15	11	8	47	45	38
Chesterfield	35	12	10	13	45	42	37
Sheffield Wed.	34	14	12	8	56	49	36
Luton	34	12	11	11	44	46	35
Leeds	35	11	11	13	53	56	33
Bury	33	11	14	8	36	53	32
Queen's Park R.	35	12	15	8	52	61	32
Coventry	35	13	16	6	50	54	32
Plymouth	34	11	14	9	39	48	31
Bradford	34	11	14	9	55	60	31
Grimsby	34	11	14	9	60	64	31
Barnsley	34	9	13	12	49	52	30
Brentford	33	10	13	10	34	39	30
Blackburn	35	11	17	7	46	56	29
Leicester	31	8	11	12	50	59	27
Lincoln City	36	7	18	11	20	49	25
Nottingham Forest	35	9	20	6	35	48	24

Only seven games to go and certs for the Championship – barring "unlikely disasters" was promising – "with a few days' rest, Charlie could be back in a fortnight" – the long-term truth was to prove devastating for Saints.

For the time being, though, Wayman's goal seemed poetic justice for Southampton and for Bates in particular, who had been desperately unlucky not to score earlier.

Again he had burst through strongly and beaten Ditchburn with a fierce low drive, which hit one post and flew across the line at right-angles to lodge against the base of the opposite upright before being cleared.

Sir Stanley Rous, then secretary of the FA and later to become a leading figure in FIFA, was watching the game and considered Bates's effort to be "as near as anything possible on a football field without actually being a goal."

Spurs had gone close themselves with Bennett, their inside-forward, forcing Saints goalkeeper Ian Black into a sublime one-handed save.

It was a day when commitment and ultimately courage earned Saints the two points. No-one worked harder for the cause then Len Wilkins in the middle of the field.

He was master of every situation which confronted him and some said it was his finest game for Saints.

But Wayman made the headlines in what had already been a momentous season. Five of his chart-topping 32 goals had come in the 6-0 home win against Leicester City in October, one of them being his 100th in League football. The Bishop Auckland-born striker, who had played for Portsmouth during the war and had cost Saints £10,000 (then a king's ransom) from Newcastle in 1947, would have only one more season at The Dell before moving to Preston North End.

It was with North End in 1954 that he would suffer perhaps his greatest disappointment, scoring in the FA Cup Final against West Bromwich, only to finish up on the losing side.

Meanwhile, though, Saints had business of their own to contend to with against West Brom.

TOTTENHAM HOTSPUR:

Ditchburn, Tickeridge, Ludford, Nicholson, Clarke, Burgess, Cox, Baily, Duquemin, Bennett, Jones

SOUTHAMPTON:

Black, Ellerington, Rochford, Wilkins, Webber, Mallett, Day, Curtis, Wayman, Bates, Heaton

Referee: Mr P.C. Annette (Hampshire)   *Attendance:* 69,265

Compiled by **BOB BRUNSKELL** from the *Echo* report. Charlie Wayman interviewed by **David Bull**. *Echo* photograph

SOUTHAMPTON 1
WEST BROMWICH ALBION 1

They closed the gates half-an-hour before the start of the Saints' final home game of 1948-49. There were 30,826 spectators in The Dell – a new ground record which beat the attendance for their 1937 cup-tie (Match No. 28) and which would stand for 20 years.

And yet the most significant spectator was sitting in the dug-out – or "trainers' box", as it was then called. Charlie Wayman was not fit to play. His injury at White Hart Lane, as described in the previous report, was turning out to be more of a "disaster" than the writer in the Spurs' programme could possibly have envisaged.

Charlie Wayman (left) sits out the game in the Trainer's Box with trainer Sam Warhurst

In the three weeks since his heroic goal at Tottenham, the Saints had played five games, including the traditional three over Easter, winning but one of them and that with their only goal in those 450 minutes of play. Wayman had been risked once, but otherwise manager Dodgin had been shuffling the pack, first trying left-winger Bob Veck at No. 9 and then switching Ted Bates from inside-forward.

For the game against West Brom, who had been able to close the gap between them and Saints to three points and had two games in hand, Bates was at centre-forward, flanked by Augie Scott and George Curtis. Although Bates and Curtis swapped during the second-half, the

Echo praised this trio for their "whole-hearted and often brilliant play." But the headline verdict on the Saints' failure to take both points from their performance told the story: **"Good Football Without Marksmanship Was Not Enough."** Quite simply, they had missed "the magic of Wayman's goal-scoring left foot."

But why, you may well ask – especially if you have been brought up on squad systems, substitutes and formations that managers change even during the course of a game – was Wayman so indispensable? Why was there no competent cover available? His team-mates will tell you that they had a system that revolved around Charlie, it was so successful that that was how they always played and Charlie was irreplaceable. That doesn't sound like the team that had so impressed Flamengo's coach with their "extraordinary capacity" to adjust their game, which included finding new ways of feeding a *libero*-frustrated Wayman (as you may recall from Match No. 37). But adapting to no Wayman at all was another matter. As Ian Black explains, the Club had some "very good reserves who came in and did their stuff," but you couldn't expect such cover for the unique Wayman.

Len Wilkins reasons that Alf Ramsey, who'd played centre-forward and scored a few up front – as in Matches 32-33 - was available in the Reserves. Or what of Eric Day? Unlike Ramsey, he would not get the chance prove himself as a goalscoring No. 9 for another four seasons. Meanwhile, he was not having a happy afternoon in his customary No. 7 shirt against West Brom. The lack of "fire" on both wings was a recurrent theme for "Commentator" in Saturday's *Football Echo* and it was still "puzzling" the *Echo* come Monday's review of the 1-1 draw. But, although Day had "lost his touch," he did pop up, with three minutes remaining, to score. Bates had headed on to him from Mallett and Day headed past West Brom's Sanders – thus equalising a header from the visiting outside-left.

This was not enough for Day to keep his place for the final game at Chesterfield the following Saturday. Saints' fans travelled north by rail and road – there were 10 coaches of them – hoping it wasn't true that the Club and its players *did not want to go up.* Unlikely though it may seem to younger fans, this explanation of the team's decline from a seemingly invincible position was a dominant talking point at the time and has, of course, become part of the Saints' folklore. To the players, this

Match of the Millennium

Division Two

suggestion was "ridiculous" (Bill Ellerington) and "a load of hooey" (Eric Webber). For them, the indispensability of Wayman was an overwhelming factor.

Well, Wayman was back for the showdown at The Recreation Ground, with Scott taking over Day's wing place. A "fatal" piece of shuffling by Bill Dodgin, in the opinion of reporter Harold Swan – an opinion endorsed by the players, especially since none of them thought Wayman was fit. And nor did he. But, then, as Bill Dodgin ruefully put it, almost 50 years on, "football is a game of mistakes."

And too many mistakes were made by linesmen, we're told, during that disastrous seven-game climax – not least by the fan who stepped out from the Bury crowd, after Joe Mallett had accidentally laid out the referee at Gigg Lane, to run the line and disallow what the *Football Mail* considered a "perfect goal" by Ted Bates. Only after consulting another linesman did the referee award

> It would be very, very hard to get somebody near [Wayman's] class and ability to score goals. And, even if you had, you wouldn't be able to keep him in the Reserves…
>
> They say "Well, Charlie was injured. There should have been somebody to take his place." But who are you going to get to play in the Reserves to be good enough to take Charlie's place when he's injured?
>
> Ian Black

Acclaimed by George Curtis (right), Eric Day wheels away after scoring the late equalizer. It was not enough, though, either for him to keep his place in the side the next Saturday or for Saints to keep their place in the promotion spots.

Chesterfield the only goal of that last game.

So then, their season over, Saints had to wait while the other two contenders completed their fixtures. They would finish Fulham 57 points; West Bromwich 56; Southampton 55 – a third place snatched from the jaws of the championship.

There was, though, a bigger Championship for Hampshire that season.

Portsmouth won the First Division, clinching it with a win at Bolton on the day of Saints' draw with West Bromwich.

Their Chairman was not there to see it. He had come instead to The Dell, whence he took a group that included the Southampton manager to the Pompey celebration at his hotel.

In those less hostile days, many a Saints' fan would have been pleased to join Mr Dodgin in celebrating their neighbours' success. Today's fans might see it otherwise – a case of adding insult to our Charlie's injury?

SOUTHAMPTON:

Black, Ellerington, Rochford, Wilkins, Webber, Mallett, Day, Scott, Bates, Curtis, Heaton

WEST BROMWICH ALBION:

Sanders, Pemberton, Millard, Kennedy, Vernon, Ryan, Elliott, Haines, Walsh, Barlow, Smith

Referee: A H Blythe (London)   *Attendance:* 30,826

Compiled by **DAVID BULL** from reports in the *Echo*, an unidentified national and the (Portsmouth) *Football Mail*, some of them researched by **Norman Gannaway** and **John Warren**; and from his interviews with Ian Black, Bill Dodgin, Bill Ellerington, Charlie Wayman, Eric Webber and Len Wilkins. Photographs from the *Echo*.

SOUTHAMPTON 5
LEICESTER CITY 3

They did it again in 1950. The Saints just missed out on promotion – more narrowly even than in 1949. This time, the margin of failure was but 0.065 of a goal.

And yet their road to denial was so different from that of the previous season. They started appallingly – three defeats followed by a draw - but then came with a late burst, culminating in two home games that produced 13 goals. Unfortunately, five of them went to their visitors, which proved to be three too many for the second promotion spot behind runaway Spurs.

It is not perhaps surprising that they couldn't get it together at the start. With the season about to kick off, they were without a manager. Bill Dodgin having left for Fulham, one of the teams that had pipped Saints for promotion, the Board was hurrying to appoint a replacement. It tried to find a satisfactory way of deploying all three internal candidates: Sid Cann as manager; Bill Rochford as player-coach; and Sam Warhurst as trainer.

None of the players ditched by Dodgin will tell you that Cann was the right appointment. That especially goes for the Rochford philes, like Mallett and Ellerington. And Ian Black couldn't wait to be re-united with Dodgin, his "second father," at Craven Cottage.

But wait he did – till the end of this odd season. Apart from Dodgin himself, the only close-season departure from among his nearly-men had been Alf Ramsey to Tottenham, in a deal that had brought Ernie Jones to The Dell in the continuing quest for a settled No. 11. That meant Heaton and Grant could leave during the season, the latter going to Ninian Park, in exchange for Ernie Stevenson. When Saints started March – and a 12-game run-in of W7 D4 L1 – with a home win against Cardiff City, Stevenson shone for the visitors. The next Saturday, he was at inside-forward for Southampton.

By trading in left-wingers, Sid Cann was carrying on a Dodgin custom. What was different about this season was the disruption at full-back. For the past three seasons, Rochford had been almost a fixture at left-back, while

As Charlie Wayman runs in looking for a rebound from Anderson, the Leicester goalkeeper lets the ball through his hands instead.
It had been headed by Ted Bates, turning away at the top of the picture, while Ernie Stevenson (right) watches.
The left-most Leicester defender is Norman Kirkman who would sign for the Saints in the summer.

Ramsey and Ellerington had taken it in turn to partner him and to win their first England caps. Ellerington feels that Ramsey should have stayed: the 36 year-old Rochford would not go on forever and there'd be room for both of them, probably with Ellerington at No. 3.

How right he was! Rochford and he would partner each other only seven times that season, with Ellerington spasmodically out injured and the player-coach fading out of favour. Five players would wear the No. 2 shirt and three the No. 3.

For the penultimate game of the season, at home to Leicester City, the full-backs were utility-defender Ted Ballard and Sandy Anderson, an early season signing. Otherwise, save for Stevenson and Jones as the left-wing pair, this looked very much like a Dodgin team. And it needed to score goals with the freedom of that rampant side of 1948-49.

Wayman had been true to form, coming into this game with 22 goals from 34 League games, and well supported by Bates with 14 from 31. The problem lay in too many goals being conceded – not surprising if you consider the comings and goings at full-back – but, after a 4-0 thumping at White Hart Lane, they had embarked on that 12-match run.

They had conceded only one goal in the last six matches, a spell that included successive 1-0 wins over their two promotion rivals, Sheffield United and Sheffield Wednesday. Now a couple of clean sheets in those two remaining games at The Dell should do the trick – so long as they could manage to score five.

Leicester soon messed up those calculations, going ahead through Lee after only five minutes. The Saints hit back with three goals before half-time, a header from Wayman following two from Bates.

The inside-right's first had been set up by Wayman – "a great goal in every way" as "Commentator" saw it for the *Echo* – and his second followed when, we are told, he met Day's corner "with his goal-scoring head." Quite how many other heads he happened to have about his person Commentator was not saying.

The visitors, with nothing to play for, were in no mood to roll over. Kirkman at left-back was certainly not giving up without a scrap, twice bringing Day down and provoking a rumpus that required the referee to admonish both players.

This was the second season running in which Norman Kirkman had participated in the Saints' climax: he'd been playing for Chesterfield in 1949. As if to stop him being a further nuisance, Sid Cann duly signed him: we'll see him by floodlight in Match No. 42.

A sensational nine minutes of the second-half further demonstrated Leicester's commitment. After Stevenson had laid on Wayman's second and then made it 5-1 from the penalty-spot, the visitors retaliated with two goals of their own.

You might say these two goals cost Saints promotion. But, then, what would you say about the two that West Ham would score before Southampton got going – to win 3-2 - the following Saturday?

If I'm correctly informed (by more than one of the home side) that a West Ham deputation offered not to try too hard if their hosts would hand over their win bonuses, then we can have no doubt, from the way the visitors went 2-0 up, that the offer was refused.

However you analyse and explain it, we can say, with hindsight, that the Saints needed to avoid three of the four goals they conceded between leading Leicester 5-1 and scoring their first against the Hammers.

Indeed, whichever way you like to play the "if only" game, you can see how Leicester's "consolation" goals from Lee and Barlow spelled desolation for Southampton.

It would be 15 years before Saints would finish as high again and 16 before they achieved what those end-of-season "goals against" had cost Sid Cann's late-showers.

SOUTHAMPTON:
Black, Anderson, Ballard, Curtis, Webber, Mallett, Day, Bates, Wayman, Stevenson, Jones

LEICESTER CITY:
Anderson, Jelly, Kirkman, Baldwin, Plummer, King, Griffiths, Barlow, Lee, Marsh, Adam

Referee: Mr E. W. Baker (Epsom)   *Attendance:* 21,091

Compiled by **DAVID BULL** from the *Echo* report and drawing upon several interviews: with Bill Ellerington, as quoted; and, as appropriate, upon a few more of those conducted with nine of the Saints' players from this game. *Echo* photograph

SOUTHAMPTON 5
COVENTRY CITY 4

It was my first season at The Dell and my concessionary rail ticket – 1s. 10½d (less than 10p) return - had brought me from Christchurch for my third League game. Two wins out of two so far – against Tommy Lawton's Notts County and Bury, each win by 1-0, each goal by Eddy Brown.

Like most 13 year-olds, with autograph books in satchels, I scanned the Coventry players kicking-in before the start. After-match targets would be internationals such as Bryn Allen of Wales and Norman Lockhart of Northern Ireland, plus Ken Chisholm who had played for Leicester City in the 1949 Cup Final against Wolves. How impressionable we were.

Overnight storms had left the Dell pitch heavy and surface water remained around the respective goal-mouths as the teams took the field. Early exchanges suggested both defences would be fully stretched, especially on the flanks. Each side possessed wingers of pace and guile and Eric Day began to show a clean pair of heels to Coventry's Mason. Following end-to-end skirmishes, it was Saints who made the breakthrough after 10 minutes when Ted Bates netted from close in. Brown was proving a thorn in Coventry's defence. Interchanging on either flank with Day and Jack Edwards, he was promising to ease the pain of Charlie Wayman's departure.

Wayman's two goals against Leicester City in our previous Match of the Millennium had been, alas, the last of his 77 in 107 games for Saints. Eddy Brown, Preston's exchange for Charlie, had arrived with no illusions that he might be able to replace such an idol, but a goal a game in the last four fixtures (including those two for my benefit) must have helped. He would make it five in five this afternoon, but we'd have to wait until the second-half for that. Meanwhile, Coventry would more than hold their own, as the home defence failed to protect their young 'keeper. In another exchange deal to Saints' detriment Hugh Kelly had arrived from Fulham when Ian Black went to rejoin Bill Dodgin. Now he was out injured and Eddie Thomas, 18 the week before, was in for the fourth game of his eight-match career.

Coventry drew level on 20 minutes, when a shot from Barrett, that appeared to be going wide, struck the head of centre-forward Roberts and beat Thomas. Bad luck for the young man. Undismayed, Saints swept forward once again and a header from Curtis was cleared off the line. Their continuing pressure brought a second goal in the 38th minute, when Day evaded several tackles to scoop the ball past Wood, Coventry's veteran 'keeper. Coventry's No. 7 Warner, not dissimilar to Day in style, was giving Ted Ballard a torrid time and was largely instrumental in opening up the Saints' defence just before the interval for Chisholm to make it 2-2.

Norman Lockhart duly signed for the young fan with a satchel on his back and a return ticket to Christchurch in his pocket.

Half-time and plenty for those of us in the schoolboy section under the "chocolate boxes" at the Milton Road end to talk about. We had already seen so many incidents in the first-half to delight us on this grey November afternoon: what more could we possibly expect?

Coventry took the initiative almost immediately after the restart when Thomas was again unfortunate. Ellerington got a boot to Allen's shot, only to divert the goal-ward effort beyond the despairing dive of his young team-mate. Jack Edwards, on the Saints' left touch-line, was now beginning to stamp his ball-playing abilities on the game. Signed by Dodgin, just before he left, from Forest, Edwards had played most of his first (1949-50) season at inside-forward. But he had blossomed since his recent conversion to outside-left, where he reminded you of Newcastle's Bobby Mitchell, with that skill in leaving a defender lost with the drop of a shoulder.

Coventry were not lying second in the division without good reason, though, and they constantly threatened to increase their lead. Yet it was Saints, perhaps against the run of play, who struck next. Joe Mallett tried a speculative cross into the Coventry goal-mouth and first to the ball was Brown with his head – 3-3.

Division Two

Sole district representatives for the Brooks Rupture Appliance.

FIRST PUBLISHED 1898.

REGISTERED AT THE GENERAL POST OFFICE AS A NEWSPAPER.   SOUTHAMPTON, SATURDAY, NOVEMBER 18, 1950

DING DONG DELL SAINTS WIN WELL!
Game of thrills the crowd liked

By "COMMENTATOR"

WHAT a game! What a victory! The Saints fought back when all seemed lost in the closing stages of the match with Coventry, scored two quick goals, and won by five goals to four!

The 22,000 crowd was becoming increasingly captivated by the sheer theatre of it all. Surely, with home advantage the Saints must edge the game? But no! Within minutes, Eric Webber's back-pass had stuck in the mud and Lockhart slammed the ball past the hapless Thomas.

Into the last 15 minutes. By now, the atmosphere was electric. Could the Saints at least equalise? Brown, once again out on the right, centred. Wood twice clawed at the ball but there, ever the opportunist, was Day to scramble it over the line – 4-4.

The home fans could surely expect no more from their team. Legs were visibly tired in the deteriorating conditions. The only further action must be the referee's final whistle. Not so! A through-pass into the Coventry half was collected by Edwards, with the entire visiting defence in front of him. We were spellbound as Edwards evaded one tackle after another, came into the penalty area and – with the crowd holding its breath – struck a venomous shot past Wood – 5-4.

My school cap went into space. Who cares? We had won this sensational game, twice coming from behind. If their had been any doubt before, I was now a confirmed SAINT. I retrieved my well-trodden cap, obtained the signatures of my selected Coventry players and made my journey home – the remaining 11¼d-worth, as it were – in that marvellous after-glow of having witnessed something very special.

---

*Charlie was God! When I got down to Southampton… I walked down the High Street. There's "WAYMAN" in one shop and then I go another 500 yards: "CHARLIE WAYMAN." How will I ever replace this fellow? And I never did. Charlie was a very, very great player… a wonderful player… He understood **football**. Charlie was a footballing man – steeped in it, soaked in it, breathing the game… I **played** football, but I was simply a right-footed runner. And most of the running was done without the ball – terribly **fast**, but I didn't take the thing with me… I'm not apologizing for myself but the whole aura around Charlie must have faded into insignificance when Brownie arrived – still learning, not ready yet and foreign to their way of caressing, holding and spraying the ball around.*

Eddy Brown

SOUTHAMPTON:
Thomas, Ellerington, Ballard, Elliott, Webber, Mallett, Day, Curtis, Brown, Bates, Edwards

COVENTRY CITY:
Wood, Timmins, Mason, Barrett, McDonnell, Alderton, Warner, Allen, Roberts, Chisholm, Lockhart

Referee: Mr W.B. Everett (Beccles)   *Attendance:* 22,438

Compiled by **TOM KELLY** from being there and from the *Echo* report. Eddy Brown interviewed by **David Bull**

SOUTHAMPTON RESERVES 0
TOTTENHAM HOTSPUR RESERVES 1

It was another first for Southampton FC. The club that had sailed away to Brazil in 1948, with an ingenuousness bordering on arrogance, had returned home wise beyond all expectations.

One of the lessons they had learned (as you may recall from Match No. 37) concerned the benefits of playing under floodlights. And so here they were, just over three years later, hosting the first-ever competitive match to be played under lights in this country.

There had been previous attempts to play football under lights – starting in Sheffield in October 1878, taking advantage of the recent introduction of electric arc lighting. The innovation reached Hampshire the following month – for two evenings of sporting entertainment at Dean Park, Bournemouth: cycling and other sports the first evening and football on the second. The next night the show was scheduled to go on at the Antelope Ground, a venue with which you'll be familiar if you joined this book for the early matches. Heavy rain washed out most of the entertainment, although there were some races and the Trojans did manage to play rugby – for which they received medals, inscribed *"in commemoration of the first electric light exhibition at Southampton, November 1878."*

There were no such mementoes for the pioneers of 1951 – just an unusually large crowd, of 13,654, for a Football Combination match. The celebrity spectators included two Saints' old boys, Reading manager, Ted Drake, and Fulham manager, Bill Dodgin, who, after taking Saints to Brazil in 1948, had returned there as Arsenal's guest the following year. Arsenal had also installed lights – which were brighter than The Dell's, Messrs Drake and Dodgin both told the *Echo*. "Commentator" was unbowed: the Highbury lights had cost £6,000; Southampton's – installed primarily for training – only £600.

Commentator was similarly unimpressed by the Club's ban on photographs: only a couple of "sighting" shots were permitted. However disconcerting players might find it initially, they would get used to it: just think, he urged, of Brazil with "batteries of cameras around the goals." The objection to flash photography had not come from the referee, who reported no problems beyond a "little dark[ness] in the centre of the field and the linesmen's

One of the "sighting" shots that the *Echo* photographer was allowed. Goalkeeper Stansbridge appears to hoping for a sighting of his own, while his full-backs, Sillett (right) and Kirkman, stand guard.

Football Combination

flags did not always stand out very clearly" - although, for their part, the linesmen could not always distinguish red-and-white stripes from the visitors' white shirts when it came to offside decisions across the full width of the pitch.

The spectators could see enough to enjoy themselves, though, even those who needed to see the full length of the pitch. Commentator felt the players obliged by keeping the ball on the deck. Indeed, Arthur Rowe's second string put on a display of passing of "speed and precision" that "exceeded almost anything" the *Echo* reporter had seen at The Dell all season, "either in first team or reserve matches." One of those passes was from Eddie Baily, in the process of playing himself back to first team fitness, to Tony Marchi who scored the only goal of the game.

Southampton fielded a standard reserve line-up of the day: a youngster or two on their way up mixed with veterans on their way out. Take the full-backs. The 18 year-old Sillett had made his first team debut only 10 days earlier, while the career of his 30 year-old partner was on hold. You may recall, from Match No. 40, how Norman Kirkman had played against Saints in the crucial climaxes of 1949 and 1950 and then joined them. He would have few first team opportunities, however, before

I had one of those games where it was 99 per cent luck and 1 per cent good play – because the floodlights were absolutely hopeless for goalkeepers. There were balls that normally, under ordinary light, I'd have swallowed, come out and got. But you just couldn't see the damn thing. So I stayed on my line. Headers were coming in from about three yards out and I just happened to be in the way… Those unknowing would say I had a marvellous game: I had the luckiest game of my life.

Ron Reynolds

featuring in an unusual trade – going to Exeter as player-manager in 1952, in an exchange deal that brought George Roughton to The Dell. Two of his contemporaries who were currently out of favour with manager Sid Cann had been on the lesson-learning exercise in Brazil: Ted Bates had had but three first team games since March and George Curtis had only four more left in his locker.

This mix came good in the second-half – good enough, anyhow, to put Spurs off their passing game if not to score. They might have had several – "there were three of four shots which seemed certain goals" to Commentator – had it not been for "a remarkable display" by Reynolds in the visitors' goal.

Ron Reynolds saw it – or, rather, never saw it – differently. This Lilleshall coaching buddy of Ted Bates – who would join him at the end of the decade for many an epic that we'll be coming to – would become the butt of team-mates' jokes, for wearing contact lenses and for being lost like a rabbit in the low-grade, low-slung Dell floodlights.

So it's a wonderful irony that Ron (pictured left in his, later, Southampton years) should be the goalkeeping hero of the night those lights led the British game into a new age.

He couldn't see the ball. It just kept hitting him.

SOUTHAMPTON RESERVES:
Stansbridge, Sillett, Kirkman, Elliott, Oakley, Bates, Brown, Curtis, Judd, McGowan, Lowder

TOTTENHAM HOTSPUR RESERVES:
Reynolds, Henty, Willmott, Robshaw, Gibbins, Brittan, Scarth, Baily, Marchi, Wetton, Spivey

Referee: Mr C.H. Hayward (Bournemouth)   *Attendance:* 13,654

Compiled by **DAVID BULL** from *Echo* reports (as researched by **John Warren**) and from his interview with Ron Reynolds. *Echo* photograph.

SOUTHAMPTON 5
FULHAM 3

The 1952-53 season was a watershed for Southampton in several ways. Ted Bates played his last game; the Club was relegated, for the first time in its history, despite scoring goals galore; and everybody says they should have beaten Blackpool by rights in the Cup and Stanley Matthews should have had to watch the Final ("Matthews Final," indeed!) on his black-and-white telly like the rest of us.

The Cup story belongs in the next report. The matter, for the moment, is the League game, two months earlier, at home to Fulham – a game that encapsulates the first two features of the watershed. The date, 27 December 1952, was the 15th anniversary of Bates's debut at Swansea. But a manager with no sense of romance had allowed Ted to play his last game the *previous* Saturday, when West Ham had won 2-1 at The Dell. He'd lately been up against three competitors – Walker, Purves and McGarrity - for an inside-forward berth. And now manager George Roughton had signed another contender: Roy Williams from Southern League Hereford.

Williams made his debut at Craven Cottage on Boxing Day – although it would be fair to say that the inside-forward playing the first of his 594 League games for Fulham was probably a more notable addition to the game's personnel. Johnny Haynes. Bill Dodgin – whose ill-timed move to Fulham you may recall – deemed The Dell too heavy for the 18 year-old protégé to play in the next day's "return" fixture, but he fielded three players with different degrees of association with the Saints. Right-back Tom Wilson was one of several untried youngsters who had followed Dodgin to Fulham in 1949. Goalkeeper Ian Black's desire to rejoin Dodgin in 1950 has been charted earlier (Match No. 40). And then there was Mitten.

Charlie Mitten was a war-time guest-player at The Dell, who received a special mention, you may have noticed, in Match No. 31.

Having won FA Cup, and narrowly missed League, honours with Manchester United, he had eloped to Bogota and returned to find himself banished from Old Trafford. 'Twas Fulham's gain. And how he demonstrated that to Southampton's defence in the opening skirmishes of this game!

My abiding memory is of Mitten gliding towards me – as I stood at the Milton Road end on the fourth anniversary of my first day at The Dell – taking advantage of the less muddy flanks to beat Bill Ellerington and lay on goals, in the first 10 minutes, for Bedford Jezzard and Geoff Taylor.

What I didn't know at the time, of course, was how the Saints' right-back then contrived to close that route. Ellerington has recently explained, though. The cardinal rule for full-backs was to restrict your winger to his line: "if you can keep balls wide, it's marvellous, isn't it? It's when balls get played inside you, you're in trouble." But Mitten revelled in that space and Ellerington figured he'd have to "mark him much tighter", even if that meant taking a risk - "if you're two-down, you might as well be six-down" – by playing further from his centre-half than was the rule.

Frank Dudley has lost his marker, Jim Taylor (right), and Jimmy Hill, to beat Ian Black for the first goal of his hat-trick

Division Two

Then it was just a matter of getting from two-down to 3-2 up by half-time. In three moves that involved all five forwards, Frank Dudley scored twice, either side of a home debut goal for Williams. In the second-half, Dudley completed his hat-trick and set up the fifth for Walker. A second goal for Jezzard made it 5-3.

In describing Frank Dudley's hat-trick goal for his *Echo* readers, "Commentator" credited left-half Alex Simpson who had "carried the ball forward." And too far forward, far too often, centre-half Henry Horton and left-back Peter Sillett both reckoned.

When he was not admiring the way Dudley was troubling England international Jim Taylor at the other end, Horton was worrying about troubles of his own: never mind Mitten on the wing; gaps were occurring centrally because Simpson – the captain who'd arrived a month earlier from Notts County – was being too adventurous.

Henry's own great adventure of that season was yet to come – in the FA Cup at Bloomfield Road, as we shall see in the next report.

In the 16 months he'd been at The Dell, Horton had worn all three half-back shirts and the No. 10. He was currently in one of his No. 5 phases.

They scored twice in the first [10] minutes and we were all at sixes and sevens. Simpson wasn't covering his man at all. He wasn't having a bad game: he just wasn't marking …There was one man loose and it was [his] inside-forward and there was Jimmy Hill coming through [from right-half] with the ball. We were all pulled out of position… He was a good player, Alec; but on this particular occasion, he wasn't in touch. He wasn't in touch with his man or the game… Frank [Dudley] gave Jim Taylor a real roasting… I remember the ball was hit through and Frank had to chase it with Jim Taylor. And it was just like a horse coming up the home straight and leaving the field, because every pace that they took, Frank was drawing away from Jim Taylor. I think this must have happened twice and each time he thumped the ball and it really rocketed in the back of the net and we won 5-3

Henry Horton

The fight-back against Fulham brought Dudley, signed from Leeds two seasons earlier, the second hat-trick of his best season – 14 League goals in 23 games – for the Saints. But, then, as I say, the side scored a lot going down, including seven in the two games against Sheffield United, who won the Division. And the five against Fulham was their third five of the season – to say nothing of a 6-1 win against Blackburn at the death. They were relegated, having scored 68 goals, four more than when they fractionally missed promotion three seasons earlier (again, see Match No. 40).

The irony for Dudley is that his contribution to the season will be remembered less for the goals he scored than for those he missed in the (coming-up-next) Blackpool replay. As one of the schoolboys who actually went to school on that replay afternoon, my own special memory of that odd season is of the Fulham game: of seeing Mitten – "a player-and-a-half" as Johnny Walker recalls – flashing towards me and of my conversation with Bedford Jezzard, as he signed my autograph book at the station afterwards.

Wouldn't I like the signature of the lad standing next to him? Yes, please.

The youth duly obliged: "J. Haynes" it says.

SOUTHAMPTON:

Christie, Ellerington, Sillett, Elliott, Horton, Simpson, Day, Williams, Dudley, Walker, Hoskins

FULHAM:

Black, Wilson, R.Lowe, E.Lowe, J.Taylor, Hill, Stevens, G.Taylor, Jezzard, Brennan, Mitten

Referee: Mr H. Pearce (Luton)   *Attendance:* 21,935

Compiled by **DAVID BULL** from being there; from the *Echo* report; and from interviews with Bill Ellerington, Henry Horton, Peter Sillett and Johnny Walker. Photograph from the *Echo*.

SOUTHAMPTON 1
BLACKPOOL 2

I suppose no football fan of 50 or more will ever forget the last 20 minutes of the 1953 Blackpool v Bolton Cup Final, although sympathy must be felt for Bolton who had, by then, been reduced to nine fit men. If ever a man won a game off his own bat it was Matthews that day, but it wasn't the first occasion he ensured Cup success for the Tangerines that season. The contribution he made in the Fifth Round replay at The Dell in February was equally crucial.

Without it, Blackpool would never have been at Wembley in the first place. Whether Saints would have been there instead is doubtful as 1952-53 was one of their poorest seasons post-war and, at the end of it, they lost their Second Division status for the first time since they had achieved it – thanks ultimately to Match No. 19 – in 1922.

Saints had earned the replay by drawing the first game at Bloomfield Road the previous Saturday, Henry Horton scoring a late equaliser against their illustrious First Division opponents. Fans started queuing in Milton Road at three o'clock the following Tuesday morning to buy tickets for the return game. What is it that makes a replay so special? The expectation, despite bitter experience, that it will end in a home victory? It is logical, of course, but since when has logic ever played a part in football?

The next afternoon, in front of over 29,000 spectators paying record receipts of £4,123 – an awful lot of grandmothers must have been buried that day – the Saints certainly played as if they were going to be victors.

They were simply all over Blackpool, wave after wave of red-and-white surging towards the Archers Road goal only to be frustrated by those triple wreckers of expectation – good goal-keeping (Farm would have a poor game in the Final, but had a good one at The Dell), bad luck and poor finishing.

Charlie Purves was their inspiration in these 45 minutes. I hope I am not being unfair to Charlie, but he followed a relatively undistinguished five years with Charlton Athletic with an equally unremarkable three years with us during which time he made 36 appearances and scored a modest six goals. Every dog has his day, however, and Charlie certainly had his in the first 45 minutes that afternoon. He was not the same man after half-time. This may have been due to tiredness because he had been everywhere in the first-half. With almost total control in mid-field Saints were able to mount attack after attack and most of them seemed to involve Charlie. He caused Blackpool's defence no end of problems, probing first down one wing, then the other, then through the middle, once rounding Farm to "score" only to have it disallowed for offside, and on another occasion, with the goal at his mercy, being called back for a Blackpool foul.

All Saints had for a storming half was a Johnny Walker goal scored in the 17th minute. I can see Purves today as he came off at half-time, grinning broadly as he acknowledged the acclaim of the crowd, his shirt soaked in sweat. Surely, he seemed to be saying, Blackpool cannot withstand another such pounding in the second-half?

That pounding did not materialise, however, because, immediately after the interval and before Saints had a

Promenading in Blackpool are 10 of the side – plus reserves Gregory and Clements – who took Blackpool to two games. The missing man was Sillett, whose RAF duties meant he seldom travelled, let alone trained, with his team-mates – which makes his taming of Matthews even more creditable. Left to right: Gregory, Ellerington, Purves, Day, Clements, Christie, Elliott, Dudley, Hoskins, Walker, Simpson and Horton

FA Cup Fifth Round (Replay)

The side played above themselves – there's no doubt about it. We all did. We played really well… We were so overwhelmingly superior that I thought we must score a few more goals here. And we felt when we went in at half-time that we'd robbed ourselves… I think it was one of the most disappointing results that I figured in.

Frank Dudley

We murdered 'em… we ploughed them into the ground… Frank Dudley could have stood there picking dirt, getting a hat-trick… We got one goal… Out they come half-time… and what happened? Stan Matthews just drifted into the middle of the field – you know, anywhere - and he created havoc and they beat us 2-1.

Bill Ellerington

We should have been at least four or five up at half-time without question. It was absolutely ridiculous that we lost… I can see George Farm standing on the goal-line and Dudley absolutely blasted it past him and it hit the crossbar and nearly came up to the other end.

John Christie

I can describe the game in three words – we were lucky…In the first-half… Peter Sillett played me very well and I struggled to make any impact at all on the game… As we took the pitch [for the second-half, I told] Harry Johnson… "I'm going to roam about this half, …OK?"…and as luck would have it, it paid off… Free from the attentions of Sillett, I prodded and probed from midfield, went on runs on both wings and managed to pull the Southampton defence about.

Stanley Matthews

chance to build up any momentum, Blackpool were ahead. First, a Perry centre was deflected over the line by Horton's lunge and then Matthews linked up with Perry, Mudie and Taylor to set up Allan Brown, all in the first four minutes. After that Matthews controlled the game and Saints just faded away.

I am not sure how many times Stanley Matthews appeared at The Dell post-war. I can remember only this one occasion, although 10 years later when he was with Stoke and nearing his 50th birthday, he did come out onto the pitch before the game to take a bow as Footballer of the Year, before retiring to the stand injured, or perhaps just too tired to play.

On this occasion, however, he was anything but too tired or injured although he could have been either in the first-half when the Blackpool mid-field had been far too pre-occupied to get him the ball. In the second-half, however, Matthews simply went inside and got it for himself. Thereafter, the middle of the pitch was always more Blackpool's than Southampton's.

I had seen Matthews a number of times at Portsmouth in the forties, thinking each time that, in view of his advancing years, it might be the last. He had always seemed to me then to be the quintessential winger, too slight to withstand the hurly-burly of midfield. How wrong I was. Great players can play in almost any position, within reason, because – as Terry Paine and Alan Ball were to prove later – all they need is the ball, no matter where they are on the pitch.

Saints supporters left the ground disappointed and disillusioned, the "if only" brigade in full spate – blaming this or that player, the ref or just their wretched luck. But in truth, they had been beaten by one of the game's greatest exponents.

They had had their chance and they hadn't taken it, and Matthews had denied them a second one. He certainly won the cup for Blackpool that year, twice in fact, and the first time was at The Dell that February afternoon.

SOUTHAMPTON:
Christie, Ellerington, Sillett, Elliott, Horton, Simpson, Day, Purves, Dudley, Walker, Hoskins

BLACKPOOL:
Farm, Shimwell, Garrett, Johnson, Crosland, Fenton, Matthews, Mudie, Brown, Taylor, Perry

Referee: Mr. B.J. Flanagan (Sheffield)   *Attendance:* 29,223

Compiled by **ROB HOLLEY** from being there and from the *Echo* report. John Christie, Frank Dudley and Bill Ellerington interviewed by **David Bull**. Stanley Matthews quoted from his latest autobiography.

SOUTHAMPTON RESERVES 3
NORWICH CITY RESERVES 1

For the crowd of just under 10,000 who turned up to watch Southampton Reserves beat Norwich City Reserves in the Combination Cup Final of 1954, this was an opportunity to attend a one-legged Final in which the Saints had not only home advantage but their lights. The team that had pioneered floodlit Combination football in Match No. 42 were entertaining floodlight novices.

And yet this game was about more than that. It was a triumph for the former player who'd been in charge of the Reserves since the start of the previous season. Shortly before his retirement in December 1952, as recorded in Match No. 43, Ted Bates had assumed joint-coaching duties with Jimmy Easson. Then, in May 1953, he was appointed "2nd Team Trainer and Coach," at a weekly wage of £12 in season and £10 in the summer.

When judged by bald statistics, there was no compelling reason to get especially excited about winning the Combination Cup. It was the Saints' fourth final in five years and they had won it in 1952. And yet, having set out that record in the *Echo* and charted their high strike-rate in the competition, "Observer" offered a "special word of praise for… Ted Bates, whose enthusiasm has done so much to inspire the members of the team." That inspiration had manifested itself in the way that 10 men

had won the trophy after losing their centre-forward and leading Cup scorer, Doug Millward, in only the third minute. True, Millward had returned to hobble on his sprained ankle for an hour, but this still ranks as the game that made Ted Bates.

If Southampton had started favourites under their suspect lights, the injury to Millward reversed the odds and made the game a test of their spirit. The *Echo* did not find them wanting:

> What one admired most about their play was the unquenchable drive and enthusiasm. Each and every man was always challenging for the ball; the hardest tackle was never shirked and the handicap of being virtually a man short throughout the game was overcome by intelligent positional play and smooth co-ordination between the backs and halves and forwards.

The Cup-winning squad with trainer-coach Ted Bates (left) and manager George Roughton (right)
Standing (left to right) Turner, Gregory, Clements, Christie, Oakley, Parker
Front: Elliott, Flood, Millward, McGowan, Williams, Digby, Gaynor

Football Combination Cup Final

Bryn Elliott opened the scoring for the Saints in the 16th minute when his long-range effort went in off the head of Norwich's centre-half. They held out until half-time. But then, on 47 minutes, the visitors equalised. With John Flood having moved from the wing to centre-forward, the ten-and-a-bit men were still coming forward at the end. They were rewarded with two goals, from Flood and Gaynor, in the last eight minutes.

It had been, said the *Echo,* "a grand match – worthy to rank with some of the most exciting and keenly-contested battles seen on the ground in recent years... The Saints had won a real thriller on their merits and given their supporters something to talk about for a very long time." And the players, too. Forty-odd years later, some of them recalled the game for me and elaborated on the *Echo's* tribute to trainer-coach Bates. Step forward John Christie, Bryn Elliott and Pat Parker, each of whom made more than 100 first team appearances for the Saints (Flood being the only other member of this side to do so).

This was the fourth of five seasons in which Christie shared the 'keeper's jersey with Fred Kiernan. He had started it in possession but was dropped after a 6-4 opening-day win. You'll find John today at many a home game, chatting away in the car-park before the kick-off about his memories (cue that Blackpool replay, again) and enunciating his fundamental beliefs – like why a manager who sits in the dug-out is in no position to judge his goalkeeper. If Ted Bates persistently failed him in that regard, Christie is generous in his assessment of the impact he had on the Reserves:

> He got everybody involved in various moves, set-pieces, certain things to do and he became very successful at it. The launching pad, so to speak, would be the set things that we did. If I collected the ball on the left, the right-winger would be back to change the play... He was always trying to introduce something – even if it was simple – if it was successful.

> *Ted made you want to win games. We met the Norwich players at Wembley the same season [watching the FA Cup Final]. They said "You must have been on a big bonus the way you played that day." They couldn't believe that we only had 10 men and we beat them quite easily. Everybody ran themselves into the ground that night – tremendous, honestly!*
>
> Pat Parker

In the seven seasons from 1950-51 to 1956-57, this would be the only one in which wing-half Elliott would miss more than half of the first team's games. He recalls how directors re-acted to the defeat of Norwich – "Well done, Ted!", "Well done, Ted!" – and feels that this gave credit where it was due: "There must have been a helluva team spirit for 10 men to beat 11 for 85 minutes. It's got to have something to do with the chap who was in charge ...That was probably the match that made the Directors realise that Ted was the chappie for the [first team] job." If that is so, then they were taking their time: it would be 10 months before Bates would be appointed Manager.

Elliott and Parker both talk of Ted's determination to win – even to the extent of needing to beat the first team in practice. Not that this impressed Bill Ellerington: "a Reserve team is there not to win but to bring the youngsters on." Fair enough, but there were no under-20s in this Cup-winning side. This rag-bag of a team had some who were temporarily out-of-1st XI-favour, like the four centurions mentioned, and the likes of Oakley, Digby, Gaynor and Millward, who would get fewer than a season's worth of senior outings between them.

Which makes it all the more creditable that their trainer-coach could motivate them to function as a team. And which is why this game has become part of Saints' folklore, less for being final than for being the beginning. It was the beginning of the Club's climb back from Division Three, by virtue of its being the Making of the Manager that would take them up and up.

SOUTHAMPTON RESERVES:
Christie, Oakley, Gregory, McGowan, Parker, Elliott, Flood, Gaynor, Millward, Williams, Digby

NORWICH CITY RESERVES:
Oxford, Holmes, Hepple, Carberry, Norman, Ashman, McMillan, Woan, Kearns, Englefield, Collins

Referee: Mr K.G. Aston (Ilford)   *Attendance:* 9,808

Compiled by **DAVID BULL** from *Echo* reports, the Club Minutes and his interviews with John Christie, Bill Ellerington, Bryn Elliott and Pat Parker. Photograph from the *Echo.*

MANCHESTER UNITED YOUTH 2
SOUTHAMPTON YOUTH 3

When the FA introduced a Youth Cup competition in 1953, it was tailor-made for showing off the products of Matt Busby's Old Trafford youth policy.

So much so that when the Busby Babes came to The Dell for the first leg of the Youth Cup semi-final in April 1957, they had not only won the thing four years on the trot, they had never even lost a leg. There was to be no change in that record that evening. The excitement generated in the town by Ted Bates's own babes was captured by "Nomad" in his eve-of-match rejoicing in a cup run that had peaked with a 6-0 quarter-final trouncing of Spurs before a Dell crowd of 8,500. Since that win was still the talk of the town, Nomad reflected, he jolly well hoped his readers would turn up in twice that number and send the lads off to the second leg "with a useful balance of goals in their favour."

The fans did their bit for Nomad. The crowd of 19,320 amply exceeded his exhortation. The players could not, however, get the "balance" right. It started badly when Terry Simpson hit the post with a penalty in the first minute and David Scurr, following up, had his shot saved by Gaskell. But then a "perfect centre" from Terry Paine was met with a "gem of a header" by Wesley Maughan to give the young Saints a ninth-minute lead. It did not last long. Tony Godfrey "made his only mistake of the game"

when he dropped a centre and Colin Holmes, trying to clear, put the ball into his own net.

Now, if you've followed the career development of this Youth XI, you'll have noticed that each of the home players so far mentioned went on to play for the first team; in fact, Paine had made his debut the previous month. And so would two others in that line-up – John Sydenham, who would join Paine in the first team, by the season's end, and Peter Vine – to make a remarkable eight in all. On the night, though, these starlets faltered against the probings of United's "fast, clever attack," led by Alex Dawson, whose substantial career would be mainly with Preston, and with captain Ken Morgans, who would survive the Munich crash, at outside-right.

Although Scurr managed a second, the visitors took a 5-2 advantage back to Old Trafford. Never mind that the second leg should have been a formality, there were still 17,000 wanting to see it. They saw a first-half dominated by "the Manchester machine moving smoothly, effortlessly and remorselessly" towards what Nomad assumed would be "the inevitable conclusion, a triumph of skill over honest endeavour." It was "an exhibition,"

As a United attack gets past David Scurr (right) and Colin Holmes, Mick Stickler comes in from the left intent on intercepting.

FA Youth Cup Semi-Final, second leg

said one of the nationals, "right out of the Busby textbook." But the "brilliant goalkeeping" of Godfrey restricted the Babes to a 1-0 interval lead and kept the leg alive.

With five minutes to go the leg indeed appeared to be Southampton's and even the tie seemed capable of being prised from United. Saints were leading 3-1 on the night and trailing only 5-6 on aggregate. The comeback had begun when Paine headed home. Well, that's how one of the nationals saw it. Another perceived him to have "bustled through" the corner from Sydenham, while Paine himself will tell you, with a wicked chuckle, that he punched it in. And then Maughan scored twice to set up a hectic last five minutes.

Could the "miracle" that Nomad had suggested it would take to come back from 5-2 be in the offing? Could Saints level at 6-6 and maintain the momentum in extra-time? Sadly, no. In the dying seconds, Dawson made it 7-5. United were in their fifth successive final. But they had lost a game for the first time in the first five seasons of the competition

That warranted a visit by Matt Busby to the visitors' dressing room for a congratulatory word that still excites Ernie Jones (whom we last met, as a player, in Match

> *We were all local boys… Busby couldn't understand that a bunch of yokels had beaten his star players. He used to inquire after Schoolboy internationals – England, Scotland and Wales. There were some very good players in that [Southampton] Youth side.*
>
> Peter Vine

Terry Paine (right) interrupts Mick Stickler's private photo call in Manchester

No. 40) when he recalls with pride the exploits of the side he had coached for Ted Bates. And a memorable moment for the 11 heroes of the hour. For Walker, Stickler and Harley, that was perhaps as big as it got. For the likes of Holmes and Vine (both capped at Youth level) and Scurr, it was something of a false dawn: they would play but five first team games between them. Maughan would manage only a few more than that, despite scoring as freely for the Reserves as he had for the Youth team. Simpson would be let go after 25 first team outings, but would play in the First Division (with West Brom) ahead of any of them. Godfrey would never make the top flight: after 149 appearances, unluckily missing out on all of the great Cup feats from 1960 to 1963 (see Matches 47 and 51-53), he would leave during the promotion run of 1965-66.

That leaves Paine and Sydenham, who would between them make 1206 appearances for Southampton. Nearly all of these would be in tandem and all bar Paine's last 30 would be under Ted Bates – a manager whose faith in youth had this memorable early moment at Old Trafford.

Its ultimate vindication, though, would surely be the way in which teams built around these constant wingers took the Club from the Third Division to the First.

MANCHESTER UNITED YOUTH:

Gaskell, Smith, Gibson, English, Holland, Bratt, Morgans, Lawton, Dawson, Pearson, Hunter

SOUTHAMPTON YOUTH:

Godfrey, Walker, Stickler, Harley, Holmes, Scurr, Paine, Simpson, Maughan, Vine, Sydenham

Referee: Mr. R. Ryalls (Sheffield)   *Attendance:* 16,876

Compiled by **DAVID BULL** from reports in the *Echo*, and in national newspapers not identified in the cuttings of Wesley Maughan and Mick Stickler, and supplemented by interviews with eight of the team and coach Ernie Jones. Photographs from Mick Stickler's collection

MANCHESTER CITY 1
SOUTHAMPTON 5

The *Echo* hailed it as "Saints' finest hour in 66 years of cup fighting." And until they beat Manchester United 1-0 at Wembley Stadium some 16 years and a bit later, their 5-1 win at Manchester City in January 1960 ranked as their greatest achievement in the FA Cup.

In that 1959-60 season of great hope and ultimate fulfilment, Saints went to Maine Road as a high-riding Third Division side taking on a Manchester City who were comfortably riding along in the top flight and rightly regarded as one of the great cup-fighting teams of the day.

After all, in the mid-1950s the Light Blues had made two trips to Wembley, once to fail 3-1 to Newcastle United only to come back the following season and gloriously beat Birmingham City in a final which threw up one of the great heroic stories of the FA Cup.

For those of us old enough to remember – and how could we forget it? – City's German goalkeeper Bert Trautmann soldiered on between the sticks after breaking his neck, stoically helping City to a 3-1 victory over a battling Birmingham side.

When Saints journeyed to Maine Road for a Third Round tie in those early days of 1960, they had to face a City side bristling with confidence after a 4-1 Division I victory over Sheffield Wednesday the Saturday before.

Seizing a rare chance to watch Saints in action against a top team, over 2,000 fans made the long journey to Manchester.

They gave the men in red-and-white stripes a rousing reception when they came out.

Cliff Huxford, the Saints skipper, recalled:

When we came out of the tunnel and heard them roar, we were lifted and inspired. We might have been playing at The Dell and from that moment I sensed we were in with a great chance.

Derek Reeves, whose four goals underpinned a result which sent shockwaves throughout the length and breadth of English football, dedicated his own personal finest hour to those fans. He said: "I was determined to run myself into the ground just to thank them for their wonderful support."

In his report for the *Echo,* "Nomad" pulled no punches:

First Division City were humbled, humiliated, outplayed and reduced to a shambles. From first to last Saints played with assurance, determination and speed which was a joy to behold.

The skill and the spirit which was to carry Saints to a Division III title win (of which more in the next report) burned bright that day, even after City hit them with an 18th minute goal. Lesser sides would have crumbled, especially after dictating the early stages as Saints had done so audaciously. But adversity served only to spur them on.

Within five minutes they were back on level terms and another nine minutes on had taken the lead. The sudden desperate nature of the City tackling betrayed the sudden panic which had set in in the City ranks. The score stayed that way until half-time and during the break there was still a smug smile on the faces of many City fans. They had a knack in those days of turning the tide with a sudden burst of goals. There was a strong feeling among the light blue hordes that Saints would pay for their impudence.

But it never happened. Instead Saints silenced the crowd and stunned City

Celebrating the "finest hour"
Standing (left to right) Charles, Conner, Jimmy Gallagher, Traynor, Page, Huxford, Davies, Paine.
Crouching: Ted Bates, Reeves, Mulgrew, O'Brien, Sydenham.

FA Cup Third Round

into submission with goals from George O'Brien and Reeves (to complete his hat-trick) on 64 and 67 minutes. City, with a handful of the side who had so famously won the cup just four years before, were a battered, broken side. And as the Maine Road floodlights dimmed, with a bemused official prematurely anticipating the final whistle, Reeves hammered the final nail in the City coffin, with a searing right-foot drive from just inside the penalty area.

Reeves was given a hero's reception by Saints' ecstatic band of fans who had seen a game which would live forever in their memory. But alongside Reeves, at the top of the bill, stood right-winger Terry Paine, then just a tender slip of a lad at 20. Paine had laid on four of the goals and had run City's Welsh Under-23 left-back Cliff Sear ragged. Saints manager Ted Bates described Paine's performance as the best he had ever seen from an outside-right. Another unsung hero was wing-half Huxford who had battled on for 30 minutes with a dead leg after a kick on the thigh.

Yet their Cup heroics would end in anti-climax. Saints' reward for victory at Maine Road was a home draw with Fourth Division Watford in the next round. It finished 2-2 at The Dell, with the Hornets winning the replay 1-0 in front of a huge 27,000 crowd at Vicarage Road.

It was just as well there was a League title to be won…

The Reserved Party for Manchester included
(left to right) George O'Brien, Cliff Huxford and Tommy Mulgrew.

I said to Pagie, "I hope they don't get a cricket score, here."… I was [soon] picking the ball out. I thought "Bloody hell! 'Ere we go!" Then Reevesie got one… We've gone in at half-time [leading 2-1] and Ted's gone round and seen all the lads… "You all right, Bobby?" I said "Yeah!" And he said "Right, get out and, if you get a quick one here, this side's finished." We've gone out there and… bang! 3-1! And when it got to 4-1, I thought "We can win this." That's how nervous I was: I still couldn't see us beating them. I looked up at the clock… and she's twenty past four. I thought "Bloody hell! Another 20 minutes yet." Then it's 5-1. And at twenty-five to five, I thought "They're done now! They're finished, this side." After the game,… Bert Trautmann came up to me and he said "Well done! What a load of rubbish I had in front of me!" …Three of them were his fault

Bob Charles

I made a mistake and we were one-down. After [that], we murdered them, we really did. Sydenham and Paine just ran riot. Terry absolutely skinned his left-back… One of the big disappointments was… Bert Trautmann… I was very disappointed with his display.

John Page

A wonderful day. I've actually got the ball from that game here with me in Australia… Derek Reeves got presented with the ball afterwards, that was autographed by all the players. And when I was back home [a few] years ago, a supporter approached me… He'd won the ball in a raffle and he said, as he had no family, he'd like me to have it…[It] now sits in my office and there's not many days that I don't look at it and recall that game…Obviously a very, very special day. Derek Reeves's performance was incredible. Terry Paine had a wonderful day. I had quite a good one.

John Sydenham

MANCHESTER CITY:

Trautmann, Branagan, Sear, Oakes, McTavish, Barnes, Fagan, Barlow, McAdams, Hayes, Colbridge

SOUTHAMPTON:

Charles, Davies, Traynor, Conner, Page, Huxford, Paine, O'Brien, Reeves, Mulgrew, Sydenham

Referee: E T Jennings (Stourbridge)   *Attendance:* 42,065

Compiled by **BOB BRUNSKELL** from the *Echo* report. Bob Charles, John Page and John Sydenham interviewed by **David Bull**. *Echo* photographs

SOUTHAMPTON 1
READING 0

Saints' graduation from promotion-certainties to Third Division champions spanned three crucial games during an intriguing run-in to the momentous 1959-60 season.

The one which longstanding fans will perhaps remember the most was the Easter Monday derby with Reading. The teams had met at Elm Park on Good Friday with Reading winning 2-0. Saints had whacked Accrington Stanley 5-1 on the Saturday and the scent of revenge was very much in the air as Reading ran out for the return at The Dell which was a cauldron of excitement with a 25,000 crowd packed in.

They were to witness something which was much more than a grudge match. It all hung on one goal from Brian Clifton which was enough to clinch a Southampton victory and with it the prize of promotion back to Division Two.

It was the first time Saints and their supporters had had something tangible to celebrate since the Club had capped their second Football League season, in Match No. 19, with promotion from the Third Division (South) in 1922.

They had lost their Second Division status in 1953 and hadn't seriously threatened to regain it until 1960 dawned. Even as late as March that first year of the Swinging Sixties no-one would have put serious money on Saints going up. That was certainly the case after a grim two-game sequence when they crashed 5-1 at Newport County then went to Coventry a week later on 12 March and suffered a comprehensive 4-1 reverse.

Seeing their promotion hopes slipping down the pan, manager Ted Bates reacted promptly by signing an experienced replacement for Bob Charles. The young goalkeeper had so enjoyed his big day out at Maine Road in January but has no complaints about being called into the office after the Coventry defeat to be told "You're only 18. I think the strain is beginning to tell on you." The man to replace him was the star of The Dell's pioneering floodlit match (No. 42), Ron Reynolds from Tottenham.

A Spurs reserve he might have been, but his new team-mates welcomed what he brought to the team – not only as a "very, very experienced goalkeeper," but, as John Sydenham goes on, for "lots of input into team discussions" (Match No. 51 being a case in point). Reynolds immediately steadied the boat. Saints went through their next four games unbeaten and when Reading made the short journey down the A33 for that important Easter Monday game, they found the Saints 'keeper in a uncompromising mood. It was just as well, for a side who were fast closing in on a century of League goals were remarkably shot-shy on the day. And it wasn't through lack of opportunity because John Sydenham had run Reading ragged down the left flank.

But when his crosses came raining in, Saints were uncharacteristically wasteful. Thankfully, with Reynolds

"That goal's going to be remembered forever" said George O'Brien (No. 8) to Brian Clifton (stripes, right), the scorer

in commanding form and the club captain Cliff Huxford marshalling his defensive troops in masterful fashion, one goal was to prove enough.

It came from the trusty head of Clifton, a Whitchurch-born inside-forward who was never really to establish himself in the side but who nevertheless had a remarkable goalscoring record, particularly during the 1959-60 season. The Reading game was only his sixth of the season, but in the five he had played in a more attacking role, Clifton had scored six goals. His most important came 15 minutes into the match. Clifton was regarded as the best header of the ball in the club and proved it as he soared to reach a left-wing corner to head firmly beyond the acrobatic leap of the visiting 'keeper, David Jones.

Jones had tried all he knew to spike Southampton's guns and, after Clifton's successful strike, the Reading goalkeeper made sure they wouldn't have any more. All the time there was the threat of a Reading counter, but it never came and the result ensured Saints at least were going up. Now they had to go on and win what remains their one and only Football League championship.

The next game was at Bournemouth's Dean Court where a 21,657 crowd watched Cherries take the lead through Ray Bumstead before the trusty Clifton struck again with his head. John Page gave Saints a 3-1 win with

It seemed to go right through Jonesie. It went so quick. We went in afterwards and George O'Brien ... said "You lucky so-and-so! You know that goal's going to be remembered forever." It's true! If I speak to anybody from down there [in Southampton], they'll always remember that goal, because it put us in the Second Division. [And yet, when you think] of all the goals that Derek [Reeves] got – 39 of them!

Brian Clifton

two second-half penalties and they went into their last match of the season, at home to Bradford City, needing a point to claim the crown.

And like the Reading game before, it was a tense affair with Saints making heavy weather of it in attack. They had more of the first-half play, passing the ball about in quick, creative patterns but without an end product. Derek Reeves changed that on the half-hour, when the Bradford defenders, convinced he was offside, stopped playing, as the former Bournemouth Gasworks man sped through on to a ball lobbed over the top from the left.

As the linesman's flag stayed down, Reeves ran on to shoot past a dismayed 'keeper. It was his 45th of the season, 39 of them coming in the League, a feat which up to then had been surpassed in Division Three only by Ipswich Town's Ted Phillips with 41.

Bradford were incensed that the goal was given, and they were stung into trying to balance the scales of justice. And it was the Saints defence who were to emerge with the laurels as they held them back – a stout effort which reaped its reward 10 minutes from time when George O'Brien, the best forward on the day, swept forward to make it 2-0.

The title had gone to Southampton by two points from Norwich City and they had done it in style with a haul of 106 goals, creating a new record for the Third Division.

SOUTHAMPTON:
Reynolds, Davies, Traynor, Conner, Page, Huxford, Paine, O'Brien, Reeves, Clifton, Sydenham.

READING:
Jones, Goodall, Reeves, Spiers, Davies, Walker, McIlvenney, Wheeler, Ayre, Whitehouse, McLuckie.

Referee: J E Cooke (Cambridge)   *Attendance:* 25,042

Compiled by **BOB BRUNSKELL** from the *Echo* report, with additional material – from interviews with Charles, Clifton and Sydenham – by **David Bull**. Oz cartoon by permission of the late Don Osmond and Mrs Osmond

SOUTHAMPTON 4
LIVERPOOL 1

I had been ever-present during the traumas of the 1952-53 season when Saints had lost their Second Division status for the first time in 31 years. Up to then this division had been our home, our rightful place, that we seemed destined never to leave. Then fate decreed otherwise and we had to rub shoulders with the Halifaxes and the Accringtons so that, by 1960, our Second Division credibility had gone - apart from which, except for Tommy Traynor, there had been a total turn-over of players. We were now a Third Division side - albeit an outstanding one, having won the championship in April and been clear of the third spot by nine points, but we were young and untested and doubt remained.

There must always be some anxiety in the minds of promoted clubs, particularly the players: are we good enough for the new division; or are we going to be out of our depth and return whence we came?

The first game, away to Rotherham, had not been very re-assuring. We had lost and not even scored a goal. Now we were home to mighty Liverpool, not quite as mighty as they were later to become but testing opponents nonetheless – and well capable, under the recently-appointed Bill Shankly, of answering our self-doubt.

We did not have to wait very long for the first crucial moment: after 11 minutes Liverpool scored following a free-kick. Although much against the run of play it seemed portentous. We had seen that Southampton could play a bit only to have it demonstrated by these aristocrats from Merseyside that it was finishing that counted.

Terry Paine finding space, in the Second Division, to cross...

We waited for the seemingly inevitable footballing lesson, but it didn't happen, perhaps because the Gods had decided this was an occasion, if not for the weird and supernatural, then certainly for the highly unusual: a John Sydenham goal. And not the result of a cut-in from the left wing but a flying raid down the middle followed by a stunning prod from – or does my memory play me tricks? – his right foot. The indignity seemed too much for Liverpool.

The first home goal always sorts out the optimists from the pessimists. For the optimist the first goal is the prelude to others and a spanking win, but to the pessimist it is a potential goal to the opposition who might now go up a gear and sweep us from the field. Better to have stayed as we were and gone for the last-minute draw when it would be too late for the opposition to repay the insult.

Yet, to the surprise of the lily-livered amongst us, it was Liverpool who folded, and before our disbelieving eyes, Saints scored again, and then again.

First, a quick pass from Paine found O'Brien who had the ball in the net before several defenders around him could, in today's jargon, "close him down." A typical George O'Brien goal.

Then Derek Reeves headed in a rebound off the crossbar to suggest (at least for now) that he wasn't just a lower-division goal-scoring wonder.

Surely Liverpool would not accept being two goals in arrears to these upstarts from the Third Division? But they had no choice. Southampton were in the ascendant and even the unwelcome sound of the half-time whistle did not break the spell. To the pessimists, half-time when Saints are in a comfortable lead is almost a crisis. It is an opportunity for the players to realise how easy it had been, and, despite the warnings of the manager, to think the match won.

The visitor's manager, however, shrewd football brain that he must be, will have spotted something and there will be a change of tactics or an adjustment here or there which will wreak a transformation in the game.

To the optimists, of course, the second-half is going to be a repetition of the first, and on this memorable night, the optimists had it, and Saints actually scored a fourth. After seven minutes, Reeves crossed to Paine who rounded his full-back, Moran, Liverpool's legendary trainer of the future, and beat the goalkeeper with a cracking shot. Six years later he was to score a somewhat similar goal in our first game in the First Division. And at the same end, too: Archers Road.

So, now, we were not just two-up with 45 minutes to go, but three-up and only 38 minutes to go. This was clearly the night for miracles, so there might be more to come.

But it was not to be. Saints noticeably relaxed and Liverpool came more into the game and Ron Reynolds, he of the contact lenses, was forced into several saves including one where he had to dive at the feet of Liverpool's centre-forward, Dave Hickson.

On those occasions I always expected him to be frantically waving away his team-mates as he got to his feet, lest they trampled one of his lost lenses into the mud. He never did, however, and I never knew how he managed it.

At the final whistle Saints were applauded from the field by spectators who seemed reluctant to leave.

I remember scoring from quite a long way out. Not that they all didn't give you pleasure, but I've got especially fond memories of that goal.

John Sydenham

We scored first and were so full of ourselves. Before half-time, we're down 3-1 and, as we walked into the dressing room, Tommy Leishman, who scored the goal, was the first one in. The manager, Bill Shankly, was so mad with us. He tore into Tommy and gave him such a hard time. Tommy couldn't believe it.

Jimmy Melia, then of Liverpool

It had been a super game and a super result, a moment to savour and prolong.

We walked up Archers Road with the special feeling that only an unexpected, overwhelming victory can bring – happy recollections in the pub to come, followed by the pleasures of the late report on television and of the newspaper headlines the next morning.

Even the pessimists were luxuriating in the belief we had proved ourselves good enough for this division.

The confidence gained that evening took us on, before the month was out, to a thumping 5-1 win against Portsmouth and, wonder of wonders, a second victory over what must have been a shell-shocked Liverpool at Anfield.

We were back where we all thought we belonged. We did not know, we could not have imagined, even on that magical night when we blitzed Liverpool after going behind, that we were destined for even higher things.

...but Derek Reeves had two men to close him down

SOUTHAMPTON:
Reynolds, Davies, Traynor, Clifton, Page, Huxford, Paine, O'Brien, Reeves, Mulgrew, Sydenham

LIVERPOOL:
Slater, Byrne, Moran, Wheeler, White, Leishman, Lewis, Hunt, Hickson, Melia, A'Court

Referee: Mr. R.H. Mann (Worcester)   *Attendance:* 24,823

Compiled by **ROB HOLLEY** from being there and from the *Echo* report. Jimmy Melia and John Sydenham interviewed by **David Bull**. *Echo* photographs

SOUTHAMPTON 5
LEEDS UNITED 4

It was the longest match ever played at The Dell and in every aspect one of the most remarkable. Southampton's 5-4 victory over Leeds United in the Fourth Round of the Football League Cup in December 1960 lasted two hours and 40 minutes.

Two floodlight failures plunged The Dell into darkness, forcing 28-minute then 34-minute delays during the first-half of the cup-tie. The fault, which had developed in the public supply output at the ground, clearly threatened the game. But electricians refused to be beaten and so did the Saints.

When light was eventually restored they overcame the loss of injured 'keeper Ron Reynolds after just 20 minutes to power into a four-goal lead. But this was no ordinary night and Leeds fought back to equalise before Derek Reeves completed an extraordinary personal performance with the winning goal 25 seconds from the final whistle. The centre-forward, who had been finding it harder to score in the Second Division than the Third – only five goals in 17 games to date – scored all five of Saints' goals that night, courtesy of five assists from irrepressible right-winger Terry Paine.

Four times in recent seasons Reeves had scored four for Saints – most notably, of course, 11 months earlier in Match No. 47 at Maine Road. But this was his best-ever performance and would remain a League Cup record (although equalled in 1967) until Oldham's Frank Bunn put six past Scarborough in 1989. It was even more special on a night when his strike partner George O'Brien was reduced to a hobbling passenger relatively early in the

game – although you could say this showed Paine's ability simply to switch his sights to Reeves in a season when the Paine-O'Brien wing would bag 52 of the team's 115 goals. Paine had so far scored in each round of this competition, including both goals at Anfield in the Third Round when Saints cheekily rubbed home their League double (of the previous report) by winning 2-1.

The *Echo*'s "Observer" summed up the events of the Leeds cup-tie simply and effectively:

> Saints reached the last eight of the League Cup by beating Leeds 5-4 in one of the most remarkable matches in the history of football that will be talked about for years to come.

The tie was just 10 minutes old and goalless when the lights went out for the first time. While electricians grappled to solve the problem, the players stayed out on the pitch making ghostly shapes in the gloom as they kept themselves warm by passing the ball about. After 28 minutes there were cheers of relief from the 13,000 crowd as light flooded the ground again and Saints just about had time to take the lead through Reeves – a firm header from a pinpoint cross by Paine – before the lights went out again.

Never having played in goal before, Huxford dons the jersey against Leeds United, hoping that nobody will be able to see him anyhow

League Cup Fourth Round

> *What a remarkable game! What a night! The lights kept going out…and we were back in the dressing room, having a good old chat and I think even the cigarettes were going there…[Then] the lights back on, out we'd go again…It was just an incredible night and I don't think there was **one** of the crowd that left that game until the lights really went out at the end.*
>
> John Sydenham

But unfortunately for Saints during that first resumption, which lasted just 11 minutes, Reynolds was injured diving bravely at the feet of Leeds centre-forward McCole. As Reynolds was stretchered off, skipper Cliff Huxford pulled on the green jersey and went between the posts for the first time in his career.

There were groans when darkness enveloped the ground again. This time the players didn't hang about. They made for the sanctuary of the dressing-rooms where they stayed for 34 minutes before the light was again restored – this time, thankfully, for keeps.

And Saints saw their way clear to establish what looked like a stranglehold on the tie. Substitutes were still seven seasons away; so with Reynolds off and O'Brien struggling, Saints were effectively reduced to nine men. Yet by 50 minutes, they were four goals ahead.

Leeds to be fair had one of their full-backs, Jones, struggling with a first-half knock. He eventually went off for good and being reduced to 10 men seemed to galvanise the Yorkshire side.

Peyton gave them a whiff of hope when he scored after 53 minutes and with spirits soaring they went for Southampton's throat. McCole added a second on 64 minutes and then Jack Charlton, a young beanpole of a centre-half, made a dramatic intervention.

Frequently up supporting his attack, Charlton scored a third for Leeds in the 69th minute then won them a penalty when he fell under challenge in the box and Cameron beat Huxford from the spot.

There were still 11 minutes left on the clock and it was developing into a potential nightmare for makeshift 'keeper Huxford, but he heroically stopped two danger efforts as Leeds went for a late winner. And in doing so he laid the foundation for a grandstand finish from the Saints.

When Paine played the ball through to him, Reeves set off for goal, drew the Leeds goalkeeper Humphries and beat him with a well-placed drive. There was only time to restart the game when referee Thorpe blew the final whistle.

The clock had ticked on to ten past ten. The tie had finished two hours and 40 minutes after it had begun. Fans greeted the last whistle with a mix of euphoria and relief – euphoria for Saints and Reeves, who had capped such a wondrous night so dramatically, and relief that the game itself had managed to run its course.

Once out of the ground came the problem of finding a way home, especially with your last bus or train perhaps already gone.

And once home, the need to explain such a late arrival to your nearest and dearest.

Five-goal Reeves

SOUTHAMPTON:
Reynolds, Davies, Traynor, Conner, Page, Huxford, Paine, O'Brien, Reeves, Mulgrew, Sydenham

LEEDS UNITED:
Humphries, Jones, Hair, Cameron, Charlton, Goodwin, Francis, Bremner, McCole, Peyton, Grainger

Referee: G W Thorpe (Swindon)   *Attendance:* 13,448

Compiled by **BOB BRUNSKELL** from the *Echo* report. John Sydenham interviewed by **David Bull**. Photograph from the *Echo*. Oz cartoon by permission of the late Don Osmond and Mrs Osmond

SOUTHAMPTON 7
IPSWICH TOWN 1

Saints made club history in 1960-61. Their record achievement in the FA Cup remains their 14-0 win against Newbury at the Qualifying stage in 1894. But when they routed Ipswich Town 7-1 in the Third Round at The Dell in January 1961, this was their biggest win in the competition Proper, overtaking the 6-1 defeat of Walton and Hersham three years previously.

Yet what was most remarkable about the result was that it was achieved against THE up-and-coming club in the Football League. Ipswich, managed by former Saints right-back Alf Ramsey, were destined to go on and win the Division Two title in May – and more. They strode into the top flight and promptly won that as well in 1962.

Ramsey sullenly summed up: "Collectively we had a bad day at The Dell." His opposite number Ted Bates had a huge smile of satisfaction on his face – and why not?

Only a year before, Saints had won 5-1 in the same round of the cup at Manchester City – regarded almost unanimously as the Club's best performance in the competition. But on a day when Saints stung Ipswich with six first-half goals, four of them in a quite remarkable seven-minute spell, Bates was moved to suggest that "in the first-half the team played even better than they did at Maine Road."

According to "Observer", in the *Echo,* "half chances were turned into goals by quickness of mind and foot.

There was determination going for the ball and deadly shooting from the home side." Support had to be there from the back and after helping Saints establish early control, the men in defence held their ground stoically after the break when the home side, six goals to the good, eased off the throttle and Ipswich tried to pull some pride out of the wreckage.

Up front the nimble and the prolific George O'Brien was Southampton's inspiration. He scored three goals, hit the woodwork and played a leading role in some of the other strikes. The first came after a seven-minute opening spell when Ipswich had looked the livelier of the two sides, driving forward in a bid to seek out early weaknesses in the home rearguard.

There were none and it was Ipswich's turn to be put under the hammer as O'Brien pounced on a mistake by the Town centre-half and captain Andy Nelson and went on to shoot past 'keeper Roy Bailey who had hurried out to narrow the angle.

Tommy Mulgrew heads Saints' record-breaking seventh goal.

FA Cup Third Round

Tommy Mulgrew, adept at being in the right place at the right time, was first on to a well-flighted corner from Terry Paine to hit goal number two. And O'Brien quickly added his second after Paine had been fouled and Saints awarded a penalty. John Page, Saints' regular penalty-taker, had missed out with his previous two efforts from the spot, and had asked to be relieved of penalty-taking duties. O'Brien, who fed on goals, gladly grabbed the job and the cool, ruthless manner in which he despatched the kick made it his for keeps.

Mulgrew's goal had come in 23 minutes, O'Brien's penalty on 27 and his third moments later, as he again darted through the Ipswich defence as though they weren't there and beat Bailey. Two minutes later and Saints were five goals to the good, this time left-winger Harry Penk grabbing himself a piece of the glory. Penk, a cover for John Sydenham away on National Service, was the only change to the side that had won the Third Division nine months earlier. This was his first senior goal for Saints at The Dell.

Ipswich were chasing shadows. Their marking had disintegrated, their passing lacked any sort of conviction. They were wide open for more punishment and Paine made it six of the best with a quality delivery just before half-time. Out of the chaos, Ipswich had created just one first-half chance, a Jimmy Leadbetter effort which right-back Ron Davies cleared off the line.

*One of Ted [Bates]'s strengths was that he invited experienced players to discuss tactics... Alf Ramsey was playing this method where Crawford [No. 9] moved back to **lure** defences away and create the gaps for Phillips – the inside-left – to come in. And it was so successful... Ted got Cliff Huxford, Tommy Traynor and myself and said " Phillips is the danger-man. I'm thinking, Cliff, to switch you over to right-half" – because Dick Conner was the attacking wing-half, as we know – "What do you think?"... The three of us discussed this... and suggested to Ted that, instead of this, he would have a word with Dick and say "Look! You know this fellow's the one who comes through the middle. Do you think you can [cover his runs]?" [We suspected that] Dick would make sure that he could prove to everybody that he could do it. This is what we did and Phillips never had a look-in... There was only really one side in it .*

Ron Reynolds

*Ramsey went on to get the England job. So we used to say **Ted** would've got that job – if he had done what he should have [in buying defenders]. I think we were a better team than Ipswich. I'm sure Ipswich thought that as well! After all, we stuffed them 7-1.*

George O'Brien

It was no surprise when Saints eased up after the break. But Ipswich saw it as a chance to retrieve some of their damaged pride and within two minutes of the restart they opened their account, or – to be exact – a Southampton player opened it for them. Yes, Saints players scored all eight goals. But in this case, John Page unwittingly deflected the ball past his own 'keeper Ron Reynolds.

Before Saints scored their seventh goal twelve minutes from time, Reynolds had become one of the busiest figures on the pitch, pulling off a string of saves as Ipswich, spearheaded by deadly strike duo Crawford and Phillips, strove to give the scoreline some respectability. As noted in the previous report, Saints' own strike-force were having a contrasting season. While O'Brien was still banging them in, Derek Reeves had all but dried up.

After his record-breaking five a month earlier, he would score only six more goals in the rest of the season. But although the other four forwards shared the seven against Ipswich, Reeves was still playing his part – no more so than in the last goal, the result of his pinpoint centre which Mulgrew headed home.

It was the last nail in the Ipswich coffin and Saints were left to celebrate their first-ever win over Ipswich.

And how!

SOUTHAMPTON:

Reynolds, Davies, Traynor, Conner, Page, Huxford, Paine, O'Brien, Reeves, Mulgrew, Penk.

IPSWICH TOWN:

Bailey, Carberry, Malcolm, Pickett, Nelson, Elsworthy, Stephenson, Millward, Crawford, Phillips, Leadbetter.

Referee: Mr C.H. Rogers (London)   *Attendance:* 20,422

Compiled by **BOB BRUNSKELL** from the *Echo* report. George O'Brien and Ron Reynolds interviewed by **David Bull**. *Echo* photograph

SOUTHAMPTON 3
NOTTINGHAM FOREST 3

It was the fightback to cap all Cup fightbacks. There were Saints three goals down with just 16 minutes of their FA Cup quarter-final replay against Nottingham Forest left to play – but refusing to throw in the towel.

The manner in which they went on to wipe out the deficit thrilled a huge 29,479 so much on that April night in 1963 that "Observer" wrote for the *Echo*, "I have never seen nor heard a crowd at The Dell so enthusiastic as they were in those closing minutes."

Saints pulled it back to 3-3 with less than a minute of normal time left on the clock. They had driven so much fear and uncertainty into the Forest defensive ranks in those final, spell-binding moments that it seemed inevitable that they would go on and win the tie in extra-time. That they didn't was down to some inspired goalkeeping by Forest's Peter Grummitt and the fact that their players had given so much in normal time that, come the extra period, there was next to nothing left in the tank.

Those fans who after 120 minutes of unbearable tension finally escaped the crush inside the ground must have staggered home with their own minds and bodies consumed with a mixture of euphoria and exhaustion. Forest were a top flight side who had won the FA Cup in 1959. Three members of that side figured in this unforgettable contest, one of them, Joe Quigley, with potentially devastating consequences during the first hour.

This was a cup-tie with an explosive start and a quite astonishing sting in the tail. Saints expected Forest to come out in ultra-defensive mode when they announced just before the kick-off that they were sacrificing winger Trevor Hockey for an extra defender. But those expecting them to sit back, with the intention of catching Southampton on the break, were stunned by the manner of their start. The visiting side stormed forward, were two up after just four minutes and after holding back the first tide of Saints' attacks, added a third with the second-half less than 10 minutes old.

Colin Addison was first to silence the big, hopeful crowd, hooking a shot just inside the post after two minutes. When Geoff Vowden soared above the home defence to bury a fourth-minute header, Saints had a mini-mountain to climb. Having established a bridgehead, Forest packed their defence and Southampton, in the gold-shirts of this Cup run, went through a long period of frustration. Strong headers from David Burnside and George Kirby, both from Terry Paine crosses, were warning shots across the Nottingham Forest bows. Just before half-time, George O'Brien penetrated the massed Forest ranks only to be denied by a terrific save from Grummitt.

But as the clock ticked past 54 minutes, Saints sustained what looked like a mortal blow – a third Forest goal, again from the head of Vowden. Quigley, their Wembley winner of four years before, had played a part in all three goals. Forest, it seemed, had booked their ticket to Villa Park for a semi-final appointment with Manchester United, whose manager Matt Busby was watching the game from the West Stand.

Understandably Forest were by now adopting a "what we have, we hold" policy but, all credit to Saints, they refused to give up the ghost. They had been chasing the game from virtually the first kick but, remarkably on this night, they never lost the desire. They kept piling forward, looking for the breakthrough which would give them a spark of hope. When it came, the spark soon fanned into flaming passion which swept panic throughout the Forest ranks.

Paine found the net with a header which was disallowed for offside. But with Tony Knapp, their vociferous captain driving them on, Saints increased the tempo of their attacks and when Kirby emerged from a goal-mouth scramble to force the ball home in the 74th minute, the die had been cast.

Saints, with the scent of blood in their nostrils and a huge noise from the crowd at their backs, went for the kill, with Paine the peerless provider and Kirby the battering ram.

The side that played, unchanged, throughout
the seven-game Cup run and won the Giant Killers of the Year trophy
Back row (left to right) Williams, Reynolds, Traynor
Middle row: Wimshurst, Knapp, Huxford
Front row: Paine, O'Brien, Kirby, Burnside, Sydenham

FA Cup Sixth Round (Replay)

Arriving from Plymouth as part of Ted Bates's spending spree that also brought in David Burnside and Stuart Williams, the former Everton and Sheffield Wednesday powerhouse had initially made a regular habit of scoring in home games. That he had scored only twice at The Dell in the last two months – both of them in the Cup – owed much to the freeze-out of football in January and most of February.

This night will be remembered, though, not for the goal he scored (or two, if you believe his story) but for the way George the Dragon terrorised, even as Paine tantalised and tormented, the Forest defence.

Poor John Winfield, whipped into a frenzy of self-doubt by Paine's

The body count for the late equaliser is as described by the scorer below

As Terry [Paine] comes in the box again... George O'Brien is on the front post and I think George Kirby is at the back somewhere, so I think "I'll be in the middle... The ball comes to me, about eight yards from the goal... I always remember a lot of bodies there and the ball arriving to me and it sat there ... I can remember just concentrating on seeing the ball and striking it as hard as I can between the posts and under the crossbar [and] I remember it just disappearing through one or two players and into the net... The mood, that night, of the crowd was enormous.

David Burnside

pressure, lobbed a hopeful ball back to his 'keeper. Under pressure from Kirby, who always claimed the goal, Grummitt spilled it over his own goal-line....3-2.

Then, with just seconds left, Burnside a skilful, creative midfield player with a panache for striking quality goals, pulled one out of his locker, a perfectly aimed, powerful shot which arrowed its way beyond Grummitt's reach.

In extra-time, though, Grummitt dug deep and found the inspiration to deny Sydenham, Burnside and O'Brien.

When the last whistle went the players barely had the strength to make it back to the dressing-rooms. They had but five days in which to recover for a third attempt at a semi-final spot.

...a bizarre game. We fancied our chances [at the start and] we always felt, at half-time, that we could come out and get a goal ... Of course, George [Kirby] absolutely terrorized the Notts Forest back four. Paine was hitting corners in and George was steaming in – you know, anything goes – and they were all looking at him. They made so many mistakes that we cashed in on them.

Ken Wimshurst

We went three-up and I suppose we relaxed a bit too much ... As goalkeepers in those days, we used to know that, if we were going up for the ball, we were going to get hit. But it was always fair and square and we used to enjoy it. It was part and parcel of the game ... As far as I can see [Kirby's challenges were] not that dirty. It doesn't worry me. It didn't worry me at the time.

Peter Grummitt, the Forest 'keeper

SOUTHAMPTON:
Reynolds, Williams, Traynor, Wimshurst, Knapp, Huxford, Paine, O'Brien, Kirby, Burnside, Sydenham

NOTTINGHAM FOREST:
Grummitt, Wilson, Mochan, Whitefoot, McKinlay, Hindley, Addison, Quigley, Vowden, Winfield, Cobb

Referee: Denis Howell MP (Birmingham)　　　　　　　　　　　　　*Attendance:* 29,479

Compiled by **BOB BRUNSKELL** from the *Echo* report. Burnside, Grummitt and Wimshurst interviewed by **David Bull**. *Echo* photographs

SOUTHAMPTON 5
NOTTINGHAM FOREST 0

So how do you follow that? Brian James, who'd predicted that whatever Southampton did next would be an anti-climax, admitted to his readers that he was "wrong … very, very wrong." And how!

Saints, on something of a roll, continued where they had left off, winning 5-0, to make it eight goals without reply. Yet, when David Burnside put them 1-0 up in the 40th minute of the second replay at White Hart Lane, it meant that Saints were leading for the first time in the 250th minute of this adjective-defying cup-tie.

It was as well that the Second Division underdogs delayed their opening goal until then, since so many of their travelling fans arrived late: an estimated 3,000 had not made it by half-time and some never got in at all. There were three reasons for this.

First, as the *Echo* reported on the Monday afternoon of the match, there had not been enough coaches to go round. As firm upon firm – Mullards, Follands, Pirelli – confirmed that it was closing and had hired transport to take employees to this North London show-down, coach company after coach company was complaining that it had been unable to meet demand. So, secondly, many were obliged to go by car and jam the pre-M3 route to London. My father, a bricklayer, watched this endless stream of red-and-white humanity from a roof-top on the A30 in Blackwater: "it didn't seem to stop," he recalls. And then, when it did stop in Tottenham, White Hart Lane wasn't ready for it. There weren't enough turnstiles open to admit this exodus from Southampton.

Saints were unchanged. Forest were without their injured right-half, Jeff Whitefoot, who was being tipped – along with Ken Wimshurst, his Southampton counterpart – for England honours. But they changed their defensive formation, too. Whether their deployment of seven at the back was intended to combat the Paine-O'Brien wing – as George O'Brien saw it – or the threat of George Kirby, as Donald Saunders of the *Daily Telegraph* perceived it, the outcome was the same: Wimshurst had the room in which to put on what was "one of the best wing-half displays" the *Echo* Sports Editor had "ever seen in a Saints side or almost any other." He was, for Saunders, "the great difference between the teams."

It was he who scored the second, soon after Burnside's volley from Tommy Traynor's run and pass had put Saints ahead. From suddenly being 2-0 up at half-time, they came out and quickly made it five: another for Burnside and two for O'Brien.

Wimshurst had what James called "a havoc-making hand in all three of these goals." Forest may have tamed the Paine-Kirby axis, but at the price of giving Wimshurst the run of White Hart Lane.

Paine barely rated a mention, save when he slid inside to take a pass from Wimshurst but just failed to make it six. Kirby got the head-down for O'Brien's first and deserved a goal, in James's book, for his "menacing" contribution: "he caused trouble wherever he wandered. Half the Forest defence were watching him and not the ball when four of the goals went in."

Matt Busby was watching, too. Whatever plans he formed for stopping the flow when Manchester United faced Saints in the semi-final, these did not stop Wimshurst being "the sole constructive Southampton player of any quality" in the first-half at Villa Park. That's a verdict cited by United's captain, Noel Cantwell, on a

George O'Brien (hidden by McKinlay) scores Saints' fifth, with Wimshurst (black shorts) as ever up with the action

poor game all-round, won by "a sloppy affair" of a goal – and that's according to Denis Law who scored it.

The defeated Saints side has not burst into autobiographical accounts of that game and I have no intention of spoiling the party by quoting from any of the interviews I had the privilege to record with 11 of them.

As John Arlott wrote, in the *Hampshire Magazine* that summer, the defeat was not necessarily failure: the players and supporters had shared, in those two Sixth Round replays, "a triumph which nothing can ever take from them."

The second of those replays had been a memorable night out, indeed, for those fans who made the journey *and* got in. But then they all had to get home.

Cliff Huxford had taken a knock on the leg and was resting it by standing in the stairwell at the front of the coach:

They played with a man withdrawn. They didnae play with an inside-left; they played with two left-halves… a normal left-half and somebody behind him. So Ken [Wimshurst] had the freedom of the field … I think it was for [stopping] me and Terry [Paine]…Everything was going in. We were that kind of side. If we got a goal, we took a bit of stopping.

George O'Brien

Southampton closed down on the afternoon. Everybody just left … We didn't change from the first game to the second game to the next game. We played exactly the same because that was the only way the team that Ted [Bates] had accumulated understood how to play. He just let people go on and play … We demoralized them. They came to play it tight. I remember coming out of the game and Ron Reynolds was talking to Danny Blanchflower outside the ground … I went over and I remember Danny Blanchflower saying "It's a good job they didn't come here to attack you or it might've been 10."
That was the way we were!

Ken Wimshurst

I could see, for miles in front of us, the tail-lights of cars, in streams going back to Southampton. It was brilliant. We had a fantastic following that night.

I was not a part of it at all, I'm afraid. I was out playing bridge in Exeter, but was back at my digs in time to see the highlights. My landlord, the kind of sports-fan who told you the result before he invited you to watch his TV with him, announced that the game had finished 5-0.

I'm sure I spluttered something courageous, but limp, about how well our lads had done to take a First Division side to three games. This set him up perfectly: "Who said they lost? What kind of supporter are you?"

I'd like to be able to recall and report that I was shamed by these questions. But, be honest, now: would you have expected a 5-0 win?

Any more than the contrite Mr James did?

Ted Bates (right) congratulates his team on their epic performance.
Top row (left to right) Kirby, Huxford, Reynolds, Wimshurst
Bottom row: Sydenham, O'Brien, Traynor, Gallagher (trainer), Burnside, Paine, Williams, Knapp

---

SOUTHAMPTON:
Reynolds, Williams, Traynor, Wimshurst, Knapp, Huxford, Paine, O'Brien, Kirby, Burnside, Sydenham

NOTTINGHAM FOREST:
Grummitt, Wilson, Grant, Palmer, McKinlay, Hindley, Addison, Quigley, Vowden, Winfield, Cobb

Referee: Jack Taylor (Wolverhampton)　　　　　　　　　　　　　*Attendance:* 42,256

Compiled by **DAVID BULL** from reports in the *Echo, Daily Telegraph* and Brian James's unidentified newspaper; the autobiographies of Cantwell and Law; John Arlott's essay; and interviews with Cliff Huxford, George O'Brien and Ken Wimshurst. *Echo* photographs

SOUTHAMPTON 6
DERBY COUNTY 4

April Fools Day 1964 was to throw up an extraordinary game at The Dell when Derby County were Saints' visitors. On paper there seemed to be nothing potentially remarkable about this match but that wasn't at all the way things turned out.

With only seven games to go and with little for either side to play for, this promised to be no more than an end-of-season affair. Saints had had something of a chequered season. Blasting off with a 6-1 victory over Charlton, they recorded another six against Grimsby and then went one better by sticking seven past Scunthorpe.

This was balanced, though, by a shattering home defeat in the Third Round of the FA Cup by holders, Manchester United, after Saints had led by two at half-time, and an unthinkable two League defeats at the hands of Portsmouth.

When Saints and Derby ran out on a pleasant April evening, they were greeted by a smallish crowd of 11,392, although that was 96 more than had watched the two sides at the Baseball Ground two days earlier. Having won that Easter Monday match 2-1, Derby wasted no time taking the lead in this one. Rams' outside-left John Bowers outpaced Stuart Williams to score with a fine shot. Saints weren't out of it for long, though. Terry Paine was notorious, it will be remembered, for needling opponents. He would wind up full-backs and goalkeepers alike until they either lost their rag or were harried into error. One of Paine's victims was Derby's sometime England 'keeper, Reg Matthews. Terry cast his spell, Matthews fluffed a simple back pass, Terry had a simple tap-in and Saints were level.

Then came Martin Chivers. Having made his debut, at 17 the season before, Chivers was now

fully installed (as you will see from the end-of-term report that follows at Match No. 55). Now, taking a well-judged through-ball from utility player, John McGuigan, who was enjoying the longest run of games (11) he would ever have for Southampton, he slammed Saints in front. The lead was, however, short-lived and it was at this point that the drama began to unfold. Saints 'keeper, Tony Godfrey, well into an extended run after an injury to Reynolds at Portsmouth in September, came off his line to punch clear and received a nasty blow to the face for his troubles. The ball hadn't travelled far and Bowers smacked it home for his second.

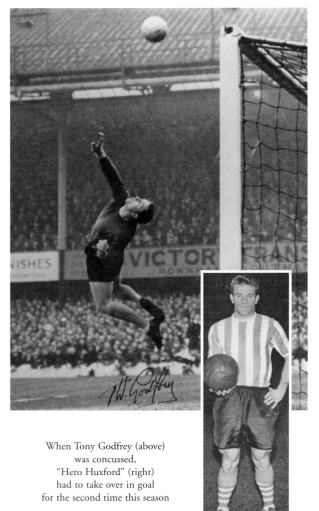

When Tony Godfrey (above) was concussed, "Hero Huxford" (right) had to take over in goal for the second time this season

Godfrey, later taken to hospital with concussion, couldn't have known what day it was, let alone who the opponents were, and this may have contributed to his letting in a Barrowcliffe 40-yarder that put Derby 3-2 up two minutes before the break. Within a minute, though, Paine had dispatched a penalty after being brought down by Derby left-back, Ferguson.

"Hero Huxford" took over in goal for the second-half. His debut as substitute 'keeper, three seasons earlier in Match No. 50, is, of course, famous. This was the second time this season that he had been called for duty between the sticks, the first being at Fratton when – as already mentioned – Reynolds was injured. He had prevented Pompey adding to their two goals without reply. This time he would be beaten, but he brought off many fine saves, one of which especially impressed the *Echo*'s "Observer" as a save of which "any goalkeeper would have been proud." Saints' injury agony was further compounded by the loss of centre-half Mike Hennigan. Standing in for skipper Tony Knapp it was Hennigan's third outing of the season and on his home debut he had the misfortune to dislocate an elbow after performing well.

Saints, then, were down to nine. By now, though, Chivers had made it 4-3. Even without a two-man advantage, Derby had looked dangerous going forward. Now they should surely go on to win with something to spare. It looked that way when centre-forward Bill Curry, in for the versatile Ian Buxton who was away preparing himself for the upcoming County Cricket season, levelled the scores at four-apiece.

But Saints had not read the script. Paine was not finished with Matthews yet and, having worried the goalkeeper into an infringement, duly knocked in his second penalty of the match to complete his hat-trick.

Derby then launched wave upon wave of attacks tearing their hair out to find an equaliser, not that their nippy winger, Gordon Hughes, had an abundance to begin with. In fact, Derby probably tried too hard and, as they became over-hurried in their work, panic set in as the nine men defended demonically, one of these demons obviously possessing Cliff Huxford.

A couple of unusual breaks in play only added to the tension. Referee Smith wanted the ball changed and phantom whistlers, quite commonplace back then, caused another intervention as Mr. Smith asked for a loudspeaker announcement taking the warblers to task.

Why anyone would want to blow a whistle in the crowd to interrupt such a feast of entertainment is really quite beyond me.

Derby's forwards had done their worst and blown themselves out. Enter the darting John Sydenham.

In the final minute, he scored with a typical burst as he sprinted from the half-way line. His solo effort which gave Saints an amazing 6-4 advantage that had never seemed possible completed Derby's humiliation.

The *Saints Go Marching In* anthem rang out loud and clear and at the whistle a good many of a crowd that had been at fever pitch flooded on – and came off, chairing their man-of-the-hour Huxford all the way to the dressing room on an emotion-charged and memorable night.

The teenage Martin Chivers, "now fully installed," is pictured earlier in this season's precocious run of scoring

---

SOUTHAMPTON:

Godfrey, Williams, Hollywood, Wimshurst, Hennigan, Huxford, Paine, O'Brien, Chivers, McGuigan, Sydenham

DERBY COUNTY:

Matthews, Barrowcliffe, Ferguson, Webster, Young, Parry, Hughes, Cullen, Curry, Waller, Bowers

Referee: Mr. D.W. Smith, (Stonehouse, Glos.)   *Attendance:* 11,392

Compiled by **CHRIS NEWMAN** from being there and from the *Echo* report. *Echo* photographs

SOUTHAMPTON 6
ROTHERHAM UNITED 1

It may have been previously postponed and it may have been the last match of the season between two sides out of the honours, but in terms of goal scoring this was a meeting of the Second Division's big guns. Rotherham had a goals-for tally of 89 going into this game while the Saints were perched tantalisingly on 94.

I can't recall any great sense of anticipation that Southampton might once more reach the magic hundred – which they'd not achieved since promotion four seasons before – but their having belted in 14 in the three previous games, perhaps we should have expected another riotous display of attacking football from the home side.

Rotherham had a useful outfit at the time and their attack, spearheaded by Brian Tiler with Bennett and Houghton working inside wingers Barry Lyons and Ian Butler, was more than capable of giving Saints a run for their money and it was the "Merry Millers" who started as brightly as their nickname. First, Ken Houghton bothered Tony Godfrey into a second grab anxiety and then Albert Bennett, later famous for his huge "Pickwick" sideburns, sent a rasping shot against a post.

It was shortly after this, though, that the prolific Southampton opened their account for the evening, George O'Brien in typical predatory fashion connecting from supplier-in-chief Terry Paine. Six minutes later, maker turned taker as Paine scored himself to put Saints two-up and cruising to half-time.

After the break, Rotherham decided they were going to make a fight of it and, coming more into it, they forced a passage of evenly balanced play but this was broken as O'Brien poached his second, neatly latching on to a John Sydenham corner on 61 minutes. Another perfect cross from

George O'Brien scored a hat-trick to round off a season whose middle he had lost

Paine found David Burnside – restored at the death after an injury-troubled season and characteristically taking up a goalscoring position – who planted a header past Rotherham 'keeper Roy Ironside and Saints were four up.

At some point during a game that the fans were obviously thoroughly enjoying, they began to speculate as to whether the Saints' well-oiled goal machine could actually reach the hundred. The seed had been well and truly planted, the noise levels began to increase having started as an excited murmur and the team reflecting the crowd's enthusiasm responded brilliantly. Tiler had briefly stemmed the Saints tide with a headed goal on 68 minutes but with Southampton still comfortably in front it was to be no more than scant consolation. The fuse had already been ignited… Saints wanted that hundred and set about pursuing it as if it had been promotion itself. The catalyst was a quite remarkable goal by O'Brien who completed his hat-trick, firing in from an almost impossible angle in the 81st minute when right on the by-line, catching Ironside out completely.

Other than *"Oh When The Saints"* or *"Glory Hallelujah"* (initially pinched from Tottenham) or the Bill Bray-instigated 2-4-6-8 chant, crowds never sang or chanted anything like as much in those days as they do now. Nine minutes from the end of yet another amazing match, however, the loyal twelve and a half

Division Two

David Burnside returned to score from a "perfect cross" from Paine

room for a Chivers-O'Brien strike-force that would be formidable in 1964-65.

Meanwhile, after three seasons as top scorer, O'Brien was obliged to cede the honour, in 1963-64, jointly to Chivers and Paine, with 22 goals each. While Terry missed only one League game – to win his sixth cap for England at Hampden Park – Martin scored his 22 in but 29 games.

In this high-scoring climax to what had been a roller-coaster season for the team (as highlighted in the previous report), Chivers unfittingly failed to celebrate his 19th birthday with a goal after the Dell's resident Albion Band had played for his many happy returns.

Not that this mattered to a crowd that returned home almost as happy as if Saints had notched a trophy.

thousand struck up with the one-hit wonder, "We Want The Ton" and this got huge airplay topping the crowd's own personal chart until the Dell floodlights beamed down on what everyone was waiting for.

There may have been an air of inevitability about the final strike but that was in itself only a celebration of Saints' fine form. It was Terry Paine (well, who else?) who fittingly in the 84th minute grabbed the honour of achieving Saints' century, although had George O'Brien not been flattened in the area, causing the ball to run on, it might well have been his.

It had been a disappointing season for O'Brien who had lost his place in November to a local youngster with an eye for goal: Martin Chivers, who was briefly introduced in the previous report. The sale of Kirby in March had made

Terry Paine scored twice to finish as joint-top scorer in a season that saw him miss only one League game – in order to play for England

---

SOUTHAMPTON:

Godfrey, Williams, Hollywood, Wimshurst, Knapp, Huxford, Paine, O'Brien, Chivers, Burnside, Sydenham

ROTHERHAM UNITED:

Ironside, Carver, Lambert, Lancaster, Madden, Jackson, Lyons, Bennett, Tiler, Houghton, Butler

Referee: Mr T.W. Dawes (Norwich)   *Attendance:* 12, 539

Compiled by **CHRIS NEWMAN** from being there and from *Echo* reports. Photographs from the *Echo* and *Duncan Holley*'s collection

SOUTHAMPTON 9
WOLVERHAMPTON WANDERERS 3

Saints sat proudly at the top of Division Two in the early autumn of 1965 after humiliating Wolverhampton Wanderers, the former aristocrats of English football. The gold and black Wolves flag, which had been hoisted proudly to acclaim three League Championship wins in the 1950s, was at half mast after a 9-3 pummelling at The Dell on 18 September.

With a brand of high speed, precision football, the like of which had rarely been seen at The Dell before, Saints powered to a club scoring-high in the League which still stands today. It gave *Echo* reporter "Argus" a problem:

Finding superlatives to describe the Saints wonder display presents an exercise as elusive as beset the team in their efforts to score a tenth goal. But what does it matter. Had the magic double figures been reached, it would not have made it a greater victory.

Ironically, it required the shock of an own goal by Tony Knapp, conceded in less than a minute, to galvanise and then propel Saints to an unforgettable performance. It had been nip and tuck early on with four goals coming in the first 12 minutes, two from each side. But even this was no real foretaste of what was to come. By half-time Saints had thrust themselves into the driving seat, building a 5-2 advantage. By the hour-mark the scored had accelerated on, astonishingly, to 9-3. And yes, for the last 30 minutes, there wasn't a goal. How the sides, and Saints in particular, failed to add to the scoreline was in a way as remarkable as what had gone before.

In essence Saints could easily have had another five or six. Post and then bar kept out shots but it was the Wolves goalkeeper Dave MacLaren who stopped it becoming a cricket score. Although he'd let in nine, MacLaren brilliantly kept out at least six more goal-worthy efforts.

Such was his performance that Saints manager Ted Bates was sufficiently impressed to sign him a year later. It was a transfer which raised more than a few eyebrows, but Bates was no mug on the transfer market. In fact, few managers of the day had a better reputation for making shrewd buys. What MacLaren's contribution did confirm was just how irresistible Saints were on that extraordinary day in what was to become an landmark season for Saints – as they marched on to the First Division, as demonstrated in the next few reports.

In many ways Wolves had become whipping boys even before the game. Saints were smarting after a 5-1 defeat at Coventry. They were looking for someone to take it out on, and Wolves were the next in line. But Wolves weren't exactly short on confidence going into the game. They had won three of their last four games, scoring 15 goals in the process. Saints had also won three on the trot, with 11 goals to show for it, before the setback at Highfield Road. So there were no panic changes from manager Bates. The defence remained intact, which meant a home debut for right-back Ken Jones, a close season signing from Bradford Park Avenue. The only change was upfront where George O'Brien returned from injury at the expense of Norman Dean, the young centre-forward whose home debut would have to wait.

In the shuffling of forward positions that this required, the No. 9 shirt went to midfield general Jimmy Melia, the former Liverpool player (as in Match No. 49) who had

Terry Paine rounds MacLaren to score Saints' third goal. The ninth would be almost identical in its execution.

Division Two

arrived at The Dell, via Molineux, nine months earlier. There are various theories as to how Melia ended up wearing the No. 9 – his own version is reproduced here – but the upshot was that he played a deep-lying centre-forward role, with Martin Chivers and George O'Brien going through the inside-forward channels as a two-pronged spearhead.

This bamboozled Wolves and reduced them to a defensive shambles. Melia especially wanted to do well against his old club and although he was the only Saints forward not to score, his contribution to the debacle was profound. Wherever he went, Wolves centre-half David Woodfield followed. And with Woodfield drawn from the heart of defence, Saints exploited the extra space. With Melia spraying the passes and Terry Paine and John Sydenham rampaging down the flanks, Chivers and O'Brien had the ammunition to wreak havoc.

Wolves were heading for their heaviest defeat in 45 years but who would have known it when Knapp, trying to head a probing ball from Bobby Thomson out of harm's way, succeeded only in finding his own net after just 35 seconds? Saints were badly stung but within four minutes were on level terms, Chivers rounding England international Ron Flowers to score the first of four goals with a perfectly placed shot. After 11 minutes Melia began the move which led to Sydenham speeding past three players before arrowing a shot just inside the far post. Wolves replied within a minute, Bobby Woodruff hooking the ball home from a Terry Wharton corner.

Southampton regained the lead on 25 minutes and never looked back. It was a sweeping move from one side of the pitch to the other involving four players before

> *Martin Chivers, who was playing No.9, came to Ted Bates and said "I don't want to play with that number on my back"… On the Friday, before we played Wolverhampton, [Ted] said "Jimmy, will you put No.9 on?" I said "I don't care what number I wear. It doesn't make any difference to me." So, for the first time, I put No.9 on and I'll never forget this game. Because I had No.9 on, David Woodfield marked me all over the field, so he left a big gap right through the middle and every time we went down, we scored goals … I probably had one of my best games **ever** and I didn't score a goal.*
>
> Jimmy Melia

Paine latched on to O'Brien's pass and rounded MacLaren to score. O'Brien scored himself four minutes later when he jabbed home from close range after a Chivers centre had been deflected into his path. The roles were reversed in the 33rd minute when O'Brien dispossessed Flowers and Chivers scored from his pinpoint pass.

Saints fans were glad of a breather at half-time. They needed it because between the 47th and 60th minutes of the second-half, there had been five more goals, four from Saints. Chivers began the deluge, racing on to a fine pass from Melia to shoot past MacLaren. After 50 minutes Chivers's enterprise earned him another. Both he and O'Brien gave chase to a Woodfield back-pass intended for his 'keeper. Chivers won the race, scoring his fourth and Saints' seventh goal. Wolves refused to give up the ghost and Peter Knowles, a gifted young forward who was soon to turn his back on football to become a Jehovah's Witness, notched their third goal on 54 minutes. Saints answered that isolated moment of impudence with their eighth goal within 60 seconds. This time it was Sydenham driving the ball home after Paine had worked his way into the penalty area. Paine completed the scoring after again weaving his way into the box but this time going the whole hog and rounding the 'keeper to steer his second goal past a couple of defenders who had scrambled back to cover the line.

"We want ten" was the chant from the terraces. Paine hit the post, Sydenham the bar and Chivers demanded a stunning save from the shell-shocked MacLaren.

But Wolves escaped the ultimate humiliation of a double-figure defeat.

SOUTHAMPTON:
Godfrey, Jones, Williams, Walker, Knapp, Huxford, Paine, O'Brien, Melia, Chivers, Sydenham

WOLVERHAMPTON:
MacLaren, Wilson, Thomson, Flowers, Woodfield, Miller, Wharton, Woodruff, McIlmoyle, Knowles, Wagstaffe

Referee: A E Dimond (Harlow New Town)   *Attendance:* 23,226

Compiled by **BOB BRUNSKELL** from the *Echo* report. Jimmy Melia interviewed by **David Bull.** *Echo* photograph

PORTSMOUTH 2
SOUTHAMPTON 5

The "derby" match at Fratton on an inclement Saturday in early February was greatly anticipated, the excitement almost tangible, growing in both camps in the few days leading up to the match.

For the Saints, promotion to the First Division was still on the agenda and the team appeared brimming with confidence after demolishing Derby County 3-1 at The Dell the previous Saturday. Pompey, for their part, may well have had revenge on their minds after Saints had beaten them easily 3-0 at Fratton early in the previous season, although two Dell clashes since then had left things finely balanced with two draws.

In this match, Saints wasted no time in taking the game to the home side, roaring in front with two opportunist goals from the newish striking partnership of Martin Chivers and Norman Dean. The latter had waited a long time for the opportunity to partner his good friend upfront. Seven months younger than Dean, Chivers had got in a whole year earlier and, as you may recall from Matches 54-55, had booked one of the striker roles with a blazing run in 1963-64, which he had followed up twinned with George O'Brien in 1964-65. But now O'Brien was out with hepatitis and Dean had been taking his chance in style with five goals in as many games.

He made that six after 21 minutes. John Sydenham, endeavouring to mark his 300th appearance with a goal, drove a fierce shot goalwards from a tight angle but Dean got himself in the way and diverted the ball into the net, the ball cannoning in off his leg. Within a couple of minutes, Chivers had made it two. Taking advantage of a fumble by Pompey 'keeper, John Armstrong, he captured the ball and coolly tapped it home. Saints then became over-generous in their finishing and instead of going into what at that stage would surely have proved an unassailable lead they found themselves pegged back by Brian Lewis's fine flying header after a cross by the home side's danger-man, the speedy John McClelland.

Pompey's appetite to have a go and make a real fight of it was obviously not diminished by the interruption of the half-time interval and playing, as the *Echo*'s "Observer" noted, "with great zest," they got right back in it after a typically scorching drive from popular inside-left, "Albie" McCann. Picking up a ball threaded through by Johnny Gordon, McCann raced for goal pursued by Terry Paine, back-tracking like a hare. Paine finally caught up with McCann around the penalty area but in trying to dispossess him with a crafty back-heel, he didn't get enough on it. McCann seized his chance and rifled a rising shot into the far corner. Having been out-shouted and out-sung by the huge travelling Saints' contingent,

Ted Bates would need to call upon 22 members of this 1965-66 squad – and sign Forsyth and Webb – to gain promotion.
1 Kemp **2** Hollowbread **3** Godfrey **4** Walker **5** Hare **6** Traynor **7** Huxford **8** White **9** Williams **10** Wimshurst **11** Knapp **12** Chivers **13** Channon **14** Dean **15** Jones **16** Chadwick **17** Hollywood **18** Spencer **19** O'Brien **20** Paine **21** Melia **22** Sydenham

Division Two

the typically partisan Fratton Park hordes were re-awakened and Pompey responded as, for the next 10 minutes or more, the "Chimes" rang out.

It was, though, Saints' ability on the counter that was ultimately to see them come marching in. In the wind and rain and with Armstrong looking ever more uncertain in goal, Saints were able to use the pace of Paine, Chivers and Sydenham, the prompting of Jimmy Melia and the predatory instincts of Norman Dean.

So it was that, after 70 minutes, Saints snatched back the lead. Forsaking his right-wing, Paine drifted over to the left to centre for Jimmy Melia. Whether by accident or design, Melia dropped it straight to the feet of Dean. Norman, for the second time in the match, became "Johnny on-the-spot," gleefully notching his second goal in what was probably the turning point in a close-fought match. Saints now had their tails up and had rediscovered the confidence and the extra class they had shown in the game's opening stages. It was no real surprise, therefore, when Paine sent Dean scampering on a long run through the middle to shoot Saints 4-2 ahead, as he completed what *Observer* described as "the hat-trick of an opportunist." It was his first – with, of course, the added spice of being against the local rivals.

Those rivals were now, surely, beaten. There was going to be only one winner and the voices, red-and-white scarves, banners and golfing umbrellas were already being

Great! A local derby. It was a good win because there was a big atmosphere there … We didn't play very well the first-half and, the second-half, we were under a bit of pressure, but we came out on top… [My] first goal was Sydenham: it was one of them [where] I ran to the near post; Siddie had just hit it and it was coming over like a bullet about waist-high; so I just stuck my leg out. I either had to stick my leg out or keep out of the way. The second one Jimmy Melia made. He did a little jink inside the box and pulled it back and I just side-footed inside the near post where it had come from. And the third one, Terry [Paine] made. He put me through from the halfway-line for a hat-trick. I went through and, as the 'keeper came out, I just slid it past him. It was exciting.

Norman Dean

raised in celebration at Fratton's Milton End. Then Chivers joined the carnival with a goal at that end.

Receiving a throw-in, Pompey centre-half Frank Haydock, a recent big-money signing from Charlton Athletic, passed back to John Armstrong. This wasn't the smartest thing for Haydock to have done, as Armstrong was having something of a "Frank Haffey" afternoon.

For Armstrong, the ball once again took on the properties of petroleum jelly and once again it was "Big Chiv" who was to be his tormentor, wresting the ball away and seeming to take forever as he meandered round the unfortunate goalkeeper to slot the ball into a gaping, billowing net, behind which the Southampton fans paid homage.

Perhaps the Saints' win ended up being more emphatic than had looked likely at the time of Pompey's stirring fight-back. However, with the exception of the two spectacular efforts by Lewis and McCann, it was the Saints who had the more professional edge to their finishing and it was their eye for converting the half-chance that became the decisive factor in another excellent and historic victory over their deadly rivals.

Significantly, and most importantly, Saints' march toward promotion was firmly on track.

They could at last be playing in the Division from which their neighbours had once looked down at them for 30 long years.

PORTSMOUTH:

Armstrong, Wilson, Tindall, Gordon, Haydock, Harris, Lewis, Portwood, Edwards, McCann, McClelland

SOUTHAMPTON:

Forsyth, Hare, Williams, Wimshurst (Walker 73), Knapp, Huxford, Paine, Chivers, Dean, Melia, Sydenham

Referee: Mr E.D. Wallace (Swindon)   *Attendance:* 25,860

Compiled by **CHRIS NEWMAN** from being there and from the *Echo* report. Norman Dean interviewed by **David Bull**. *Echo* photograph

PLYMOUTH ARGYLE 2
SOUTHAMPTON 3

Saturday 7 May was scheduled to be the final day of the 1965-66 season for Division Two. But, thanks to postponements, the Saints went into it with three games to play - all of them away from home.

It tends to be the second game of the three - the following Monday at Brisbane Road (which is the match coming up next, of course) - that everybody talks about. But that is to under-value the other games in an unbeaten 12-match run-in, like the win at Plymouth on 7 May.

It was a gorgeous day when an epidemic of Saints' fans, breaking out in a red-and-white promotion-fever rash, set out on every excursion available for Plymouth. Saints had not enjoyed the best of fortunes at Home Park in recent years, so it was a tough enough assignment in any case, without the added pressure of the promotion issue and the fact that, for Argyle, their clashes with Saints were something of a derby match.

The air before kick-off crackled like static in an atmosphere similar to a cup-tie. Indeed, one Plymouth follower was led away by the local constabulary before a ball was even kicked. Two Saints' fans had got into the middle of the ground, proudly displaying a banner. This was too much for the local cove who ripped the standard apart in a riot of sticks and cloth.

Saints made a nervy start. This was to be another day when goalkeepers were susceptible to the wobblies. Ted Bates had tried to insure against frailties between the posts with his mid-season acquisition of Scottish international, Campbell Forsyth. But his insurance policy hadn't covered Forsyth's slipping in the tunnel as the team took the field and being shaken after hurting his head and knee.

This may well have accounted for the tentativeness in Saints' early play but there was no doubting the quality of Plymouth's opener as Argyle's left-winger, Cliff Jackson, lashed the ball high into the net to an appreciative roar from the home fans, who, like their team, were well and truly up for this game.

The Saints had been developing some durable qualities, though, this season. They now had a refusal-to-lie-down mentality to match their characteristic attractive football. They settled and Paine equalised, put in cleverly by Jimmy Melia, ably assisted by David Walker, back in, at No.6, for the injured Huxford.

On 37 minutes, Plymouth swept in front again. Local hero Mike Bickle, the footballing milkman who had scored on his debut at The Dell, scored again, suckering Saints into falling for a cleverly worked set-piece from a throw-in.

Obviously annoyed with themselves, Southampton came back strongly and a menacing John Sydenham hit a post. Within three minutes Saints were level with some delightful football, as a thrilling match see-sawed to and fro. It was left-back Denis Hollywood who shot through a narrow angle to score his first goal of the season, after some neat inter-change between Terry Paine and Martin Chivers.

Hollywood had returned in April, after a long injury, to form a mobile partnership at full-back with new signing David Webb from Leyton Orient. That's when the versatile Webb was not standing-in for Tony Knapp at centre-half in a season when nobody was ever-present and Ted Bates was constantly shuffling a pack of 24 to cope with the vagaries of form and fitness.

After a greatly entertaining first-half, the question, upon the resumption, was which team wanted it more?

It had been a game which could, indeed, have gone either way at one stage and, as Ted Bates pointed out, "the most dangerous period of the match for us, came when Plymouth took a 2-1 lead." He also praised the team's ability to hit back quickly and it was those

Possibly unaware that they were being photographed for a coaching manual,
Saints demonstrate a two-man wall for a Plymouth free-kick

Jimmy Melia runs through the Argyle defence to perform "a silly goal" for the coaching manual

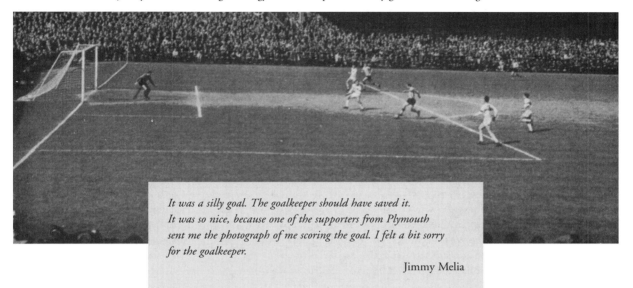

It was a silly goal. The goalkeeper should have saved it. It was so nice, because one of the supporters from Plymouth sent me the photograph of me scoring the goal. I felt a bit sorry for the goalkeeper.

Jimmy Melia

boomerang qualities that were to prove decisive here against the battling Pilgrims.

We Saints fans had become used, over the season, to some memorable goals, initially from Chivers and O'Brien and latterly from Dean and Paine.

This game, though, produced a more unlikely hero in the shape of bubbling Jimmy Melia, arch-schemer and master of the slide-rule pass, who'd not scored since September. He seemed to pop up everywhere on the Home Park pitch this afternoon and now did so running clear in the area and latching on to Sydenham's pass.

In all honesty, the shot didn't look anything like good enough but it turned out to be the winner. Melia might well have snatched at his effort and although the accuracy was there the power wasn't.

This was where a goalkeeping blip intervened. Plymouth 'keeper John Leiper appeared to have the ball covered but he let it slip under his body and it rolled agonisingly over the line as a mass of Saints' fans behind his goal encouraged it into the net.

It wasn't quite the final curtain. Melia had an opportunity for another but cramp claimed him as he was shaping up. And, as Argyle pressed hard to try and salvage something from the game, Jackson drew a magnificent save from the now fully-recovered Forsyth.

Saints, holding on to the end, were superbly marshalled from the centre of defence by skipper Tony Knapp.

So, it was Saints who whipped the Devon Cream and Jimmy Melia, when interviewed afterwards, who wore a grin as wide as Plymouth Sound.

Perhaps, though, it was summed up best by an Argyle regular who thought it the "best match we've had here this season."

And for Saints, as we shall see in the next report, it was more than good enough.

PLYMOUTH ARGYLE:

Lieper, Book, Baird, Hoare, Nelson, Newman, Jones, Neale, Bickle, Piper, Jackson

SOUTHAMPTON:

Forsyth, Webb, Hollywood, White, Knapp, Walker, Paine, Chivers, Dean, Melia, Sydenham

Referee: Mr L. Callaghan (Merthyr Tydfil)   *Attendance:* 18,992

Compiled by **CHRIS NEWMAN** from being there and from the *Echo* report. Jimmy Melia interviewed by **David Bull**. Photographs by kind permission of John Barlee – two of his several photos of this game to be found in D.F. Rowe's coaching manual

LEYTON ORIENT 1
SOUTHAMPTON 1

Leyton Orient's Brisbane Road pitch was transformed into a boiling, dancing sea of red and white on a balmy spring night in 1966 as thousands of jubilant Saints fans celebrated a result which brought top-flight football to Southampton for the first time.

Players were carried shoulder high to the dressing-room but the main focus for hero worship was one of the club's all-time favourites Terry Paine, whose goal clinched a 1-1 draw and the point Saints needed to join Manchester City in the First Division. It was the dawning of an extraordinary period in Paine's life for two months later he was to figure in the final stages of England's World Cup-winning effort.

At Leyton Orient on Monday 9 May, Paine, who normally laid goals on with his precision- crossing, headed a priceless one himself to make promotion a near certainty. Barring a six-goal defeat in their last game at Manchester City, Saints had arrived in Division I for the first time in their 81-year history. The fact that their last game was away to the leaders, and that they began the game at Orient a point behind their main promotion rivals Coventry, underlined just how important it was.

They had a better goal average than Coventry, and knew that a draw would almost certainly be enough. But the way Orient started up and their continuing determination for long into the game, made for a tough, tense night for Saints and their supporters. One of the most nerve-wracking perhaps in their history.

Saints had to fight their way from behind before they could glimpse the promised land. Much to the consternation of the team and their fans, Orient scored after just seven minutes. In what had been a nerve-jangling run-in to the season, it was the third game running that Saints had fallen behind. They'd come back twice before. Would they do it again?

David Webb, a bright young Cockney prospect with the pugnacious crew-cutted looks of a street urchin, had never finished in a losing Saints side since his transfer from Orient two months before. He had the honour of leading Saints out against his old club and even got to toss the coin. But after that the true captain Tony Knapp took over and the powerful, whole-hearted centre-half led by example, as usual.

Saints made a nervous start and were forced back by lively opponents who were rock bottom of the Second Division and playing only for their pride. Campbell Forsyth had to come racing off his line to save at the feet of Gregory as he broke through. When Allan ran clear in Orient's next attack, out came Forsyth again but this time the Scot was well beaten by the midfield man's cool, precise finish.

Many of the 12,000 Saints supporters who had made the mass pilgrimage to East London missed it. They were still battling to get through the clogged-up approach roads to the ground. The game was fast and furious and the great volume of sound coming from the packed terraces was from the away fans and it roused Saints from their early malaise.

> *A fluke I think. It was a punt from Campbell Forsyth. And, as it's coming, I read it – everybody might miss it. I've got on my bike early and it's bounced. It's bounced over the top of them and I just head it and stick it in the back of the net*
>
> Terry Paine

Terry Paine reads the bounce to head the vital equaliser

Division Two

Paine and Jimmy Melia had Orient back-pedalling as they swapped passes with Melia driving on and forcing a mass scramble in front of Rouse's Orient goal. It was cut and thrust but much of the thrust came from Orient's tricky left-winger Dick Flem whose pace and trickery was a constant threat. There was a roar of anticipation when Paine forced a free-kick on the edge of the box and picked himself up to plant the ball on Norman Dean's head, but the centre-forward was high and wide. Le Flem responded with a scorching 30-yarder which fizzed past the post.

Several minutes of sustained Orient pressure brought the best out of Knapp, who was a man mountain at the heart of the defence repulsing the aerial threat from the men in blue shirts. But Orient could have gone two up when Saints checked expecting an offside against David Metchick. But to their mortification the flag stayed down and Metchick went on, letting Saints off the hook by shooting over the bar. Not until the 30th minute did Saints test Orient 'keeper Rouse with Paine demanding a relatively straight-forward save. Forsyth then had to produce the save of the match to keep out another menacing effort from Le Flem, who was later to make a name for himself with Nottingham Forest.

Orient were still carrying the game to Saints after the break but all that changed on 52 minutes when Saints equalised. Forsyth punted a long clearance upfield and Ferry, the Orient centre-half, badly miscued his header back to his own 'keeper. As the ball hung in the air, Paine was in like a flash to nod home.

The massed ranks of Saints fans erupted with a volume of sound which they kept up for fully 10 minutes. And as they shook the rooftops around the ground, Saints visibly grew in confidence. They took control of the game, beginning to play it at their own pace. Dean then Martin Chivers extended Rouse and although Orient remained a danger, Saints were containing them with a strengthening grip at the back.

When Gregory and Le Flem threatened, David Walker tidied up immaculately. As the final seconds ticked away, the referee blew for a throw-in. Many Saints fans, thinking he had blown for time, invaded the pitch and had to be sent back. The moment Walker took the throw, the last whistle went and celebrations, unprecedented in Saints history, began.

With a disciplined defensive display, Saints held Manchester City to a goalless draw in the last match at Maine Road.

It left them five points behind the champions but, more important, one ahead of third-placed Coventry.

And then the fans came onto the pitch, confident that their team would not lose by six goals at Maine Road

LEYTON ORIENT:
Rouse, Jones, Forsyth, Allan, Ferry, Sorrell, Gregory, Carter, Smith, Metchick, Le Flem

SOUTHAMPTON:
Forsyth, Webb, Hollywood, White, Knapp, Walker, Paine, Chivers, Dean, Melia, Sydenham

Referee: D Laing (Preston)   *Attendance:* 19,839

Compiled by **BOB BRUNSKELL** from the *Echo* report. Terry Paine interviewed by **David Bull.** *Echo* photographs

SOUTHAMPTON 6
WEST HAM UNITED 2

SAINTS HAMMER THE WORLD CUP WINNERS! No, I haven't just received a severe bump on the head, been indulging in fantasy football or over-indulging in the bottle, for this is in effect what happened one winter's Saturday early in 1967, when the Saints' compact, yet atmospheric, home ground once more became a ding-dong Dell for a seething full house of 30,123.

West Ham United were the visitors. In the Hammers' team that afternoon were Bobby Moore, Geoff Hurst and Martin Peters - the famous trio who had had such a massive part to play in England's historic World Cup Final triumph over arch-rivals West Germany six months earlier. West Ham were rather more than a three-man show, though. FA Cup-winners in 1964 and winners of the European Cup-Winners-Cup in 1965, their star-studded line-up included box-of-tricks striker Johnny Byrne, with 11 England caps to his credit; two other England caps, in winger Peter Brabrook and centre-half Ken Brown; and the agile Jim Standen who doubled as West Ham 'keeper and Worcestershire cricketer. For good

measure, a promising young midfielder by the name of Trevor Brooking warmed the subs' bench.

Saints, too, had their very own World Cup winner, of course, in the shape of Terry Paine, who had played with credit, despite concussion, in a memorable group match against Mexico. And it had been mainly from his crosses that Ron Davies had been finding First Division nets and was keeping neck-and-neck with Geoff Hurst for the Division's top scorer. Saints had taken to the top flight well enough for early doors wins over Sunderland, Blackpool and Villa and to follow this, in October, by demolishing Sheffield Wednesday and by turning the form-book upside down to win at Leeds.

Manager Bates and trainer Gallagher inspect their squad – with two new players in Ron Davies and David Thompson – for the First Division.
Back row (left to right) Webb, Davies, Forsyth, Gurr, Chivers, Walker.
Middle row: Huxford, Dean, Paton, Jones, Wimshurst, Knapp, Channon,.
Front: Hare, White, Thompson, Hollywood, Paine, Melia, Sydenham, Kemp

Division One

But in truth they had at times struggled. The best teams and players in the country had more than once exploited Saints' shortage of top-level experience at the back, where they had not been helped by losing Campbell Forsyth long-term. When he broke his leg in mid-September, Ted Bates had made the famous signing (of which you were forewarned at Match No. 56) of Dave MacLaren.

There could be little doubt that many of those in the capacity crowd – their largest yet in the First Division – had come more for a look at the glamorous visitors, the Division's leading exponents of attacking football, than to watch a home side with only one point from their last four games.

And yet West Ham were perhaps there for the taking, still reeling, as they were, from the midweek shock of a 3-1 FA Cup defeat at Third Division Swindon. Evidence of Hammers' hangover was there for all to see when "Budgie" Byrne danced through on his own in the first minute; but, with bags of time to beat MacLaren, he completely messed up his shot. The Hammers were made to pay almost instantly, for Saints built a multi-player attack which finished with left-back Denis Hollywood driving firmly past Standen.

Tasting first blood, Saints began to pour forward, looking dangerously hungry for more goals. If MacLaren could be erratic among flashes of brilliance, one thing he did have was a decent long kick. Davies took advantage of one of those clearances on 18 minutes. Although known better for his command of football's airways, he showed good ground control and composure after beating Brown to the ball, before shooting Saints two ahead. Nine minutes later, Paine's dribbling skills had West Ham all of a dither with the normally ice-cool Bobby Moore conceding a penalty which Paine himself converted. An irresistible player in this sort of mood, Paine then crossed for Chivers to head number four after what had been an amazing 31 minutes.

Twelve minutes after the break Hammer's frustration with Paine surfaced again, this time Eddie Bovington

bringing down the tormentor. Terry clinically despatched his second penalty and Saints' fifth goal and it wasn't until Saints had gained this unassailable nap-hand that West Ham finally broke their duck through Hurst on the hour. Chivers made it six, though, when after a build-up in which John Sydenham was prominent, he showed the deftness of footwork for which this gentle giant had become renowned. Jack Burkett's 25-yarder, a minute later, was spectacular but no more than academic.

West Ham's pride had taken a severe 6-2 pounding. There would be no "bubble blowing" in East London come the evening.

Ironically, in the final shake-down, West Ham finished only a couple of points ahead of Saints. But that mere statistic disguises the drama of the relegation battle that was to become a Saints' trademark in those early First Division years – and again, of course, in the 1990s. Despite not being awarded the credit that they had deserved, Southampton had brought some marvellous entertainment to the top division.

Yet it was to go almost to the wire, when the second last game - coming up next - would decide whether the Saints' obvious talent in attack would again grace the elite the following season.

Martin Chivers makes it six

SOUTHAMPTON:

MacLaren, Webb, Hollywood, Wimshurst, Knapp, Walker, Paine, Chivers, Davies, Melia, Sydenham

WEST HAM:

Standen, Bovington, Burkett, Peters, Brown, Moore, Brabrook, Boyce, Byrne, Hurst, Sissons

Referee: Mr K.A. Wynn (Wolverhampton)　　　　　　　　　　　　　　　*Attendance:* 30,123

Compiled by **CHRIS NEWMAN** from being there and from the *Echo* report. *Echo* photographs

---

SOUTHAMPTON 2
NOTTINGHAM FOREST 1

Previous reports have illustrated how Southampton had gained their top flight status in style, only to experience problems in retaining it. Saints had some of the finest forwards in the country; but even in their final days as a Second Division club, before the giant upward step was made, pundits were tut-tutting, knowing glances were exchanged across bar-rooms and fingers were wagged at what was seen as a suspect defence. This despite the likes of barnstorming full-back David Webb and the boundlessly energetic centre-half and captain, Tony Knapp.

At the start of the campaign, the fixture list stretched out like an Archers Road laden with cup-ties. For a small club like the Saints, entering the big time of the First Division - in those days truly one of the great Leagues of world football, containing the very best that the British Isles could offer, with stars like Best, Law and Charlton, Gilzean and Greaves and the West Ham trio of the previous report – it was much like having a Cup game every week.

Every team had its match-winners. Even Newcastle, Villa and Blackpool, who were destined to contest the two dreaded relegation spots with Saints, all had players capable of turning a particular match on their day. Despite their defensive shortcomings, as charted in the previous report, and their dependence on how many goals they could get out of the golden-maned Davies, Saints had eked out three wins and a draw in the 12 games since the West Ham show and were still in with a chance of staying in the top division. This really was the only place for the likes of Davies, Paine and Chivers.

The big problem was that, if Saints dazzled in one game, thrilling supporters with a prize scalp, they would inevitably follow this with a losing sequence – three defeats on the trot after that West Ham game – and, although more evenly contested than today's plastic Premiership, this was a ruthless First Division, with no prisoners taken. Manager Ted Bates did what he always did in tight situations. He went out and bought modestly but masterfully. I often think of Ted as something of a star-maker and the new 'keeper, Eric Martin from Dunfermline, did not disappoint. Joining him was a creative and brave midfielder from Blackpool, Hugh Fisher. The "Hughie shuffle" was about to become another Dell byword.

The turning point, however, in a heart-pounding survival struggle, was reached on the Wednesday after Easter when West Bromwich, 3-2 winners at the Hawthorns on the Monday, came to The Dell for the "return" and took a 2-0 lead. Saints fought back to gain a priceless point, the equaliser coming from the unlikely source of "Docker" Walker, who swept home from within a packed penalty area for what would remain, after 231 games, his only goal for the Club. Once more, though, the

side flattered to deceive, going out and losing four of their next five games.

It was all then down to the penultimate wire, with Nottingham Forest visiting The Dell on a sunny May Saturday. Despite being without England forwards Joe Baker and Frank Wignall on the day, Forest were not to be sniffed at. Having lost an FA Cup semi-final, the previous Saturday, they would finish runners-up to champions Manchester United.

It's down to Terry Paine again, this time to preserve the side's First Division status. Some of his team-mates can hardly bear to look as he walks back in readiness to take the fateful penalty.

There was a predictably good crowd for this vital game and there seemed to be a confident air around the ground as from the outset the Dell faithful roared them on. Inspired by their expectant excitement, the Saints took the lead when Martin Chivers steered in a superb header making the most of a cross in a career of zillions made by Terry Paine. Southampton were playing with a confident flow and defensively this may well have been the day they earned their First Division wings. Indeed the *Echo's* "Observer" reported that Webb "was a tower of strength," while Knapp, back after injury, "held the middle well." There were accolades, too, for the defensive efforts of Fisher and Hollywood. Fisher was also praised for his contribution to "an attacking triangle that puzzled the Forest a good deal," – a triangle completed by Paine, with "an outstanding display," and Chivers, who "had a particularly good game" alongside Davies, "a constant threat" with both head and feet. It looked good for Saints.

Division One

Until the 66th minute that is. Then Forest inside-forward John Barnwell (still influential in the game today as Chief Executive of the League Managers Association) drove in firmly after collecting a wayward Knapp clearance. All credit to the Saints: they kept their composure and perhaps fortune does indeed favour the brave. During the second-half and before the Forest equalised, Walker had handled on the blind side of referee Bye. No pen. Ten minutes after Barnwell's goal, however, Jimmy Melia fell to earth after a penalty box tackle by Terry Hennessey and the coveted spot-kick was to the Saints awarded.

Paine, with his usual cocksure attitude, placed the ball on the spot. Facing him was Peter Grummitt, a goalkeeper with good reasons to remember facing Paine and Southampton – and if you don't remember those nine reasons, then you've allowed those two memorable Matches of the Millennium (Nos. 52-53) to pass you by: "I always remember going back down there. They always used to sing about the 5-0 drubbing," Grummitt recalls.

It all made for a tense wait. I seem to recall that it was Walker (among one or two others) who knelt in silent prayer, not bearing to look, head bowed and looking towards the several-shillings enclosure in hope of salvation. After all, Terry had been known to miss.

Salvation came rolling in like the sound of thunder. It was in fact the Dell crowd erupting in joyous celebration as Paine, so often the saviour, dispatched the penalty-kick

beyond Grummitt's reach – and also put the Saints beyond the reach of Aston Villa who had lost 4-2 at Everton and would be joining Blackpool in the long drop to the Second Division.

To rub it in, Saints would see off Villa 6-2 in the remaining game, when four goals from Davies would give him, outright, the top-scorer spot that he had been contesting with Geoff Hurst. The 1966-67 season will always be remembered for Davies's remarkable 37 goals in his inaugural season in the First Division – exactly half of the team's tally as they completed that awesome fixture list with 74 goals, only 11 fewer than their promotion total the season before and 10 more than runners-up Forest.

That goals-for total is a testimony to the way the side went about retaining their new found status: by never once burying their principles and by always trying therefore to play attacking, entertaining and - in the finest tradition of Ted Bates's sides – *good* football.

Ron Davies, Ted Bates's signing
of the season
and, indeed, of the Millennium

End-of-term report

We have learned many things during our first look at the First Division. I like to think we have learned our lessons well. In fact it is fair to say that a few months ago we would not perhaps have beaten Forest… We knew it would be hard in the First Division. The standard is tremendously high and there is not such a thing as an easy game. But I believe we would have finished in a much healthier position in the table but for the injury that robbed us of goalkeeper Campbell Forsyth. That was a bad blow for us and it took us quite some time to recover. Now we end this season a lot wiser than we started and hopeful that we shall do better next season.

Ted Bates

SOUTHAMPTON:
Martin, Webb, Hollywood, Fisher, Knapp, Walker, Paine, Chivers, Davies, Melia, Sydenham

NOTTINGHAM FOREST:
Grummitt, Hindley, Winfield, Hennessey, McKinley, Newton (Brindley, 55), Kear, Barnwell, Chapman, Lyons, Moore

Referee: Mr P. Bye (Bedford)   *Attendance:* 25,305

Compiled by **CHRIS NEWMAN** from being there and from the *Echo* report. Ted Bates's post-match comments recorded by Norman Giller for an unidentified national. Peter Grummitt's recollection recorded by **David Bull.** *Echo* photographs

CHELSEA 2
SOUTHAMPTON 6

They called it capital punishment. For Chelsea, a 6-2 defeat by Saints in their own Stamford Bridge fortress in September 1967, was nothing short of humiliating and quite literally something they had never experienced before. The margin of the scoreline represented a record First Division defeat for the Blues at Stamford Bridge.

For Saints it was such sweet revenge for two comprehensive defeats by Chelsea in 1966-67, their debut season in Division I. And Ron Davies, who had scored against every team except Chelsea in his first sensational season in the top flight, perhaps had a point of his own to make. And he made it in some style, destroying the home side with a 17-minute hat-trick.

Then Chivers nipped a possible Blues revival firmly in the bud after Peter Osgood had magically stirred up hope for his side with a goal just after the break.

Chelsea had almost caught Saints cold in the first minute when Bobby Tambling intercepted a clearance from Jimmy Gabriel only to drag his shot wide from a good position. Ironically, Ted Bates had reported to his Board in August 1966 that he would like to buy Tambling for £80,000 – but he had settled instead for Davies at £55,000. The Chelsea attack boasted an abundance of talent – not only Osgood and Tambling, but Charlie Cooke and Tommy Baldwin, too.

Yet Saints contained them superbly, turning defence into attack with speed and vision. The ploy of midfield general Jimmy Melia was to sweep the ball out to the flanks where Paine and John Sydenham ran Chelsea ragged. And when they crossed balls into the box, Davies and Chivers wreaked havoc.

Ron Davies demonstrates how to score "with a soaring, downward header"

That was brilliant! Like Rimmer [in Match No. 64], he stayed on his line. Thanks, Bonetti! Whoosh!

Ron Davies

I broke my leg. My first game back was against Southampton. at home and we lost 6-2. I scored two goals – but Ron Davies scored four! Great player, wasn't he? Ron wasn't the biggest centre-forward, but he just used to hang in the air there. He'd get up there about five minutes before the ball was coming and say "Just stick it there and I'll knock it in for you." Unbelievable!

Peter Osgood

Davies began his incredible goal burst after six minutes, stabbing home after an astute flick across goal by Chivers had disarmed the Chelsea defence. The Welshman was renowned for his great power in the air, but for a big fellow he was nimble with the ball at his feet. He scored his second after robbing his marker Colin Waldron and outsmarting goalkeeper Peter Bonetti before shooting calmly into an empty net. His third on 23 minutes was pure Davies, Paine placing a corner with perfection and Davies striking with a soaring, downward header.

But Chelsea were not through. Osgood, who had spent much of the previous season out with a broken leg, showed that he had lost none of his old magic as Chelsea looked for a way back after the interval. Three minutes later, Ossie wrong-footed four Southampton defenders then took the ball around Campbell Forsyth to open his side's account.

For 15 minutes Saints had their backs against the wall but the defence held out. It was superbly marshalled by Jimmy Gabriel, who had arrived in the close season from Everton.

Initially displacing Tony Knapp, he was being watched at Stamford Bridge by the Scottish selectors.

The Chelsea storm was gathering when Saints, or to be more precise Chivers, struck with a double counter-

CHELSEA ROUTED BY 6-2 SAINTS

By " OBSERVER "

punch which had the London side reeling on the ropes. Big Chiv made it 5-1 with goals in the 63rd and 65th minutes, both laid on by Paine, the first with valuable assistance from Melia. Chivers looked like joining Davies on a hat-trick when he powered through the entire Chelsea defence only to be denied at the last by a brave Bonetti. Chelsea, who had begun the game with a sweeper and reverted, in panic, to 4-2-4 after Davies's early burst, were in disarray.

Osgood provided a glimmer of respect to the scoreline when he rose to head a second goal but two minutes later and with just seven minutes left on the clock, Davies nodded his fourth, and Saints' sixth, goal to underline their total supremacy on the day.

Chelsea supporters, like their players, didn't like being taken to the cleaners on their own patch. In the days when the gathering clouds of football hooliganism were beginning to take shape, several trouble-makers were ejected from the ground. Genial Bill Rawlings, then the *Echo* reporter on Saints, was at pains to point out that, "of those who were led out, I was relieved to see that none wore the red and white of Southampton."

So the match verdict can focus on events on the pitch and on Davies's contribution in particular. Every Southampton player was a hero, but none more so than their centre-forward who had again demonstrated how wise Ted Bates had been to sign him rather than Tambling – and to save £25,000 into the bargain.

Martin Chivers, whose two goals – like those of Osgood – were overshadowed by Davies's four

CHELSEA:

Bonetti, Hinton, McCreadie, Hollins, Waldron, Harris, Cooke, Baldwin, Osgood, McMillan, Tambling

SOUTHAMPTON:

Forsyth, Webb, Hollywood, Fisher, Gabriel, Walker, Paine, Chivers, Davies, Melia, Sydenham

Referee: N.C.H. Burtenshaw (Great Yarmouth)   *Attendance:* 31,876

Compiled by **BOB BRUNSKELL** from the *Echo* report – with additional material, from the Club's minutes and interviews with Ron Davies and Peter Osgood – by **David Bull.** *Echo* photographs

SOUTHAMPTON 1
LEICESTER CITY 5

If this fine compendium does nothing else it does at least establish beyond reasonable doubt that when, and wherever, two or more Saints' supporters are gathered together, be it over a couple of beers or more in the local, round a blazing domestic hearth, across a restaurant table with brandy and cigars, or even clinging to a raft in the Indian Ocean, there is no shortage of memorable games to reminisce over. Awesome goals, scintillating runs, majestic passing movements, all are there to be picked over, dissected and relished. Quite naturally, along with the good, comes the bad: the "if only" moments, the inexplicable individual performances from Hell, the refereeing decision that cost "us" the game, and… buried deep in the subconscious of 20,000-odd seasoned campaigners there is the match that, like the "Scottish play", must not be mentioned.

We break that taboo here because a publication such as this cannot flinch the awful truth and, while we regret any trauma that may be relived, we pray that the sufferers will understand that younger devotees must learn that there is more to supporting Saints than watching their heroes smack three late, unexpected goals past Liverpool.

Saints' second term in Division One, 1967–68, had got off to a fairly good start. The 6-2 win at Chelsea may have been exceptional but the goals were generally flowing in both directions (with Ron Davies and Martin Chivers just about keeping the goals-for column in the black) and by October, having been as high as sixth, Saints were settling comfortably into mid-table. The arrival of Jimmy Gabriel from Everton had been a distinct plus, and the return of goalkeeper Campbell Forsyth, who had spent most of he previous season recovering from a broken leg, was welcome; though many thought that the young Eric Martin, having survived the previous season's baptism of fire, should have started the season in goal.

The visitors on 14 October were Leicester City, who had been a mid-table side since anyone could remember. It comes as a surprise to go back through the records and find that Leicester hadn't been mid-table perpetually since the Football League was founded. In fact the only remarkable thing about Leicester had been their consistency at staying in mid-table and the fact that they possessed, arguably, the world's greatest goalkeeper, Gordon Banks; or rather had possessed, because that season Banks had been sold to Stoke City for an earth-shattering £52,000, to make way for the precocious, teenage, Peter Shilton.

The game kicked-off on a wet, slippery pitch with a strong, gusting wind blowing driving rain in over the Milton End. Saints dominated the early play and Leicester appeared to be reconciled to their doing so. In fact, in an age when so many sides went away with no higher aim than going home with a point, City gave the impression they would have been delighted just to go home —sooner rather than later.

Saints opened the scoring with a scrappy Davies goal, and continued to plough through the mud quite happily and the drenched spectators on the Archers and Milton ends perhaps decided that, while this was never going to be a classic, Leicester were there for the taking.

This said, Shilton was confirming Leicester's confidence in him with every attack and, with the surface becoming increasingly saturated, the game began to slow and the ball started to sink so deep into the turf the players were having to dig it out with their feet. It was not a pretty spectacle. Then, as the first-half dragged to a close, Leicester's centre-forward, converted winger Mike Stringfellow, equalised.

The second-half went much like the first, although Saints had lost the advantage of the wind. The *Echo's* "Observer" attested to Saints having "80 per cent of the play territorially.

"For long periods there was no one but Forsyth in the Saints' half of the field as everything was thrown into attack in an effort to wipe out Leicester's lead." Lead? Well yes, it would seem that every time Shilton made a save the ball would be cleared up field for a Leicester attack that would end up with the ball in the back of the Archer's net.

Stringfellow netted twice, Tewley had put Leicester ahead and Jackie Sinclair knocked the ball past a stranded Forsyth for the fourth. Saints continued to press, but appeared incapable of getting the ball past Shilton, as much through mischance as any brilliance on the part of the young 'keeper.

The crowd, as bemused as the Leicester players by the score-line, began a steady drift out of the ground and not many who had left when the *coup de grace* was delivered will regret it, while many of those who were witness still, on occasion, sit bolt upright in the middle of the night, the hairs on the back of their neck bristling, and make an involuntary exclamation; such as "NO!"

Observer, a man of iron nerve, described it thus:

> Shilton was no doubt as surprised as anyone when his hefty clearance, carried by the wind, caught Forsyth in no-man's land, unable to reach the bounce of the ball and powerless to stop it going over his head into the net.

Division One

> *I've been asked about it hundreds of times. I blame another ex-goalkeeper, Len Stansbridge [by then the Dell groundsman]. Whitening was no good to him. He didn't do it with a wheel and a barrow. He had to paint the lines… You may think it an excuse, but I'm convinced, to this day, that the ball hit one of those hard-baked, painted lines and it* **shot.** *It didn't just bounce high: I've been beaten with weaker shots, but this was unbelievable!*
>
> Campbell Forsyth

> *I smacked it down the middle and it landed more or less on the edge of the box and it bounced but skidded and the wind took it and it took off and went over his head and bounced in the net… I felt very sorry for Campbell Forsyth, actually – not at the time I didn't because I didn't realise I'd scored. I thought Mike Stringfellow had knocked it in… I don't take any satisfaction from it because I know how I'd feel if it happened to me… It was just a complete fluke and the conditions added to it.*
>
> Peter Shilton

Forsyth has excused himself by placing the blame on the "hard-baked lines" of groundsman Len Stansbridge. Quoting him in *Dell Diamond*, David Bull cruelly refutes the claim:

> Nice try, Campbell,
> but the video evidence appears
> to be against you. Watch the Saints' video again
> and try convincing me that the ball bounces anywhere
> near any line.

Which misses the point entirely. Shilton's clearance was dropping on the edge of the penalty area, Stringfellow was ambling after it and, given the conditions, Forsyth had to beat him to the ball or stick on his line and wait for the Leicester forward to scoop the ball out of the slime and, unopposed, have a free run at goal. Forsyth did the obvious and attacked the ball. Neither Forsyth nor

Stringfellow could have anticipated what actually happened. And what happened was that the ball *bounced.*

It was probably the first time in the game: it certainly was the first time in the second-half that it had rebounded high enough to pass over somebody's head.

Every time the ball had hit the ground previously it had sunk in the mud, so Forsyth's claim that it had hit the pitch-marking was an obvious deduction. If not the line, then what did the ball ricochet off?

Forsyth vindicated then? Not entirely, though it was somewhat harsh, given that the rest of the defence had gone AWOL for the goals, that he was selected for the drop, along with John Sydenham, for the following fixture away to West Ham.

Eric Martin was given the posts, and Saints won, 1-0. Their first clean sheet of the season.

SOUTHAMPTON:
Forsyth, Webb, Hollywood, Fisher, Gabriel, Walker, Paine, Chivers, Davies, Melia, Sydenham

LEICESTER CITY:
Shilton, Rodrigues, Norman, Roberts, Sjoberg, Bell, Sinclair, Nish, Stringfellow, Gibson, Trewley

Referee: Mr W.J. Gow (Swansea)   *Attendance:* 21,719

Compiled by **DAVE JUSON** from being there and from the *Echo* report; and with reference to *Dell Diamond*. Peter Shilton interviewed by John Hughes for the Saints' *Official History* video. Campbell Forsyth interviewed by **David Bull.** Photographs from **Duncan Holley**'s collection

MANCHESTER UNITED 1
SOUTHAMPTON 4

"The finest centre-forward in Europe"

That's how the great old Manchester United manager Matt Busby described Ron Davies after the blond-haired bomber destroyed the Red Devils with an awesome four-goal display at Old Trafford in August 1969.

Saints had begun the 1969-70 season badly, losing their first two games (home to West Bromwich Albion and away to Wolverhampton Wanderers) and a trip to Manchester United, still bathing in the after-glow of their European Cup triumph, was daunting to say the least.

To put the match more into perspective the great United side who had beaten Benfica in the European Cup Final at Wembley just 15 months before, was starting to fray around the edges and Wilf McGuinness had just taken over, with Busby stepping upstairs. The side who plunged 4-1 to Saints in front of 47,000 shell-shocked United fans still contained the likes of Best, Law, Charlton, Crerand and Kidd but some of the older hands, like the redoubtable centre-half Billy Foulkes who had survived the Munich air disaster, were getting long in the tooth.

The ruthless manner in which Davies exploited Foulkes's slowing reactions hastened the end of his career at Old Trafford, something which Davies derived no pleasure from. "It was a memorable game for me," he said, "but it probably finished Bill and I was sad about that because he was a fine old centre-half." Ian Ure would arrive from Arsenal the next week and Foulkes would never play for United again.

That Saints were to turn the tables so dramatically on United was down to a number of circumstances. Manager Ted Bates had radically changed the team's preparation for a game by taking them to train at the Lilleshall Recreation Centre a couple of days beforehand. Saints had struck on a problem, rare under Bates, of how to score goals. After a 2-1 midweek defeat at Wolverhampton, the manager left out two young forwards Mick Judd and Bobby Stokes –

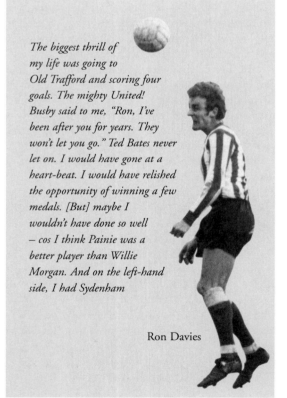

The biggest thrill of my life was going to Old Trafford and scoring four goals. The mighty United! Busby said to me, "Ron, I've been after you for years. They won't let you go." Ted Bates never let on. I would have gone at a heart-beat. I would have relished the opportunity of winning a few medals. [But] maybe I wouldn't have done so well – cos I think Painie was a better player than Willie Morgan. And on the left-hand side, I had Sydenham

Ron Davies

who'd made respective Easter Monday debuts in 1968 and 1969 - and recalled Frank Saul and John Sydenham.

Arriving from Tottenham in exchange for Chivers at the start of 1968, Saul had seldom kept Mick Channon out of the No. 8 shirt. But Channon's season was yet to start, so Saul had another chance. Sydenham had a different problem: in the First Division, manager Bates had often been prepared to sacrifice his attacking assets in order to play the more defensively-equipped David Thompson or even to play a defender like Jimmy Gabriel at No.11.

So it was a bold move to opt for Sydenham's attacking speed at Old Trafford. Speed had always been his greatest asset. Had he been able to harness that with a greater percentage of accurate crosses, he would, like Paine, have achieved acclaim.

But against Manchester United everything clicked into place for the Saints No. 11. His crossing was precise and deadly and Davies, with his peerless power and potency in the air, did the rest with his head. Collectively the two of them enjoyed perhaps their finest hour at Old Trafford.

On a superb playing surface, Saints boldly carried the game to United and reaped a bonus surely beyond their wildest dreams. To a degree their hand had been forced by an early United goal, whipped home from close range by Willie Morgan after Kidd had flicked on a free kick.

Saints' response was devastating. Within four minutes they had equalised. Fisher picked out Sydenham with a cross-field pass and the winger went full tilt at Shay Brennan, sweeping past him on the outside and carrying on to the by-line from where he cut back a centre which Davies headed home.

Division One

From that point Saints took control and poor Brennan was to have no answer to Sydenham's pace and footwork while the veteran Foulkes was constantly outfought and outjumped by Davies whose extraordinary spring off the ground had been perfected during his early footballing days at Chester where the coach had him jumping over hurdles with sandbags strapped to his back.

After 16 minutes the same combination gave Saints the lead. Sydenham, receiving a diagonal ball from Paine, got in an early cross from which Davies produced a sharp downward header. United 'keeper Jimmy Rimmer laid a hand on the ball and Burns, scrambling back, succeeded only in helping it over the line. It looked like an own goal but later it was ascertained that Davies's header had crossed the line before Rimmer touched it.

United fans weren't used to seeing their side go behind and didn't like it and they soon turned on their own players. Ironically the main target of their jeers was the great Denis Law who was getting short-changed by a relatively untried Saints defender, a young Irishman Tony Byrne.

Southampton's third goal came on the hour. By now Sydenham was on fire. He had wings on his heels. When Jimmy Gabriel picked him out, Sydenham carried the ball up to Brennan, stopped and invited him to take it, then impudently side-stepped the bemused right-back before clipping it on to Davies's head....3-1. The Welshman scored his fourth goal in the last minute, reminding us that he could get them on the ground as well as in the air.

Foulkes was stranded by a quick Southampton break-out from defence. Davies, confronted by the hapless Brennan, turned past him before slipping a shot beyond Rimmer.

It was the second time Davies had scored four times for Saints in a match. When he had previously done this in Match No. 62 – that 6-2 win at Chelsea early in the 1967-68 season - he had gone on to finish as joint top-scorer in the First Division, alongside George Best with 28 goals. But not this time. He would score only eight more goals in 1969-70. His superstar scoring days were over but he would still total 153 goals in 277 games for Southampton.

Big Ron certainly gave Saints his best years before joining Portsmouth.

He was eventually signed by United in 1974 – after Matt Busby, his great admirer, had gone for a second time – but he never started a game at Old Trafford.

For Davies the move had come five years too late.

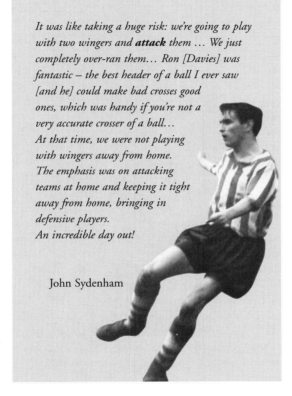

*It was like taking a huge risk: we're going to play with two wingers and **attack** them ... We just completely over-ran them... Ron [Davies] was fantastic – the best header of a ball I ever saw [and he] could make bad crosses good ones, which was handy if you're not a very accurate crosser of a ball...*
At that time, we were not playing with wingers away from home. The emphasis was on attacking teams at home and keeping it tight away from home, bringing in defensive players.
An incredible day out!

John Sydenham

MANCHESTER UNITED:
Rimmer, Brennan, Burns, Crerand, Foulkes, Sadler, Morgan, Kidd, Charlton, Law, Best

SOUTHAMPTON:
Gurr, Jones, Hollywood, Fisher, McGrath, Gabriel, Paine, Saul, Davies, Byrne, Sydenham

Referee: E P Jennings (Worcester)   *Attendance:* 47,436

Compiled by **BOB BRUNSKELL** from the *Echo* report and an interview with Ron Davies. The boxed reflections by Davies have been composited from that interview and another one by **David Bull**, who also interviewed John Sydenham. *Echo* photographs

SOUTHAMPTON 2
ROSENBORG 0

Saints made their European debut in the 1969-70 season courtesy of a top seven finish in the First Division. What had started out as the Inter-City Fairs Cup and would become the UEFA Cup was then known as the European Fairs Cup and under the one team per city rule of the original competition, Saints got in despite finishing seventh and in the wake of three London clubs.

As the head of a capital trio which included Spurs and Chelsea, it was Arsenal who represented London. Saints might have squeezed in by the back door, as it were, but their baptism in Europe was no passing fancy.

They made it through two difficult two-legged ties before going out on the away-goals rule to Newcastle United who by chance were defending the trophy.

The Saints fans had their first taste of European football at The Dell on 1 October 1969 and it proved a night of tension for players and supporters alike as Ted Bates's team overturned a 1-0 deficit from the first leg against Rosenborg of Trondheim to win 2-1 on aggregate. Today the Norwegian club have become redoubtable players in the European Champions League. Thirty years ago they were a bunch of enthusiastic amateurs coached by a former Saints favourite George Curtis, a veteran like Ted Bates of the Club's dramatic late 1940s as illustrated at Matches 37-40.

They had shocked the soccer world by beating Saints 1-0 on their home patch and at The Dell they made life difficult for a Saints side who were struggling at the lower end of Division I. *Echo* correspondent Brian Hayward wrote: "The amateurs from Trondheim made Southampton's passage into round two as hazardous as the mountain terrain of their homeland."

Apart from trying to put poor domestic form behind them as they took their first nervous steps in Europe, Saints had come out of the first leg in Norway with an unwelcome legacy. Their tough-tackling wing-half Dave Walker had cracked a bone in his foot, and centre-forward Ron Davies had sustained a groin strain.

The Welsh international, who had been in and out, and out of goals, since his famous four described in the previous report, had rested the injury between the two games but within five minutes of the second leg, he realised he had come back too soon.

Davies aggravated the injury and eventually had to go off, but not before playing a monumental role in lowering the barricades put up by the uncompromising opposition from the land of the Northern Lights. The Welshman's majestic qualities in the air brought him the honour of scoring his club's first goal in Europe after they had battled feverishly for 30 minutes to wipe out Rosenborg's one-goal advantage.

Saints swept forward from the kick-off, their ploy to get the ball to the flanks from where Terry Paine and John Sydenham delivered a stream of crosses. Rosenborg at times packed all 11 men back into their own penalty area as Saints pounded their goal, with Davies, Sydenham, Bobby Stokes and Fred Kemp (who had been keeping Fisher out at No.4) all either going close or being denied by the unorthodox and at times shaky 'keeping of Tor Fossen.

The vital breakthrough came on 33 minutes when Joe Kirkup – who'd generally been preferred to Jones at right-back since arriving in an exchange deal with David Webb – centred sweetly and Davies, despite his injury, soared like a salmon to head powerfully home from 10 yards.

George Curtis (left) and Ted Bates had competed alongside each other overseas – as here in Rio in 1948.

If anybody thought to photograph their reunion, in European opposition 21 years later, we have yet to locate a copy

European Fairs Cup First Round, second leg

Saints quickly tried to press home their advantage and Fossen had to cling on to headers from Jimmy Gabriel, often a centre-back but playing in midfield on this night, and Stokes.

Rosenborg were relieved to reach the break still level on aggregate. They had defended doggedly but with no shortage of ability. After all, they had come into the tie as leaders of the Norwegian First Division. As Ted Bates gave his half-time talk, he knew there was still a lot of work to be done.

Most of the Norwegians' best work had come in the last third of the field and early in the second-half the pattern stayed the same. A shot from Paine flashed a yard wide and a Davies, Paine, Kemp link-up ended with Fossen again saving well from Stokes. After 50 minutes another Davies header, this time from a Paine free-kick, rattled the post and in the ensuing scramble the gritty Gabriel thought he had pressed the ball over the line. But the French referee, after consulting his linesman, turned down Southampton's appeals.

When Eggen tried to pass back, Kemp pounced on the ball and went on to kick it into the side-netting with the furious Davies standing unmarked in the middle. But on the hour Saints took the aggregate lead for the first time. Another half-hearted pass back, this time by Jon Christiansen, was seized on by Paine. Fossen came out and

Jimmy Gabriel appeals in vain for a goal, while Joe Kirkup keeps his eye on the ball

drove him wide but Paine recovered his balance, turned back in towards goal and cracked the ball home from a narrow angle.

Saints had the chance to kill off the Norwegians for good after Paine had been brought down in the box on 67 minutes.

It seemed like an interminable time before Davies could take the kick and the delay may well have affected him because he screwed the spot-kick wide. The miss was to cause Saints much anxiety because, for the first time in the game, Rosenborg showed an appetite for going forward.

They launched a flurry of attacks but Saints held their ground. The fact that the game had six minutes of injury time added to the tension all round.

Ted Bates admitted afterwards that Saints "had made hard work of it, but had learned some valuable lessons about Europe in the two legs." George Curtis was proud of his Rosenborg amateurs, saying with a wry smile, "they died standing up. You can't ask for any more than that."

The game was significant for one other unusual incident – a booking for Sydenham. He seemed to run into his opponent, but referee Robert Helies took out his notebook and cautioned the winger. It was the first time in a long career that Sydenham had been booked.

SOUTHAMPTON:

Martin, Kirkup, McGrath, Byrne, Hollywood, Kemp, Gabriel, Paine, Stokes, Davies (Fisher 84), Sydenham

ROSENBORG:

Fossen, Ronnes, Rime, Eggen, Avidsand, Christiansen, Naess, Pedersen, Sunde, Iversen, Oiasler

Referee: Robert Helies (France)   *Attendance:* 22,329

Compiled by **BOB BRUNSKELL** from the *Echo* report. Photographs from Ted Bates's collection (Rio) and the *Echo*

LEEDS UNITED 7
SOUTHAMPTON 0

Leeds United, with a display of awesome passing and finishing, gave Southampton their greatest battering of the millennium

Southampton trotted out for a match at Elland Road on 4 March 1972 with heads in the clouds – clouds of doubt over whether they could ward off the growing threat of relegation from the top flight. Those doubts became demons as their survival prospects took a body-blow of monumental proportions as they suffered one of the most humiliating defeats in their history.

Don Revie's Leeds were without doubt the team of the moment, winning the title twice and never finishing out of the top three in the six seasons from 1968-69 to 1973-74. Against Saints they were simply superb, the complete team who were expert at all aspects of the game. Leeds won 7-0 and though Saints had suffered heavier defeats than that – just three months beforehand they had crashed 8-0 at Everton – none was as emphatic as this one in West Yorkshire.

Yorkshiremen may be notoriously hard to please but the manner in which the men in white toyed with Saints, especially in the second-half when Ted Bates's side seemed to be forever chasing shadows, sparked off joyous celebration throughout the length and breadth of Elland Road. Their young fans chanted "Superwhites, Superwhites" as United's exhilarating passing and movement cut great swathes through the Southampton defence. Even their hordes of hard-bitten season ticket-holders leapt to their feet to give them a standing ovation. Saints centre-half Jimmy Gabriel, whose experience of First Division football spanned more than a decade, summed up: "It was as if we had gone to another world and found superior beings."

The home side needed to win to keep in touch with League leaders Manchester City and Revie had issued a pre-match warning to his players: "Southampton are in a false position in the table. They possess players like Terry Paine, Ron Davies and Mike Channon who can easily turn a match against you." This theme was maintained in the match-day programme, where Leeds fans were reminded

of Saints' 2-1 win at The Dell in November and warned that "today's game promises to be a difficult one": the visitors were one of four clubs who might yet do the double over their hosts – even though Leeds were undefeated at home. Leeds fans reading this in the match-day programme on Saturday night must have had a wicked grin on their faces: "Who were you kidding, Don?"

Messrs Paine, Channon and Davies and for that matter everyone else in the Saints team were helpless to turn back the tide. Long before the end the whole Saints team had laid down and died.

With their goal average already unhealthy after the drubbing at Everton, Saints hurtled down to third from the bottom after this latest rout. But as Revie had pointed out, Davies and Channon were potential match-winners. Davies had managed only four goals in 20 League games when he found his head for the crucial run-in to the season, with seven goals in as many games to save the club's First Division skins.

Leeds effectively did them a favour. Saints were rudely awakened to the fact that if they didn't pull up their socks, they would go down. The Leeds team to face Southampton was minus England left-back Terry Cooper (now of course an important part of the Saints staff), but his absence went unnoticed as the home side still managed to field 11 internationals.

The fact that Leeds were so wound up for the match might have had something to do with the fact that they had lost at The Dell in November. Bursting for revenge, they put Saints on the rack and the final whistle, when it came, brought blessed relief. It spared them further punishment. Leeds had hammered five past Manchester United in their last home game. All seven of their goals against Saints came in the space of 38 minutes – one every five minutes – although to be fair to Saints, there had been few signs, early on in, of what was to come.

Southampton have chance of a League "Double"

That thrilling and memorable 5—1 victory over our old rivals Manchester United two weeks ago gave us a double-double over the two Manchester clubs but today we welcome Southampton to Elland Road with the knowledge that they are one of four clubs who have a chance of completing a League double over us.

To achieve that at our expense the Saints will have to succeed where all other sides have failed on visiting Elland Road in the League this season.

We have, of course, been beaten twice on our own pitch this time but those defeats were in cup matches, first when the little-known Belgian side, Lierse triumphed 4—0 in the first round of the new U.E.F.A. Cup and then when West Ham United knocked our League Cup hopes with an extra time goal from Clyde Best. In the League, however, we have prevented any of our visitors returning home with maximum points.

Out of 11 matches played at Elland Road only two sides, West Ham United and Ipswich Town have returned home with anything to show for their efforts, although in two of the four early season home games which were played on neutral grounds, Wolves and Tottenham Hotspur, won a point.

NO SURRENDER

Nevertheless our record at Elland Road this season is one of

COVER PICTURE
LEEDS UNITED v. MANCHESTER UNITED
SATURDAY, 19th FEBRUARY
at ELLAND ROAD

Leeds forward Mick Jones beating Manchester United 'keeper Stepney to score Leeds 4th goal and his hat-trick.

The programme alerted Leeds fans to the threat from Southampton, while reminding them that the front cover illustrated a 5-1 win over Manchester United

Division One

Leeds had the early initiative but Saints defended with dogged determination, refusing their rivals a clear-cut opportunity. Saints made a number of counter attacks, but with nothing on the end of them, Gary Sprake in the Leeds goal was largely unemployed. Once the floodgates were opened, though, Saints were swept away. There were still 13 minutes left when Leeds scored their seventh goal. Thankfully for Saints, Leeds seemed to settle for that, throttle back and play pure exhibition stuff, with the crowd baying in delight like they were at a bull fight.

Saints at one stage failed to get near the ball as Leeds strung together 24 passes. It was humiliating for the visitors and no-one felt it more than Terry Paine, who was substituted – at his own request, he insists – for the first time in his career.

Southampton's biggest tormentors were the Leeds wingers Eddie Gray and Peter Lorimer. After 39 minutes it was Gray who laid on the first goal for Allan Clarke whose angled drive was helped over the line by beleaguered left-back Roger Fry, a local lad trying to establish himself in the side. The second Leeds goal came on 42 minutes with Gray and right-back Paul Reaney combining to send Lorimer striding through to shoot past Eric Martin. Leeds made it 3-0 on the hour when Clarke, fed by a sublime Johnny Giles pass, rifled home left-footed. Within five minutes Lorimer had turned inside Fry and unleashed a shot which Saints' other young full-back, Bob McCarthy, helped into the net.

Saints were in a hopeless tangle at the back when Lorimer went through for number five but on 73 minutes came the ultimate humiliation as one Leeds centre-back, Norman Hunter, crossed for the other, Jack Charlton, to head home. Leeds went seven up after 77 minutes when Mick Jones gleefully joined in on the scoring act, after Lorimer had again eluded Fry to head down to him from Gray's cross.

Lorimer ran his marker ragged and Fry never played in the first team again. He claims he was made the scapegoat

After about five minutes, Terry Paine put Micky Channon through and Micky only had the 'keeper to beat and I think he sliced it wide. We could have been 1-0 up … [Roger Fry and I] were the ones that took the can for it. Actually, I had quite a good game. I was disappointed that I was dropped for the next game. I did reasonably well in that game, because we all took a thumping…

Forget that! They keep showing it on the telly.

Bob McCarthy

*We had a great run in the League, with some famous victories: 5-1 over…Manchester United, 6-1 over Nottingham Forest, and, most famous of all, 7-0 over Southampton…We absolutely murdered them that day. The movement, the pattern, everything seemed to go right… The game was shown on **Match of the Day,** and people started looking at us in a different way. They started calling us "Super Leeds" and comparing us to Real Madrid. I reckon that was the game when people took a look at us and finally said, "Yeah, this is a good team."*

Jack Charlton

for the whole sorry episode. And who could blame him? No-one in red and white could hold his head up on the way home.

LEEDS UNITED:
Sprake, Reaney, Madeley, Bremner, Charlton, Hunter, Lorimer, Clarke, Jones, Giles, Gray

SOUTHAMPTON:
Martin, McCarthy, Fry, Stokes, Gabriel, Steele, Paine (Byrne 71), Channon, Davies, O'Neil, Jenkins

Referee: Referee: D A Corbett (Wolverhampton)   *Attendance:* 34,275

Compiled by **BOB BRUNSKELL** from the *Echo* report and his interview with Roger Fry. Additional material by **David Bull**, from his interview with Bob McCarthy and from Jack Charlton's autobiography. *Echo* photograph

GLASGOW RANGERS 1
SOUTHAMPTON 3

Glasgow Rangers were humiliated in front of their own fanatical Ibrox fans by a Saints side who were battling to stay afloat in the Second Division.

Freshly relegated from the top flight and floundering round the lower reaches of the division after a poor start to the 1974-75 season, they were desperately in need of a tonic as indeed was manager Lawrie McMenemy. The further Saints' star declined, the more abuse the manager had to take in the long walk from tunnel to dug-out.

A trip to meet the might of Rangers in their own intimidating lair of Ibrox for a Texaco Cup quarter-final in mid-September was daunting to say the least. But Saints gloriously illustrated what a good side they could become with a comprehensive 3-1 win over the Scottish giants. They finished so much in the ascendancy that they could have taken a four- or five-goal lead back to The Dell for the return leg.

Solid defence, visionary midfield play from Gerry O'Brien and pace and skill up front from Mike Channon and Peter Osgood, sent Saints sweeping to a famous victory. Yet early on Rangers, urged on by a passionate 33,000 crowd, had been asking all the questions. This was a joust with the auld enemy and although the Texaco Cup was not to be a long-lived competition, it brought English and Scottish clubs into direct opposition and in doing so invoked a good deal of national pride.

There was certainly a good deal of urgency from Rangers as they set out to sweep Southampton back across the border. Alec MacDonald and Quintin Young went close as the blue shirts poured forward, and Ian Turner had to dive bravely at the feet of Graham Fyfe after MacDonald's piercing downward header had opened up the Saints defence.

This defence had just taken on a significant new shape with Mel Blyth, an important new signing from Crystal Palace, making his debut alongside Paul Bennett, a young home-grown product who had taken over from John McGrath the previous season.

So Jim Steele, who had been partnering Bennett in central defence, was deployed in a deep midfield role, the former Dundee man revelling in his return to his native Scotland. His abrasive qualities proved a key factor on the night.

Rangers were generally restricted to speculative efforts from distance. On the run up to half-time, the game was waiting for somebody to take the initiative, and it was Saints who struck the important first blow, thanks to another Scot, the former Clydebank midfielder Gerry O'Brien. Presented to the Board as potentially "a younger edition of Paine," he had never lived up to that billing.

But now, back in his native Glasgow and watched by his family, O'Brien didn't need a better stage to display his ball-playing skills and it was he who brilliantly opened the door for the first goal after 40 minutes.

O'Brien released Channon down the right wing with a sublimely flighted lob and Channon's inch-perfect centre was headed home powerfully by Peter Osgood. The lead lasted only four minutes. Osgood turned from hero to villain when he fouled Tommy Forsyth wide left and deep in his own half. Scottish international full-back Sandy Jardine flighted the free-kick dangerously into the box where Colin Jackson rose to head the equaliser.

It was the last action of the first-half and having struck such an important blow just before the break, Rangers were expected to come out for the second-half breathing fire. Exactly the opposite happened.

Two minutes into the resumption Hugh Fisher found Channon running in to oceans of space down the right and he squared to Osgood, whose 12-yard drive spun off the 'keeper Kennedy and into the net. It was Osgood's eighth goal of the season, his sixth in four games, and it broke Rangers.

After 56 minutes it was virtually all over bar the shouting when Osgood won the ball in midfield and picked out O'Brien who again sent Channon sweeping forward. O'Brien carried on his run, too, veering into the middle to pick up Channon's return pass and stab a close-range shot past Kennedy.

From then on there was menace and meaning in almost every Saints attack. O'Brien was spoon-feeding Channon like he was a hungry young cub, and the England international apologised when he passed up a great chance laid on by the irrepressible Scot.

Osgood did the same and missed out on his hat-trick after a great prompt from Fisher, another Glasgow-born player who was loving every minute of playing in his native city and beating the side that had been the "enemy" in his Celtic-supporting boyhood.

He was fortunate when Jardine's cross hit his hand and the referee turned down roars for a penalty from the terraces. Rangers skipper John Greig appealed so forcefully for the spot-kick that he was booked. That's how seriously Rangers were taking it.

When Steele mishit a back pass, another of Rangers' internationals Derek Parlane seized on it only to drag his shot into the side-netting. That was the extent of Rangers' late retaliation and when it was all over McMenemy was

Texaco Anglo-Scottish Cup Quarter-Final, first leg

justifiably proud. "Not many teams win at Ibrox let alone do it so convincingly," he beamed. "Ibrox is a big park and our front-runners revelled in the wide open spaces."

The Saints boss also threw in a word of praise for the new boy Blyth: "He steadied things down at the back and did the job I bought him to do." He was to do that and much more in the days and seasons to come, once he'd taken over Bennett's No. 5 shirt and Steele had returned to No. 6.

Meanwhile, Saints were on their way to the Texaco Cup Final, via a 2-0 home leg (to make it 5-1) against Rangers and a 5-2 aggregate win over Oldham in the semi-finals. The final with Newcastle United proved a close-run affair. Channon shot them to a 1-0 win in the home leg, but Newcastle turned it round at St James's Park where they needed extra-time before completing a 3-0 win on the night, and a 3-1 aggregate success.

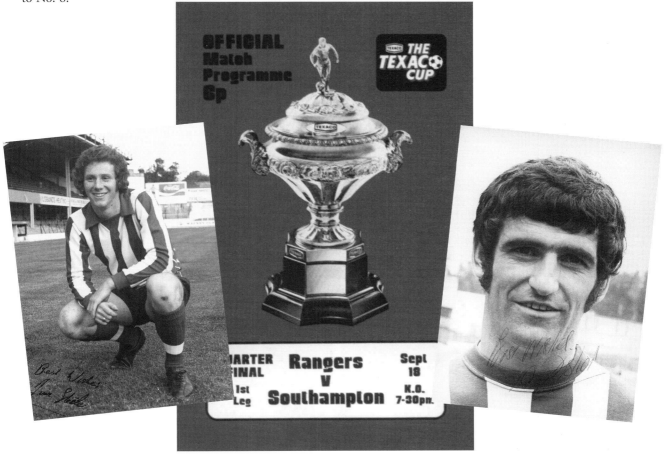

Two of Saints' returning Scots – Jim Steele (left) and Hugh Fisher

---

GLASGOW RANGERS:

Kennedy, Jardine, Greig, McDougall, Jackson, Forsyth, Young, Johnstone, Parlane, MacDonald, Fyfe (McLean 76)

SOUTHAMPTON:

Turner, Mills, Peach, Fisher, Bennett, Blyth, O'Brien, Channon, Osgood, O'Neil (Gilchrist 75), Steele

Referee: R H Davidson (Airdrie)   *Attendance:* 33,000

Compiled by **BOB BRUNSKELL** from the *Echo* report, with additional material, from the Club minutes, by **David Bull**. *Echo* photographs

SOUTHAMPTON 4
WEST BROMWICH ALBION 0

The value of confidence is beyond estimation in football. When one looks back in a more detached manner to the fervour, passion and glory of the wonderful 1976 FA Cup campaign, it's clear how big a role it played.

Before the Fifth Round clash with fellow Second Divisioners, West Bromwich Albion, Saints had gone a dozen League and Cup games unbeaten. At the Hawthorns it could so easily have been unlucky thirteen. Saints had had no problem beating the Throstles 3-0 at The Dell in the first game of the season – their first opening-day win since their promotion campaign 10 years previously – and had completed a League double with a 2-1 away victory in December. Even so, the teams appeared to be very evenly matched. And, anyhow, we all know that, in the FA Cup, you can chuck stats and form-books away.

A wildly enthusiastic Saints' following of 10,000 made its way by coach, car and chartered train to the Black Country on Saturday 14 February, helping to create a sizzling atmosphere in a 36,634 crowd at West Brom's famous old ground.

The Saints' fans were at the Smethwick Road End, complete with its old-fashioned pillars, and spreading also along the side, with West Brom's vocal hordes steeply banked behind the opposite Birmingham Road goal. However, as the balloons went up and ticker tape misted the air before the start, those away supporters were unaware of the drama the night before. Half our heroes were suffering from a stomach bug, with the strike-force of Bobby Stokes and Mike Channon among the victims. At that time, Channon was one of football's biggest stars and about to win his 25th consecutive cap for England; and, had he not played, which he most certainly shouldn't have, the psychological boost to Albion could have been immeasurable. And Stokes, always such a gutsy little player, would also rise to the occasion in this pulsating cup-tie.

They call it cup luck and the away fans must have thought that the trophy engraver had already prepared his tools when 'keeper Ian Turner misjudged a cross. For a moment, time stood still and, in what seemed like a slow motion replay, Albion's right-winger, Mick Martin, found a post with his effort.

West Brom had further efforts – from centre-forward Ally Brown and midfielder Tony Brown (twice) – blocked by Turner, who was enjoying a good season. But Saints were dangerous from David Peach's corners. First, he found Jim Steele, whose header flashed across the face of the goal. Next, he picked out Channon, whose own excellent header was scrambled off the line by Paddy Mulligan.

On the home left wing, Willie Johnstone had so far been kept reasonably quiet but on 58 minutes his jinking run created a simple chance for the always dangerous Tony Brown, celebrating his 600th Albion appearance. The goal seemed only to increase Saints' resolve and "Jack-in-the-Box" Stokes sent the Saints' fans behind John Osborne's goal into raptures when, set up by Channon, he drove firmly beyond the goalkeeper's outstretched hand.

David Peach (No. 3) caused havoc with his corners and Paul Gilchrist scored a spectacular goal

"Had we lost," said Lawrie McMenemy, "I wouldn't have mentioned the illness of the players, but we didn't lose, so I think it only right that the truth be told." The replay, that Saints had thoroughly and heroically earned, took place four nights later at The Dell.

Channon was feeling a touch better, I gather, for after 52 seconds he had the ball in the net, Stokes having repaid the compliment for Saturday. West Brom, to their credit, didn't buckle. Well not at first, anyway. David Peach made an uncharacteristically nervous start as, in a super-charged

FA Cup Fifth Round (Replay)

atmosphere, he undersold Ian Turner with a backward chip but Ally Brown, ever alert to a goal chance, failed for once to capitalise.

Saints soon settled, however, and got their second with one of The Dell's all-time great goals. After receiving a cross from captain Peter Rodrigues, Channon touched a ball to partner-in-crime Stokes. Bobby goes for goal but his shot, coming off a defender, tantalisingly falls for Paul Gilchrist. 'Gilly' was perhaps sometimes under-rated and although he should have indeed scored a lot more, this night he struck with a goal Pelé himself would have been pleased with. Taking the rebound, he deftly clipped the ball into the air and with the aplomb of a ballet dancer he pirouetted, hooking the ball back over his shoulder, raising the roof of the net and those of the stands at the same time.

Then it was three, Channon taking the ball around Osborne after running on to Peach's pass. A certain Bryan Robson had come off the bench for West Bromwich at half-time and, although he managed on this occasion to reach the field of play without falling down injured, he made no real impact. Saints had the Sixth Round well and truly in their sights and we were all realising that their having been within a minute of going out of the tournament in the Third Round, having given a magnificent display in the Villa Park replay and having then overcome "Montezuma's Revenge" at the Hawthorns, then something very special was at long last on the cards in Saints' exciting but up to then unfulfilled history of FA Cup adventures.

Not, however, before this night's work was done. Mick Channon would no doubt take issue with me for saying the next goal, from a penalty, was a formality, for it completed his hat-trick. It was just reward in any case as the goal resulted from his being pushed in the back by John Wile. Jim McCalliog generously allowed Channon to take the spot-kick.

When you play the likes of Villa on a miserable day and you are a goal down with a minute to go, you think "Well, maybe not this year." But when the ball rolled across the edge of the box and Hughie Fisher mis-hit a shot which flew into the back of the net off his dodgy left foot – only my little joke, Hughie – we then slaughtered them after extra-time at Villa Park and then up at West Brom we had four players down with sickness, got a draw and then go three-up in the replay in the first half-hour, I began to think "There may be something on here."

Peter Rodrigues

Nor was there to be a consolation goal for Albion. Alistair Robertson, who had been left trailing in Channon's wake for Saints' second, was put clean through, but presented the ball to Turner after taking it right up to him. It had been that sort of night for Robertson. It had been that sort of night for West Bromwich Albion.

And the Saints marched on.

SOUTHAMPTON:
Turner, Rodrigues, Peach, Holmes, Blyth, Steele, Fisher, Channon, Gilchrist, McCalliog, Stokes (O'Brien 78)

WEST BROMWICH ALBION:
Osborne, Mulligan, Mayo, T. Brown, Wile, Robertson, Martin, Cantello, A. Brown (Robson 45), Giles, Johnstone

Referee: Alf Gray (Great Yarmouth)   *Attendance:* 27,614

Compiled by **CHRIS NEWMAN** from being there, from reports in the *Echo* and from his interview with Peter Rodrigues. *Echo* photographs from the semi-final and Final celebrations

SOUTHAMPTON 1
MANCHESTER UNITED 0

It was and will forever remain their greatest achievement of the millennium… a sunlit day at Wembley Stadium on 1 May 1976 when Saints beat Manchester United 1-0 to claim the FA Cup for the first time.

Saints had had their moments as Cup-runners, as our selected Matches of the Millennium show. Two finals at the turn of the century. Two semi-finals in the 1920s. But, since then, not a lot – apart from the 1963 semi-final for Ted Bates's exciting side.

There had, of course, been other occasions for celebration under his resourceful and far-reaching management, as promotion in 1960 and 1966 brought about that transition from Third to First Division club.

But for Southampton people nothing could match the pure, unbridled pleasure of seeing their Saints create one of the great upsets in FA Cup history.

When they brought the trophy back to town the following day, an estimated 200,000 turned out to greet them. The old Solent port had seen nothing like it since VE Day in 1945.

The nature of the victory, against one of the greatest club sides in the land, embraced all the romance of the FA Cup. The late, decisive strike from Bobby Stokes, the smallest guy on a field of attacking giants, merely added to the compelling nature of the achievement.

When it was all over, there wasn't a dry eye in Southampton. It might have been an infamous moment in Manchester United's history, but the neutrals loved it, too, and shared in this, Southampton FC's finest hour.

As a young reporter privileged to be there at Wembley covering a momentous event in Southampton's history, it was easy to get carried away on a tidal wave of hysteria. But the words I used then matched, I hope, the mood of all those connected with the Club. I make no apology for using them (give and take a tweak here and there) again…

Saints faced the might of Manchester United as one of the biggest outsiders in the the history of the Cup. Most of the critics wrote them off and even the most ardent of their fans couldn't search their soul and assuredly predict a Wembley upset, so formidable was the opposition. But they rose to meet a colossal challenge, equalled it and then, in an enthralling finale, outwitted the giant to bring the issue to a triumphant conclusion. Lawrie McMenemy had been villified by many Southampton fans for being the man at the helm when the ship foundered and then sank from the top flight just two years earlier.

But on this day a city took him to their hearts forever and he became the Club's most successful manager. As a brilliant man-manager and

Bobby Stokes, seen scoring Saints' most famous goal on the Saturday and acknowledging some of the 200,000 multitude on the Sunday

David Peach (right) contains "the menace" of Coppell while Clive Thomas, Macari and McCalliog compose their comments for the box below

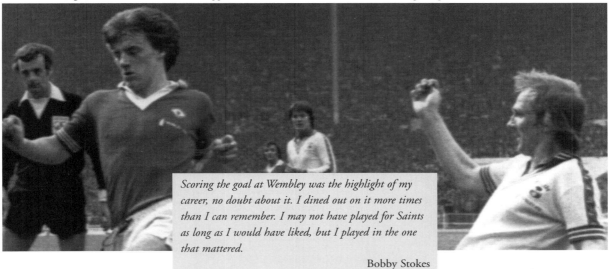

Scoring the goal at Wembley was the highlight of my career, no doubt about it. I dined out on it more times than I can remember. I may not have played for Saints as long as I would have liked, but I played in the one that mattered.

Bobby Stokes

When I got the ball from Mick Channon I looked up and spotted Bobby starting his run with at least a couple of... defenders between him and the goal. I lifted the ball over their heads and Bobby did the rest – brilliantly. I've no doubt that by the time he took the ball in his stride he was ahead of them but referee Clive Thomas was spot on in allowing it to stand.

Jim McCalliog

When Stokes... had the ball at his feet, he appeared to me possibly to be offside. I looked quickly to my linesman... and the flag stayed down. Another split-second and I saw another Manchester United defender playing Stokes onside. Then the players were jumping for joy, the supporters were going berserk and Southampton had won.

Referee Clive Thomas

You might wonder what excuses I'm going to put forward ... I'm not – I'm just going to admit that, ... on the day, we didn't do ourselves justice ... If a goal is awarded by a referee, it stands, whether you think it's offside or not. And I'm not going to start any arguments now about the one which Bobby Stokes tucked away for Saints ... I would not want anyone to think that I am giving Southampton little credit for their performance. They did the job in the best way they possibly could, and they did it effectively.

Lou Macari

motivator, he extracted the maximum from his players. They ran themselves into the lush Wembley turf to bridge the great gulf between a Southampton side still finding their feet in Division Two and one which was still riding high among the ruling class in the top flight.

Only in the early minutes of the 1975-76 Cup Final, as Saints tried to get their bearings in Wembley's vast amphitheatre, did they look uncomfortable. Gordon Hill, the United left-winger who had destroyed Derby County in the semi-final, smashed a 20-yard shot which stung 'keeper Ian Turner's fingers. Urged on by confident followers, United probed again and Lou Macari's mazy diagonal run disarmed the Saints defence and set up Gerry Daly for a shot which cannoned off Turner's legs.

But once they had established their bearings, Saints began to restrict United's attacking options. Peter Rodrigues and David Peach pushed up and began to contain the wing menace of Hill and Steve Coppell; Nick Holmes and Paul Gilchrist, all heart and motion, outfought Macari and Daly in the middle of the park.

The Southampton central defenders Mel Blyth and Jim Steele were alert to every move the United strikers Stuart Pearson and Sammy McIlroy made – or almost every move, for McIlroy later came close to spoiling the party.

In the Southampton midfield Jim McCalliog set out to prove that United manager Tommy Docherty had been wrong to sell him to McMenemy the season before. The little Scot was relishing his role as play-maker and picked out Mick Channon with a lovely pass. Goalkeeper Alex Stepney spotted the danger and raced out to block Channon's effort with his legs.

Mick Channon and Jim Clunie take their turn with the Cup
Left to right Stokes, Osgood, McCalliog, Steele, Channon, Peach, Clunie and Bill Ellerington

The longer the tense, gripping game went on, the more Saints, with their extra experience (Blyth, Rodrigues, McCalliog, Osgood and Channon) began noticeably to grow in confidence.

But not before United had gone desperately close to opening the scoring early in the second-half when Pearson, at the near post, flicked on a corner from Hill for McIlroy, leaping in at the other side of goal, to head against the outside of the upright. Channon later responded by driving past two defenders and drilling a left-footed shot narrowly over the bar. Then Osgood took out three red shirts before bringing goalkeeper Stepney to his knees to save. Stokes was looming as a threat, too, twice letting fly with efforts

It was our finest hour but not perhaps our finest side. That was the one I came back to from Manchester City, with the likes of Kevin Keegan and Alan Ball in it.

Mike Channon

It wasn't quite the same picking up a medal at Old Trafford [with Chelsea in the 1970 replayed Final]. Winning with Saints against a team of United's calibre at Wembley was personally much sweeter. Lawrie Mac's team-talk had been brilliant. We may have been the underdogs in the eyes of most people but Lawrie told us "We've got more experience in our dressing room than they've got in theirs. So why should we feel inferior?" We knew that if experienced guys like myself, Micky Channon and Peter Rodrigues did our bit, the likes of Jim Steele, Dave Peach, Nick Holmes and Paul Gilchrist would run their socks off. So we went out there convinced we had a chance.

Peter Osgood

from outside the box which were too close for Stepney's comfort.

As the final count-down began, it was Saints who were reaching out for victory, pushing forward and arousing the yellow and blue multitude that was flanking the goal they were attacking.

They could sense something special was afoot and turned up the volume. Then in one extraordinary moment in time for all Sotonians, the ball was in the back of the United net.

Again, Jim McCalliog breached the United defence with a long, raking and perfectly balanced pass which Stokes, in line with three red shirts, took in his stride. He delivered a low, left-footed shot from 22 yards which gave Stepney no chance.

SOUTHAMPTON 1
MANCHESTER UNITED 0

The debate whether Stokes was offside will rumble on forever, but Saints players and their fans will insist that the little predator was marginally on-side when he began his run to meet McCalliog's pass. One thing was for sure – United weren't going to let it rest there and with just six minutes left, they hurled themselves after an equaliser and Turner had to come bounding off his line to deny Pearson.

The clock seemed to stand still as 30,000 Saints fans held their breath and hovered tantalisingly on the threshold of a dream. Then referee Clive Thomas blew the last whistle; the dam broke and Wembley was awash with unrestrained emotion.

The fairytale had been written, none more so than for the Saints captain Peter Rodrigues who received the Cup from the Queen.

Less than a year before, the Welsh international had been given a free transfer by Sheffield Wednesday and was convinced that his long career was at an end.

Lawrie McMenemy may have seen me as a bit of a stop gap… to fill in for Steve Mills who had had been injured in a car accident. But it proved an inspired move when I stayed in the side and ended up leading them out at Wembley then up those famous steps to receive the trophy from Her Majesty.

Peter Rodrigues

I was Southampton-born and bred and had watched Saints from being a young lad… It was always my ambition to play for them one day so you can imagine how I felt when I went all the way to Wembley with them and helped them beat Manchester United in a Cup Final. It was beyond my wildest dreams.

Nick Holmes

One of my nicest memories was to hear the fans shouting "give us a wave, Lawrie." I went over to them and they raised their arms in the air. And for once they had nothing in their hands to throw at me. But seriously, I saw it as the dawn of a new era for Southampton FC and indeed, from that point on we made great strides as a club.

Lawrie McMenemy

SOUTHAMPTON:
Turner, Rodrigues, Peach, Holmes, Blyth, Steele, Gilchrist, Channon, Osgood, McCalliog, Stokes

MANCHESTER UNITED:
Stepney, Forsyth, Houston, Daly, Greenhoff, Buchan, Coppell, McIlroy, Pearson, Macari, Hill (McCreery)

Referee: Clive Thomas (Treorchy)   *Attendance:* 100,000

Adapted by **BOB BRUNSKELL** from his own *Echo* report and from interviews with Mick Channon, Nick Holmes, Jim McCalliog Lawrie McMenemy, Peter Osgood, Peter Rodrigues and Bobby Stokes. Additional material, from the autobiographies of Lou Macari and Clive Thomas, by **David Bull.** *Echo* photographs

SOUTHAMPTON 2
QUEENS PARK RANGERS 2

It has been said, by those of an impressionable age when it was going on, that "If you can remember what happened during the '60s, you weren't there!" A few weeks of 1976 were something like that. After Saints' defeat of Crystal Palace in the Stamford Bridge FA Cup semi-final on 3 April, the city of Southampton took on a Mardi Gras atmosphere, and even its ubiquitous population of curmudgeons were having trouble keeping a straight face during their doom-laden pontifications.

Then there was that Bobby Stokes goal and… and after that, it all gets somewhat confusing. Collating information for the early Matches of the Millennium has been a matter of trying to make sense of a jigsaw puzzle without the benefit of pictures, or all the pieces. But an account of what occurred in the aftermath of the 1976 Cup Final is rather like having all the pieces of six or seven jigsaws mixed up in one box, and a quick glimpse of a couple of pictures.

Having been there isn't necessarily a great help; discussing it with others, who may, or may not, have been more clear-headed over the period in question, obscures rather than clarifies, as recollections tend to consist mainly of hazy speculations concerning how much was drunk, where and when, followed by where the subject woke up afterwards. This is met with a chorus of "That's nothing! I…" because, if anything defines a Sotonian, or a Mush, it is an ability to top a story – however outlandish.

Some 200,000 of us, so we're told, remember watching the open-top bus bearing the triumphant Saints go past the end of our street, and another thirty to fifty thousand have distinct memories of the squash outside the Civic Centre when the bus arrived a couple of hours late for the civic reception. Many of those witnesses will hazard that it was on the day after the Cup was won, and can say, fairly certainly, that it was a Sunday. Then there was Monday evening.

Tickets for the Mike Channon testimonial had been on sale for the best part of a month and were, apparently, selling quite briskly, but it dimly occurred to quite a few people – quite a few thousand in fact – that as Saints were now FA Cup-holders, queuing at the turnstiles to get in on the night might just be a tad problematical.

The crowd was over 29,000 – about two thousand in excess of what was by now The Dell's official capacity – and another 5,000 were reported as being turned away.

The atmosphere was, as Peter East (quite possibly the only sane person in town?) noted in his *Echo* report, "bedlam." And that was before the Romsey Old Boys Band took to the pitch to add their own, eccentric, brand of celebration to the proceedings.

They paraded up and down blowing their bugles and banging their drums, in the time-honoured Boys' Brigade fashion, dressed as bumble bees.

Intermittently, some joker dressed as a bee-keeper would blow them up.

By the time that Mike Channon led the team onto the pitch the crowd's mood had gone from carnivalesque to "Wilder than VE Day!" That was the consensus among older Saints' fans at least.

Channon was presented with the *Daily Express* Sportsman of the Year award and the Ford Motor Company presented Bobby Stokes with a brand new Grenada Ghia. Ford had originally offered the incentive of a car for any Saint scoring a Cup Final hat-trick, but in the euphoria of the win their hard-headed executives had gone as daft as everyone else. It's a pity Stokes couldn't drive, but the gesture was undoubtedly appreciated.

Amid all this, somewhere, was a game of football.

Queens Park Rangers were the opposition – as if anyone cared! They were leading the First Division at the time (they'd end the season runners-up, a point behind Liverpool) and it was evident early on that, on the night, they were the better team.

In fact, to those few who were taking an interest in the football, it was soon apparent that at least a few of the Saints' side, like the vast majority of spectators, had been partying until quite soon before the game kicked off. Fortunately for this account, Peter East was the acme of professionalism over the weekend, and it is interesting to be reminded that Saints actually opened the scoring: Stokes, just outside the six-yard box, converted from an Osgood knock-down in the 30th minute. Frank McLintock levelled just before half-time.

> I had to be at The Dell early that morning to sort out one or two things and I found people had been queuing for tickets since 6 o'clock in the morning. It frightened me to death because there were a lot of season ticket holders there screaming for my head… It was a sell out! It had to be a case of first there, first served. There was nothing I could do about it. That night as I walked into the ground some spivs were busy selling tickets on the black market. They even approached me to see if I could let them have some more to flog … bloody hell!
>
> Mike Channon

Mike Channon Testimonial

As the game went on the crush on the terraces was being relieved by allowing spectators to sit on the running track and, with the second-half under way, quite a number of the evacuees found bum-space in the back of the Milton End goal, a situation that didn't appear to worry Rangers' 'keeper Phil Parkes unduly. Not even when a well-worked move, orchestrated by Osgood, put Stokes through to score a second. This got a thunderous reception, which Stokes received somewhat sheepishly.

QPR were the perfect guests.

Their forwards had earlier passed up a couple of opportunities to go ahead, steering the ball wide rather than testing Ian Turner, but honour had to be satisfied and, with only 11 minutes left on the clock, Peter Eastoe "pounced on a pass from Stan Bowles to level the scores."

Those interested had to get next day's *Echo* to discover the actual result. As the final minutes ticked by, more and more spectators spilled over the walls and a knot of players, of both persuasions, was growing near the tunnel. Among them Peter Osgood, who found the ball, delivered by Stokes, at his feet on the corner of the penalty area, and lashed it goalwards.

Even as he let fly hundreds of spectators were charging forward, the contingent from the Milton goal in the vanguard, and the players instantly evacuated the pitch with a turn of speed far in excess of anything they had exhibited in the previous 90 minutes.

Was it a goal?

Local legend insists that Channon went looking for the referee after the game to find out the score, but found him too drunk to communicate. Peter East had more luck in the chaos that ended the game:

Had Osgood's goal counted Saints would have won the game. But referee Robinson explained: "I blew the whistle before the ball hit the spectator. The game was all over."

The game may indeed have been "all over," but the Bacchanal went on. The crowd tarried to applaud their heroes once again.

As they appeared with the Cup in the Directors' Box, there were quite a few choruses of *"We'll support you evermore."*

And then it was into the streets, as the publicans of Southampton braced themselves for yet another, profitable, onslaught.

Referee Robinson blows his whistle before an invading spectator can come between Osgood's shot and the goal

---

SOUTHAMPTON:

Turner, Rodrigues, Peach (Mills 63), Holmes, Blyth (Bennett 45) Steele (Waldron 45) Gilchrist (Earles 74), Channon, Osgood, McCalliog (Fisher 45), Stokes

QUEENS PARK RANGERS:

Parkes, Clements, Gillard, Hollins, McLintock, Webb, Thomas, Leach, Beck, Bowles, Givens (Eastoe 45)

Referee: Alan Robinson (Waterlooville)   *Attendance:* 29,508

Compiled by **DAVE JUSON** from being there, from the *Echo* report and from both of Mike Channon's autobiographies (of which *Home and Away* is quoted). *Echo* photograph

SOUTHAMPTON 4
OLYMPIQUE MARSEILLE 0

Olympique Marseille have been one of the leading players on the European stage for three decades. In September 1976, though, the French giants had to eat humble pie after suffering a comprehensive 4-0 defeat by Saints in the opening game of the season's Cup-Winners' Cup at The Dell.

It was Southampton's first appearance in the competition after their fairy-tale FA Cup Final win – and it couldn't have been a more impressive, more emphatic success over a club who boasted nine cup final wins in their own country.

Yet glory was born out of uncertain origins. Unknown to Marseille, Saints were taking a huge gamble with their 'keeper Ian Turner, who was thrown into the action nursing a knee ligament injury which began to play him up so much that at half-time he required a pain-killing injection. Had Marseille set about Saints in a more positive manner rather than setting out to stop them more by foul means than fair, it might have been a different story. Certainly the game opened up in an unsavoury way with almost a foul a minute (most of them seemingly against Mike Channon who was regarded by Marseille as the man most likely to cause them a problem). They were not wrong.

It needed some drastic action by the Spanish referee to stop the early rot. In days when bookings were few and far between, the official took the name of Marseille defender Alonso for a dubious challenge on Fisher. The referee had needed to stamp his mark on the game and, thankfully, with a flourish of his little notebook after 11 minutes, he had done just that. From that moment cynicism made way for skill, much of it from Saints who wrapped the tie up with a devastating burst of three goals in seven minutes just over halfway through the first-half.

The warning signs had been flashing for Marseille, marshalled by the great French international centre-half Marius Tresor. Peter Osgood, who was to have one of his finest games for Saints, tested out 'keeper Migeon with a strong header. The centre-forward showed majestic control when he chested down a corner from Jim Steele and produced a shot which demanded an even better save from Migeon. But between the 30th and 35th minutes, Migeon, Tresor and everyone else in the Marseille ranks were pulled apart by a breath-taking Saints onslaught.

Bobby Stokes began it all by sending Channon bounding forward and trying to pick out Osgood with his firmly-struck cross. Osgood challenged for the ball, didn't connect but in doing so distracted the Marseille defence who failed to pick out Malcolm Waldron running in at the far post to drive home.

With Marseille's resolve shaken and anxiety taking over their players, Saints went for the jugular. Within three minutes they were two-up. Zvunka was drawn into another foul on the speedy Channon and when Steele sent the free-kick across goal, it was Channon himself who got there to send a stooping header just inside his near post. Saints were marching in, backed up by a loud chorus from the terraces, and the party continued when a firm left-wing cross from Nick Holmes found its way through a crowded goalmouth to Steve Williams on the far side. The young midfielder, who had just broken into the side on a regular basis, showed great poise and control by bringing the ball down, glancing up and picking out Osgood with the most precise of crosses. Ossie was a purist who didn't pass up service like that and he gave the 'keeper no chance with a classic far-post header.

Mike Channon stoops among his markers to score Saints' second goal

European Cup-Winners' Cup First Round, first leg

With a the luxury of a three-goal cushion, the sight of the lamed Turner having to face a penalty wasn't quite as bad as it might have been for Saints. The action was still at boiling point on 37 minutes when Steele handled from a corner and Marseille got a penalty which Alonso tucked firmly past the Saints 'keeper. But to Marseille's consternation Emon had carelessly encroached into the box while the kick was being taken so Alonso had to try again and this time Turner saved, diving to his right to push the ball away for a corner.

Fortunately for the Saints and Turner it was to prove an isolated threat.

Into the second-half, they were still carving chances with some creative and innovative play. Williams and Osgood were the main architects and one memorable centre, curved in by Osgood with the outside of his right foot, brought a sharp close-range shot from Channon which was beaten away by the busy, bemused Migeon.

Saints kept plugging away and scored a fourth goal after 70 minutes with right-back and captain Rodrigues doing the spadework. He intercepted a pass in his own defence and in one sweeping move looped a long ball forward to send Channon galloping into the box where he was floored by Zvunka who had been given a torrid time by the England man.

The special newspaper for the away leg carried a health warning: this man Channon is dangerous

Channon picked himself up and scored from the penalty.

Marseille's late attempt to limit the damage was fairly muted. A shot from Nogues dropped on top of Turner's bar but Saints, closing ranks, comfortably contained the French who to all intents and purposes had given up the ghost. It was the night perhaps when Romford-born Williams arrived as a star of the future. Osgood's peerless skills had never been in doubt. Against Marseille he produced a wide repertoire of them to entrance the crowd.

Ted MacDougall, watching from the stands after just completing a £50,000 move from Norwich City, must have wondered how he was going to get into the side. But he would be in on the Saturday, initially at the expense of McCalliog.

The second leg of the Marseille tie was an unappetising brutal affair from which Saints were relieved to escape with a 2-1 defeat and life and limb intact. When David Peach scored to scotch Marseille's hopes of a comeback, they took it badly and according to eyewitnesses "kicked everything in sight." To add insult to injury the Saints' coach was stoned as they left the ground.

The notorious old French port had truly lived up to its fearsome reputation – even if the reputation of its famous club had been dented by the newcomers to the Cup-Winners' Cup.

SOUTHAMPTON:

Turner, Rodrigues, Steele, Holmes, Waldron, Blyth, Fisher, Channon (Earles 84), Osgood, Stokes, Williams

OLYMPIQUE MARSEILLE:

Migeon, Baulier, Tresor, Zvunka, Bracci, Fernandez, Nogues, Emon, Yazalde, Alonso, Bereta

Referee: Pedro Urrestarazu (Spain)   *Attendance:* 19,150

Compiled by **BOB BRUNSKELL** from the *Echo* report. *Echo* photograph

WOLVERHAMPTON WANDERERS 2
SOUTHAMPTON 6

Saints went into a Division II match at Molineux in October 1976 on the back of a 6-2 defeat at Charlton Athletic and without their record-signing Peter Osgood. The defeat at The Valley had been an unplanned setback of huge proportions; the loss of Osgood a calculated gamble on the part of manager Lawrie McMenemy.

In between the six-goal hiding at Charlton and the match at Wolves, Saints had moved off the bottom of the Second Division with a 4-1 home win over Fulham, George Best and all (at least until he was sent off).

Wolves, meantime, were in second place and on a course which by the end of the season would lead them back into the First Division.

So when Saints trotted out at Molineux for the midweek game against the men in old gold, they were deemed by most to be on a hiding to nothing. It was a sobering backdrop for young local product Pat Earles to make one of his few first team appearances, especially as he was stepping into the formidable boots of Peter Osgood.

But the pale, slight figure of Earles was one of many in red-and-white stripes to haunt Wolves on a great night for Saints.

They won 6-2 to give a temporary fillip to a season which had begun very poorly and had soon developed into a major anti-climax after all the hope and glory generated by Saints' Cup Final victory only four months beforehand.

The side was already showing significant change with only Peter Rodrigues, David Peach, Nick Holmes, Mel Blyth, Jim McCalliog and Mike Channon of the Wembley winners remaining for this particular game. Before the match McMenemy, quizzed on Osgood's omission, explained: "I pick teams to win matches." It was a bit of an understatement even by the big fella's standings in the light of what actually happened on the night.

The victory proved McMenemy's best away success so far. Amazingly his Saints side was to set new marks that same season by winning 6-0 at Carlisle in January (coming up next).

But back to Wolverhampton. *Echo* reporter Peter East summed up:

Pat Earles runs clear to score Saints' fourth goal

It was a performance of sheer determination crowned by wonderful opportunism. Every shot on target went in and the Wolves keeper Gary Pierce didn't make a single save. It wasn't that he had an off day; he just didn't have a chance with any of the goals.

Channon and Holmes scored two goals apiece, Earles and McCalliog one each, but the unsung hero of the night was ironically one of the finest goal poachers of the lot, Ted MacDougall – and he didn't score!

In our previous report, of a game three weeks earlier, SuperMac had just signed and was raring to score. And so he did. Saints had managed only two goals in their first five games. With MacDougall in tow, they got 13 in their next four.

But as Peter East pointed out, "Ted the taker became Mac the Maker at Wolves." MacDougall didn't put his name on the scoresheet, but he played his part in all six goals. McMenemy joked afterwards: "I buy a player to score goals, we get six and he doesn't get one!" Needless to say, the Saints boss followed up with credit where credit was due: "Ted worked as hard as anyone. He had a blinder." MacDougall's impudent flicks and touches, Channon's brilliant runs and Earles's determined foraging prevented Wolves settling at the back.

Saints plucked unceasingly at their nerve ends and, to the alarm of their own fans, the home side cracked up in the second-half.

It had been nip and tuck beforehand and it was Colin Boulton, the goalkeeper on loan from Derby, who provided the launch-pad for success. He saved heroically from Kenny Hibbitt, Steve Kindon and Alan Sunderland and, even when Wolves had him struggling, Peach and Holmes were on hand to make last-ditch clearances.

Division Two

Holmes, just back in the side after a five-week lay-off with knee trouble, ran his socks off for Saints, covering, tackling, creating and scoring twice. His first goal came just three minutes into the game after a free-kick from McCalliog had triggered panic in the Wolverhampton goalmouth where MacDougall and Channon had shots blocked by Mike Bailey before Holmes powerfully despatched the loose ball.

Saints were perhaps awaiting half-time with nervy anticipation when Hugh Fisher's midfield perseverance presented them with an unexpected bonus of a second goal. He robbed Bobby Gould on the halfway line and played a one-two with Earles before bringing Channon, Peach and MacDougall into play. Holmes joined in and, spotting that Channon had continued his run, laid the ball into his path. Pierce came out but had no chance.

Wolves were back in the game just four minutes into the second-half when Blyth fouled Gould and Hibbitt scored from the penalty spot. But Fisher's midfield industry again set the home side back on their haunches in the 55th minute. As he challenged Steve Daley, the ball spun loose and MacDougall swept it forward to Earles, who went on to tuck it gleefully past Pierce from 15 yards. It broke the Wolverhampton spirit and, as they tentatively probed Saints in the 78th minute, Peach cleared, Channon turned the ball inside to MacDougall and his first-time flick let in Holmes to drive home.

Daley scored on the break with just two minutes left on the clock but Saints reserved the best till last. Their sixth goal, in the last minute, iced the cake quite beautifully. Tormentor Ted MacDougall made a run down the right touchline, picked out McCalliog in-field who in turn moved the ball on to Channon who, in one breathless moment, had put the finishing touch to a superb move.

So in just two away games Saints had gone from the ridiculous to the sublime and McMenemy, the great orator, summed it up perfectly. Referring to the previous 6-2 defeat at Charlton he said that he had "never managed a team who played as badly as that away from home. But on the other hand, I'd never managed a team who had won 6-2 away either."

The books, you felt, had been balanced beautifully.

Although involved in all six goals, Ted MacDougall did not get on the scoresheet – not even with this overhead effort

WOLVERHAMPTON WANDERERS:
Pierce, Palmer, Parkin, Daley, Bailey, McAlle, Hibbitt, Carr, Gould (Patching 68), Kindon, Sunderland

SOUTHAMPTON:
Boulton, Rodrigues, Peach, Holmes, Waldron, Blyth, MacDougall, Channon, Earles, McCalliog, Fisher

Referee: Derek Lloyd (Fernhill)   *Attendance:* 21,286

Compiled by **BOB BRUNSKELL** from the *Echo* report. *Echo* photographs

CARLISLE UNITED 0
SOUTHAMPTON 6

A January afternoon on the north-west frontier of the Football League is not perhaps the most obvious setting for Saints both to establish a Club record and to lay to rest a jinx of the period.

Their 6-0 win at Brunton Park in January 1977 became, and remains, their best-ever score away from home (not counting a war-time frivolity or two). As you know from the previous report, they'd already had a 6-2 away victory that season at Molineux; and you may not need reminding, either, of that same scoreline at Stamford Bridge in Match No. 62.

If Mansfield Town fans will forgive our saying so, we didn't rate, among our Matches of the Millennium, the 6-1 win at Field Mill on the first day of the 1958-59 season, even if it was the kind of start that puts you top of the table for the weekend.

What makes the win at Carlisle special, of course, is not that they're a cut above Mansfield, but that this is the only time Saints have scored as many as six away goals without reply.

The jinx that had "haunted them," as Peter East put it in the *Echo,* was their tendency, at that time, to fail against "unfashionable, struggling opponents." But, then, what humble club was not keenly looking for an opportunity, in 1976-77, to take a pop at the Cup-holders with their Channons and their Osgoods – the "violinists", as Lawrie McMenemy called his silkier stars – who harmonised on good days with his "road-sweepers", the likes of David Peach and Nick Holmes? Indeed, Carlisle had been the first team that season to beat the holders, coming to The Dell on the first day of the season and winning 2-1.

Although goalkeeper Ian Turner played in that opening game – along with nine outfield members of the Wembley team – he was injured in it and had made only three appearances since. Portsmouth-born Steve Middleton had come in for half-a-dozen games but manager McMenemy had borrowed a couple of 'keepers – Colin Boulton from

Derby, as you may recall from the last report, and Jim Montgomery, the romantic hero of Sunderland's 1973 Cup win. So by the eleventh game of their League season, Saints were on to their fourth goalkeeper.

And soon it was five. A week before Christmas, Peter Wells, an £8,000 buy from Nottingham Forest, came in for the rest of the season. And before there was any score at Brunton Park, the 20 year-old goalkeeper made an outstanding save.

A 14th minute header from Frank Clarke looked a goal all the way, but Wells took off to push the ball over for a corner.

It was the kind of save that can lift a team and so it was that Saints began to mesmerise a Carlisle side that had gone into the game knowing that a win would lift them above their visitors and ease their relegation worries.

Saints now began to look the part, as the violinists and road-sweepers got it together.

Peter Wells, the new goalkeeper, whose "outstanding save" enabled Saints to weather the initial storm

Within a minute of Wells's save, they were one-up and, as Peter East observed, the goal "typified" the abilities of the four players involved in it.

Alan Ball's vision and distribution skill set things moving as he steered a pass through the middle and there was a perfectly-timed run by Mike Channon to beat the offside trap.

Next, after Channon had flicked a pass out to him on the right, Ted MacDougall showed all his penalty area ruthlessness as he let Carlisle defenders scamper back across his path and then tormented them with a chip to the far post.

There the energetic Nick Holmes, whose powerful runs so often took him through rearguards unmarked, was on hand to head home.

Division Two

Carlisle did their best to get back into the game and Rafferty and Clarke, prompted by Bonnyman, posed a problem or two. But the odd "mistimed tackle and missed clearance" – and there weren't many, Peter East noted – was as nothing to "the happy sight of players running and working for one another." And, if there were any danger of the visitors being flustered by this pressure, there was Peter Osgood, putting his foot on the ball and giving team-mates the chance to settle and regroup – "almost like a thermostat in keeping the engine nicely warm and efficient on the odd occasion it threatened to overheat."

Then, when the moment took him, he could demonstrate his "inch-perfect flicked pass."

Vintage Ossie, then? Well, not entirely. In his Chelsea prime, Osgood had scored goals as well. But he hadn't scored since that opening-day defeat by Carlisle. On 31 minutes, however, he came good. It was a flowing team move and the best of the six in that regard. To be more precise, there were two flowing moves, but after the home centre-half, MacDonald, had interrupted the first one, Holmes regained possession and another six passes were put together before Steve Williams set Osgood up.

By half-time, Carlisle were looking a very different side from the one that had won at The Dell. While their summer-look had been so "cool", it was "a sorry, disjointed side" that Peter East watched troop back to their dressing room. Whatever their player-manager Bobby Moncur said to them during the interval, they certainly came out firing – twice in the person of Billy Rafferty and twice wide of the post.

Having ridden that storm for a few minutes, Saints then made it three with a 51st minute penalty. Running onto a pass from Williams, Channon had his legs pulled from under him by goalkeeper Martin Burleigh. Peach made no mistake from the spot. Two minutes later, Peach was setting up a fourth with a diagonal pass from the left for MacDougall to finish.

With Carlisle now lacking in morale and cohesion, McMenemy could afford the luxury of bringing on young substitute Trevor Hebberd for his first taste of senior football.

Osgood, coming off, went out of his way to encourage the 18-year old from Alresford by changing direction to give him a good luck handshake and pat on the back on his way back to the bench.

Hebberd had 26 minutes in which to enjoy himself but needed only three to start the fifth goal. From his short pass, Alan Ball sent Channon galloping through for his 150th League goal.

Channon almost scored again and Bonnyman nearly conceded an own goal with a back pass that went narrowly wide.

But there was a second goal for Holmes in the 84th minute, when his unstoppable 30-yard shot made it 6-0. Saints needed to hold out for only six minutes for this scoreline to enter the record books.

It also kick-started a good run in the League as they went the next 10 games with only one defeat.

There was still much to be done, though, to rebuild a side that had proved fit for Wembley into one capable of getting back to Division One.

CARLISLE UNITED:
Burleigh, Hoolickin, Carr, Bonnyman, MacDonald, Moncur, Smith, Barry, Clarke, Rafferty, McVitie

SOUTHAMPTON:
Wells, Andruszewski, Peach, Holmes, Blyth, Steele, Ball, Channon, Osgood (Hebberd 64), MacDougall, Williams

Referee: Eric Garner (Maghull, Liverpool)   *Attendance:* 9,617

Compiled by **BOB BRUNSKELL** and **DAVID BULL** from the *Echo* report. Photograph from **Duncan Holley**'s collection

SOUTHAMPTON 2
ANDERLECHT 1

It was a case of so near, so far on a rainy March night in 1977 when Saints went within seven minutes of forcing one of the giants of European football into extra-time when the mouth-watering prize for victory was a place in the semi-finals of the European Cup-Winners' Cup.

Their opponents at a soggy Dell were Anderlecht, the great Belgian club side who had won the competition the year before and had followed up by scooping the European Super Cup as well.

Anderlecht were a powerful blend of Belgian and Dutch stars, every one of them an international. When they stepped out to a suitable fanfare at The Dell, they were two goals to the good after the first leg.

But for Saints, the FA Cup Final conquerors of Manchester United who had already removed Olympique Marseille from this competition, nothing was impossible. They built up slowly to a crescendo, whipping their fans into a frenzy before letting them down right at the death with an elementary and oh so costly mistake. Saints, after a goalless first-half, wiped out the two-goal deficit and were pushing hard for a winner when they lost possession, lost their shape at the back, lost a goal and with it all hope of going through to the last four.

The clock was ticking down to the end of normal time when full-back Manny Andruszewski tried to set up another attack, skipping down the right and dragging the ball inside to a midfield colleague. But the ball stuck in the mud and Anderlecht suddenly had possession. Jean Dockz quickly hit a pass forward for the great Belgian international Francois Van der Elst who produced a devastating burst into the penalty area. There, though, to the huge relief of the big crowd, he let the ball roll too far ahead of him to the feet of Jim Steele, a no-nonsense central defender, who had played heroically all night. The crisis it seemed had passed. But inexplicably Steele miscued his clearance and as the ball slithered under his boot, Van der Elst, who had continued his run, latched on to it and shot low into the corner of the goal.

It was a sickening blow for Saints who had fought their way back into the tie with great character and no small measure of skill on a pitch saturated by hours of heavy rain. The game had not shaped up too well early on as Mick Channon and Ted MacDougall repeatedly got snared up in Anderlecht's offside trap and Steele and Peter Osgood found themselves running the gauntlet with the East German referee after collecting first-half bookings.

The referee's over-vigilant handling of a huge game badly riled the 24,337 crowd, who slow hand-clapped him and became further incensed when he disallowed a

Peter Osgood challenges in the air as Mick Channon (right) waits for the head-down

European Cup-Winners' Cup Third Round, second leg

37th minute "goal" by MacDougall for offside after Osgood had opened up the Belgians' defence with a superb pass. Anderlecht had kept Saints on their toes with sudden breaks out of defence and Peter Wells, in the Southampton goal, had to pull off a fine save from Ressel after a cross from Dockx had skimmed off Mel Blyth's head.

> *It was as muddy as hell. I suppose I slipped. It was after that McMenemy and I definitely fell apart*
>
> Jim Steele

Defences, though, had dominated the first-half but all that changed after the break when chances began to flow. At half-time, the manager had pulled off midfielder, Jim McCalliog - an anti-climactic exit for the hero of that slide-rule Wembley pass to Bobby Stokes, who would never appear for the Saints again. He was replaced wide on the left by Austin Hayes, who had scored twice on his debut – in the previous round against Carrick Rangers. He wouldn't get many chances to shine, but he did in this game. Channon hurried a half-chance over the bar and Hayes just failed to get a toe to a MacDougall cross as it flashed across the face of the goal. Then Vanden Daele, the Anderlecht skipper, needed a last-gasp tackle to deny Hayes a clear run at goal.

Saints were upping the tempo and Anderlecht were looking rattled. Again referee Glockner took a tirade of boos as he turned down penalty appeals after Vanden Daele carelessly knocked MacDougall off the ball. But on 61 minutes the unpopular official didn't say no. Channon went sprawling as he challenged for a MacDougall knock-down after another Hayes cross with Vanden Daele again the offender. David Peach stepped up to take the penalty and sent the 'keeper the wrong way from the spot.

The goal stung Anderlecht into an immediate counter-attack with Ressel bursting through and having a shot cleared off the line by Steele. But Saints had the sniff of glory in their nostrils and Thissen had to throw himself in front of a shot by Channon to stop it going in. A desperate tackle by Dockx took out Williams in full flight before Saints hit goal number two on 77 minutes. Peach paved the way with a dash down the left touchline and a cross which was helped on by Channon into the path of MacDougall who made no mistake.

It stoked Saints up for one last big push but just as the excitement and the anticipation was starting to shake the old ground, the wind was taken right out of the Southampton sails by Van der Elst's ruthless exploitation of the slip by Steele.

Channon's persistence "won" a penalty

A large crowd had paid a club record £44,000 to see Saints go out 3-2 on aggregate, despite winning on the night. In fact, Anderlecht had become the fifth national cup-holders they had beaten that season. On their way to their meetings with the Belgian Cup-winners, they had eliminated Olympique Marseille (Match No. 71) and Carrick Rangers of Northern Ireland; and they had earlier beaten Rangers in the Tennent-Caledonian Cup and Napoli in the home leg of the Anglo-Italian Cup.

Anderlecht? They went on to reach the Final but lost their grip on the trophy as SV Hamburg beat them 2-0.

SOUTHAMPTON:

Wells, Andruszewski (Stokes), Peach, Holmes, Blyth, Steele, Williams, Channon, Osgood, McCalliog (Hayes), MacDougall

ANDERLECHT:

Ruiter, Van Binsts, Broos, Vanden Daele, Thissen, Dockx, Van der Elst, Haan, Ressel, Coeck, Rensenbrink

Referee: Rudi Glockner (East Germany)   *Attendance:* 24,337

Compiled by **BOB BRUNSKELL** from the *Echo* report. Jim Steele interviewed by **David Bull**. *Echo* photographs

ORIENT 1
SOUTHAMPTON 1

It was another of those spring evenings when Southampton emptied into London. It had happened in 1963 and again in 1966 – but, then, you'll hardly need reminding of Matches 53 and 59 - and it was happening again at the end of April 1978. And, just as in 1966, the dual destination was Brisbane Road and Division One.

After that visit from the Saints in 1966, Leyton Orient had dropped their geographical label (until they re-adopted it in 1987). While, in 1966, they had already been relegated when Southampton invaded, this time they had everything to play for, lying a place above the drop-zone but with games in hand – thanks to a Cup run that had ended in semi-final defeat earlier in the month. For Saints, on the other hand, this was 1966 re-visited: this was again their penultimate game and they were on the verge of promotion to the top flight. Of the 18,000 present, travelling support filled two sides of the ground, ensuring that the match was played out to a constant backdrop of *"When The Saints Go Marching In."*

With but seven defeats in a 42-game season, 1977-78 ranks among Saints' best-ever campaigns. In the final two months of the season, they played 13 League games, losing only once, to Cardiff City.

Notwithstanding the six-goal frolics described in previous reports, 1976-77 was a mediocre League season for a team distracted, by a European adventure that lasted until March, from the routines of Division Two. You will be aware, from the reports of that disappointing campaign, of how McMenemy brought in two experienced internationals in Ted MacDougall and Alan Ball. By the time the 1977-78 season began, most of the Cup-winning team had left the Club, including Mike Channon for Manchester City. To fill his boots, the manager signed Phil Boyer, which meant a reunion (right) with MacDougall, previously his strike-partner at York, Bournemouth and Norwich. And in came a new pair at centre-back in Chris Nicholl, who assured McMenemy that he would win promotion, just as he had in his first full season with his three previous clubs, and Mike Pickering, who would have the misfortune during the Orient game to get injured and so miss being the one ever-present player in this promotion season.

Despite early-season optimism, however, Saints failed to impose themselves on the promotion race early on and it wasn't until mid-October that they joined the group of five or six clubs with realistic hopes of making Division I. As the season gathered momentum there were several matches that remain in the memories of the those who

followed the side around the country. Not all were glorious victories: the low points included a 3-0 defeat at Millwall, where Saints supporters were intimidated into watching in silence; a 2-1 defeat at Blackburn, where the home side's John Bailey conspired to get both Steve Williams and Peter Osgood sent off, thus establishing himself as The Dell's public enemy No.1 during the late seventies; not to mention a Cup defeat at Bristol Rovers.

Defeats were rare, however, and the team put together a formidable run as the season reached its climax. The Dell crowd saw Saints take revenge for the perceived injustice they suffered at Blackburn – a 5-0 win ending Rovers' fading promotion challenge.

During the last three weeks of the season increasing numbers of travelling fans witnessed a 1-1 draw at Fulham, a 3-0 win at Hull City and David Peach's last minute penalty at Luton, which gave Southampton a 2-1 win and sparked a celebratory pitch invasion by some of those supporters.

Other results, notably promotion rivals Tottenham faltering against both Brighton and Sunderland, meant Saints went to Orient knowing that a victory would put them in pole position for the Second Division Championship, while a draw would avert the need to win their final game.

The game itself was not a classic. It was certainly memorable for the atmosphere generated by the Saints support and because the more confident fans (and players, it seemed) felt that the point gained would be enough, but the game was characterised by what the *Times* described as "an untidy jumble of mistakes and inconsequential midfield activity." This did not concern those Saints' fans who were inclined to believe the omens: not only was Chris Nicholl in the team, but going to Orient for a 1-1 draw in the penultimate game was a replica of 1966 and all that.

And just as Terry Paine's equalising header had secured the draw in 1966, a headed goal again brought the score back to 1-1 in 1978. The unlikely hero was Tony Funnell, plucked out of non-league football the previous year to seize the moment with seven goals in that 13-match run-in, including both goals in a 2-0 home win over Crystal Palace after coming off the bench.

Division Two

Orient scored early through Mayo. Saints equalised just before half-time with a rare moment of class amongst the mediocrity. Alan Ball played the ball wide to David Peach, who crossed for Funnell to head in from close range.

Once the 1-1 scoreline was established, both teams were happy to pack the midfield, close down the game and allow the away fans to party on the terraces, a celebration that could have turned to tragedy as, not for the first time that season at Brisbane Road, a perimeter wall collapsed. Fortunately, those taken to hospital with minor injuries were discharged in good time to return to Southampton for the final match of the season, at home to Tottenham.

Spurs came to The Dell needing a point to be sure of the third promotion place, at the expense of Brighton, who had overtaken them during the run-in. Almost 29,000 packed the ground, with the Tottenham fans enclosed behind hastily-erected fences at the Archers Road end of the ground. A tense, error-ridden game petered out in a 0-0 stalemate, allowing Bolton Wanderers to take the Second Division title. Both sides were happy with the outcome. Brighton, whom Tottenham pipped to promotion on goal average, were less happy and you still hear an occasional mutter from their fans about a conspiracy to keep them down.

For a new wave of Saints followers, who see Premiership football as the norm, the excitement of promotion is something that can only be imagined.

Good as the memories are, let's hope that promotion is not an issue that Southampton have ever to concern themselves with again.

Lawrie McMenemy supervises the celebratory bath.
Back row (left to right) Funnell, Boyer, Williams, Ball, Peach, Nicholl. Front row: MacDougall, Wells, Andruszewski, Hebberd

ORIENT:
Jackson, Fisher, Roffey, Payne, Hoadley, Roeder, Clarke, Gray, Bennett, Kitchen, Mayo

SOUTHAMPTON:
Wells, Andruszewski, Peach, Williams, Nicholl, Pickering (Hebberd), Ball, Boyer, MacDougall, Holmes, Funnell

Referee: L.B. White (Harrow)

Attendance: 18,000

Compiled by **ANDY MERCER** from being there and from reports in the *Times. Echo* photographs

SOUTHAMPTON 1
LEEDS UNITED 0

Saints were looking to march on to those twin towers of Wembley again in 1978-79, but they had to negotiate an unfamiliar hurdle: a two-legged semi-final. Victory would take them into the League Cup Final.

A powerful Leeds United, lying fifth in the First Division, stood in their way and the first leg was at the fiercely partisan cauldron that is Elland Road. When Saints had been there in the League in November, they had been soundly beaten 4-0 and *Match of the Day* had glorified a perfectly-flighted goal by midfielder Tony Currie over the head of 'keeper Terry Gennoe.

The approaches to the ground were snow-covered and treacherous as 500 Southampton supporters made their way into Elland Road to be huddled into an exposed windy corner of the ground.

The pitch was, however, immaculate, looking green and lush and a testimony to the under-soil heating. As befits a semi-final, the game was a tense scrappy affair and after 47 minutes, courtesy of Currie and Ray Hankin, Saints were 2-0 down. Things were not looking good.

Then, however, the game began to turn. Perhaps it was those famous yellow-and-blue shirts worn at Wembley three years earlier? Or maybe it was the fierce determination of those 500 brave Saints fans to stick behind their team? Whatever, but when Terry Curran ran down the wing and crossed for Nick Holmes to head home, you could sense that perhaps this might be Saints' night after all. With a large, demanding, home crowd, Leeds were beginning to feel the pressure and when Steve Williams sent a perfect volley into the net to equalise, the away contingent went wild.

After that, there was no doubt that Saints would grind out a result, even when Phil Boyer was sent off in the closing stages and a 110 per cent effort was required. The final whistle was greeted with derision by a home crowd that had not perhaps adjusted to Life-after-Revie and had expected their team to steamroller a Saints side still finding its feet back in the First Division.

That side came over to our small corner of Elland Road and celebrated with the fans – even though there were still 90 minutes to go.

Saints' heroic comeback had surely given them the psychological edge. The Leeds manager, Jimmy Adamson, was having none of it, seemingly suggesting that his team's lapse had been something of a blip that would soon be rectified at The Dell – no matter that many a "big team" has run aground within the compact walls and somewhat unique atmosphere of the Saints' claustrophobic ground.

As I made my way into it that evening, I was in two minds. Since the run in the League Cup had begun with a convincing 5-2 victory at Birmingham in late August, I had been discussing with friends and work-mates the possibility of Saints going all the way to another Wembley final. It just felt right. The other side of my brain, though, was extremely worried about the non-availability of the suspended Boyer.

Who would replace him? The smart money (and mine) was on promising young afro-haired, reserve team forward, Tony Sealy.

He lacked big game experience but was a good little player who, if given his chance, would surely run until the Dell floodlights were switched off. But this was another of those occasions when Saints manager, Lawrie

Alan Ball (right) gets closer to Tony Currie at The Dell than Nick Holmes felt he managed at Elland Road

At Leeds, I was playing against Tony Currie, one of the hardest players I've ever marked. Skill - ever so good! … We were getting soundly beaten, to be fair … Then we went down the right and the ball came over from Terry Curran and I scored with a header … All of a sudden, we were buzzing … In the second game, we were without Phil Boyer, who had a magnificent season for us – the most under-rated striker I ever played with … Andruszewski went man-to-man on Currie – Lawrie obviously didn't think I was up to it. And he was quite right! We were under the cosh. We scored early and we hung on … The atmosphere was fabulous and we'd done it. We'd got to Wembley again and we felt we were up for it again.

Nick Holmes

Football League Cup Semi-Final, second leg

McMenemy, timed his trump card to perfection. Coming back into the side was not young Sealy at all but versatile local hero, Manny Andruszewski.

Dependable Manny had been used in a variety of roles by McMenemy, including both full- and centre-back. Now he was assigned the difficult task of man-marking playmaker Currie. It was this tactic more than anything that ultimately won Saints this game. Manny not only prevented any further "quality goals by a quality player" but virtually nullified Tony Currie's silky skills altogether.

I wasn't to know that, though, as the match kicked off: overwhelming tension gripped the cold night air and I had something the size of a match-ball pounding in my chest. Leeds obviously thought they could still win it, but McMenemy had done his homework so that one of Saints' classiest central defensive pairings of Chris Nicholl and Malcolm Waldron reduced the effectiveness of Leeds's dangerous twin strike-force of John Hawley and Ray Hankin.

The other significant factor over the course of the two games was the form of Saints' enigmatic winger, the exciting but unpredictable Terry Curran. He had first impressed us at The Dell as a member of one of Cloughie's Forest teams but it was after a move to Derby County that McMenemy decided to bring him to The Dell at more or less the same time as Partizan Belgrade right-back, Ivan Golac. These two players, plus the likes of Boyer, had given Saints that vital dimension of pace going forward. Despite his erratic ways,

Terry Gennoe celebrates a Wembley date

I always liked Terry Curran. It was obvious that he possessed the trickery to match his speed. His only real fault was that too many crosses found their way onto the Milton Terrace or said hello to buses passing down Archers Road. But this night - like those of the first leg and the rain-lashed Fifth Round win over Mike Channon's Man City before that - was to be one of those nights that Terry Curran set alight.

As early as the 11th minute, skipper Alan Ball linked with Nick Holmes and Trevor Hebberd to carve Leeds open. The dainty Hebberd drove the ball across the box and with Leeds's Frank Gray failing to clear, Curran was on it in a flash, first sorting his footwork, then crashing the ball into the roof of the net. Curran had delivered the killer blow in the blink of an eye. It seemed to those of us looking on, though, to take an age. But that didn't matter – Curran had recorded his first and only goal for Saints. It had been a cracking build-up, a strike to remember and proved enough on the night.

Leeds did have their moments. That match-ball felt as though it had moved from my chest and up into my mouth when Welsh international, Bryan Flynn, went close and when Terry Gennoe made a terrific full-length save when the sublime Currie escaped Andruszewski's attention for long enough to have a dip at goal.

But Saints and their relieved though ecstatic followers had survived their first two-legged semi-final and had another Wembley date.

SOUTHAMPTON:

Gennoe, Golac, Peach, Williams, Nicholl, Waldron, Ball, Andruszewski (Baker 86), Hebberd, Holmes, Curran

LEEDS UTD:

Harvey, Cherry, F. Gray, Flynn, Hart, Madeley, E.Gray, Hankin, Hawley (Harris 64), Currie, Graham

Referee: Clive Thomas (Treorchy)   *Attendance:* 23,646

Compiled by **CHRIS NEWMAN** from being there and from *Echo* reports – with **Nick Illingsworth** reporting from Elland Road. Nick Holmes interviewed by **David Bull**. *Echo* photographs

NOTTINGHAM FOREST 3
SOUTHAMPTON 2

Saints had the all-conquering Nottingham Forest – Football League champions and League Cup winners in 1978 and well on their way to being European Club champions in 1979 - on the rack for 30 minutes of the 1978-79 League Cup Final. But, like the great side they had become under Brian Clough's legendary management, Forest fought back like true champions to win the trophy 3-2.

There was no stopping Forest that season – unless you count finishing only runners-up in the First Division - but Saints came closer than most at the end of a bitterly cold week in mid-March 1979. Looking back over 20 years, you sense that Saints' contribution to what *Rothmans* hailed as "one of the best finals for years" may have been understated a tad.

Remember that while Forest were finishing second in the top flight, Southampton had just got back into it after four seasons in the Second Division. Yet Clough's men had come off at half-time having been outfought and outplayed by the underdogs from the south coast.

Of course, it was to turn dramatically after the interval when Forest's mercurial midfield genius, Scottish international Archie Gemmill, began to pull the strings although it took a crucial mistake to unlock a battling Saints defence. Once they had made the breakthrough, Forest were rampant, turning a one-goal deficit into a 3-1 lead before conceding a late goal to Nick Holmes. The quality of Holmes's strike rendered it one of the finest consolation goals ever scored at the old stadium.

Sadly, it came too late to save a Saints side who, for an hour, had begun to think of Wembley as their lucky ground, where they might repeat their previous underdog appearance in a cup final (Match No. 69 of which you'll hardly need reminding). Here, after a week of snow and sleet and on a Wembley pitch flanked by banks of cleared snow and cutting up rough, they had the crown princes of Europe rocking on their haunches. Sporting their favoured yellow-and-blue Cup Final kit and roared on by a huge following in the 100,000 Wembley crowd, they made the best possible start, taking the lead with a top-drawer goal crafted between left-back David Peach and skipper Alan Ball after just 16 minutes.

Peach pushed a short pass to Ball on the edge of the Forest penalty area and bounded forward on to the return pass before adroitly rounding Peter Shilton to score. Shilton was at the peak of his goalkeeping powers and basked in clean sheets. The fact that he was to be beaten twice by quality strikes on this day, spoke highly of the skill and commitment which Lawrie McMenemy's men put into the game.

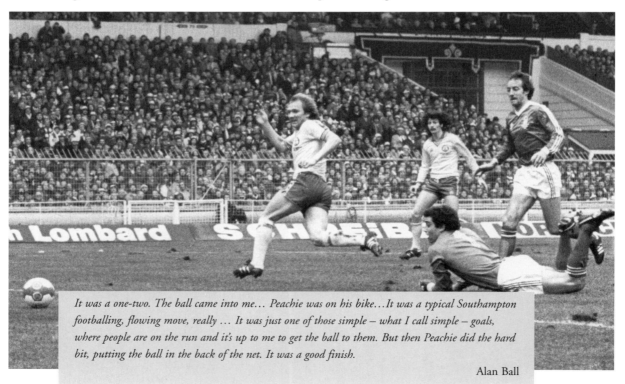

It was a one-two. The ball came into me… Peachie was on his bike…It was a typical Southampton footballing, flowing move, really … It was just one of those simple – what I call simple – goals, where people are on the run and it's up to me to get the ball to them. But then Peachie did the hard bit, putting the ball in the back of the net. It was a good finish.

Alan Ball

But by the time Holmes had struck the second explosive blow with just three minutes left on the clock, the game had been lost with Forest's dark, lean and classy striker Garry Birtles hailed as the hero of the hour. Birtles turned the game on its head with opportunist goals in the 50th and 77th minutes and Tony Woodcock tied Forest's red-and-white ribbon on the trophy with a sweet effort on 82 minutes.

The pivotal moment of the match came just five minutes into the second-half when Chris Nicholl, normally a tower of strength in the middle of the Saints defence, got his wires fatally crossed with his 'keeper, Terry Gennoe. Saints were clinging bravely onto their lead despite growing Forest pressure, which had gathered momentum late in the first-half. Then Forest's Scottish left-winger John Robertson, who had been given little scope by Ivan Golac, drove the ball in low from the left and as Saints 'keeper prepared for a routine pick-up, Nicholl put his foot in the way of the ball. Gennoe was suddenly stranded and, as the ball broke loose, Birtles pounced on it and and powered it home.

Nicholl had twice been a League Cup winner with Aston Villa but his chances of a third winner's medal were fast disappearing on 77 minutes when Birtles sped on to a pass from Woodcock to get the better of him again and make it 2-1 to Forest. Saints' hopes collapsed completely when Gemmill threaded a pass through to Woodcock, a skilful, beautifully balanced striker who steadied himself before arrowing a terrific shot past the helpless Gennoe.

When the game was seemingly beyond them, Saints suddenly roused their deflated followers with a goal of high quality. A cross from Terry Curran was turned back by Malcolm Waldron for Holmes to crash home an unstoppable shot. It came too late to save Saints who, to be fair, had finished a clear second-best.

> *The ball kept coming to me. I cleared one off the line and I scored the goal. It was a nice feeling to have beaten the best goalkeeper in the world with a good, long shot.*
>
> Nick Holmes

Yet in the first-half they had been worthy of their lead. Waldron had kept a tight rein on Woodcock and Nicholl clamped down strongly on Birtles. Golac was cutting out Robertson's supply to the front men and, perhaps most significantly, Saints were containing the Forest midfield which boasted the likes of Gemmill and Martin O'Neill.

Ball and John McGovern were having a rare old battle of wits and, up to half-time, Ball had had the better of it. Forest's towering centre-halves, Larry Lloyd and David Needham, though, were giving Saints' lightweight strike force of Phil Boyer and Austin Hayes little scope although Curran was posing a problem or two for Frank Clarke down the right wing.

It was when Gemmill, the play-maker of this great Forest side, started to see a lot more of the ball that the pattern of the game changed. As the little Scot began to stamp his mark, McGovern and O'Neill came into the picture, too. Robertson was suddenly a major presence down the left and Saints were starting to get stretched out at the back.

There were just seven minutes left when Saints sent on their substitute, the chunky Geordie striker Tony Sealy, for Hayes, but there were many critics among the Saints' followers who claimed Manny Andruszewski would have been a better choice on the bench. The curly-haired kid from Eastleigh had a superb motor and could run forever. One of his specialities – demonstrated in the semi-final, as we saw – was marking jobs. He could stick to a predator like glue. Perhaps with him on the bench, McMenemy would have had an antedote for Gemmill.

It was pure hypothesis of course and the manager typically went for the positive option of a striker on the bench. No-one questioned it too much when the teams were announced.

NOTTINGHAM FOREST:
Shilton, Barrett, Clarke, McGovern, Lloyd, Needham, O'Neill, Gemmill, Birtles, Woodcock, Robertson

SOUTHAMPTON:
Gennoe, Golac, Peach, Williams, Nicholl, Waldron, Ball, Boyer, Hayes (Sealy 83), Holmes, Curran

Referee: Peter Reeves (Leicester)   *Attendance:* 100,000

Adapted by **BOB BRUNSKELL** from his original *Echo* report, with additional material – from *Rothmans Football Yearbook 1979-80* and an interview with Nick Holmes – by **David Bull**. Alan Ball interviewed by John Hughes for the *Saints' Official History* video. *Echo* photograph

SOUTHAMPTON 4
NOTTINGHAM FOREST 1

When Nottingham Forest came to The Dell in November 1979, there were some significant changes to the Southampton side that had gone down to them at Wembley in March.

England centre-half, Dave Watson, had been wooed back to English football from Werder Bremen – a dry-run, you might say, for the sensational signing, come February, of Kevin Keegan from Hamburg.

And Keegan's good friend, Mick Channon, had returned from Manchester City to team up with Phil Boyer, the man Lawrie McMenemy had bought to replace him. The afternoon's goals would be shared between those two signings and Boyer.

The side had lost four games on the trot, the third of them being Terry Gennoe's last game for the Saints, with Peter Wells coming in. And yet they proceeded to take Forest to pieces. Brian Clough's side had been beaten in their last two away games – each time by 1-0 – but they were opponents to be reckoned with. Ten weeks after winning the League Cup for the second successive season, they had beaten Malmo to win the European Cup. Trevor Francis, the first £1m signing, had displaced Martin O'Neill from the Wembley winning line-up to score the only goal in Munich. And they had finished runners-up in the League to Liverpool. Now they were on their way to retaining their European trophy, having won the second leg of their second round tie (for a 4-1 aggregate) in Rumania in midweek. And if you think I've been delving into the records to prepare some context for this match report, you're only partly right: most of these statistics were adduced by journalists trying to convey the magnitude of Southampton's affrontery.

The demolition began in the 27th minute when Watson headed in a cross from Holmes. "Elementary!", exclaimed Jack Welling, ho! ho! – maybe not appreciating that Conan Doyle had played for Portsmouth (albeit a team of Victorian gentlemen with no ancestral link to the current Fratton outfit, I'm assured). Two minutes later, it was 2-0 when Shilton parried a shot from Graham Baker, the young midfielder who'd been finding it hard to get a game while Alan Ball and Steve Williams were in regular residence. Channon picked up the rebound and worked the space to score.

The best was yet to come in the form of Boyer's two second-half goals – memorable both in their build-up and in the finishing of the Saints' No.9, who had been a Clough reject as a 19 year-old at Derby. It is the way that the Southampton forwards swept majestically towards the Milton Road end to beat Shilton twice more that lives with me from this game – my recall having been reinforced, of course, by video evidence. If ever I had the time and inclination to sit and watch football videos for as long as it took, one of my first projects would be to determine when the "early ball" into the box replaced the "pull-back" from the by-line as the centre of choice. We had been spoiled as Saints fans by the by-line mastery of Terry Paine, whose art had been carried on by Mick Channon. But now here was the disciple setting up Boyer with an early ball slid between back-tracking defenders and a stranded goalkeeper.

Boyer completes the scoring with a goal that had "reporters reaching for their superlatives"

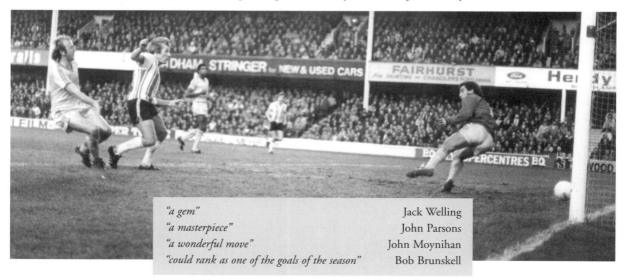

"a gem"	Jack Welling
"a masterpiece"	John Parsons
"a wonderful move"	John Moynihan
"could rank as one of the goals of the season"	Bob Brunskell

Division One

This magic moment in the 64th minute was an elaborate version of what Ball had done on 57, a minute after Birtles had got one back for the visitors. Ball's run and pass merely required that he dispossess Kenny Burns and skuttle 40 yards before sliding the ball in low and early for Boyer. If the subsequent Channon-and- Boyer effort ended in the same sweet way, this goal was special for the orchestration of a move started in their own half by Williams and on to Ball to Boyer to Baker to Channon and Boyer again, a goal that had the reporters reaching for their superlatives and which remains one of my all-time favourites.

It seemed to be agreed that this was Channon's finest game since coming home and Boyer was hot.

It was the ninth consecutive game in which he had scored at The Dell and his two goals kept him top of the First Division's scorers. He would continue to slot them in at home, bringing the sequence to 12 games at the year's end. And, although he would tail off seriously after that, his 23 goals would still make him the Division's top man.

> *We destroyed them. No problem at all! If we'd played Forest [at Wembley] only a year later, I know that it would have been us! ... We had needed [to fill] a couple of positions, which we had with Channon coming back. That's when we started to build something special on the right-hand side: Channon, Bally and myself [with] some terrific football ...That was the kind of game which really would have suited us at Wembley ... It was a special time*
>
> Ivan Golac

Forest had not conceded three League goals – let alone four – for more than two years. Describing the result as "a near thrashing," John Moynihan paid tribute to "a thorough team performance." In recalling "wonderful" goals, we tend to forget the defensive contributions. So well had Trevor Hebberd, the dependable utility player, man-marked his £1m opponent that John Parsons described him as "Trevor Francis's jailer."

Like Moynihan, Parsons praised the team effort, all the way back to goalkeeper Wells, the former Forest player who'd been sold by Clough to Southampton.

On a day when two of his rejects had the last laugh, Brian Clough could not have been more generous in defeat. Not for him a Fergiesque whine about some tiring midweek expedition in Europe. He was content to acknowledge that "Southampton were incredible, better than us in every department."

And he added, in a bulletin on Kenny Burns's broken nose that had caused him to be substituted, that this would improve his centre-back's looks: "so out of disaster comes something good."

Mike Channon wriggles the ball round Shilton's feet to score Saints' second

---

SOUTHAMPTON:

Wells, Golac, Holmes, Williams, Watson, Waldron, Ball, Channon, Boyer, Baker, Hebberd

NOTTINGHAM FOREST:

Shilton, Anderson, Gray, McGovern, Lloyd, Burns (Needham, 79), Francis, Bowyer, Birtles, Woodcock, Robertson

Referee: Mr S. Bates (Bristol)   *Attendance:* 22,072

Compiled by **DAVID BULL** from Bob Brunskell's reports in the *Echo;* from the accounts of the three cited journalists (Moynihan, Parsons and Welling), writing in their respective unidentified nationals; and from an interview with Ivan Golac. Photographs from the *Echo*

WATFORD 7
SOUTHAMPTON 1

Even their manager Graham Taylor gave Watford no realistic chance of retrieving a four-goal deficit as they met Saints for what appeared a purely academic second leg of their League Cup Second Round tie at Vicarage Road in September 1980.

Taylor, then in his first spell as Watford manager, described his team's 4-0 defeat in the first leg at The Dell as "the worst performance of any team I have managed. Now my players owe it to themselves to put some pride back in their game."

Those words were to be chillingly repeated by his opposite number Lawrie McMenemy as Saints suffered surely the most extraordinary set-back in their entire history. Watford won the second leg at Vicarage Road 7-1 to go through 7-5 on aggregate amid scenes of utter astonishment, some of it deliriously happy, some of it stunned and shameful disbelief.

It was a result which astounded English soccer because Saints, with European Footballer of the Year Kevin Keegan having an immediate influence on the side, had won three of their first four games and were a whisker away from the top of the First Division. The 4-0 demolition of Watford in Southampton's opening League Cup game of 1980-81 was nothing less than their followers were expecting, so well were the side playing.

The fact that Graham Taylor had got Watford accelerating up through the leagues, from Division Four to Division Three to Division Two in successive seasons, was a sign that here was a young side very much on the move forward. Maybe it should have served as a warning just as Keegan's withdrawal from the return leg at Vicarage Road through injury should have. But it didn't. The big reputation which Saints had built up over their first five games was reduced to rubble by the Second Division club on a night when the formbook went haywire.

Saints came out as though their place in the Third Round was already secured and, as I reported on the night, "it will go down as one of the worst cases of overconfidence in the history of the League Cup competition."

For Watford, struggling in the depths of the Second Division, it was a night of sheer fantasy. Taylor admitted that he would have settled, before the game, for a draw:

> I was so knocked back by what had happened at The Dell, but it's nothing to the way Lawrie must have been feeling after that. Despite the score he went up and faced the Press. That must have taken a lot of guts.

McMenemy had warned his players against complacency. But complacency was rife. Instead of setting about Watford and finishing the job, they showed Watford, with their proud cup-fighting history, far too much respect and the Hertfordshire men, their confidence soaring with every goal that went in, humiliated them.

By the time they realised their first leg advantage was in danger, it was too late. Watford are nicknamed the Hornets but they stung the First Division side with the venom of a rattlesnake.

All Watford needed was an early goal to spark a ray of hope. They got it and the spark became a roaring flame as Watford launched wave upon wave of attacks and made them tell. Taylor's tactical ploy was to get the ball into the box as much as possible to unnerve Southampton's unpredictable 'keeper Ivan Katalinic. And as the balls rained in from the flanks, the Saints' defence, so organised in the recent past, fell apart.

Saints surrendered the midfield to their opponents from the outset and Watford capitalised with a 10th-minute goal from Malcolm Poskett, made by Watford's lanky centre-forward Ross Jenkins with the most delicate of back-headers. Jenkins's great height and aerial dominance was the key to the extraordinary outcome of the match. And before half-time he had disarmed Saints again with a ball to Ray Train which he despatched after 35 minutes.

McMenemy's half-time orders were for Saints to push forward and impose themselves on the game and early in the second-half there were more positive signs as Steve Williams tested the Watford 'keeper Eric Steele and Charlie George shook the bar with a vicious half-volley.

For a spell everything looked to be under control but Jenkins awakened Watford to the belief that they could yet save the tie when he drove the ball low into the box where Luther Blissett fumbled but Patching followed up to lash a low shot beyond Katalinic. The 67th-minute goal didn't look half so grave when midfielder Graham Baker, who had just been booked for a foul on Mick Henderson, pulled a goal back after 73 minutes. George made it with a delightful flick and Baker struck a firm right-foot shot which Steve Sims deflected into his own net.

Watford's reply was stunning. Within seconds Chris Nicholl had brought down Jenkins in full flight and Ian Bolton stepped up to tuck away the penalty — 4-1. McMenemy, who had hurried down from his seat in the directors' box to join his anxious trainers in the dug-out, hung his head in desperation when Jenkins, afforded all the time in the world, scored the crucial fifth goal with just four of the 90 minutes remaining.

League Cup Second Round, second leg

But even then there was one last twist of drama in normal time when Williams curled a free kick into the net only for it to be disallowed for offside against Mike Channon. Extra time had barely begun when Train limped off to be replaced by Nigel Callaghan, a 17-year-old winger who was getting only his second taste of first team football.

And it was Callaghan who turned an unthinkable defeat into a harsh reality, again after a powerful assist from Jenkins. When the big centre-forward's shot came back off Katalinic, Callaghan bounded in to rip a murderous shot into the top of the net. Poskett completed Saints'

nightmare when Henderson sent him clear and he made no mistake with just six minutes left to play. Before that George had limped off, Channon had been denied by a superb fingertip save from Steele and young sub Steve Moran had scooped a half chance over the bar.

It was one of the most hurtful results of McMenemy's generally successful managerial career and he summed up as only he could: "It's like trying to climb up Niagara Falls. Right then I couldn't recall many worst performances from teams I had managed, but really the fault was mine. There's no way a team should surrender a four-goal advantage in a cup tie."

A picture that tells its own lamentable story

WATFORD:
Steele, Henderson, Jackett, Patching, Sims, Bolton, Blissett, Poskett, Jenkins, Train (Callaghan 96), Rostron

SOUTHAMPTON:
Katalinic, Waldron, McCartney, Williams, Watson, Nicholl, Hebberd, Channon, George (Moran 99), Holmes, Baker

Referee: Brian Martin (Keyworth)   *Attendance:* 15,992

Adapted by **BOB BRUNSKELL** from his own *Echo* report. *Echo* photograph

Tottenham Hotspur 4
Southampton 4

Two teams primed with attacking ideals made goalscoring look easy at White Hart Lane on Boxing Day 1980 when Spurs and Saints drew 4-4. It's the kind of scoreline that has managers despairing at their team's lack of defensive resiliance, yet chances were created so expertly and executed so clinically that this holiday showcase was a great victory for football.

Among the game's principal creators was Tottenham's Glenn Hoddle, linking superlatively well with his Argentine midfield partner Ricky Villa. Hoddle was one of two future Southampton managers on view. Don't ask what the other one, Saints' perfectionist defender Chris Nicholl, thought about eight goals being conceded.

In those days, though, League football was fighting to claw back missing fans and this was just the sort of game to bring them flocking back to the terraces. Two pocket-sized teenage strikers were the heroes of the hour. Gary Brooke, who had scored a hat-trick in a Football Combination match against Saints Reserves just four days before, was rewarded with his first start for Spurs. He more than justified it with two fine goals.

But his opposite number Steve Moran was not to be outdone. The bright-eyed hot-shot had burst off the bench in January, when just 19, to score against Manchester City, but had been kept waiting for a start until October. He'd responded with six goals in five games and was shaping up as one of the finds of the season. And this day he showed marvellous opportunism to bring Saints a point which for two extraordinary periods of the game seemed to have been beyond them.

The game was full of festive fayre and Hoddle and his midfield adversary Steve Williams were the central characters. They bubbled like vintage champagne. Their creativity, their vision and their ability to pass a ball with such perfection tore great holes in the respective defences and the abundance of goalmouth activity left the holiday crowd breathless.

McMenemy's sides were never afraid to attack away from home, and this one was a case in point. The full-backs Ivan Golac and Nick Holmes had a natural instinct to get forward and even their young sweeper Reuben Agboola, who had just recently cut his teeth in an awe-inspiring debut at Old Trafford, liked to bound forward and pass the ball.

For Saints the die had been cast early in the game. The home side scored twice in the first 20 minutes and McMenemy's men had no option but to push forward and try and save it.

The first goal arrived after 12 minutes, majestically forged by Villa who went through a wall of defenders as though they were not there to set up the pale-faced Scottish predator Steve Archibald for a fierce shot into the corner of the goal.

Charlie George makes it 2-2 from an acute angle

Division One

Saints were looking nervous and ragged as Spurs sprayed the ball about and after 20 minutes they were two down, Brooke bulging the net after Hoddle had combined with Garth Crooks to open up the defence down the forward from his defensive duties. He in turn picked out Brooke who had the time and space to chip 'keeper Peter Wells as he came off his line. Hoddle was again the architect as Spurs scored the fourth and surely the decisive

Steve Moran sweeps in front of Spurs No. 11 Garth Crooks to score Saints' late point-saver, with Agboola and George (right) in attendance

right. If Saints hadn't found a spark of hope there and then, they would have been sunk big time. They found it five minutes later, albeit through a lucky break. The Tottenham 'keeper Milija Aleksic failed to hold on to a shot from Williams and when the ball squirmed loose, Moran was on to it in a flash, jabbing it shoulder high. Aleksic parried the ball and as it sailed up, Graham Baker ran in to head it into the unguarded net.

Then, after 36 minutes, Saints were level. Dave Watson, again demonstrating that he was one of the game's more creative centre-halves, threaded a well-weighted pass down the left to send Williams clear. And when Spurs dabbed half-heartedly at the cross, Charlie George hit an acute-angled effort past Aleksic.

After the interval Spurs, and Hoddle in particular, regained the initiative. On 52 minutes the England star brilliantly picked out Steve Perryman who was driving

goal. He exchanged passes with Brooke and Archibald following a short corner and the beneficiary was Crooks who was left to convert the simplest of chances.

Saints had a mountain to climb and little time to do it in. But there was no shortage of character in the side. No cause was a lost one and Moran epitomised that never-say-die spirit by chasing like a greyhound to reach Channon's long, probing pass before the 'keeper. He made it and from a tight angle rifled a low shot just inside the far post.

It was a marvellous finish, but Moran wasn't done. Three minutes from time Channon struck a deep corner from the right which created mayhem in the penalty area, Moran emerging like a terrier from the ensuing scramble to volley a superb equaliser.

It was another step towards his becoming the season's top scorer for the Saints, despite giving the ever-present Channon 12 games' start.

TOTTENHAM HOTSPUR:
Aleksic, Yorath, Hughton (O'Reilly 43), Roberts, Lacy, Perryman, Brooke, Archibald, Villa, Hoddle, Crooks

SOUTHAMPTON:
Wells, Golac, Agboola, Williams, Watson, Nicholl, Moran, Channon, George, Holmes, Baker

Referee: Derek Civil (Birmingham)   *Attendance:* 28,792

Adapted by **BOB BRUNSKELL** from his own *Echo* report. *Echo* photographs

LIVERPOOL 0
SOUTHAMPTON 1

The tireless resolution which had carried Saints through 450 minutes of defensive invincibility baffled and eventually destroyed European champions Liverpool at Anfield in November 1981. Saints battled like demons for what looked like being a draw but was turned into glorious victory by a late, late strike from young Steve Moran. And while their fans celebrated deliriously, The Kop was stunned into silence. A precious moment indeed.

Liverpool were still the dominant force in English football and although some claimed their star was waning after this 1-0 defeat by Southampton on a misty, murky autumn day, the Red Army were able to shake it off and march on to their second Championship in three years. Indeed, four more title wins were to follow in the 1980s.

Yet Saints were no slouches themselves in those days and their first victory at Anfield in the top flight carried them hard on the heels of the leaders during a season in which they were to finish seventh with only Liverpool and runners-up Ipswich scoring more goals.

They had gone into the Liverpool game on the back of clean sheets against Stoke, Leeds and Wolves, preceded by Sporting Lisbon in the UEFA Cup, but this ranked as one of their all-time great shut-outs, achieved against a Liverpool side who would lose only seven League games all season and who were just days away from a World Club title showdown against the Brazilian champions, Flamengo.

Saints owed their success most of all to an inspirational goalkeeping display. Ivan Katalinic won't figure on your all-time list of great Southampton 'keepers, but at Anfield and against a Liverpool attack in full spate, the dark, brooding Yugoslav turned in a truly brilliant display. Agile, spectacular and at times unpredictable, Ivan was nicknamed "The Kat" by his team-mates, and he lived up to it that day. Many doubts had been raised about his overall ability but he emphatically rammed them back down the throats of his critics. Two saves from Graeme Souness were breathtaking and the Liverpool raiders who kept up a constant battery of the visiting goal, were left shaking their heads in resigned disbelief as The Kat sprung

Mark Lawrenson (right) is unable to catch Kevin Keegan to welcome him back to Anfield

between his goalposts fending off everything they could throw at him.

When Ian Rush, then an explosive new weapon in the Liverpool armoury, ran through the Saints defence just before half-time, Katalinic's resistance looked set to snap. But the Yugoslav's defiant charge from his line seemed to unnerve the Welshman who checked in his stride and hurried his shot the wrong side of the post. There was another thrusting new talent in the Liverpool side, the bustling Irish midfielder Ronnie Whelan. Rush and he gave Liverpool extra direction and pace and became increasingly the focal point as Liverpool looked to turn their unerring possession into a last, decisive sweep at goal.

Liverpool's passing, movement and ability to keep the ball was unsurpassed in English football. Although Saints were on the brink of achieving one of their finest results, they were to do it without seeing too much of the ball. Alan Ball, back for a second spell as midfield general, was seemingly forever in retreat as Liverpool attacks beat down on the Southampton defence like a relentless tide.

The back four, marshalled by Chris Nicholl, were besieged at times and glad of reinforcements from midfield. No-one provided greater support that day than David Armstrong who ceaselessly funnelled back, particularly to help Nick Holmes as Whelan, Phil Neal and Terry McDermott probed down the right flank.

All the time, though, Liverpool had to keep half a mind to the quality in the Saints attack. Former Anfield legend Kevin Keegan was always capable of disarming them on the break and so was Mike Channon, stalking the touchline, where he provided their best attacking outlet.

Division One

Liverpool at times had to rely on some perceptive last-ditch defending by Mark Lawrenson to defuse the threat of the long-striding Saints and England striker but it was from an unlikely source, the right foot of central defender Malcolm Waldron, that Saints had come closest to breaking the deadlock just before half-time.

Phil Thompson caught Keegan high with a tackle and Waldron stepped forward to crack a ferocious free-kick which was scrambled inches over the bar.

When Nicholl later moved up for another set piece, a free-kick from Ball which was nodded on by Keegan, the Northern Ireland centre-half put his own header narrowly over. As the clock ticked on and Liverpool's pressure increased, Saints wore the look of a side who would happily settle for a draw. But there was to be one last dramatic twist of the tail.

Just three minutes were left when Steve Williams broke from deep in midfield, skilfully evading two challenges and finding Keegan whose first-time flick caught the Liverpool defence square. Suddenly Moran was behind them bearing down on goal. To a man Liverpool appealed for offside but the flag stayed down and the young striker kept his cool, fending off Alan Hansen who was snapping at his heels before rounding Bruce Grobbelaar and slipping the ball into the empty net. Later video clips showed that Phil Neal had played Moran onside.

No-one was more delighted with the victory than Keegan who had been warmly welcomed back to his old domain but derided by The Kop after he had helped Saints achieve an audacious victory which the shell-shocked Liverpool supporters saw as daylight robbery.

Keegan admitted that

> it would have been nice to have won in more style but we had to match them for effort, try and contain them and then try and convert one of our chances. To do it so late in the game, when they didn't have much time to do anything about it, was just about perfect. People were accusing us of being a negative side afterwards but it's worth remembering that we went to Anfield as one of the leading scorers in the First Division. Liverpool had the misfortune to catch us in a very determined mood.

And although it was a *team* mood, the scoring record to which Keegan referred would see him crowned as the Division's top scorer (with 26) and as the PFA Player of the Year. And Moran would be the PFA's Young Player of the Year, despite being sidelined from mid-January by a back injury.

Steve Moran loses the pursuing Hansen and rounds the prostrate Grobbelaar to score

---

LIVERPOOL:
Grobbelaar, Neal, Lawrenson, Thompson, Kennedy, Hansen, Dalglish, Whelan, Rush, McDermott (Johnson 79) Souness

SOUTHAMPTON:
Katalinic, Golac, Holmes, Williams, Nicholl, Waldron, Keegan, Channon, Moran, Armstrong, Ball

Referee: M.G. Peck (Kendall)   *Attendance:* 35,189

Adapted by **BOB BRUNSKELL** from his own *Echo* report. *Echo* photographs

MIDDLESBROUGH 0
SOUTHAMPTON 1

High-flying Saints and their manager Lawrie McMenemy were enjoying the view from the top of the League at the end of January 1982. A hard-earned 1-0 win at Middlesbrough's crumbling old fortress at Ayresome Park achieved a landmark in the club's 97-year history. It was the first time they had topped the First Division.

Two years before McMenemy had brought in the man with the class to lead them to the top. And against Middlesbrough, former European Footballer of the Year Kevin Keegan turned the dream into reality with the golden goal that carried the club to No. 1 position.

It was a heady time for club and supporters spanning three more games (a 2-1 home win over Manchester City, a 1-1 draw at Aston Villa and a 2-0 success against Nottingham Forest at The Dell) before Ipswich sent them tumbling down in spectacular fashion at Portman Road. They lost 5-2, beaten and bemused by Alan Brazil's stunning five-goal salvo.

But they had enjoyed their moment of glory. When the news had come through at Middlesbrough that Manchester United and Ipswich Town had lost and Saints were top, McMenemy vividly recalls the euphoria which swept through the dressing room:

> It was like winning the Cup all over again and I was certainly going to enjoy the moment. We had won the Cup and played in the League Cup Final but it's the ambition of every club to go top of the League and to do it in January was no mean achievement. Brian Clough had struck first blow for the smaller clubs taking Derby and Nottingham Forest to the top and we had followed suit. I would have been happier if we had been top three months later but it wasn't to be. But nothing could take away how good we felt that day at Middlesbrough. When I looked around the dressing room I was especially pleased for players like Mick Channon, Nick Holmes and Malcolm Waldron. They were at The Dell when I first arrived and they could never have dreamed then that one day we would be top.

Keegan's goal after just eight minutes of the game at Middlesbrough was worthy of the milestone it created. It was conceived out of a half-chance and taken very much against the mathematical odds. Alan Ball was the architect, disarming the Boro defence with a telling first-time ball which sent Keegan accelerating towards goal. With defenders snapping at his heels and the Boro 'keeper Jim Platt racing out to meet him, the former Liverpool and Hamburg star was driven wide, too wide it seemed. As he almost hit the by-line the angle seemed too acute but somehow Keegan got his angles just right, cutting the ball back so that it rolled just inside the post and across

the line before a back-pedalling Boro defender could retrieve it.

Bobby Thomson, the Boro midfielder, could have denied Saints their moment of glory but made the penalty miss of the season. Even the Boro fans wore sheepish grins when Terry Cochrane's theatrical dive over a combined challenge by Holmes and Graham Baker earned the approval of referee Arthur Robinson in the 64th minute. But in a reckless act of justice Thomson stepped up and screwed the penalty-kick 10 yards wide.

It was a day, I suppose, when fortune favoured the brave. Saints began boldly and grabbed the initiative against a Boro side locked in the jaws of a relegation struggle and very low on confidence. Having grabbed the initiative they held against a Boro challenge which grew in determination through the second-half.

Elsewhere the leading players in Division I were having a bad day at the office. Manchester United's brief reign as leaders ended with defeat at Swansea, who, under the management of John Toshack, were to make their own special piece of history as League leaders later in the season. Ipswich Town could have gone top if they had won their home game against Notts County. But County turned the form-book upside down with a 3-1 win at Portman Road.

Kevin Keegan rounds goalkeeper Platt to score the historic goal

Division One

Boro hadn't won a League game since September and the Southampton game-plan was to make a fast start and try and further undermine their confidence – which they succeeded in doing.

David Armstrong, making his first return journey to the ground where he had been a Boro hero, would have been first on to the scoresheet, but Platt smothered his close-range shot and Baker, who was to fill in solidly for the transfer-listed Steve Williams, sent the rebound wide.

Keegan, having broken the deadlock, promised a second when he pounced on a careless backpass from Irving Nattrass, but Platt dashed out to deny the England star with a double save. Boro's pressure began to grow and Dave Hodgson fired the first warning shot which grazed the Southampton bar. Cochrane tested their Yugoslav 'keeper Ivan Katalinic and burly defender John Craggs beat him with a thunderous shot which Holmes manfully blocked.

For Saints it was not so much a glorious charge to the top; more a well organised climb with the defence taking the strain superbly as Boro came back at them. For much of the second-half the Saints wore a harassed look which hardly befitted a side about to take the biggest step in their League history.

But they got there in the end and Trevor Hebberd, who was standing in for the injured Steve Moran, might have made it a more comfortable passage had he converted one of the few chances that came the way of the visiting side in the closing stages of the game.

The story made the front page of the *Echo*.
Mr Perkins, the Chairman of Southern Newspapers, presents Lawrie McMenemy with a gold medallion and a framed copy of the page

As noted in the previous report, Moran's season ended between his goal at Liverpool and the win at Middlesbrough, by which time he had already done enough (nine goals in his 18 League games) to be the PFA's Young Player of the Year.

That is surely a measure of how much he had contributed to the side in half a season and a suggestion of what might have been had he been able to maintain his partnership with Keegan now that the Saints were on top.

MIDDLESBROUGH:

Platt, Craggs, Bailey, Ross, Nattrass, McAndrew, Cochrane, Otto, Hodgson, Bell, Thomson

SOUTHAMPTON:

Katalinic, Golac, Holmes, Baker, Nicholl, Waldron, Keegan, Channon, Hebberd, Armstrong, Ball

Referee: Arthur Robinson (Radcliffe)

Attendance: 12,682

Adapted by **BOB BRUNSKELL** from his own *Echo* report and a subsequent interview with Lawrie McMenemy. *Echo* photographs

SOUTHAMPTON 5
COVENTRY CITY 5

Mistakes they say make for entertainment in football and as defenders dithered Saints and Coventry City served up a feast of epic proportions at The Dell near the end of the heady season of 1981-82. All the goals in an extraordinary 5-5 draw were taken with such precision and style it would be easy to overlook two defences who constantly defied the Trades Description Act through their utter failure to do the job required of them.

The moments of quite alarming Southampton vulnerability were perhaps easier to comprehend because they had lost one of their centre-backs with a bad facial injury just before half-time, the result of a crunching head-to-head with City's big, awkward striker Steve Whitton. This was bad luck for the 20 year-old Mark Whitlock, who was just getting a bit of a run in his debut season. And with Danny Wallace coming off the bench, it required some redeployment, Holmes going into the centre and Armstrong dropping back to fill his vacancy.

But individuals compounded basic errors of judgment which were punished savagely by two athletic young giants in the Coventry attack, an inspired Mark Hateley and the rampaging Whitton himself. In many ways, though, the game was above criticism. In the second-half particularly it reached the realms of fantasy as Saints turned a 2-4 deficit into a 5-4 lead.

On a night when there was a war raging in the far-off Falklands, the 18,000 crowd poured into The Dell looking for some light relief. For 90 minutes they were transformed on to another plain. The football was at times exquisite and the goals were magnificent, none of them better than a 64th minute chip from Keith Cassells, delivered by the ex-postman which such precision that Les Sealey, the Coventry 'keeper, was reduced to a groping, floundering figure near his own goal-line.

Cassells hadn't long arrived from Oxford – as the latest attempt to fill the hole left by Steve Moran - and the goal rated among the best of a 1981-82 season where the volume, and the variety of, goals had been immense (as already noted – even if two 1-0 wins have been selected to highlight this exciting campaign).

Matching Cassells for quality finishing was Kevin Keegan. Twice, the dark curls were a blur as he ghosted in behind the Sky Blues defence and twice bewitched Sealey with some clinical finishing, completing his tally of 26 for the season, the highest (as previously observed) in the Division. Yet, at the end of a mild, breathless early summer

Kevin Keegan falls under a challenge from Paul Dyson, but no penalty was given

night, the real hero was Hateley, the tall, pencil-slim Coventry centre-forward who had been a doubt because of flu. When he contracted a bad nose bleed just before the game, he was tempted to throw in the towel but pluckily gave it a go and finished up with a superb hat-trick.

His third and last goal made it 5-5 and left Southampton's hopes of qualifying for the UEFA Cup dangling by a thread. Fortunately for them, they drew in their horns for the next match against Sunderland. They cagily beat the Wearsiders 1-0 at The Dell and a fifth season in Europe was theirs.

Cassells gave the first hint of what was to come in the Coventry game with a header that was cleared off the line. But the Sky Blues drew first blood after 11 minutes when Whitton darted unseen into the six-yard box to sweep in Steve Hunt's left-wing cross. The gangling Paul Dyson was lucky to survive penalty appeals after dragging Keegan away from the ball, but if there was a little smirk on the centre-half's face, it was wiped away as Steve Williams latched onto an Ivan Golac clearance and hoisted the ball over his head for Keegan to go on and shoot low past Sealey's right hand.

After Whitlock's departure and while Saints were still trying to reorganise, Alan Ball lost possession and Hunt squared for Hateley to squeeze the ball under the body of Ivan Katalinic. And still the goals kept coming with Saints equalising four minutes into the second-half as Williams again deceived the Coventry defence with a cunningly flighted free-kick which Cassells despatched with a glancing header into the right-hand corner.

Cassells barely had time to celebrate his first goal for Saints. A delicate flick by the powerful figure of Garry

> *A memorable match. The score at half-time was 1-2 when a very young Danny Wallace came on to make one of his first appearances for the club. Suddenly the floodgates opened and the goals poured in from all angles. Afterwards Danny stormed into the dressing room and hurled his boots on to the floor.*
> *"What's the matter?" asked Dave Watson.*
> *"You had a good game, son. You played your part."*
> *" I just cannot believe that we lost that game," said Danny.*
> *For a moment we were puzzled. There had been so many goals that he had lost count and thought we'd been beaten 5-4.*
>
> Kevin Keegan

Thompson had Hateley skipping past Golac and shooting past beyond a hesitant Katalinic. Worse was to come for Saints as Ball of all people erred again, losing possession to Whitton who cut in from the right to explode a vicious right-foot shot past the bemused Katalinic on the hour.

It was a measure of Ball's tenacity that, with his pride badly stung, he instantly set out to make amends. When the little fella next had the ball, he tore through the Coventry ranks, sending a 25-yard drive screaming past the startled Sealey. At 3-4, and with The Dell a heaving mass of noisy expectation, Cassells delivered his exquisite chip to tie the scores up in the 69th minute. Saints, you felt, could go on and win it. And they thought they had when the irrepressible Cassells sent Keegan through to drive low into the left-hand corner with just seven minutes left.

But it was no night and no match to take anything for granted and Hateley had the last word in the 88th minute. He took two Yugoslav prisoners in one fell swoop, going past Golac as though he wasn't there then catching the hapless Katalinic again in two minds before slipping the ball gleefully into the back of the net.

It wasn't a good night for the coaching purist, but Saints manager Lawrie McMenemy had to admit:

> It was great entertainment. The only pity was that the crowd was 5,000 down on our last match against Liverpool. I can't understand it. We had scored 43 goals at The Dell before this game, and it looks like we're going to be the top scorer at home for the third season running.

And so they were!

SOUTHAMPTON:
Katalinic, Golac, Holmes, Williams, Nicholl, Whitlock (Wallace 43), Keegan, Channon, Cassells, Armstrong, Ball

COVENTRY CITY:
Sealey, Thomas, Jacobs, Butterworth, Dyson, Gillespie, Whitton, Francis, Hateley, Thompson, Hunt

Referee: Tom Bune (Cranleigh)   *Attendance:* 18,522

Adapted by **BOB BRUNSKELL** from his own *Echo* report. Additional material, by **David Bull**, from Kevin Keegan's autobiography. *Echo* photograph

PORTSMOUTH 0
SOUTHAMPTON 1

A third world war may well have broken out in Southampton during the dark winter days of 1984 but for the "divine intervention" of Steve Moran.

The potentially explosive FA Cup Fourth Round derby clash between Pompey and Saints at Fratton Park was heading, with excruciating tension, towards a goalless draw. The dreaded prospect of a mass invasion of Pompey fans into Southampton for a replay at The Dell was looming large and fearfully in the thoughts of many.

For those were the bad old days when football hooliganism was rife and when the hatred between the two sets of fans down the Solent burned stronger and more sinister than ever. So when Moran struck the match-winning goal deep into time added on, it averted a crisis on two fronts. It wiped out the prospects of a replay and left 25,000 Pompey fans so stunned that Saints and most of their followers were able to slip blissfully and peacefully out of the ground and high-tail it back to the sanctuary of Southampton.

There had been fears of great bloodshed in and around Fratton Park before and after the game but thanks to a superb policing operation and Moran's own devastating means of silencing the Pompey hordes, the game passed without anywhere near the carnage that had been feared.

Moran, who had grown up between the two great Solent towns in Warsash, had been the target of much abuse from Pompey fans during the cup-tie. The previous season he and Saints team-mate Mark Wright had been caught up in unproven rape allegations by a nurse after a UEFA Cup-tie in Sweden. Throughout the match Moran in particular was the object of some crude jibes from the Pompey followers. His retort was perfect. His match-winning goal silenced them in the best possible way.

In time added on for crowd violence, instigated ironically by Pompey followers, Moran produced a whiplash volley from a David Armstrong cross and Alan Knight could do nothing but help the ball into the net. Little Moran had often been described as the pocket battleship of the Southampton attack and this was his most damaging broadside.

The match itself had not reached great heights, but its joyous climax will never be forgotten by those Southampton followers who were brave enough to venture into the lion's den that day. Saints fans had sometimes been criticised for lack of passion, but their joyous acclaim of that last explosive kill turned the Milton End of Fratton Park into a big, boiling sea of red and white while down on the touchline manager Lawrie McMenemy did a dance of glee.

Steve Moran scores in "injury-time"

FA Cup Fourth Round

Pompey were blue in every way. Bobby Campbell's warriors slumped to the turf like broken men. Second Division Portsmouth were very much the poor relations in those days, firmly overshadowed by Saints who had been moulded by McMenemy into one of the top six teams in the land and who would finish second to Liverpool that season. Yet here was a decent-looking Pompey side in the making with the promise of Neil Webb and Kevin Dillon in midfield and a potentially lethal attacking spearhead of Mark Hateley (starring for Coventry in the previous report) and Alan Biley. With quality service from midfield, Hateley's power in the air and Biley's capacity to tuck away the half-chance suggested a testing afternoon for the Southampton defence. But Mark Wright and Reuben Agboola were up for it. And so was their new full-back pairing of Mark Dennis, recently arrived from Birmingham, and Mick Mills who'd moved in a year earlier after such a distinguished career with Ipswich and England and who was back at the ground where he had been an apprentice 20 years before.

Mark Dennis required treatment when home fans threw money at him

But on two occasions Biley let them off the hook. Pompey had had the best of the opening exchanges when Biley squandered gift number one which came courtesy of a flick on by Mick Tait from a John McLaughlin corner. The range was no more than three yards yet Biley headed over the bar. McMenemy admitted later that he couldn't bear to look when Biley had an equally good chance to settle it with just three minutes left. A cross from winger Alan Rogers found Biley unmarked on the six-yard line and this time he volleyed the ball over the bar.

That had something to do with the presence of Peter Shilton, another of McMenemy's experienced imports who'd arrived shortly before Mills. The sight of the great hulk of England goalkeeper Peter Shilton prancing on his line, with those great long arms of his protecting his net, clearly intimidated the little blond Pompey striker who normally accepted gifts like that. Pompey claimed with justification that they deserved to be ahead by then. Webb had let another late chance go begging and Hateley protested he should have had a penalty after being floored early on by an Agboola challenge.

The atmosphere inside the ground was like a pressure cooker. Saints had looked the tenser of the two sides and had created only a half-chance in the first-half, with Frank Worthington – yet another England international enjoying his one majestic season with the Saints - failing to muster enough venom to test Knight with his favoured left foot. But there was better from the visitors in the second-half. A long clearance by Mills and a touch-on by Danny Wallace put Steve Williams in for a chance which he chipped wide. Knight saved well from Mills then Williams drove wide from 25 yards before Moran settled it.

A fine angled pass by Worthington put Armstrong clear in unfamiliar territory for him down the right wing. When his cross arrived, Moran's left foot did the rest. The goal came in the time added on by referee Lester Shapter to let the trainer on to treat Dennis who had been felled by a coin thrown from the terraces.

There was whiff of great justice in the air as well as delirium as Saints celebrated one of their most extraordinary derby wins of them all. There would be two more rounds to celebrate as the side reached the Club's first semi-final since 1976, when they lost to Everton and an extra-time goal by Adrian Heath.

PORTSMOUTH:
Knight, McLaughlin, Sullivan, Doyle, Tait, Aizlewood, Webb, Dillon, Hateley, Biley, Rogers

SOUTHAMPTON:
Shilton, Mills, Dennis, Williams, Wright, Agboola, Holmes, Moran, Worthington, Armstrong, Wallace

Referee: Lester Shapter (Torquay)   *Attendance:* 36,000

Adapted by **BOB BRUNSKELL** from his own *Echo* report. Photographs from the *Echo* and **Duncan Holley**'s collection

SOUTHAMPTON 2
LIVERPOOL 0

"Just what," Saints devotees have often been heard to demand, "is Alan Hansen's problem?" In an attempt to discover this psychiatrists have watched all the tapes of his punditry on _Match of the Day_ and delved deep into the former Scottish defender's childhood, seeking to isolate that traumatic incident that makes him so antipathetic towards Southampton in general and Matthew Le Tissier in particular.

And yet the harrowing experience that lies buried deep in Hansen's id is easily identified. It took place on the evening of Friday 16 March 1984, and the metaphorical scar was inflicted by Danny Wallace.

Liverpool were reigning champions, they were top of the League and Clive White of the _Times_ issued a warning on the morning of the game:

> Woe betide Southampton, Manchester United, Everton or anyone else interested in disputing honours with Liverpool this season. Ian Rush, the League's leading goalscorer was yesterday pronounced fit from groin trouble and will resume with Kenny Dalglish the most feared partnership in British football at The Dell tonight.

From early on that season the "experts" had been promoting the First Division as a two-horse race between Liverpool and Manchester United and, as the final furlong post came into view, the two favourites were well ahead, on 63 and 61 points respectively. Tucked in behind them were Nottingham Forest, West Ham United and Southampton, with Saints trailing the leaders by 11 points – before the game. There was something else worth considering too: Saints had two games in hand on all the clubs ahead of them. Not something that the national press had picked up on.

In short, the faithful made their pilgrimages to The Dell that evening anticipating one of the hottest six-pointers of all time. There were two sound reasons for optimism. First: Saints, no matter how outstanding the Liverpool form, and

how indifferent their own, had a knack of beating the Reds at The Dell; they had even snatched a point at Anfield earlier in the season. Second: Lawrie McMenemy had built the Club's best side since the indomitable Harry Wood had captained them at the turn of the century.

Steve Williams and David Armstrong were the midfield anchors and at the top of their game. Behind them, Ken Armstrong, Reuben Agboola, Nick Holmes and Mark Wright were competing for the three central defensive positions, with Holmes and Agboola each seeing service as sweeper, while Mick Mills and Mark Dennis operated as wing-halves or backs. Up front Steve Moran and Danny Wallace were the favourite options to flank the evergreen Frank Worthington.

The only problem was that the squad lacked quality in depth and an injury crisis in October and November had seen them struggling for points. This was not a problem Liverpool often suffered from, although a family bereavement had denied them the presence of Graeme Souness for this game.

Nearly 20,000 turned up to watch - 2,000 in excess of the average gate that season - on a night the BBC chose to broadcast live. So not only was The Dell crowded, but pubs and living rooms all over the city were packed to near-capacity.

It is surprising, after all these years, to read Bob Brunskell's comments in the next day's _Echo_, claiming that the match "was on the verge of becoming a big switch off." True, there was not much activity in either penalty area in the first-half, but a fascinating game of chess was being enacted in the middle of

Frank Worthington "nonchalantly" contributed to
Wallace's spectacular goal

the park, with both defences efficiently snuffing out the rare breakthroughs on either side. Everyone appeared to be playing out of their skins, with one exception. Danny Wallace, seemingly exiled on the right wing, just couldn't get anything right. He hadn't scored for three months and Brunskell noted that "the crowd were venting their frustration on him" (well, some of them) when he "turned, dramatically, from villain to hero."

In first-half injury-time, Wright played the ball up to Worthington. He nonchalantly fed Dennis breaking down the left who, almost on the Liverpool by-line, sent over a telling cross. True, it needed two attempts, but the looping ball that came over to the far post was one that Terry Paine would have been proud of. Mark Wright, incredibly, met the ball, heading it out towards the penalty spot, high and beyond the advancing Wallace, who turned, span in the air and, with a spectacular overhead kick, hammered it past Grobbelaar into the Archers End net.

It was a goal breathtaking in its delivery and execution, the sort of strike that should win European Cup and World Cup finals, and, frankly, far too good for a mere clash of English League Championship contenders. But that's football for you.

Danny Wallace of the "spectacular" goal

particular, that neither Dalglish nor Rush got any opportunity to demonstrate their international pedigree in front of goal and Saints' one player of proven world-class ability, Peter Shilton, had a quiet time of it.

It was the 85th minute when Hansen's humiliation was manifested. Puckett, who had come on for Worthington five minutes previously, latched on to the ball to the left of the Liverpool goal and knocked it back for "Dennis to hit another superb cross."

Great though the cross was it was Hansen's all the way, until the pocket-sized Wallace, all 5 foot 5 inches of him, darted in front of the towering, Scottish centre-half and met the ball with the firmest of headers, thus confounding Grobbelaar, Hansen, the rest of the Liverpool team and several million television viewers.

When the League tables were published in the Sunday papers, Manchester United, who had defeated Arsenal 4-0 that Saturday, had elbowed Liverpool out of the top spot by one point, while the Saints were showing in fourth, nine points in arrears, but still with those two precious games in hand.

If they could just win those the title race would be wide open. And the following Tuesday, they had an FA Cup Sixth Round replay with Second Division Sheffield Wednesday coming up at The Dell. Saints were chasing the double!

Liverpool pulled out all the stops in the second-half, but so effective were the Saints midfield, Williams in

---

SOUTHAMPTON:

Shilton, Mills, Dennis, Williams, Agboola, Wright, Holmes, Moran, Worthington (Puckett 80), D. Armstrong, Wallace

LIVERPOOL:

Grobbelaar, Neal, Kennedy, Lawrenson, Whelen, Hansen, Dalglish, Lee, Rush, Johnston, Nicol (Robins)

Referee: B.T. Stevens (Stonehouse)   *Attendance:* 19,698

Compiled by **DAVE JUSON** from reports in the *Echo* and the *Times*. Photographs from **Duncan Holley**'s collection

SOUTHAMPTON 8
COVENTRY 2

Saints knocked eight bells out of Coventry City at The Dell in April 1984 and sent elated statisticians racing back to the record books to rewrite a special piece of Club history.

A dazzling 8-2 victory created a Club record in Division I and the winning margin against the not so bright Sky Blues matched a 6-0 demolition of Crystal Palace at The Dell in 1971. It was Saints' biggest haul since the all-time high 9-3 victory over Wolverhampton Wanderers in Division II in 1963 (as recorded at Match No. 56).

It was Coventry's biggest defeat for 54 years and as they trudged, dispirited and demoralised off The Dell pitch, they looked a side destined for the drop. And yet, in what has been a trademark of their long survival in the top flight, they performed a Houdini act and escaped relegation by two points. It was hard to believe that this same Coventry side had been running strongly in the top six over the first half of the season.

From Southampton's point of view this, a most spectacular of wins, headlined a ten-match unbeaten finish which carried them to second place in the League – another, more telling, Club record. Achieved a year after Kevin Keegan's departure, their best-ever finish is the topic of the next report. There can be no doubt that the incisive manner in which they dismantled Coventry gave them the confidence and the momentum to end the season in such style.

Steve Moran and Danny Wallace were at the top table in the goal feast with a hat-trick apiece. Wallace, though, took the star billing after playing a part in seven of the goals. His electrifying pace destroyed Stuart Pearce, a raw-boned newcomer who had just moved into Highfield Road from non-league football. Wallace ran rings round him, turning Pearce into a bemused, bewildered figure – hardly resembling the man who was destined to become one of England's finest and most feared left-backs.

On the day Wallace was a demon in the air as well as on the ground. Moran was close behind as he took his tally for the season to an impressive 22 goals. Yet it was with some irony that the biggest cheer of the day was reserved for a goal from Frank Worthington, his first for the club in two months.

Bohemian in appearance, a worldly and well-travelled England international who was blessed with sublime skills, Worthington was a ball-playing artiste who may not have been a prolific goalscorer for the Saints but who ingeniously made things happen for others.

With Saints two up by the break, the game had looked nothing out of the ordinary. But the second-half most certainly was. It produced eight goals, one every four minutes, from the moment Moran scored his first and Saints' third. There was such an explosive burst of activity that the fans were left both elated and breathless – and maybe a little forgetful of what had gone before.

Ironically, Coventry had fired the first warning shot with little Terry Gibson forcing Peter Shilton to turn a sharp effort past the post. It jolted Saints out of an early malaise and Wallace zipped away down the left to curl in a cross which David Armstrong, at full pelt, nodded home at the far post.

Danny Wallace completes his hat-trick with a header

Division One

Just over 28 minutes had gone and barely six more had ticked by when centre-back Mark Whitlock gave the ball some air and little Wallace sprung above his static Coventry markers to curl an exquisite header past 'keeper Perry Suckling from 12 yards.

For Suckling, who had kept a clean sheet on his debut against Saints the previous season, it was the start of a torrid spell. Just 12 minutes into the second-half Moran headed home from Ivan Golac's free-kick. All Saints' goals had come from headers, two from two of the smallest men on the pitch. But Wallace showed he could do the business on the ground when, in the 64th minute, he controlled a pass from right-back Mick Mills, turned past Pearce and beat Suckling with a searing right-foot shot.

Shilton, who had been enjoying the floor show from the other end, was caught out by a long shot from Ashley Grimes but the Coventry spirits, temporarily raised, were crushed three minutes later when Worthington swept in at the far post to head in Wallace's cross.

Pearce failed in a desperate bid to scoop it off the line, much to the delight of the crowd who

Steve Moran (left) and Danny Wallace celebrate their hat-tricks

It was one of those days when everything you touch turns to goals. …[I]t was just one of those days. You wish you knew what the secret was, so you could bottle it up and get it out for every game … I remember getting an early touch and from then on it never seemed to leave my feet … The crowd gave us a standing ovation and it was the greatest feeling, walking off after scoring a hat-trick and having had a hand in a few others. But it had been easy. We had a good side with David Armstrong and Steve Williams running everything in midfield and Frank Worthington showing some great touches. What a player.

Danny Wallace

had seen Worthington score only once before at The Dell since his move from Sunderland.

The Coventry defence was flapping open like a barn door and when Suckling only parried a shot from David Puckett, a 65th minute substitute for the injured Alan Curtis, Moran darted in to score his side's sixth goal. He completed his hat-trick by heading in another Wallace centre and, with five minutes left, Wallace completed his treble with a header from Puckett's pinpoint cross.

It was a measure of Saints' superiority that home-grown product Puckett could have had two goals himself, one effort coming back off the post, the other just missing the target. But Coventry had the last say when little midfielder Micky Gynn fired in a long-range shot which went across the line off the underside of the bar.

For Sky Blues it merely papered over the cracks opened up by the remorseless Wallace and Moran, who graciously conceded the match ball to his team-mate.

After all, Moran already had one in his collection, courtesy of a hat-trick against Manchester City the previous season.

SOUTHAMPTON:

Shilton, Mills, Golac, Curtis (Puckett 65), Whitlock, Wright, Holmes, Moran, Worthington, Armstrong, Wallace

COVENTRY CITY:

Suckling, Butterworth, Pearce, Daly, McGrath (Hendrie 65), Jacobs, Gibson, Grimes, Ferguson, Gynn, Platnauer

Referee: H W King (Merthyr)　　　　　　　　　　　　　　　*Attendance:* 16,740

Adapted by **BOB BRUNSKELL** from his own *Echo* report. Additional material by **David Bull,** drawing upon Danny Wallace's account, for Bob Holmes, of "The Match of my Life." *Echo* photographs

NOTTS COUNTY 1
SOUTHAMPTON 3

The 1983-84 season has to be one of my most memorable as a Southampton supporter, as it is the only season that I managed to get to every single home and away game. It will, of course, be more memorable to you for reasons highlighted in the last few reports: this was the season when Saints reached the FA Cup semi-finals and finished runners-up in the League, with a team packed full of Dell legends.

It is no coincidence that the '84 side features heavily when people pick their best-ever Saints XI. The personnel of its 5-2-3 formation were introduced in Match No. 85. England 'keeper Peter Shilton was the last line in a tight defence, which averaged less than a goal a game. The central midfield combined the strong running and goalscoring of David Armstrong with the aggression and ball play of Steve Williams. And with Frank Worthington such an elegant target man, Danny Wallace and Steve Moran provided the pace and the goals.

The back three and wingback system was a revolutionary concept at a time when the rest of the League were playing 4-4-2. And every single player could control and pass the ball. If you've watched England recently, you'll appreciate just what a revolutionary concept *this* was, too.

Despite being drawn away in every round, Saints had seen off Forest and Portsmouth – Match No. 84 can surely not have passed you by – and then Blackburn and Sheffield Wednesday on the way to their first semi-final since 1976, and with the aid of only one replay, and everyone felt that our name was on the cup.

That was until the last minute of extra-time when the ball struck something – Peter Shilton blamed it on the sanding of the disgraceful Highbury surface – and bounced up for Everton's Heath to head home. To say that we were shattered by this would be a massive understatement. Could the team lift themselves, and the supporters, to qualify for Europe?

Some small revenge was gained, three days later, when Everton were beaten 3-1 at The Dell in a real bear-pit atmosphere, with the bad feeling that had erupted on the terraces at Highbury carried onto the pitch. Williams had played the semi-final with an injury that would keep him out for the rest of the season, but even without him Saints went on an unbeaten run of seven matches, going into the last scheduled week of the season.

In the days before Sky TV, it was not, of course, uncommon for teams to play on throughout May, even after the rest of the League had finished. So it was that on Saturday 12 May, while Liverpool picked up the Championship trophy, Saints drew at St Andrew's.

This both sent Birmingham down and left Southampton lying in fifth spot, with two away trips to come, and knowing that four points would see them finish in second place (this being the third season of three points for a win).

They safely negotiated the first hurdle, the following Monday at West Brom, with a very professional 2-0 win. They seemed to have done the hard part and now required only a draw at Notts County.

This may not have sounded too difficult on paper; but, Saints being Saints, you never knew quite what to expect. County had already been relegated and might now relax and start playing good football. They had already beaten Saints at The Dell in November.

So it was more in hope than expectation that we set off for Nottingham that Thursday lunch-time to join the 2,000 Southampton supporters in the away end at Meadow Lane to cheer the boys on for the 51st and final time that season.

Whatever it was that happened in a hotel the weekend after the Coventry goalfest, it meant that Frank Worthington had played his last match for Southampton and Dave Puckett was seeing out the season at No. 9. Mark Wright and Mark Dennis were injured, but the shape of the side was much the same.

The game got off to a perfect start when, in only the second minute, Steve Moran latched onto a back pass, calmly rounded the 'keeper and slotted the ball into the empty net. Unperturbed by this, County fought back hard and seven minutes later, Trevor Christie, their leading scorer, got on the end of a right-wing cross to equalise. From then on it seemed like constant County pressure until half-time; and Saints had a Kenny Armstrong clearance and a frantic Shilton save from a corner to thank for going in on level terms. Could they hold out for the point?

After the interval, Southampton camped out in the County half, attacking the away end. The lead was restored in the 56th minute when Moran headed home a Nick Holmes corner. Saints kept up the pressure and went further ahead when Puckett played a one-two with Wallace and his cross was knocked in by Armstrong, on one of his trademark runs to the far post.

It could have been more, as goalkeeper Leonard smothered at Wallace's feet and Puckett and Moran tackled each other going for the same ball. County threatened to pull one back in the last five minutes, but the result was never in doubt.

Division One

At the final whistle the team all came over to our end to celebrate.

A small scrum broke out over David Armstrong's shirt, which was thrown into the crowd, but our Sunday League 'keeper missed out on it, as his handling let him down once more.

Although this game was certainly not a classic, in

DIVISION 1	P	W	D	L	F	A	Pt
Liverpool	42	22	14	6	73	32	80
Southmptn	42	22	11	9	66	38	77
Nottm. F.	42	22	8	12	76	45	74
Man. U.	42	20	14	8	71	41	74
Q.P.R.	42	22	7	13	67	37	73
Arsenal.......	42	18	9	15	74	60	63
Everton	42	16	14	12	44	42	62
Tottenham	42	17	10	15	64	65	61
West Ham	42	17	9	16	60	55	60
Aston V.	42	17	9	16	59	61	60
Watford......	42	16	9	17	68	77	57
Ipswich......	42	15	8	19	55	57	53
Sunderland	43	13	16	42	52		

terms of the goals scored or the football played, it deserves a mention in any anthology of the club. There may have been no Champions League place at stake, just a cheque for £25,000 from the League sponsors, but finishing runners-up was, and still is, a wonderful achievement and one that I fear we may never see again.

Steve Moran (right) and David Armstrong scored the goals at Meadow Lane to complete a season in which they were the Saints' top scorers

NOTTS COUNTY:

Leonard, Hodson, Clarke, Richards, Hunt, Goodwin, O'Neill, McParland, Christie, Mair (Jones 80), Chiedozie

SOUTHAMPTON:

Shilton, K.Armstrong, Whitlock, Agboola, Mills, Golac, D. Armstrong, Holmes, Wallace, Puckett, Moran

Referee: Mr L.R Dilkes (Mossley, Lancs)

Attendance: 6,035

Compiled by **KEITH TREVIS** from being there and from the *Echo* report. Photographs from **Duncan Holley**'s collection. Shilton quoted from *Official History* Video

SOUTHAMPTON 4
MANCHESTER UNITED 1

Raise the subject of cup-ties against Manchester United with any Saints' fan and the conversation is likely to turn to 1976 and probably 1992, as well. But there was also a Dell night in November 1986, the only occasion when Southampton have beaten United in the "other" Cup.

Earlier that season, Saints had been on the end of a 5-1 battering in the League at Old Trafford. So when they were drawn away to United in the Third Round of the Littlewoods (League) Cup, few could have under-estimated the daunting task facing them. Yet not only did Southampton gain a highly creditable draw, but Danny Wallace missed a good chance to put them into the next round at the first time of asking – although, of course, our appetites were now whetted for a replay at The Dell.

If Liverpool were emphatically the team of the 1980s, while their great Manchester rivals still sought their first Championship since 1967, United remained a Cup-force to be reckoned with. Since losing to Saints in 1976, they had appeared in four FA Cup Finals, winning three of them. And they had reached the League Cup Final in 1983, losing, naturally, to Liverpool. Their manager at this time was Mr Bojangles himself, the talented, bejewelled and charismatic Big Ron Atkinson, who had taken them to two of those winning Finals. The United squad as always was packed with big names and they included classy defender, Paul McGrath; flying Dane, Jesper Olsen; bustling striker, Norman Whiteside; and oh, er, midfielder Bryan Robson - or they would have done had he not of course been injured.

United looked the part for most of the first-half of this replay. They played with the greater cohesion and I particularly liked the look of Olsen's pace and skill. But they were all frills and no finish and were made to pay for it in deadly fashion. For those of you who do not remember George Lawrence, he was a huge black winger who could really motor once into his stride and, by virtue of sheer momentum and physique, could be very difficult to shake off the ball. Two minutes before the interval he was to demonstrate his other talent - one helluva shot. Receiving the ball from pass-master Jimmy Case, Lawrence unleashed a 25-yard screamer which had it not been for the netting would have ended up on the Common. Saints consequently went in at the break one very splendid goal up.

He would be one of two Saints stars this night, but George Lawrence was surely enjoying his finest hour, running United's Arthur Albiston ragged. George almost had another goal early in the second period, when, again taking a fine ball from Case, he attempted an audacious long-range chip which just drifted away from goal at the death. United were now on the rack and first-half injuries to Whiteside and Colin Gibson had obviously taken their toll. It was Lawrence again, his effectiveness in carrying the ball forward being fully exploited, who crossed for Danny Wallace to squander the chance. Wallace then made up for his misses in this and the previous tussle, cashing in with a great team goal. Glenn Cockerill headed from the left, Colin Clarke knocked down and Wallace, so often a scorer of spectacular goals (just think back to Match 85), took off through the air and smacked the ball home right-footed. Having battled on, carrying an ankle injury, until the 75th minute, Danny would make way for the second star of the night.

Matthew Le Tissier lofts his first-ever goal for Southampton

League Cup Third Round (Replay)

Cometh the hour-and-a-quarter, cometh a very special young man.

Welcome to the spotlight of what was going to be an extremely well-trodden centre-stage. A player that was going to become as synonymous with Southampton's recent history as the likes of Paine, Davies and Channon. Enter one Matthew Le Tissier. Having come on as a sub in the 4-3 defeat at Norwich on 30 August, Matty had made his full debut three days later, in a 2-0 win over Spurs, when he tantalised us Dell fans with our first glimpses of his sparkling ball skill, his precocious body swerve and an obvious talent.

Now, on this November night, the befringed 18 year-old was to rise from the bench and leave his mark on the tie with something he was going to become renowned for – scoring goals. Since the Spurs game, he'd had one more start and five substitutions, in which to show us more of his magic. Tonight there was a little bit extra in the air. Somehow you had that feeling that something was going to happen for this Sorcerer's Apprentice. After just 75

A very special day for me. I came on as a sub … I scored the first one from a Colin Clarke flick-on – I'm not sure if he did flick it; I think if he'd have flicked it, I'd have been offside…I had to wait a little bit before the referee actually gave it. And then I scored a rare header for my second one – straight from a corner. I think it's about the only time I've ever scored with a header straight from a corner…I had a chance with a shot from about 25 yards, about two minutes later, to get my hat-trick and it sort of flew over the bar… I was on a roll. My first-ever goals for the Club.

Matthew Le Tissier

Just forty-eight hours before I entered the unemployment statistics, we got whupped 4-1, courtesy of [an 18] year-old called Matthew Le Tissier in a League Cup replay… at The Dell… Business was very brief in the execution chamber that morning, I can assure you.

Ron Atkinson

seconds of his taking the field it did happen. Matty scored his first goal for Saints, one of so many since. United stopped, obviously wanting the offside. Even he remains unsure as to whom the ball touched or missed on the way to him but, on the night, he just kept running and cheekily lofted a shot over United 'keeper Chris Turner. The goal stood. And he added another with a decisive downward header from Jimmy Case's corner nine minutes later.

As the Dell crowd welcomed its new Messiah the only thing left for Man Utd was a Peter Davenport consolation goal. For Ron Atkinson, despite his two FA Cups, the sack was to follow two days later.

While I certainly have some sympathy for the circumstances surrounding an Atkinson demise that seemed harsh at the time, he had become the victim of a right caning at the hands of little old Saints, a 4-1 going over that sent the Old Trafford aristos packing back North and a victory that was gleefully and quite rightly celebrated to the full in Southampton as fans looked happily forward to the next round or three.

SOUTHAMPTON:

Shilton, Forrest, Dennis, Case, Wright, Gittens, Lawrence, Cockerill, Clarke, S. Baker, D.Wallace (Le Tissier 75)

MANCHESTER UNITED:

Turner, Duxbury, Albiston, Whiteside (Wood), McGrath, Hogg, Moses, Olsen, Stapleton, Davenport, Gibson (Moran)

Referee: Lester Shapter (Torquay)   *Attendance:* 17,915

Compiled by **CHRIS NEWMAN** from being there and from the *Echo* report. Additional material – from an interview with Matthew Le Tissier and Ron Atkinson's autobiography – by **David Bull**. Photographs from the *Echo* and **Duncan Holley**'s collection

SOUTHAMPTON 4
LEICESTER CITY 0

On a bitter day and on a paddyfield of a pitch totally unsuited to his ball-playing skills, a willowy teenager from the sunshine island of Guernsey came of age.

The 1986-87 season had been a proving ground for 18-year-old Matthew Le Tissier with Saints struggling for First Division survival and crying out for inspiration. Before they played Leicester City at The Dell on 7 March, Chris Nicholl's side had failed to score in four games, including a two-legged Littlewoods League Cup semi-final against Liverpool which the Red Army had taken 3-0 on aggregate.

More worrying for Nicholl was Saints' League position, fourth from the bottom and on a decidedly downward spiral after a run of three defeats. Le Tissier had shown himself to be a young footballer of exceptional talent playing for Dave Merrington's youth side. He virtually sidestepped the reserves into Nicholl's first team squad but the fans had only rare sightings of him usually as a substitute introduced too late to rescue some lost cause – with the exception, of course, of that November evening (of the previous report) when he had come off the bench with 15 minutes to go and almost scored a hat-trick.

They wanted to see more of the kid who just oozed confidence and whose lazy style of dribbling left defenders on their backsides. Most important of all he'd shown that he could score goals – from anywhere in and around the penalty box.

Nicholl, though, erred on the side of caution and kept him on the bench until Saints, at a low ebb after their League Cup defeat at Liverpool, were in desperate need of freshening up as they returned to Anfield just three days later for a League game. Le Tissier played and did well enough in a 1-0 defeat to stay in for the home game with Leicester City, a crucial affair with both sides desperate for the points.

It was a day when actions spoke louder than words and Le Tissier's stunning hat-trick performance in a 4-0 win for Saints sent a strident message to his manager – leave me out at your peril! Le Tissier's was a magical, heart-warming display which quite simply swept away two months of gloom at the Club. Saints had sore need of a tonic and he provided it.

Those who talked about the player in the future tense now needed to look no further than the present. Le Tissier showed he had the talent, the confidence and most of all the physical strength to be a supreme asset to the team. In what was only his fifth full appearance, his hat-trick lifted his goalscoring tally to six (or eight in six games if you count the Full Members Cup). The manner in which he completed that hat-trick will never be forgotten by those fortunate enough to witness it. And there weren't that

Mark Wright (second left) celebrates as Matthew Le Tissier scores from his header-down

Division One

many because the bleak weather restricted the crowd to just over 11,000.

The hardy souls who did stand shivering through one of the last, icy blasts of that winter were rewarded by one of the best solo goals seen at the ground. Le Tissier was a lean strippling of a lad in those days and his stamina had already been brought into question by some so-called wise old heads.

Yet here he now was, ploughing through a swamp of a pitch, side-stepping and bludgeoning his way past past five challenges before applying the *coup de grace*. He had already scored twice and been denied by a fine piece of goalkeeping from Ian Andrews, later to become a clubmate, so it was a remarkable effort coming as it did in the last eight minutes of a strength-sapping contest.

A mix of rain and snow made the pitch slippery in places and a sticky, cloying morass in others. Both sides, fearful of defeat, were like a couple of bull terriers, snapping and snarling at each other, hustling and bustling from first to last. Very little separated the sides during a first-half in which conditions were so bad that there were real doubts as to whether the game would finish.

I remember [the game] well. My Dad was actually over. It was probably the worst conditions I've ever played a match in. I scored one in the first-half. Mark Wright knocked a ball down for me to score from a cross — left-footed. The second one, Danny Wallace crossed a ball over from the left and I sort of came in from the right-hand side and side-footed it past Ian Andrews…I reminded him of that quite a lot while he was here. And the third one…I took a dribble just inside [their] half and I got a couple of lucky bounces off a couple of their players and I hit a shot with my left foot and Ian Andrews saved it, but it came straight back to me, and I managed to hit the rebound in. It was my first ever hat-trick for the Club and I was fairly ecstatic, you could say. I got the match ball and gave it straight to my Dad after — it was a nice moment.

Matthew Le Tissier

just after the interval. But on 58 minutes the striker, just shipped in from Lincoln City, had made amends, driving in the rebound after a Danny Wallace shot had come back off the underside of the crossbar.

Wallace underpinned a telling display down the left wing by looping over a cross which Le Tissier converted with an instinctive sweep of his right foot on 62 minutes. Then followed that marvellous solo effort and the game

Le Tissier broke the deadlock after 29 minutes, firing home from close range after Mark Wright had headed back to him from a Gerry Forrest free-kick. It was Saints' first goal in 412 minutes of action and they went on to vindicate referee Alf Buksh's decision to play on with a tremendous second-half performance.

The mud denied Gordon Hobson a certain goal when his shot stuck fast a yard from the line

had been won handsomely.

There were 11 Saints heroes out there, but one match-winner.

Matthew Le Tissier had won a special place in the hearts of the fans which was to grow and grow through the last decade of the millennium.

Ian Andrews surrenders to Matthew Le Tissier's second goal

SOUTHAMPTON:
Shilton, Forrest, Armstrong, Townsend, Wright, Bond, Le Tissier, Cockerill, Lawrence, Hobson, Wallace

LEICESTER CITY:
Andrews, Feeley, Morgan, Osman, O'Neill, McAllister, Mauchlen, Reid (Alleyne 63), Smith, Ramsey, Wilson

Referee: Alf Buksh (London)   *Attendance:* 11,611

Adapted by **BOB BRUNSKELL** from his own *Echo* report. Matthew Le Tissier interviewed by **David Bull**. *Echo* photographs

SOUTHAMPTON 4
ARSENAL 2

It was in keeping with the extraordinary player that Alan Shearer was to become that he should make a truly grand entrance on to the Football League stage.

A prolific youth team striker who had been tipped by his coach to become a leading player in the game, Shearer made his Saints debut as a 17 year-old in April 1988 and marked the occasion with a remarkable 49-minute hat-trick in a 4-2 victory over Arsenal at The Dell.

Shearer, young, lean and hungry, revitalised an ailing Saints side with a performance which upstaged even Roy of the Rovers.

Chris Nicholl's team had gone through a low-key start to 1988, failing to win a home game before a tricky Dell encounter with former League leaders, Arsenal. Confidence was low, on the pitch and on the terraces. The club needed a tonic and Shearer, hailed for months by youth team coach Dave Merrington as a natural goalscorer who was rich in potential, provided it in triple measure.

He instantly became part of Dell folklore. Not even their greatest players of old had bowed in with such a flourish. Not only did he re-ignite Southampton's season; he condemned high-riding Arsenal to their heaviest defeat of the 1987-88 campaign.

Yet Shearer had got into the side only by chance. Danny Wallace failed a late fitness test on an ankle injury and at noon, just three hours before kick-off, Nicholl drew Shearer aside and said "you're playing son." Nicholl recalls vividly how Shearer took the news. "He was calm and assured. Just as I thought he would be."

Nothing fazed the man, not even in those early formative days. Once he got on to the park, Shearer exploded and the Gunners were blown to pieces. Manager George Graham said that history would have told a different story of Shearer's debut had not his side been shorn of their two central defenders.

England international Tony Adams pulled out with influenza to join his regular centre-back partner David O'Leary on the sidelines. To be fair, that was a helluva swathe through the Arsenal defence and it meant that they had to go in with the young, inexperienced pairing of Gus Caesar and Michael Thomas.

Graham insisted: "It would have been different if Adams and O'Leary had played. Alan wouldn't have got his goals so easy." But his opposite number Nicholl put Shearer's achievement into clearer perspective when he retorted: "Arsenal may have had two inexperienced centre-backs, but remember that Shearer was making his debut. You could hardly have called him experienced. Really you couldn't take anything away from the lad. He took his chances well and Colin Clarke gave him brilliant support for two of his goals."

Shearer took only five minutes to score his first League goal. Andy Townsend and Graham Baker had done the spadework, Baker with a precise cross which Shearer, surging forward at great pace, headed in from close range.

Alan Shearer surges in to head his first goal for Saints

Match of the Millennium

Division One

Even Kevin Bond's gift of an own goal to Arsenal just six minutes later could not dampen the spirits of the young Geordie, likened by Merrington to Nat Lofthouse, one of the great centre-forwards of the 1950s with Bolton

Lukic, with a desperate challenge, made the block. Seconds later Shearer turned the tables. Clarke's initial cross was blocked but his persistence gave him the chance to get over a second ball which found Shearer whose shot

I was still feeling pretty nervous when the unthinkable happened. After five minutes a cross came over…and I just managed to get in front of Arsenal's Michael Thomas to get my head to the ball. I thought I had placed it too close to the goalkeeper, John Lukic, but it squeezed through his legs into the back of the net. I was overcome with excitement… One thing I had not considered beforehand was how to celebrate in front of so many people so I just ran around for a while flapping my arms about and savouring the moment. [Next] Colin Clarke provided a centre from the right and I stooped down through the crowd of players to score another header. We were moving into fantasy football territory now. [Then] another chance came my way. Again I thought I had fluffed it. My first shot from Colin Clarke's pass hit the underside of the crossbar but I reacted first and volleyed in the rebound. I don't think I realised the enormity of what I had done to begin with.

Alan Shearer

Wanderers. Shearer chased, hustled and showed the natural instincts of a quality striker by holding the line and picking up good positions in and around the box. His enthusiasm that day was infectious. Shearer lifted everyone around him, Clarke in particular. The stocky leader with the capacity for skilful and prodigious goalscoring, had gone through a lean, lethargic spell of form but with young Shearer alongside him, the Northern Ireland international was a transformed figure. They instantly struck up a perfect partnership. Clarke took the fledgling under his wing and soon had him flying high.

The two linked superbly for the second goal on 33 minutes. Shearer chased hard after a probing ball from Glenn Cockerill, claimed it and swept it out to Clarke who was powering down the right wing. Clarke cut the ball back in and there was Shearer, bravely ducking in among a cluster of Arsenal defenders, to nod home.

Mark Blake, a young and able deputy for Kevin Moore who was absent nursing an injury, came up for a corner just before half-time and made it 3-1 with a powerful left-foot drive past the Arsenal goalkeeper John Lukic.

The second-half had only just begun when Lukic denied Shearer his hat-trick. Again Clarke was the architect with a quality cross ball to Shearer's feet, but

hit the underside of the bar. Before Lukic could turn and retrieve the situation, Shearer had pounced on the rebound and despatched it into the net.

For Saints and their success-starved fans, the game with Arsenal had reached the realms of fantasy. But they were brought back down to earth as the Gunners were stung into trying to claw back what was becoming an embarrassing deficit. They took command for the last 30 minutes but Saints held out until the 82nd minute when David Rocastle set up Paul Davis for Arsenal's second.

Shearer, who had run himself into the ground, made way for another of Southampton's exciting youngsters Rodney Wallace for the last eight minutes, and the lightning-quick younger brother of Danny almost put his name on the scoresheet with a powerful effort which fully extended Lukic.

At 17 years and 240 days, Shearer had become the youngest player to score a hat-trick in the First Division, ousting the great Jimmy Greaves from the record books.

But Shearer had done it on his debut, whereas Greaves, having played his first game at the start of the 1957-58 season, had had to wait for Portsmouth to come along so that he might enjoy a Christmas Day treat in the shape of four goals.

SOUTHAMPTON:

Burridge, Forrest, Statham, Case, Blake, Bond, Baker, Cockerill, Clarke, Townsend, Shearer (R Wallace 82)

ARSENAL:

Lukic, Winterburn, Sansom, Williams, Caeser, Thomas, Rocastle, Davis, Smith, Groves (Merson 58), Hayes

Referee: Keith Burge (Tonypandy)   *Attendance:* 14,528

Adapted by **BOB BRUNSKELL** from his own *Echo* report and a recent interview with Chris Nicholl. Additional material, mainly from Alan Shearer's autobiography, by **David Bull**. *Echo* photograph

SOUTHAMPTON 4
LIVERPOOL 1

Liverpool arrived at The Dell in October 1989 as unbeaten leaders of the First Division. They left with their record in tatters.

The Red Army had been outplayed, outthought and outfought by a collection of young Southampton players, some destined for greater things and sadly not all of them in Saints colours.

Liverpool were hammered 4-1 by a team which included the youthful promise of Tim Flowers, Matthew Le Tissier, Alan Shearer and Rodney Wallace. For the Saints fans who luxuriated in the overwhelming eclipse of one of Europe's great powers, it should have been a glowing look into the future. Sadly, within a year or two, the likes of Flowers, Shearer and Wallace had gone on to new, bigger and more rewarding pastures and the promise of a great Saints team of the future had gone with them.

But for 90 minutes on this autumn day in 1989, Saints were the talking point in pubs and clubs up and down the country.

The quality of their football, and the desire which burned within their ranks, swept Kenny Dalglish's aristocrats away.

The journey for them back to Merseyside must have been a sombre affair because it was an alien experience for Liverpool players and their officials to take such a beating. In fact, they hadn't lost an away game since the first day of the year and they hadn't lost so heavily for three years.

In contrast Saints had not enjoyed such a winning margin over Liverpool for over quarter of a century – back in Match No. 49 in 1960. *Echo* reporter Graham Hiley wrote: "storms had lashed the city the night before the game but were nothing compared to the whirlwind which which blew the Anfield aces away. Yet the entire Saints team had cost less to assemble than Liverpool had splashed on one single player, John Barnes."

Barnes took a back seat as the four men in an attacking formation sent out by Saints manager Chris Nicholl cut

Rodney Wallace resists Barry Venison to score Saints' second goal

loose. The pace of Rodney Wallace down the left wing, the cunning of Le Tissier down the right and the cut and thrust of Paul Rideout and Shearer through the middle was all too much for the Liverpool rearguard, Alan Hansen and all, to contain. Hansen had always been noted for his poise and control (leave aside his Dell embarrassment, six seasons earlier, as reported at Match No. 85) but even his calming influence could not help hold back the tide of Southampton attacks.

Liverpool, who had perfected the art of keeping the ball better than any other side in England, for a change had to do the chasing themselves and there were spells in the game when they just couldn't get out of their own half.

Glenn Cockerill and Jimmy Case established an iron grip in midfield and Liverpool, completely out of character for them, were reduced to playing long, hopeful balls which were food and drink to the big Southampton centre-backs Russell Osman and Neil Ruddock.

Dalglish predictably handed no laurels to the victors, complaining that his side had had an off-day and had played badly. The Saints viewpoint was that Liverpool had been made to look ordinary. As Graham Hiley went on, "Wallace and Le Tissier had turned the clock back to the fine Saints sides of the early 1980s as they repeatedly carved open the Liverpool defence."

New Forest-born and bred Rideout, who later in his career played successfully on the other half of Merseyside, gave Liverpool an early bout of the blues. He scored once and might easily have had a hat-trick, grazing the bar with a drive then being denied by a bizarre little cameo, inevitably feating Bruce Grobbelaar. For the unpredictable Liverpool 'keeper it proved an astonishing escape as Rideout's shot hit a post and rebounded off the bemused

Division One

Grobbelaar on to the other upright before the ball was scrambled to safety.

Rideout had already opened the scoring, rising at the near post to bury a header from a pinpoint centre by Jason Dodd, an 18-year-old right-back who was relatively new in from Bath. The man destined to become the Saints captain was making his home debut.

Partnering him at left-back was another youngster Francis Benali who had come in earlier in the season, after switching from the left-sided midfield role in which he had shone for the youth team. For young Franny it was literally another backward step because he had started out as a striker in schoolboy football and had been selected by England Boys for his goal-punching ability.

It was on the flanks that Saints' second goal, after 29 minutes, was fashioned. In an electrifying move Wallace fed Le Tissier, bounded on to the return pass and accelerated past Barry Venison to fire home. It was pure quality and it raised the roof but it stung Liverpool who began at last to play the way Bill Shankly had ordained. The difference here was that they were two goals down and chasing the game with a desperation which grew as the clock ticked on.

Even so Saints needed to nip an impending recovery in the bud and they did it in the best possible way with a third goal after 56 minutes. Le Tissier was again the architect with a piercing cross which Wallace met on the far side of the box with a first-time shot which went through Grobbelaar's legs.

Peter Beardsley scored from a penalty after Case had fouled David Burrows but, five minutes from the end, match stars Le Tissier and Wallace fittingly had the final say. Wallace crossed and there was the rare sight of Le Tissier soaring to head home. It was indeed a day when Saints had proved that anything was possible.

Liverpool went on to win the League, Saints finished seventh, their best season under Nicholl and a finish which hasn't been bettered since.

On the day of our biggest game of the season – at home to Liverpool who were flying high… – there was me, Le Tiss, Barry Horne and Mickey Adams all filling our faces at the local McDonald's just a couple of hours before kick-off… We were all in hysterics when Barry piped up with "Do you think John Barnes, Ian Rush and the boys will be tucking into a McDonald's?" Highly unlikely, but the unusual preparations obviously didn't do us any harm because we turned in our best performance of the season to beat the mighty Reds 4-1 to go third in the table. Jason Dodd,…playing in only his second game, was outstanding that day and virtually marked the great Barnesy out of the match, and he will never forget how John came…to shake his hand and congratulate him.

Neil Ruddock

I didn't know I was playing in the Liverpool game until half past one, quarter to two, and as you can imagine, I was a very nervous young lad. But…I managed to put the ball across for the first goal when Paul Rideout put it in the top corner, so it definitely settled me down a bit…After the game John Barnes came and shook my hand and said, "very well done." He didn't have to do that. Obviously he was the top man in the country at the time,…so to keep him quiet and for him to come up and say "well done" was quite nice and…obviously speaks volumes for him.

Jason Dodd

I saw David Burrows coming just out of the corner of my eye, so I just controlled it and flicked it over him. I was never blessed with blistering pace but if a defender is coming at you so quick you can knock it round him and get round him and you actually make yourself look quicker than you are…And then Rodney really finished it well – through Brucie's legs, I think it was, [for the third goal].

Matthew Le Tissier

SOUTHAMPTON:

Flowers, Dodd, Benali, Case, Ruddock, Osman, Le Tissier, Cockerill, Shearer (Baker 72), Rideout, Rod Wallace

LIVERPOOL:

Grobbelaar, Hysen, Burrows, Nicol, Whelan, Hansen, Beardsley, Venison (Houghton 68), Rush, McMahon, Barnes

Referee: Ray Lewis (Great Bookham)   *Attendance:* 20,081

Compiled by **BOB BRUNSKELL** from the *Echo* report, with additional material – from Neil Ruddock's autobiography and interviews with Jason Dodd and Matthew Le Tissier – by **David Bull.** *Echo* photograph.

MANCHESTER UNITED 2
SOUTHAMPTON 2
(SOUTHAMPTON WON 4-2 ON PENALTIES)

Saints went through the full gamut of emotions before beating Manchester United 4-2 in a penalty shoot-out in February 1992 to decide a classic, cliff-hanger of an FA Cup Fourth Round tie at Old Trafford.

Graham Hiley wrote of one of the last great great cup-tie thrillers in Saints history: "the pendulum swung from joy to despair to utter elation."

Saints stormed into a two-goal lead only to be pegged back by a bizarre United equaliser deep into injury-time. Having led the game for so long Saints could have buckled, but with spirit intact and maybe figuring that a penalty shoot-out might be their best passport to a major upset, they rolled their sleeves up even further and battled towards that goal.

And having achieved it in a goalless extra-time period, they grasped the nettle. A crucial save by Tim Flowers from Ryan Giggs ensured that Saints secured the penalty shoot-out and with it a famous victory over the Red Devils.

United might well have settled for a shoot-out themselves after completely losing the early initiative to Ian Branfoot's Saints. Goals by Stuart Gray (his first for the Club) and Alan Shearer (his 17th of the season) put the visiting side firmly in the driving seat.

Gray struck after just eight minutes, capitalising on a mix-up between Peter Schmeichel and Paul Parker as to who should deal with a long, probing ball played through the inside-left channel by Micky Adams, who was playing on that side of midfield.

Adams also did the spadework for the second goal on 22 minutes, forcing the free-kick which Matthew Le Tissier flighted quickly and accurately for Shearer to head home. That's the way it stayed until two minutes before half-time when a mistake by Kenna let in Giggs, who was quickly brought to earth by Flowers. It looked a penalty if nothing else but Andre Kanchelskis made it academic as he swept home the loose ball.

Shearer almost restored Saints' two-goal cushion with a shot which forced a fingertip save from Schmeichel but, in the second-half, with the deficit cut to just one, it was

Alan Shearer's header bounces down and up beyond Peter Schmeichel for Saints' second goal

United who were asking the questions and Saints, for their part, were coping remarkably well with a back four of an average age of just 22.

They repelled wave upon wave of United attacks and as the tie moved into injury-time, it looked as though they had survived the onslaught. But even in those days United had a reputation for plucking lost causes from the dying embers of a game.

They did it this time with an extraordinary piece of good fortune. An overhead kick by Giggs sent Lee Sharpe racing away down the left to deliver a cross which Neil Ruddock tried to head clear. To the big centre-half's horror, the ball slammed into Jeff Kenna's forehead and rebounded back across goal where Brian McClair gratefully accepted a gift from the heavens.

There was barely time to restart the game and when the final whistle sounded, Saints collectively slumped to their knees in utter despair.

Relief and elation put United on the scent of victory in extra-time and who would have bet against them achieving it?

The determined Flowers maybe. He scrambled an effort from Bryan Robson up off the line (Robson claiming the ball had already crossed it) then went down bravely at the feet of Mark Hughes, who had come on as a substitute late in normal time for Kanchelskis.

Saints had played three games in a week and would have been excused for wilting. But with Ruddock and Richard Hall magnificent at the heart of the defence and the likes of Adams and Barry Horne clearly prepared to run until they dropped in midfield, United actually didn't create too many clear-cut chances.

With the scores locked together at 2-2, the players trudged wearily to the Stretford Road end to slug out the sudden death shoot-out. It was an intimidating prospect for the Saints penalty-takers, but they refused to be

FA Cup Fourth Round (Replay)

Neil Ruddock (left) can hardly believe it, as Iain Dowie and Matthew Le Tissier congratulate Tim Flowers.
Glenn Cockerill can be seen at the rear, although there is no sign of his cup of tea

un-nerved by the vitriol hurled down from the packed terraces. If the atmosphere got to anybody, it was to the United players themselves.

After Ruddock had opened the penalty competition by coolly sending Schmeichel the wrong way, Neil Webb stepped up and blasted his effort high and wide. 1-0 to Saints. They must have derived an enormous psychological boost from Webb's miss, for Shearer, Horne and Adams all found the target, Shearer with a take which would have gone straight down Schmeichel's throat had he not decided to dive right. Horne and Adams took the more traditional route,

shrewdly wrong-footing the big, blond Dane.

Denis Irwin and Sharpe both beat Flowers to make it 2-4 and keep the pressure on Saints, but when Flowers, springing to his left, saved from Giggs, the tie was Southampton's and Flowers celebrated by sprinting the full length of the field to receive a hero's acclaim from his team-mates and 1,900 delirous Saints suppporters.

Saints went on to reach the Sixth Round before going out 2-1 in a replay at Norwich City – their best FA Cup run since making the semi-finals under Chris Nicholl in 1986.

And sadly they haven't gone close to bettering it since then.

That was the only penalty shoot-out I have been involved in in my career; and I never needed to take a penalty ... I wanted to go last, because I wanted to be the one that scored the winning penalty. I like getting the glory at the end: that's what goal-scorers do. I chose to go last and we didn't need it, because our penalty-takers that night were brilliant: Micky Adams; Barry Horne; Alan Shearer; and Neil Ruddock. And all four [had] what I'd call good nerve and good bottle. And that's what you need ... [Then, when] Ryan Giggs smashed it down the middle, Timmy just stood [and saved it]. And then Timmy's famous run down the touch-line with Glenn Cockerill chasing him, while Glenn still had a cup of tea in his hand ... It was cracking. Great night!

Matthew Le Tissier

MANCHESTER UNITED:
Schmeichel, Donaghy (Sharpe), Parker, Pallister, Irwin, Kanchelskis (Hughes), Webb, Robson, Ince, McClair, Giggs

SOUTHAMPTON:
Flowers, Kenna, Ruddock, Hall, Benali, Le Tissier, Horne, Cockerill, Gray (Maddison), Adams, Shearer.

Referee: David Elleray (Harrow)   *Attendance:* 33,414

Compiled by **BOB BRUNSKELL** from the *Echo* report. Matthew Le Tissier interviewed by **David Bull**. *Echo* photographs

NORWICH CITY 4
SOUTHAMPTON 5

For Southampton FC comebacks they didn't come much more exciting and certainly much more important than a pulsating 5-4 victory at Norwich City on April 9, 1994. Alan Ball's men almost literally came back from the dead. They had trailed the Canaries three times in a riveting see-saw of a match, but at 3-1 down and with barely 30 minutes left on the clock, they were staring a potentially devastating defeat in the face.

They had gone to Norwich after a dismal Easter double – defeats by Chelsea then Manchester City at The Dell. It was the City reverse that had hurt most of all, for the Light Blues were tucked up just behind them in the drop zone. Saints went to Carrow Road third from the bottom and knowing they must at least draw. Indeed, they fancied a win against a Norwich side who were wallowing aimlessly in mid-table with just one win from 15 League games.

The fixture in East Anglia may not have had the makings of a classic, but for those Saints fans who made the long trek, it will remain an extraordinarily happy memory. In fact, after a last, dramatic twist of the tail they were transported into the realms of ecstasy. *Echo* reporter Graham Hiley wrote:

Heart-capturing Ken Monkou

> Saints produced a great fightback after being on the ropes for most of the game. Four times they were knocked down, four times they picked themselves up. And the Spirit of Southampton was rewarded with a finish which was almost Fantasy League stuff as they gloriously grabbed a last-minute victory.

Matthew Le Tissier inspired a stunning fightback with a second-half hat-trick as Saints at last discovered the hidden secret of scoring on their travels. They had managed only 11 goals on the road all season. But needs must and they had to dig deeper than at any time during the campaign as Norwich, belying their uninspiring form, led 1-0, 2-1, 3-1 and then 4-3.

It was a day when the men in red and white had to throw caution to the wind. They had to chase the game and left inviting gaps at the back, but in doing so, they drove great swathes through the Norwich rearguard. It wasn't a great day for defenders. The fans feasted on goals but so many chances were created that it could have finished up a rugby score.

Yet Alan Ball had packed the Southampton midfield with five players and while Le Tissier was ultimately to play the starring role and Ken Monkou was to capture the hearts of the captivated Saints followers with a last-minute winner, the foundations of this unlikely success had their origins in the middle of the park.

Jeff Kenna's driving runs down the right, Paul Allen's constant movement and Jim Magilton's diligent anchor role were crucial to Saints' ultimate success.

So congested was the midfield that Norwich bypassed it, humping long balls over the top for Chris Sutton and Mark Robins to chase. And in truth, their pace caused Saints a headache or two. As Graham Hiley added,

> When Norwich made it 3-1 Saints could easily have folded – especially after coming into the game on top of a disastrous Easter. But they refused to throw in the towel. To do so would have compromised their already frail hopes of avoiding relegation. They had gone into the game desperate for a turnaround after a string of poor results. And on a day when Manchester City and Everton, the teams below them, both won, nothing less than a win at Norwich was going to be good enough.

Saints had the best of the first half-hour, playing trademark Alan Ball football, nice one-touch stuff which had Norwich scurrying around and chasing. Yet the Canaries were first to score on 37 minutes. Sutton, an emerging talent at that time, found Robins with a shrewd flick. The former Manchester United man neatly rounded Monkou before slotting his first goal of the season.

Premier League

Saints levelled a minute before half-time when Magilton picked out Neil Maddison, marauding down the left side. The young Geordie cut inside Culverhouse and unleashed a shot which looked to be going wide until Robert Ullathorne deflected it into his own net.

Norwich were back in the driving seat just three minutes into the restart as Neil Adams side-stepped Simon Charlton and crossed for Welsh international Jeremy Goss to head home.

It looked grim for Saints on 55 minutes when Norwich added a third. Dave Beasant only parried a hot-shot from Robins and Sutton, quick as a flash, was first to the loose ball, sweeping it home. Saints needed a spark of hope from somewhere and Le Tissier provided it just two minutes later, latching on to Maddison's lay-off to shoot home left-footed from 18 yards.

One of Kenna's driving runs opened the door for the equaliser. He cut in between Eadie and Crook and powered on into the box where he was upended by the unfortunate Ullathorne. Up stepped Le Tissier to convert the penalty in the 62nd minute.

The goals were coming thick and fast now and Norwich were back in front just 60 seconds later when Crook caught Saints with their pants down with a quickly taken free-kick. Sutton peeled away from Monkou to head home jubilantly.

But Saints managed to gather themselves up for one last glorious onslaught. The industrious Allen picked out Kenna, making another of his positive thrusts, and the Irishman picked out Le Tissier at the far post.

The header was good and Saints were back on terms. And deep into injury-time they went for the kill with Le Tissier this time the provider with a corner kick which Monkou headed home to the thunderous acclaim of the Saints fans.

They would raise the roof at Carrow Road with their celebrations which went on long after the final whistle.

The win provided the launch-pad for a stirring finish to the season. Victories over Blackburn and Aston Villa followed by a desperately tense last game of the season at West Ham, coming up next...

*The most remarkable match. We were down in that game three times and just kept bouncing back. And the memory I've got is: after the game I was speaking to a reporter, doing an interview, and I said to him: "Kenny Monkou's header in the last minute might just keep us up." And, as it happened, we stayed up by a point... To come back three times in a game, that was a helluva performance. The first one [of mine], the goalkeeper made a bit of a boo-boo really. I hit a left-foot shot from the edge of the box, which I didn't hit very well. Brian Gunn got his left hand to it and just sort of palmed it into the net. The second one was a penalty. Jeff Kenna had a brilliant run from right-back, all the way through, and the most blatant penalty you are likely to get, so it wasn't a problem. Sent him the wrong way for that. Then, another header (ha! ha!) from Jeff Kenna's cross again. It was very fortunate because I didn't actually realise it had gone in, because Iain Dowie and a defender had come across me, and they both sort of challenged for the ball, and they both missed it, and all I can remember was the ball hitting my head – I'd closed my eyes – and [when] I opened my eyes the ball was in the net, and I didn't actually know how it got there until I saw it on **Match of the Day**. Because, when Iain and the defender came across me, I didn't think I was going to head it, so I closed my eyes, and it hit me on the head, then it went in. That was a helluva game. That result really gave us the belief we could stay up that year, because we were struggling at that stage.*

Matthew Le Tissier

NORWICH CITY:
Gunn, Bowen, Culverhouse, Prior, Ullathorne, Adams, Crook, Goss, Megson (Robins 25), Sutton, Eadie (Woodthorpe 67)

SOUTHAMPTON:
Beasant, Kenna, Monkou, Bound, Benali, Charlton, Allen, Magilton, Maddison, Le Tissier, Dowie

Referee: Keith Cooper (Swindon)   *Attendance:* 17,158

Compiled by **BOB BRUNSKELL** from the *Echo* report. *Echo* photograph

WEST HAM UNITED 3
SOUTHAMPTON 3

The "GREAT ESCAPE" became part of the lexicon, not to say the mentality, of Southampton fans in the 1990s – so much so that we can still debate which was the most tense final count-down.

In so far as the last day of 1999 was something of an anti-climax to the dramatic day out that was Match No. 99, then it comes down, for me, to a choice between 1994 and 1996.

If sheer absurdity were the criterion, then it would have to be 1996 – thanks to Alan Ball who, having been with us at the cliff-edge in 1994, had left a season later, so as to take Manchester City over the cliff in 1996. Saints would finish that 1995-96 season at home to Wimbledon. Away wins all-round, the previous Saturday, for Southampton, Coventry and Manchester City, would leave them level on points and contesting the one relegation place still "available." And yet, with the three contenders all at home, there was a degree of flatness about the events at The Dell on Sunday 5 May. Despite the stakes, it seemed as if the tempo would never rise to the point where either side might think about scoring – any more than Coventry and Leeds would at Highfield Road.

All the tension was coming from bulletins – courtesy of those with trannies – from Maine Road, where Man City were fighting back from 2-0 down against Liverpool. They might have fought even harder, we subsequently learned, if Alan Ball had had a transistor in his dug-out.

Or maybe he should have spent more of his time at The Dell studying the Club's history and learned from the steps taken by the Board to relay last-day scores as long ago as 1922 (Match No. 19).

Whatever - but the intelligence at Maine Road told him that a 2-2 draw would keep City up. It didn't, of course. Their inferior goal difference took them down and the Saints survived with a goalless draw.

Tense, yes, but no match for the final Saturday in 1994, when the goals were flying in at Upton Park and up-dates were coming in from Lancashire and West London. When they all kicked off on 7 May, there were essentially four sides contesting who'd go down with Swindon and Oldham – although a freakish set of scores would reprieve Oldham.

The Saints started the afternoon in 17th place, the highest position they had occupied all season. From September until Alan Ball took over from Ian Branfoot in January, they had never been out of the bottom three in a Premiership of 22 teams. Matthew Le Tissier had since been turning it on for the manager whose approach, he says, best suited him and now had exactly half of the side's 46 goals to his credit.

Yet there they were, but a point ahead of Everton in 20th place and separated only by goal difference from Sheffield United and Ipswich.

Now, every fan who's ever survived an afternoon

Matthew Le Tissier, supervised by Paul Allen, bends one round the wall

We had an early knock-back, then we equalised just before half-time. We got a free kick on the edge of the box and I bent it in from about 20 yards… I think the goalie was blocked out a little bit, because he put so many in the wall… I struck it pretty well so he couldn't get across to it… That was a big boost to us, just before half-time. To go in level was good, and we sort of got the other results. And then we went 2-1 up. We got the penalty. Iain Dowie went down. I'd put Iain through. The 'keeper went the right way but didn't get anywhere near it.

And then they got back to two-all. And then the third one: I set up Neil Maddison. I jinked on the left, and the defender didn't want to come and tackle me in case he fouled me or anything. I got a left-foot cross in, and Madda – one of the best headers I've seen actually (him and Paul Rideout) – nodded it down: 3-2.

And then the crowd invasion came, we went off the pitch, got the radio on, managed to find the results of the other games – and knew we were pretty safe really. The only way we could go down is if we conceded three goals in the final four minutes. So we managed to give them one back: Kenny put one in his own net just to keep us on our toes. But the second crowd invasion came and the ref blew the whistle. I think possibly a tad early as well. I think it was just safety reasons. But we weren't going to complain.

Yes, that was a GREAT ESCAPE.

Matthew Le Tissier

Premier League

like this knows that you need a *University Challenge* aptitude for mental arithmetic. As news filters in of events elsewhere, you rapidly re-calculate your position, assuming the scores will stay that way. And so it was that the Saints had slipped two places after half-an-hour – thanks not only to a West Ham goal, but to Sheffield United taking the lead at Stamford Bridge, while Ipswich were 0-0 at Ewood Park. The real drama, though, was coming from Goodison Park, where Everton were 2-0 adrift to Wimbledon and going down with the Latics.

But, then, on the verge of half-time and from the edge of the penalty area, Le Tissier loops a free-kick past the wall to send Southampton in level on goals and up to 18th place. Seven minutes into the second-half – with the Saints now storming towards us away fans in the Bobby Moore Stand – it's looking even better as a statuesque Matty coolly tantalises Tim Breacker before teeing up a header for Neil Maddison. 2-1 Goodbye Everton!

Well, not quite. Ten minutes later, Dave Beasant juggles a Morley shot into the path of Martin Allen. 2-2 Yet still Iain Dowie leads the charge. Gale flattens him and Le Tissier obliges from the spot. Twenty-five minutes to go and the Chicken Run's not singing any more.

The Saints are now back where they began the day: in 17th place. With 15 minutes remaining, Everton have clawed back to 2-2, but they're going down, we're not. Then, with four minutes left, the Southampton forwards have stopped coming towards us. The flow in our direction is of West Ham fans and the referee is ushering the players off. The trannies take over and we soon know all the scores that matter. Everton have won 3-2, but Sheffield United have lost in the last minute at Chelsea and are surely relegated. Even if normal service is resumed at Upton Park and West Ham then score twice – to put the Saints level with Sheffield both on points and goal difference – superior scoring (bless you, Matty) will keep Southampton up. The Saints will need to concede three to go down.

Ten minutes later, the invaders have given ground to the police and the referee has restarted the match. Ken Monkou heads past Beasant and the mob reclaims the pitch. Gerald Ashby calls it a day. But wasn't there a minute or two to go? Will Sheffield United protest? Will the match have to be replayed?

If we were soon relieved of those remaining doubts, the inquest on Everton's comeback would linger on – until the performance of Wimbledon's 'keeper was judged OK by a Winchester jury.

As Time Goes By... Who's for the Drop?

How The Bottom Six Were Placed at Intervals

HOW THEY KICKED OFF		HALF-AN-HOUR GONE		HALF-TIME		15 MINUTES TO GO		HOW THEY FINISHED	
	Pts								Pts
SAINTS	42	Sheff Utd	45	Sheff Utd	45	**SAINTS**	45	Everton	44
Ipswich	42	Ipswich	43	**SAINTS**	43	Sheff Utd	45	**SAINTS**	43
Sheff Utd	42	**SAINTS**	42	Ipswich	43	Ipswich	43	Ipswich	43
Everton	41	Oldham	42	Oldham	42	Everton	42	Sheff Utd	42
Oldham	39	Everton	41	Everton	41	Oldham	40	Oldham	40
Swindon	30	Swindon	30	Swindon	30	Swindon	30	Swindon	30

WEST HAM UNITED:

Miklosko, Breacker, Burrows, Gale, Potts, Rush, Bishop (Chapman, 70), Allen, Williamson, Marsh, Morley

SOUTHAMPTON:

Beasant, Kenna, Monkou, Widdrington, Benali, Allen, Magilton, Maddison, Charlton, Le Tissier, Dowie

Referee: G.Ashby (Worcester)   *Attendance:* 26,952

Compiled by **DAVID BULL** from the *Echo* reports and an interview with Matthew Le Tissier. *Echo* photograph. The idea of the clocks is borrowed unashamedly from that evening's *Match of the Day*

SOUTHAMPTON 2
TOTTENHAM HOTSPUR 6

Going down - and out - to your heaviest-ever defeat in the FA Cup by a team that had already been expelled from it is a fine way to treat your fans.

Not that the Southampton players were too thrilled themselves with that achievement on a March evening in 1995. In order to progress to the quarter-finals, ultimately at Saints' expense, Tottenham had to overcome two most unusual obstacles.

First, they had to be allowed back into the competition after the FA had expelled them for financial irregularities. And then they had to come back from 2-0 down with an extraordinary hat-trick by a substitute, first to level this Fifth Round replay at The Dell and then to go ahead and win in extra-time.

Saints had earned the replay by drawing 1-1 at White Hart Lane, a Matthew Le Tissier penalty having equalised a well-taken goal by Jurgen Klinsmann, the German international who had joined Spurs from Monaco during the summer and who came into the game with 18 League and Cup goals to his name. But, then, Le Tissier had 21. It wasn't with his 22nd of the season, however, that Matty made his mark on this game. It was with his wizardly attempts to create goals for others, two first-half demonstrations of artistic virtuosity in particular being worth the admission fee on their own, in the estimation of Graham Hiley, writing in Monday's *Echo*.

Which perhaps explains Spurs' line-up at The Dell. Stuart Nethercott came in to man-mark Le Tissier. This didn't inhibit the Saints who flowed forward with "an exhilarating blend of style" which Hiley found "a pure joy to watch." And so did their fans among a crowd of 15,172. We soon had a goal. On five minutes, Neil Shipperley cleverly diverted a mis-hit shot from Jason Dodd. With Jim Magilton revelling in the space created by Nethercott's remit – shades of Ken Wimshurst on that sensational Cup night that was Match No. 53 – he was free to spray the ball wide to Dodd or Neil Heaney, each of whom enjoyed a field-day.

Heaney, who'd arrived from Arsenal a year earlier, had an electric pace that prompted comparisons with John Sydenham. But there, alas, the likeness stopped. The idea of getting to the by-line and crossing with his left foot appeared often to terrify him. It seemed as if he had been waiting for the FA Cup to release him. Speeding towards us Saints fans in the Fourth Round at Kenilworth Road he'd come to the line and crossed, text-book fashion, to the nearpost for Shipperley's goal in a 1-1 draw. Having already scored in the Third Round defeat of Southend, he was on the scoresheet again in the replay against Luton and so came into this Fifth Round tie, wearing – along with Le Tissier – that coveted scored-in-every-round tag.

And now, just before half-time at The Dell, he was running his full-back again. His pace was too much for Dean Austin who felled him in the box. Le Tissier stepped up for his second penalty of the tie and his third, this season, against his friend Ian Walker. The 'keeper guessed right, as he always did, but the pace, as always, carried the ball into the net. Matty's 35th penalty goal out of 36.

The Saints trooped off at the break fully deserving the warm applause of an appreciative crowd. One of us, sitting under the East Stand, recalls the words of his neighbour as the second-half started. "This could be a very long 45 minutes," she reflected. Just how long and just how devastating none of us could have imagined.

After Saints' second goal, manager Gerry Francis had abandoned his man-marking plan, replacing Nethercott with Ronnie Rosenthal. So what? The Israeli international had hardly been setting the season alight for Spurs. He'd scored only once all season and that in the Third Round against Altrincham. So, with expectant eyes on Klinsmann and Le Tissier, who would have backed Rosenthal to steal the show? In the 56th minute he volleyed in a Barmby cross, following a neat back heel from Sheringham and

Bruce Grobbelaar surveys the damage from a position he practised thoroughly on the night

FA Cup Fifth Round (Replay)

then, two minutes later, whipped in a 25-yard shot which seemed to catch Grobbelaar by surprise. We had seen our side's lead, so impressively built, wiped out in a couple of minutes by a player trebling his season's tally.

Saints seemed to surrender the initiative. Their momentum was gone but they managed to stem a rejuvenated Spurs for the remainder of normal time.

At first, extra-time was evenly balanced, with Grobbelaar saving well from Anderton's stooping header and Shipperley's turn and shot bringing the best out of Walker. But Rosenthal was reluctant to roll the credits on his show just yet and, in the 101st minute, he unleashed another 25-yard exocet, which swerved into the left-hand corner.

The spontaneity of the launch had left Grobbelaar wrong-footed and bemused. Just what secrets of Bruce's chinks had Rosenthal learned on the Liverpool training ground? Whatever the explanation of this outlandish hat-trick, it was a case of Israel 3 Zimbabwe 0 and it looked as if Saints were heading out of the Cup.

Southampton now had to gamble and throw men forward in that time-honoured Cup tradition. We know it can work for you but, as we were about to be reminded, it can go horribly wrong. After 112 minutes, Monkou slipped and Klinsmann raced onto the ball, outpacing Benali. The German international, having been overshadowed by his Israeli colleague, made a neat reverse

It was a shocker. We were 2-0 up at half-time and cruising really. Neil Shipperley scored with a good finish. Then I got another penalty, against Walks. I had three penalties against Ian Walker that season. The one at White Hart Lane I put in the top left and he got a hand to it. The one at The Dell I put bottom left and he got his hand to it. And the previous one, [in the League game away] earlier on in the season, I put bottom right and he got his hand to it. So he must know where it's going, but he still hasn't managed to stop one... The second-half all went a bit pear-shaped. Ronnie Rosenthal came on and [scored] the most amazing hat-trick I've witnessed, really. Especially from a substitute. Two of his goals were from right outside the area and just swerved and Bruce [Grobbelaar] didn't get anywhere near them.

Matthew Le Tissier

pass to Sheringham who danced round Grobbelaar to score.

Some lacked the stomach to stay and watch it get worse. Two minutes later, Klinsmann again provided the assist, threading the ball through to Barmby, who went round Grobbelaar with ease to prod into an empty net. The Saints goalkeeper – who had returned only that morning from a funeral in Africa – was not enjoying the best of nights and salt was well and truly rubbed into the widening wounds, just seconds before the final whistle, when he lunged at Barmby but completely missed. The Spurs forward side-stepped the challenge and calmly centred.

Waiting in the middle was the Southampton-born and Portsmouth-developed Darren Anderton. Controlling the ball neatly, he left-footed the visitors' sixth.

It may be Rosenthal's hat-trick that fans and players alike will continue to talk about but the one of us present that night saw Anderton put on the most complete display of football he can recall watching from an opponent at The Dell. Now chasing back, now surging forward with the ball, now engaging the reserve tank to get into a scoring position, Anderton's magnificent display epitomised Total Football and did not deserve to be overshadowed by a freakish hat-trick.

But never mind the individual honours. Spurs had become the first side ever to put six FA Cup goals past Southampton. Floodlight robbery!

SOUTHAMPTON :

Grobbelaar, Dodd, Monkou, Benali, Kenna, Widdrington (Hughes), Magilton, Maddison, Heaney, Le Tissier, Shipperley

TOTTENHAM HOTSPUR:

Walker, Austin, Edinburgh, Nethercott (Rosenthal), Calderwood, Mabbutt, Anderton, Barmby, Klinsmann, Sheringham, Howells (Caskey)

Referee: Joe Worrall (Warrington)   *Attendance:* 15,712

Compiled by **DAVID BULL** and **DUNCAN HOLLEY** from being there (in one case), the *Echo* reports and an interview with Matthew Le Tissier. *Echo* photograph

SOUTHAMPTON 3
NEWCASTLE UNITED 1

If, as it is in my case, Saints are your first love and Newcastle are your second, then games between these two wonderful clubs take on a particular significance. Only if a fixture was a meaningless end-of-season affair would I be indifferent to the result, but since Saints so seldom play such games the situation hardly arises.

Certainly, on a March evening at The Dell in 1995, both sides had everything to play for. Newcastle, managed by Kevin Keegan, were out of the Championship race but had their eyes firmly set on Europe, while the Saints desperately needed points to get out of the bottom three. It looked as though Ipswich and Leicester were doomed but the third relegation spot was very much on offer.

The home line-up included three players especially out to prove themselves. Gordon Watson was playing his first home game since joining from Sheffield Wednesday. Matthew Le Tissier, who was producing some brilliant football for Alan Ball, the manager who he says brought the best out of him, had been left out of the England squad – a victim of the abandonment of their previous game in Dublin. And Bruce Grobbelaar was under the considerable cloud of match-fixing allegations. Even so, we assumed that their first priority was the same as ours – to get Saints out of danger.

The game as it turned out could be easily forgotten, were it not for the amazing events of the last four or five minutes and the the effect they had not only on this game but the entire season.

The home side had drawn 15 but won only six of their 31 League matches and when it soon became clear that Grobbelaar was to be the busier of the two 'keepers and Kitson gave the Magpies the lead after 18 minutes, it seemed the best we could hope for was another draw and a single point – not good enough.

After Srnicek had thwarted Watson, put through by Le Tiss, Peter Beardsley nearly increased the Newcastle lead with an audacious lob over Grobbelaar but half-time came with no further goals. Indeed, none came during the first 40 minutes of the second-half either but then …

Benali had been replaced by Neil Heaney and with four minutes to go the substitute equalized. There, then, was the draw – the hoped-for best. But that old Dell magic worked once again. The game was now in injury-time but,

Gordon Watson scores his first goal for the Saints to put them ahead in injury-time

Premier League

attacking the Archers Road, the Saints swarmed forward. Gordon Watson delivered. His first goal for the Club made it 2-1 and we knew there would be no Newcastle equalizer. Even as we were drawing breath, we had to let out another roar. Neil Shipperley added a third. Three goals in – what? – four minutes. A match transformed. Three points. Fourth from bottom now. Kevin shattered. Newcastle unable to take it in. Alan Ball the world's greatest manager. Well, no, but just then we thought so.

Truth to tell, it was not a very good game but the amazing conclusion made up for the dross and the season was turned around.

The Saints owed a good deal to their 'keeper. Back in August he had conceded five goals at St James's Park; on this occasion he had played well. Interestingly, he was one of only four foreign players to take part in the game. Ken Monkou was the other in Saints' colours, although both Grobbelaar and he had been in the English game for so long that they were hardly thought of as "strangers." Newcastle also had an imported goalkeeper in Pavel Srnicek, with the Swiss defender, Marc Hottiger, as their other foreigner.

The match highlighted a number of issues pressing at The Dell at the time – the most obvious being that, despite what happened that evening, the squad of '95 was never going to be good enough to do more than stave off relegation. Too many were not of Premiership quality. And, to state the even more obvious,

the ground was too small to sustain top-flight football indefinitely.

The two factors were equally obviously linked and, while both clubs were to invest in bringing in overseas players over the forthcoming seasons, the respective wealth of the two was always going to give Newcastle an edge in attracting the truly big names.

At The Dell this night, however, those two old Saints and England team-mates, Messrs Ball and Keegan, knew the real score. Football can be fun, it can be wonderfully exciting, it can spring the most unexpected of surprises, but it aint 'arf tough at the top.

Quite where the inspiration for that late rally came from is hard to say. Perhaps Newcastle relaxed too soon (an old failing of the Saints – that cup-tie earlier in the month a spectacular case in point) but credit to Matthew and Co. for their spirit on the night.

The result meant that the two games between the two clubs that season produced 10 goals. Not quite equalling the 11 of 1947-48.

Then Second Division sides, the Saints won 4-2 at The Dell, Newcastle 5-0 in the north-east.

The attendances were interesting too. Nearly 27,000 at home, over 57,000 at St James's Park.

The night the Saints won at The Dell in March 1995 and saved their Premiership status they were watched by less than 15,000.

We didn't half enjoy it, though!

> *That was an absolute **belter** of a last five minutes. The atmosphere in the ground that night was unbelievable. We were up against it again and one-down and nothing was really happening for us. We couldn't really get the breaks and, once we got one goal, the crowd went mad and all of a sudden all the players' energy levels just went up and people were **flying** around the pitch… The atmosphere that night! I think that last five minutes created [such] an atmosphere that I'd find it very difficult to find a game that's matched that. Liverpool [Match 100] wasn't far off – that was pretty good at the end – but the atmosphere's a bit better at night games. That was an incredible comeback.*
>
> Matthew Le Tissier

SOUTHAMPTON:

Grobbelaar, Dodd, Hall, Benali (Heaney 61), Monkou, Charlton, Magilton, Maddison, Le Tissier, Watson, Shipperley

NEWCASTLE UNITED:

Srnicek, Hottiger, Peacock, Howey, Elliott, Gillespie, Venison, Lee, Fox, Beardsley, Kitson

Referee: J Worrall (Warrington)   *Attendance:* 14,666

Compiled by **RONALD ALLISON** from being there and from the *Daily Telegraph* report. Matthew Le Tissier interviewed by **David Bull**. *Echo* photograph

SOUTHAMPTON 3
MANCHESTER UNITED 1

This could be the only game that has had a book named after a half-time incident. If I mention that the book was called *The Wrong Kind of Shirts,* then we can all be sure that we know which defeat of Ferguson's Manchester United we're talking about and which whinge their manager used to explain it.

But let's start at the beginning … Manchester United came to The Dell, having won 10 of their last 11 League matches. With four games of the 1995-96 to play, they were leading the Premiership by six points – although second-placed Newcastle did have a game in hand. Southampton, on the other hand, were lying 16th, just two above the relegation zone. They'd not been finding the net. Neil Shipperley, on six League goals, was leading the way, ahead of Matthew Le Tissier on five. And it was no use expecting them to score in the first-half – something they'd achieved only nine times all season (34 games gone) and only once in their last eight outings.

So what went wrong? Basically, Saints seemed to want it more and – although we know by now that it doesn't always follow – they got it. Graham Hiley, in the *Echo,* was impressed by their "hustling, harrying, chasing and closing down." And they scored three times before the interval.

Ken Monkou started it on 11 minutes when he met Le Tissier's free-kick with a powerful header. Peter Schmeichel stopped it but Monkou re-acted quickly to force home the rebound. Next, up stepped Alan Neilson, a grafter who tended to impress me more stepping up than closing down. On this occasion, he was crossing low on 23 minutes for Neil Shipperley to make it two. And

then Schmeichel came a flap too far. If we compare his ratings with the way he performed at The Dell in 1996 – in this match and the next one – then he must have saved all his misses for us. This time, it was a cross from Shipperley that had him over-stretching and palming the ball down to the feet of Le Tissier. One of those gifted feet flicked the ball over the stranded 'keeper and the other stroked it into the net.

Shortly after half-time, United's manager re-organised his defence, bringing on David May for Lee Sharpe. As Graham Hiley sardonically remarked, this enabled him to switch Gary Neville, their England No. 2, to right-back and Denis Irwin, Ireland's No. 3, to left-back. And Neville was in the right place to cross for Ryan Giggs to score a late consolation goal for United and ruin the day of the punter who had backed Saints to win 3-0 with Monkou scoring the first.

Alex Ferguson was not making excuses about fielding a makeshift defence. United's first-half performance could be blamed on their having the wrong shirts. They had been wearing their all-grey strip in which they had never won a Premiership match. With only one point to show for four games previously played in it, a manager would not have to be over-superstitious to bin the kit, surely.

As scorer Shipperley (left) wheels away, Peter Schmeichel looks for somebody in a grey shirt to blame for the goal

Premier League

United had a commitment, though, to Umbro, who had worked for two years on the strip: "that's how much time it takes," the manufacturer explained, "to study the design, to meet the needs of the club and its sponsor [and produce] a kit that really respects its roots and culture." But it took Ferguson only the 15-minute interval to decide that, commitment notwithstanding, his side would appear for the second-half wearing blue-and-white and giving a whole new meaning to "change strip".

If you're ever feeling sorry – as, indeed, you should - for those of us whose journey home from The Dell obliges us to use the A36, then I have to confess how much we enjoy it when Manchester United have lost so that our car radio has their manager whinging on *Sports Report* and their fans belly-aching on *Six-o-Six*. If memory serves, this was how we first heard about the obligation to Umbro and the manager's concern that his players had been unable to pick out, against the crowd, team-mates dressed in grey.

Even before this limp excuse encouraged Mark Reynolds to compile a book of "outrageous football excuses, whinges and verbal own goals" and to call it *The Wrong Kind of Shirts,* this explanation had given football fans everywhere an excuse to laugh at the Premiership leaders. Ferguson's biographer congratulates him, though, on blaming the shirts and thereby ensuring that the tabloids would enjoy the joke at his expense. He reasons that "Ferguson had cleverly taken the spotlight off his youngsters," who had a Championship to win – which they duly did. That seems generous to me although it could equally be said that, by keeping up the joke, we Saints' fans have allowed that laughable excuse to detract from how well our team played to take three vital points from United.

We dared not laugh too soon, though. Three games still to go. A defeat at Newcastle, which was of no use to them at all as United, vision restored, romped on. A win at Bolton, so they were going down. And the final day cliff-hanger, already described within Match No. 94, when Saints would survive on goal difference and send United's neighbours down.

> *Then, just before half-time, Schmeichel came for a cross, dropped it at my feet, and I took it round him and put it in at the far post. That was in April. And that was my first goal from open play that season: the only time I'd scored that season was from a free-kick or a penalty. So that was a big relief for me … That was a good day, but the next day it was "Oh! We couldn't see our players" and a bit of a shame really that we didn't get the credit we probably deserved.*
>
> Matthew Le Tissier
>
> *It really was a matter of vision. Our players said it was difficult to see their team-mates at distances when they lifted their heads.*
>
> Alex Ferguson

SOUTHAMPTON:
Beasant, Neilson, Monkou, Benali, Charlton, Dodd, Magilton, Venison, Heaney, Shipperley, Le Tissier

MANCHESTER UNITED:
Schmeichel, Irwin, Bruce, G. Neville, Sharpe (May 54), Beckham, Keane, Butt (Scholes 45), Giggs, Cantona, Cole

Referee: Graham Poll (Tring)   *Attendance:* 15,262

Compiled by **DAVID BULL** from being there, the *Echo* report, an interview with Matthew Le Tissier and Stephen Kelly's biography of Alex Ferguson. The quotations from Umbro and Alex Ferguson are both from *The Wrong Kind of Shirts,* from the front cover of which the cartoon is reproduced with permission of Fourth Estate. *Echo* photograph

SOUTHAMPTON 6
MANCHESTER UNITED 3

Saturday, 26 October 1996 will remain a day to savour for Southampton Football Club fans, a day when they whipped the cream of English football.

The football world raised a collective eyebrow when Saints hit United, the defending Premier League champions, for six.

If you were a United fan or a neutral, you had to look twice at the score: Southampton 6 Manchester United 3. But not Saints supporters. It was already up in lights and will remain forever so.

The *Echo*'s Graham Hiley joyfully reported:

> United were whipped, pulverised, smashed out of sight. The champions came into town with an arrogant swagger and were humbled 6-3 by a rampant Saints side playing breathtaking football.

It was the day the Israeli Eyal Berkovic illuminated an autumn afternoon with a dazzling repertoire of midfield skills which effectively announced his arrival as one of the most exciting new imports on the English soccer stage. Berkovic turned the screw and the blond Norwegian predator Egil Ostenstad tightened it with a hat-trick. As Berkovic alerted the Premiership to his special creative qualities, so did Ostenstad with his pace and power. Graeme Souness, the latest in an uncharacteristic turnover of managers at The Dell, had brought in two overseas players whose mutual understanding contributed so much to the afternoon's entertainment – and result.

United, or more to the point their inspirational but temperamental midfielder Roy Keane, had invited the impending disaster. Yellow-carded early for dissent and riling referee Jeff Winter by continuing to bad-mouth him, Keane went for a second bookable offence after just 21 minutes – a dubious tackle on Claus Lundekvam, another of Souness's buys from Norway.

Keane's red card and an early injury sustained by Nicky Butt effectively handed midfield territorial advantage to Saints. They exploited it ruthlessly. Jason Dodd and Alan Neilson provided a cutting edge, Berkovic was the imperious creator. And United found no inspiration from their own great creative force Eric Cantona. The Frenchman was eternally in the considerable shadow of Southampton's man mountain of a defender, the Dutchman Uli Van Gobbel. When the great but broody Cantona kicked out in frustration at Van Gobbel's persistent presence, it was a gesture of futility, Manchester United's futility.

Yet after reducing the deficit to 3-2, early in the second-half, the Red Devils began to wear the look of a side who could turn the tide and Saints, it seemed, would not be able to hold on to their slender advantage. But when they found an extra gear in the last 10 minutes, they swept away all doubts as they gloriously despatched United with three more goals.

Egil Ostenstad squeezes his first, and Saints' third, past Peter Schmeichel

Premier League

The capacity 15,253 crowd had not had long to wait for the first. Just six minutes had ticked by when a Berkovic back-heel deceived Gary Pallister and set up Ostenstad for a shot wich Peter Schmeichel only parried. Berkovic reacted faster than Phil Neville, driving the loose ball back beyond the big Danish 'keeper. If there was raw power in the first goal, there was silky finesse about the second, chipped over Schmeichel's head by Matthew Le Tissier in the 34th minute. Again Berkovic was the architect, feeding the ball to the Channel Islander who swept past David May and substitute Brian McClair before applying a cool, sublime finish.

David Beckham pulled one back for United on 41 minutes and typically it came from a free-kick, this one from 20 yards which curled into the top right-hand corner. But on the stroke of half-time, Saints restored the two-goal cushion as Berkovic played in Ostenstad down the left and he cut through to the byline before squeezing a shot past Schmeichel from the narrowest of angles.

Van Gobbel had subdued Cantona well enough, but after 56 minutes he was a fraction late picking up David May as the blond United centre-back went in bravely after another Beckham free-kick. May got in the header at the far post, it was 3-2 and United were back in the ball game, with belief suddenly welling back into their ranks.

The game swayed precariously in the balance until the 83rd minute when Le Tissier's left-wing corner was headed across goal by Richard Dryden then back by Lundekvam for Berkovic to billow the back of the net with a stunning 20-yard volley. United crumpled, going 5-2 down just two minutes later when the irrepressible Berkovic put Ostenstad in behind May and he made light of Schmeichel's advance with an emphatic finish.

There was just the slightest flutter of concern among the singing, dancing Southampton multitude when Paul Scholes stabbed in from close range following a Cantona corner on 89 minutes. It sparked whistles from three sides

Obviously we were helped by Roy Keane being sent off quite early in the game. I think things may have been a little different if they had had 11 men. But, even so, we were one-up before that. Eyal scored the first one. I scored the second one. I had a little bit of a dribble past two players – Brian McClair and David May, I think it was – and, the week before Schmeichel had been chipped by Philippe Albert. I'd seen that on the telly and it was always in my mind that Schmeichel stands out from his goal a little bit, so I didn't have to actually look up when I dribbled past the two players on the edge of the box, I immediately went "he'll be off his line" and just chipped it … That was pretty special. It's nice to do a bit of homework, and have something stick in your mind from the week before, and then to use it … Andy Gray and the panel took away the last goal that Egil scored, which I thought was extremely harsh. It was going across the face of goal and Gary Neville tried to slide in and clear it, but he got a touch and it went in. But I think Egil's still got the match ball, so I still think it's a hat-trick.

Matthew Le Tissier

of the ground for the ref to blow for time, but they forgave the delay as substitute Gordon Watson cut the ball past Denis Irwin for Ostenstad who was by now unstoppable and sidestepped past Schmeichel before completing his hat-trick – or what Saints fans still talk of as a hat-trick despite the subsequent panel verdict that the third goal be credited to "own goal."

Not since Saints had beaten United in the FA Cup Final at Wembley had their fans been happier. They sang: "Can we play you every week?" Graeme Souness smiled: "We had a good day at the office. If we could guarantee football like that every week, we'd need the new stadium to be even bigger!"

United? Well they were just glad to get out of town.

SOUTHAMPTON:
Beasant, Van Gobbel, Lundekvam, Dryden, Charlton (Potter 70), Oakley, Dodd, Neilson (Magilton 75), Berkovic, Le Tissier (Watson 89), Ostenstad

MANCHESTER UNITED:
Schmeichel, G. Neville, May, Pallister (Irwin 35), P. Neville, Beckham, Keane, Butt (McClair 16), Cruyff (Solskjaer 85), Cantona, Scholes

Referee: Jeff Winter (Durham) *Attendance:* 15,253

Compiled by **BOB BRUNSKELL** from the *Echo* report. Matthew Le Tissier interviewed by **David Bull.** *Echo* photograph

WIMBLEDON 0
SOUTHAMPTON 2

When Dave Jones reflects on his time as manager of Saints, one joyous occasion will almost certainly bring a smile to his lips – a spring day in May 1999 when his team all but secured their Premiership future in front of 10,000 adoring fans.

It was an away-day to beat all away-days. A trip to Selhurst Park, which yielded a fine 2-0 victory over a normally unyielding Wimbledon side, sparked great rejoicing among a huge army of travelling fans and provided a vital step up the survival ladder. Going into the penultimate game of that 1998-99 season, the Saints were again having to fight for their Premiership lives. No-one, apart from Coventry City, had perfected the art of top-flight survival quite so well as they had, and on this memorable occasion in South London, they lived up to their never-say-die reputation.

Robbie Earle dives across Hassan Kachloul to deflect
Matthew Le Tissier's in-swinging corner past Neil Sullivan

Although they achieved a crucial victory over Wimbledon, Saints had an agonising wait over the last week of the season before the final relegation picture unfolded, the first part of it in the middle of the week when a draw with Manchester United condemned Blackburn to join already-doomed Nottingham Forest in the big drop.

The final part of the saga came on the final Sunday of the season when Charlton Athletic, who had enjoyed a heart-stopping 4-3 win at Aston Villa on the same day as Saints beat Wimbledon, tripped up in their last game at home to Sheffield Wednesday. Saints meanwhile were coolly disposing of Everton 2-0 at The Dell.

It all ended as a bit of an anti-climax but on that penultimate Saturday of the campaign, tension invaded every pore of the travelling army of Saints supporters. There were never any guarantees against an always uncompromising Wimbledon side, even though they had managed just one win from their last 20 games.

But this was to prove more than just another game. It was a very special, almost spiritual, experience for the great big family of Saints fans who were there, each and every one of them determined to savour every minute of it. Their support for Saints from first to last was deafening; their humour infectious. Conforming with a humorous trend set the year before when they dressed in tribute to cult hero Francis Benali, they picked out Moroccan star Hassan Kachloul as the theme for this particular party.

Many fans donned fezzes and colourful robes. It was a mark of the warmth and high regard they had for the Moroccan, who had played with great style and determination since his arrival in Southampton and had scored some important goals towards the survival cause. So it was perfectly fitting that Kachloul should play a key role in forcing the goal that sealed the win against Wimbledon. He and Robbie Earle (later credited with the last touch) went for an in-swinging Matt Le Tissier corner which ended up in the net, releasing a great tidal wave of joy among the red and white army in the stands. It was a lovely playback of the Club's golden days of the 1970s and '80s.

Saints went into the game with traditional life-saver Le Tissier on the bench, the result of a nagging calf strain. But more surprising was the sight of Paul Jones restored in goal just five weeks after sustaining a nasty-looking back injury which the Club initially feared would lay him low until well beyond the finish of the season.

If Jones's fitness was in question, then Wimbledon set out looking for some early answers. The Dons lined up with an adventurous 4-3-3 formation and quickly put the Welsh international to the test. Barely 10 minutes had gone when Carl Cort's quick feet earned him a yard of space from which he hit a wicked 20-yarder which Jones, with great agility, saved at full stretch.

Saints were forced on to the back foot as the Dons kept up a brisk pace and Carl Leaburn, a huge, menacing presence, almost brushed the woodwork with a glancing, downward header. Then he wrong-footed defenders with a clever dummy from a Mark Kennedy centre and Robbie Earle charged in on the blind side to force a tremendous reaction save from Jones, who blocked the close-range shot with his feet.

All Saints had to show from the early exchanges was a 25-yard effort from Benali which was a little too close for Neil Sullivan's comfort. But after 35 minutes they thought they had drawn first blood when Marian Pahars turned the ball home from close range after Claus Lundekvam had headed down a corner from Chris Marsden. It didn't count. The Latvian was ruled offside. Pahars then forced a mistake from Chris Perry and David Hughes, presented with a decent chance in front of goal, was denied by the vigilant Sullivan. Pahars's persistence was rattling the Dons and led to Kachloul having a shot deflected into the side-netting.

But Wimbledon's attacks still carried a lot of danger as Benali found just before half-time when he was superbly placed to chest a shot from Earle off the line after Kennedy had disarmed the Saints defence with another quality ball in from the left.

The Dons had perhaps edged the first-half, but the second belonged to Saints and they were starting to build up a good head of steam when Kachloul almost forced a break in the deadlock. He outstripped Cunningham and his angled shot took a deflection, wrong-footing Sullivan. Mayhem ensued in the goalmouth as Pahars, James Beattie and David Hughes all tried to force the ball home, but between them Sullivan and Perry cleared.

Le Tissier came on as substitute for David Hughes and received his usual warm rapturous welcome from fans expecting the great man to weave some kind of magic. And, of course, he did. In a perfectly scripted ending to this tense thriller, the Channel Islander orchestrated the two crucial killer blows.

The first, after 72 minutes (just three minutes after he'd come on) followed a foul on the marauding Benali. Le Tissier swung the ball over from the left and Beattie rose to steer a fine header into the top right-hand corner of Sullivan's goal.

As Wimbledon looked for instant retribution, it was Le Tissier of all people who was back to clear in front of his own goal. Saints were hanging on when Andy Roberts powered in a 25-yard shot which Jones could only parry. Benali sliced the loose ball up in the air, John Hartson headed it wide and the visiting fans breathed a huge sigh of relief.

Then they went wild with delight when Earle, under pressure from Kachloul, put the game beyond Wimbledon's reach with less than seven minutes to go.

Again Le Tissier was the architect with a menacing in-swinging flag-kick which got the faintest of touches off Earle's head, as he dived goalward, to disarm the capable Sullivan.

> *A fantastic atmosphere. The crowd that day was the thing that sticks in my mind … An incredible turn out … It was touch and go whether I'd be fit or not. I spoke to Dave Jones on the Friday night and [suggested] it might be best if I sat on the bench and, if need be, [have] 20 minutes at the end. As it happened, it worked out perfectly. Nil-nil with 20 minutes to go and "on you go." I had half a chance before I crossed the ball for Beatts from the free-kick. That was a great header by Beatts … And then I scored direct from a corner, which took a glance off Robbie Earle's head. And Andy Gray decided to take it off me for some reason, which I haven't spoken to him about yet … The ball was going in anyway …Whether the goalie would have stopped it or not we'll never know, but it was on target – to go in the goal – and it got a slight deflection. There was a big gap at the near post … I just thought "Well, I'm going to hit it as hard as I can in there; and if anybody gets a touch on it, it goes in." As it happened, it was one of their guys.*
>
> Matthew Le Tissier

WIMBLEDON:
Sullivan, Cunningham, Blackwell, Perry, Kimble, Leaburn, Earle, Roberts, Kennedy, Cort, Hartson

SOUTHAMPTON:
Jones, Dodd, Lundekvam, Monkou, Benali, D Hughes (Le Tissier), M Hughes, Marsden, Kachloul, Beattie, Pahars

Referee: Steve Dunn (Bristol)　　　　　　　　　　　　　　　　　　　　　　　*Attendance:* 24,068

Compiled by **BOB BRUNSKELL** from the *Echo* report. Matthew Le Tissier interviewed by **David Bull**. Empics photograph

SOUTHAMPTON 3
LIVERPOOL 3

Coming back from three-down to draw 3-3 with Liverpool was not part of the plan. The plan had been to start the season away from home and to get something out of the two home games the week after.

Well, not so much a plan, maybe, as the thinking behind the Club's repeated bids to the fixture-fixers, in the late 1990s, to give Saints a break from home-starts. You can see why they were fed up with forever starting at home – since drawing at Villa Park on the opening day of 1990, they had opened at The Dell for the next eight seasons. And why they were even more fed up with forever failing to start with a win: not since 1988, when Paul Rideout bagged a pair on his debut against West Ham, had the Dell faithful seen a home win to start their season.

But then, both in 1999 and 2000, the fixture computer obliged: Saints could open away. Perversely, you will recall, they won at Coventry and drew at Derby, respectively. And then – perhaps even more perversely - they blew each Wednesday night home game against a side – Leeds and an avenging Coventry, respectively – who couldn't remember what winning away was like.

And so to two exciting weekend encounters at The Dell. In 1999, it was Newcastle and resurrection from a goal down to win 4-2 and effectively write Ruud Gullit's P45. But, then, home comebacks against Newcastle had become a commonplace of the 1990s and nothing to write home about - or even to write about more than once (as in Match No. 96) in this collection.

In August 2000, though, it was Liverpool. Saints weren't in the habit of coming back against them. True, they'd done it in 1960 (Match No. 49), in their first post-war encounter with them – but that was from only one-down and the recovery

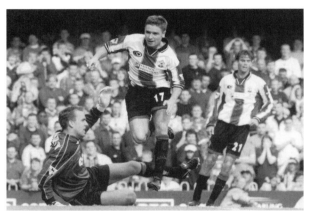

Marian Pahars levels late

started in the first-half. To leave it until you're three-down with 17 minutes remaining was like, well, pretending it was 1963 and Nottingham Forest and Match No. 52 all over again. This, though, was Liverpool, the team with the best defensive record in the Premiership in 1999-2000. OK, if you want to heap on the perverse logic, you could say that this was a good reason for expecting Saints repeatedly to dent their defences.

After all, their problem in the first hour had not been one of getting the ball into their opponents' penalty area – or into their six-yard box, for that matter – but of getting it over the goal-line from there. And their chances had even come in the air – against a beanpole Liverpool defence orchestrated by their Finnish captain, Sami Hyypia. Dean Richards had headed over the best chance, although he may have been distracted by Hassan Kachloul's floppy, rag-doll leap across his run. By contrast, Liverpool – or, to be more precise, Michael Owen – had coolly taken their chances.

Either side of a 54th-minute goal by Hyypia – an unchallenged header from a Smicer corner – Owen had run on to a Smicer pass, outpacing first Lundekvam after 23 minutes and then Richards on 64 to slot the ball past Neil Moss's left hand. You had to feel sorry for Moss. Brought in, to rapturous applause, after Paul Jones's shaky showing against Coventry, he was having to contend with a clinical young striker, proving his fancy for facing Southampton by making it seven in seven against them. And you have to feel that Glenn Hoddle was right when he reasoned afterwards that the difference between the two sides had been "Owen, with his cutting edge. His movement and sharpness were as good as I have seen for the last eight months [the length of tenure, by then, of Southampton's latest manager]."

Well, then, what made the late difference at the other end? You have to give some credit to the substitutions. Matthew Le Tissier came on for Kachloul just before Liverpool's third, which meant he was there, when Saints kicked off 3-0 down, to attempt a chip from the half-way line. Thereafter, he put himself about in his own unathletic way, generally flashed threatening balls around and specifically contributed the arching probe that resulted in Saints' injury-time equaliser. His arrival had meant that Jo Tessem could go wide and become effective – most meaningfully when he centred on 73 for Marian Pahars to head in at the far post. Hailed as the "Latvian Michael Owen," Pahars had been playing too wide and too deep to put the likeness to the test. The arrival of James Beattie

Premier League

(on after 82 minutes for Uwe Rösler) emphasised even more the need for a ferret down the centre in Owen mode. But it wasn't Pahars who popped up under Westerveld's nose on 85 to head Saints' second from Beattie's head-on. It was Tahar El Khalej, who'd come on, when Le Tissier did, for Dodd and with license, it seemed, to roam.

And then, after the fourth official's board had shone its three-minute warning, Le Tiss, over by the dug-out, looped one long and high into Liverpool's area, where Djimi Traore, challenged by Richards, headed into the path of Pahars, who coolly satisfied the Owenite label.

I suppose we all expected the media to say the visitors threw it away. They didn't. They left that to Liverpool's manager, while they themselves offered a spectrum of explanations. Take your pick from those above – from Russell Thomas's baffled agnosticism to the two-to-tango

---

Who Can Explain It?

We concede three goals in the air. When you consider the size of our defenders, that is a joke … I am very angry because we threw it away.

Gerard Houllier

Then things, most notably Liverpool's defence, unravelled in a most peculiar way.

Russell Thomas, *Guardian*

A stunning collapse by Liverpool, a rousing comeback by Southampton.

Ian Ridley, *Observer*

A comeback of remarkable spirit and self-belief.

Steve Curry, *Sunday Times*

The crowd here really lifted us. Showing that spirit, determination and character you can achieve things.

Glenn Hoddle

---

approach of Ian Ridley to Steve's Curry's outright tribute to Southampton. And note how Glenn Hoddle linked the players' "spirit" that impressed Curry to the "lift" that they received from the crowd.

The contribution of what Glenn Moore, in the *Independent*, called "the demonic roaring of 15,000 Saints" was not lost on the journalists, either.

But, as Moore insinuated, this may owe something to The Dell, "a cramped relic [that] can still crank up an atmosphere in which players are forced to reveal themselves."

Or as Ian Ridley put it, the ground "does pose an intriguing test for the bigger clubs used to grandeur and breathing space."

So a less claustrophobic new stadium will give us less chance to will a comeback next time we're three goals down at half past four, then?

Seems we'll have to be even more perverse in adversity.

---

*That was the best home comeback I've ever been involved in. That was a special comeback. The goalkeeper was at fault with the first goal. He was trying to read Marian heading it back across to Uwe … He gambled, really, and lost badly. The second one, … Beatts knocked a good header back. I don't know what Tahar was doing there: he was meant to be playing right-back and he pops up six yards out. Unbelievable! And then I crossed the ball. I was aiming for Deano. I don't know what he was trying to do, the left-back. He just came across and headed it back towards his own goal. But Marian was in the right place at the right time … From the moment the first one went in, you could see them just sort of jittering a bit. And when the second one went in, they **did** panic.*

Matthew Le Tissier

SOUTHAMPTON:

Moss, Dodd (El Khalej 61), Lundekvam, Richards, Bridge, Draper, Tessem, Oakley, Pahars, Rösler (Beattie 82), Kachloul (Le Tissier 61)

LIVERPOOL:

Westerveld, Babbel, Hyypia, Henchoz, Traore, Gerrard, Carragher, Hamann, Barmby (Staunton 82), Smicer (Murphy 73), Owen

Referee: Jeff Winter (Stockton-on-Tees)   *Attendance:* 15,502

Compiled by **DAVID BULL** from being there, from reports in the four broadsheets cited and from an interview with Matthew Le Tissier. *Echo* photograph

SOURCES

This book simply could not have been assembled without constant reference to the priceless, pioneering work of Gary Chalk and Duncan Holley in the form of *Saints: a complete record of Southampton Football Club 1885-1987* (Breedon, 1987) and *An Alphabet of Saints: A Complete Who's Who of Southampton FC* (ACL Polar, 1992).

The other reference books drawn upon constantly at the editorial stage were the relevant seasons of those two dependable annuals – *Rothmans Football Yearbook* and the *News of the World Football Annual* – and four other invaluable sources:

Mike Collett, *The Guinness Record of the FA Cup*, Guinness Publishing, 1993.
Barry J. Hugman (ed.), *The PFA Premier & Football League Players' Records 1946-1998*, Queen Anne Press, 1998.
Jack Rollin, *Rothmans Book of Football Records*, Headline, 1998.
Dennis Turner & Alex White (eds.), *The Breedon Book of Football Managers*, Breedon, 1993.

Newspapers, Journals and Handbooks

We have attempted to indicate, in the credits at the foot of each report, where we have drawn upon national newspapers, although we have sometimes had to note that the 'paper cannot be identified. This is the consequence of using players' scrapbooks in which the source has not been recorded. We have otherwise been confident in our attributions to the local *Echo* – whether a weekday edition or the *Football Echo* – and to the following newspapers, journals and handbooks, which we (mainly Dave Juson) have drawn upon, occasionally from our own collections but often from one of the public collections acknowledged in the box below:

The Athletic News; The Bournemouth Guardian; Chums (October 1899, in the Terry Gregory Collection); *The Footballer; The Hampshire Advertiser* (including several unattributed articles by F.J. Montgomery in the 1920s and 1930s); *Hampshire: the County Magazine; Hampshire Football Association Handbook; The Hampshire Independent; The Morning Leader; S. Mary's Parish Magazine; Saints Magazine; Southampton Amusements; The Southampton & District Pictorial* (notably for the 1912 series on Saints' history); *The Southampton Observer & Winchester News; The Southampton Times & Hampshire Express; The Southern Referee: an Athletic Journal for Hants, Wilts & Dorset; South Hants & Dorset FA Handbook*, 1884-85 to 1886-87; *When Saturday Comes.*

Access to libraries, archives and special collections

One or more of us (and especially Dave Juson) wishes to thank Brian Truscott for permitting, and Barry Fox and Malcolm Taylor for facilitating, access to the Minute books at The Dell and all of the others who allowed us access to their archives or libraries: the kind staff in the British Newspaper Library at Colindale; the Hampshire FA; the City Archivist's Office and the Special Collections Library, both in the Southampton Civic Centre; and, as ever, David Barber at the FA. And we are grateful for help with reports or illustrations from the *Luton News;* the *Sunderland Echo* (as kindly brokered and supplemented by Roger Shackleton and Brian Leng); and Spurs historian, Andy Porter, for information from the *Tottenham Weekly Herald.*

Reports and photographs from a weekday edition of the *Southern Daily Echo,* on the one hand, and the Saturday *Football Echo* (or *The Pink* in recent years) on the other, are all acknowledged generically as being from "the *Echo*".

Books and Articles

The full references to books and articles cited in the credits at the end of reports are:

John Arlott, "A Southampton Football Epic", *Hampshire: the County Magazine,* June 1963
  (reproduced in David Rayvern Allen, *Another Word from Arlott,* Pelham Books, 1985).
Ron Atkinson, *Big Ron: a different ball game,* Andre Deutsch, 1998.
David Barber, *We Won The Cup,* Pan, 1981.
David Bull, *Dell Diamond: Ted Bates's first 60 seasons with The Saints,* Hagiology Publishing, 1998.
Ron Burgess, *Football: My Life,* Stanley Paul, 1965.
Horatio Carter, *Footballer's Progress,* Sporting Handbooks, 1950.
Mike Channon, *Home and Away,* Stanley Paul, 1977.
Mick Channon, *Man on the Run,* Arthur Barker, 1986.
Jack Charlton, *Jack Charlton: the autobiography,* Partridge Press, 1996.
William Dawson, "A Trainer's Story", *Football Echo* (a 1924 series).
Norman Gannaway, *Association Football in Hampshire until 1914,* Hampshire Papers No.9,
  Hampshire County Council, 1996.
Alfred Gibson & William Pickford, *Association Football and the Men Who Made It* (four volumes), Caxton, 1905-06.
Maurice Golesworthy, *The Encyclopaedia of Association Football,* Hale, 1961 edn.
Geoffrey Green, *The Official History of the FA Cup,* Naldrett, 1949.
Aidan Hamilton, *An Entirely Different Game,* Mainstream, 1998.
Paul Harrison, *Southern League Football: The First Fifty Years,* Paul Harrison, 1989.
Denis Law, *Denis Law: an autobiography,* Queen Anne Press, 1979.
Simon Inglis, *League Football and the men who made it,* Willow Books, 1988.
Kevin Keegan, *Kevin Keegan: my Autobiography,* Warner Books, 1998 edn.
Stephen F. Kelly, *Fergie: the biography of Alex Ferguson,* Headline, 1997.
Lou Macari, *United – We shall not be moved,* Souvenir Press, 1976.
Tony Mason, *Association Football and English Society 1863-1915,* Harvester, 1981.
Stanley Matthews, *The Way It Was: my autobiography,* Headline, 2000.
F.J. Montgomery, *History of Deanery Cricket Club,* privately published, 1921.
William Pickford, *The Hampshire Football Association: Golden Jubilee Book,* Bournemouth Guardian, 1937.
Alf Ramsey, *Talking Football,* Stanley Paul, 1952.
Mark Reynolds, *The Wrong Kind of Shirts,* Fourth Estate, 1996.
Jack Rollin, *Soccer at War 1939-45,* Willow Books, 1985.
D.F. Rowe, *Soccer – do it this way,* John Murray, 1967 edn.
Neil Ruddock, *Hell Razor: the autobiography,* CollinsWillow, 1999.
Gordon Sewell, *Echoes of a Century: The Centenary History of Southern Newspapers Limited,* Southern Newspapers, 1964.
Alan Shearer, *My Story So Far,* Coronet, 1998.
Phil Soar and Martin Tyler, *Official History: Arsenal 1886-1995,* Hamlyn, 1995.
Clive Thomas, *By The Book,* Willow Books, 1984.
Martin Tyler, *Cup Final Extra! How the Finals were Reported 1872-1980,* Hamlyn, 1981.
Danny Wallace, "Southampton 8 Coventry City 2", in Bob Holmes, *The Match of my Life,* Kingswood Press, 1991.
Andrew Ward, *Armed with a Football: a memoir of Tim Ward,* Crowberry, 1994.
Iain Wilton, *C.B. Fry: An English Hero,* Richard Cohen Books, 1999.
Percy M. Young, *A History of British Football,* Stanley Paul, 1969.

The video cited is *The Official History of the Saints,* Meridian Films, 1990 (interviews by John Hughes).

CONTRIBUTORS

EDITORS

BOB BRUNSKELL – First Saints' match 17 December 1969 at Newcastle, EUFA Cup, 0-0, when he returned, as an *Echo* reporter, to the town of his birth – although he'd grown up in a mining village near Sunderland. From the age of six, was taken by his father to Roker Park to watch the likes of Watson, Ford and Shackleton in the early 1950s, before the family moved to Hertfordshire. Joined the *Echo* from a small weekly in Watford, where he'd covered Furphy's Watford, in 1967. While enjoying a supporting role in the 1970s to the *Echo*'s Saints writer Brian Hayward, he played a key part in covering the FA Cup triumph of 1976. Assumed coverage of Saints' matches full-time in 1979, so was privileged to chronicle the "golden years" of the early 1980s. In a more production-based position since 1988, he has retained his Saints' links through the popular "Where are They Now?" and "Match of the Century" series.

DAVID BULL – First match 27 December 1948 v. Nottingham Forest, 2-1, while attending Devizes Road Primary School, Salisbury. Moved, in 1954, to become in turn a Camberley teenager, an Exeter student and a university teacher in Exeter, Manchester and Bristol. Nowadays commutes from Bristol to the Lower East. Has written for the Saints Programme – in three spells since 1981 – and for three Southampton fanzines. Edited two collections of fans' memories, *We'll Support You Evermore* (1992) and *Football and the Commons People* (with Alastair Campbell, 1994) as fund-raisers for the Child Poverty Action Group, in which he has long been an activist. His first Hagiology Publishing venture was *Dell Diamond*, a biography of Ted Bates, in 1998. His biography of Terry Paine is due in 2002.

PRINCIPAL CONTRIBUTORS

GARY CHALK – First match 28 October 1967 v Burnley, 2-2. A native of Eastleigh, attending Chamberlayne Primary and later Alderman Quilley Schools, he has been employed at the town's Alstom Railway Works as a Coppersmith for the past 26 years. Co-author of *Saints – A Complete Record* (1987) and *Alphabet of the Saints* (1992), each with Duncan Holley, and contributor to *Hugman's Footballers Factfile*. Has helped compile Leigh Edwards's historical series in the Saints Programme. Is working on *In That Number* – an encyclopaedic history of Southampton FC, due 2003, and currently concentrating on adding Reserve team line-ups to that work. Official Historian to the Club, an original Hagiologist and something of a librarian to the collective, with a large number of items in his reference collection.

NORMAN GANNAWAY – First match 11 March 1944 v Chelsea, 1-5, while attending Brockenhurst County High School. After National Service in the RAF, worked for the Hampshire County Library service for 42 years. In addition to support of Saints, for around 60 years a follower of Lymington Town FC. Published works include histories of Hampshire, Dorset and Bournemouth Football Leagues. Club histories include those of Lymington, Pennington St. Mark's and Fordingbridge Turks. Cricket works include club histories and a history of cricket in Hampshire. Articles for football and cricket programmes etc. appear under the name of "Spectator".

DUNCAN HOLLEY – First match 20 May 1963 v Stoke, 2-0 (without Matthews). Family domiciled in Archers Road; Duncan domiciled in Dell carpark (Ron Davies's autograph over 300 times). Schools – Peter Symonds, Winchester 1966; close season transfer to Taunton's 1969. Author of *Saints – A Complete Record* (1987) and *Alphabet of the Saints* (1992), each with Gary Chalk; and *Saints' Scrapbook* (1988). Currently working on *In That Number* – an encyclopaedic history of Southampton FC, a thorough overhaul, enhancement and combination of all previous work, due 2003. Official Historian to the Club, an original Hagiologist and, time permitting, in-charge crew member on British Airways aircraft. Now residing in Winchester having spent last 20 years in London. Ambitions include eradicating small boys wearing replica Manchester United shirts in Hampshire.

DAVE JUSON – First match 3 November 1962 v Middlesborough. A dull pointless first-half followed by six goals at the Milton End in the second. It was instant love. Enthusiastic fanzine contributor; has also written for *World Soccer*, *When Saturday Comes*, BBC Radio 4 and various local publications. Attended school in a legion of establishments in Hong Kong and Southampton before ending up, gratefully, at Bitterne Park (aged thirteen). Then spent three happy months at Richard Taunton's before running away to sea. Attempted education again, aged 44, taking a diploma course at Ruskin College, Oxford, and moving on to the University of Leicester, where he graduated with a BA(hons) History in 1999. Currently planning to run away to sea again.

CHRIS NEWMAN –- First match 22 October 1960 v Norwich City, 2-2, while attending Beechwood Primary School in Southampton. Carried his Saints obsession on to Bitterne Park Seniors where he first met Dave Juson. An apprenticeship in the print trade followed, Compositor/Proof Reader/Stonehand/Layabout. Also spent the last 32 years as a local musician, Drums/Harmonica/Vocals and alcohol. Nowadays resides at Ordnance Survey's Large Scale Map Store. Writes regularly for *The Ugly Inside* fanzine and web-site, once editing a Cup/promotion souvenir special. Habitually bombards the local press with letters on Saints and was a leading new stadium campaigner at the time SFC were trying to move to Stoneham. Immediate ambition: to present a copy of this book to Mark Lawrenson live on BBC's *Football Focus*.

OTHER CONTRIBUTORS and RESEARCH ASSISTANTS

DAVID ADLEM – First match 2 November 1957 v Northampton Town, 2-1. Born and brought up in Winchester, attending Romsey Road Secondary School (same school as Terry Paine). Keen supporter of Winchester City in the 1950s. Moved to Bristol in 1962. Worked for many years as Stock Controller for a tool company. Now working in a large wholesale warehouse. A season ticket-holder and Secretary of the newly-formed Bristol & West Saints Supporters Club, he is a keen collector of Saints' programmes H&A, while his scrapbooks and other records have provided information for *Dell Diamond* and previous work by David Bull.

CLAY ALDWORTH – Taken to his first match by his uncle on 11 December 1971 v West Ham, 3-3, while attending Newlands Junior School, Millbrook. A school trip to Belgium in May 1976 meant he missed a certain game at Wembley that year. Starting out in The Chocolate Boxes, getting his first season ticket in 1978 (East Stand bench seats) and now a season ticket-holder in the Bikeshed. Currently working on *The Official Saints Yearbook*, which should be ready for June 2001, and *Saints v Pompey: The Rivalry*, which is part of the Hagiology series of books.

RONALD ALLISON – First match 15 September 1945 v Portsmouth, 3-1. Walked to Dell all the way from home in Atherley Road. Back ever since whenever possible - as Taunton's schoolboy, national serviceman, *Hampshire Chronicle* reporter, BBC broadcaster, ITV Executive, especially as Press Secretary to HM The Queen (1976 included) and, always, as a fan. Greatest pleasure has been watching the "home-growns" – Roper, Paine, Chivers, Channon, Le Tissier up front, Ellerington, Ramsey, Sillett at the back. Now living in Winchester and trying to work out best route to St Mary's. Main concern is that the "Dell spirit" will move with the Club.

AIDAN HAMILTON – First match 14 April 1973 v. Newcastle United, 1-1. A Saints scrapbook attests to his schoolboy allegiance; but proximity to his Taunton home made Bristol City his chosen team. In 1995 he began research on Brazilian football's British legacy, visiting Southampton to learn from Dave Juson about Charles Miller's historic sojourn by the Solent and then to interview members of the Southampton squad that toured Brazil in 1948. He is currently teaching English in Rio de Janeiro, where a Portuguese version of his book on Miller and Saints (*An Entirely Different Game,* 1998) is due to be published.

ROB HOLLEY – Debut at Dell, 25 August 1945, first game after War. Milton Road regular 1945-53 while at Taunton's School (truanted for mid-week cup-ties) and at Netley Hospital (national service). As a penniless teacher was a stileman at Dell 1961-63 (saw games free) but was living in Malaya when Saints toured in 1967 and entertained them to lunch (Lent a sunburned player a cotton shirt - still awaiting its return). West Stand spectator 1969 to 1990s while schoolmaster in Hampshire. Now retired from both. Was a long-time resident in Archers Road so expert at following game from crowd noise.

NORMAN HULL – First match 3 October 1942 v. Clapton Orient, 5-2, while temporarily attending St Mary's College (until Taunton's re-opened in 1945). After 20 or so years in the travel transport industry in Southampton, much of it with Aquila Airways, the country's last all flying-boat airline, he moved to Northampton as a Customs Officer. Now retired, his visits to Southampton are mostly for Aquila or Taunton's re-unions or for working on the history of Aquila. His first book on that history (*Eagles Over Water*, 1994) sold out and a second is due in 2001.

NICK ILLINGSWORTH – First match 15 January 1972 v Manchester United, FA Cup Third Round, 1-1, while attending Redbridge Junior School. A die-hard regular ever since, taking in all four of the Club's Wembley appearances. As co-founder and editor of *The Ugly Inside* fanzine and a founding committee member of The Southampton Independent Supporters Association, he has now spent the best part of 15 seasons campaigning for Saints fans to have a bigger say in how the Club is run. A financial consultant still living in the city, his ambition is to play at The Dell before its sad demise.

TOM KELLY – First match 11 January 1950 v Northampton, FA Cup 3rd Round replay, 2-3 (Charlie Wayman 2), while attending Homefield School, Bournemouth. Wednesday afternoon k.o, so went AWOL. RAF service in Iraq and Cyprus 1956-58. Played at The Dell for Christchurch v Andover, 1-2 in 1960 Hants Intermediate Cup Final. Christchurch cricketer. Author of Centenary (1985) book on Christchurch Football Club and of *The Cricket Clubs of Christchurch* (1987). Estate Agent in Christchurch for past 40 years.

ANDY MERCER – First match 9 August 1969, West Bromwich Albion, 0-2, while on summer holiday from Cranbrook School, Kent. Became a regular in the mid-70s, while attending college in Salisbury. Subsequently moved on to Bristol University (where he was taught by one David Bull), Salisbury School of Nursing, Portsmouth Polytechnic, and University College, Swansea. Now works as a senior lecturer in nursing in Bournemouth and lives near Verwood in Dorset. Contributed regularly to the *Red Stripe* fanzine and is a season ticket-holder (together with son Nick) in The Dell's family centre.

KEITH TREVIS – Taken to his first match by his father Rodney and brother Terry, both lifelong Saints fans, on 1 February 1967, v Barrow in FA Cup, 3-0, while attending Wylye infants school on Salisbury Plain. After a brief childhood flirtation with Chelsea, he suddenly got interested in Saints again in 1976. His academic career at Southampton University went rapidly downhill after Keegan signed for Saints. A founding committee member of SISA, until Ian Branfoot was successfully removed from the Club, and a regular fanzine contributor. A computer consultant, living in Salisbury and France and commuting to the East Stand.

JOHN WARREN – First match 25 August 1945 v Plymouth Argyle, 5-5, while attending Millbrook School. Following national service, joined Metropolitan Police in 1957. While attached to New Scotland Yard, designed sports-based projects to bring police into closer contact with community. Awarded British Empire Medal in 1981 for community service. Appointed FA Assistant Press Officer in 1983 and Fulham FC Community Officer 1984. Freelance sports consultant since 1987. Has been a member of management teams in World Cup, European Championship and UEFA Finals and at Olympic and Commonwealth Games. London-based, he attends Saints' matches whenever work commitments allow.

SUBSCRIBERS

Presentation Copies

The Contributors Southampton Football Club *Southern Daily Echo*

1   Ray Mursell, Bishops Waltham

2   Ted Tarbart, Shanklin.

3   Glen Williams, Sarisbury Green.

4   Ross Taylor, Andover.

5   Dave Brindley, Gosport.

6   Adrian Hayward, Guildford

7   Mr & Mrs Bruty, Whitchurch.

8   Phil Courage, Canford Heath.

9   Andy Nunn, East Molesey.

10 A.M.Quigley, Merley,Wimborne.

11 Dave Watkins, Hinkley.

12 Colin Young, Calcot, Reading.

13 Richard Trussier, Compton.

14 David Iddiols, Ealing

15 Mr.M Thear, Steyning.

16 Mark Wood,Thatcham.

17 R. Buckingham-Smith, Eastleigh.

18 G R Batchelor, Hinkley.

19 Michael Baker, Hythe.

20 Nigel Burgess, Hoddesdon.

21 Anthony Coombes, Upper Shirley.

22 Raymond Coombes, Upper Shirley

23 Mr. K.W.G. Payne, Shirley

24 Mark Fickling, Rownhams.

25 Albert Fickling. Milford on Sea

26 Bill Nicholas. Hythe.

27 R W Batchelor, Eastleigh.

28 Phill Snarr, Woolston.

29 Brian Stevens, Southampton.

30 Malcolm Lewis. West End.

31 Tim Evans, Hampstead.

32 Gareth Evans, Dorchester

33 Daniel Evans, Eltham

34 Nick Humby, Hartley Witney

35 Brian Lamerton, Hedge End.

36 Mark Clifford, West End.

37 Dorothy Hague, Fordingbridge.

38 Roger Harris, Maybush.

39 Ian Gaywood, Shirley.

40 M S Murray, Sompting.

41 Russell Beasley, Farnborough.

42 David Lance, Park Gate.

43 John Baldwin, Poole.

44 David Howard, Buxton.

45 John Priest, Winchester.

46 Irene Mitchell, Southampton.

47 David L Mitchell, Bitterne

48 Kevin MJ Hampton, Romsey

49 Ron Haylock, Sholing.

50 Richard White, Brackley.

51 Roy Martin, Thornhill.

52 Geoff Martin, Itchen

53 Ray Till, Horsham.

54 Rod Widger, Ventnor.

55 David Woodhouse, Romsey.

56 Paul Graham Sheppard, Andover.

57 Mark Taylor, South Stoke Oxon.

58 John Hammill, St.Clement Jersey.

59 Peter Humphries, Barrow in Furness.

60 Dave Monk, Bassett.

61 Jack Monk, Tavistock.

62 Andrew Soffe, Hordle.

63 Gillian Smith, Salisbury.

64 Steve Hammond, Netley

65 J P Wareham, Sholing.

66 Peter Wareham, Woolston.

67 RAJR Goble, Warsash.

68 Glenn Johnson, Arundel.

69 Martin Thompson, Dorchester

70 Gary Wilkins, Lordshill.

71 Albert Wilkins, Millbrook

72 Colin Alcock, Haslemere.

73 Tony Kerley, Eastleigh.

74 Geoff Ford, Merry Oak.

75 Stephen Northover, Millbrook.

76 Kenneth R Nicholson, Sholing.

77 Tom Bogie, Saffron Walden.

78 John Lovelock, Shirley.

79 Derek Hayter, Sixpenny Handley.

80 Gary Foyle, West End.

81 John Foyle, Southampton.

82 Harold Hunt, Southampton

83 John Hunt, France.

84 Stephen Savill, Marlborough.

85 Daniel Savill, Virginia, USA.

86 Mike Carpenter, Shaftesbury.

87 Martyn Wartski, Parkstone.

88 Paul Fulford, Chandlers Ford.

89 Clive Penny, Marlborough.

90 Trevor Defferd, Newbury.

91 Neil Catchlove, Chandlers Ford.

92 Jonathan Mundy, Romsey.

93 Ken Sherman. Hedge End.

94 Ray Gaiger, Winchester.

95 Paul Pinchbeck, Nether Wallop.

96 M J Bennett, Andover.

97 Tim Scott

98 Kevin Brown, Regents Park.

99 Vic Scott, Sholing.

100 Maurice O'Connor, Bassett.

101 Joy Lyman, Cardiff.

102 Andrew Chinery, Andover.

103 E P Feast, Seaford, East Sussex.

104 G Feast, London.

105 Leon Phillips, Southampton.

106 Neil Osborne, Portswood.

107 David Osborne, Portswood.

108 R A D Foyle, Bournemouth.

109 Paul Streeter, Basingstoke.

110 Garry Denton, Nursling.

111 David Marshall, St.Denys.

112 A.J. Borowiec, Totton.

113 Mark Shortland, New Milton.

114 Malcolm Chamberlain, New Milton.

115 Nigel McAllen, New Milton.

116 Don McAllen, Lymington.

117 Steve Seeley, Blackpool.

118 Thomas Seeley, Shirley.

119 Lee Curtis, Bournemouth.

120 Les Butters, Western Australia.

121 Peter Davis, Fair Oak.

122 Brian Joslin, Fair Oak.

123 Ken Joslin, Fair Oak.

124 Andrew Kershaw, Chandlers Ford.

125 Graham Watford, Locksheath.

126 Ken Griffin OBE, Bassett.

127 Jackie Leach, Preston.

128 Karl Mitchell, Solihull.

129 Andrew Beach, Christchurch.

130 Bill Beach, Christchurch.

131 Luke Kelsey, Southampton.

132 Brian Dawkins, Romsey

133 Christopher Dawkins, Romsey.

134 Neale Adams, Basingstoke.

135 Steve Weston, Plymouth.

136 Mark Jones, Chandlers Ford.

137 Roger Williams, Freemantle.

138 W.A.Williams, Woolston.

139 May Irwin, Winterslow.

140 Douglas Hull. Southampton.

141 F.J.Brown, Marchwood.

142 Paul Dyke, Bournemouth.

143 Paul Wilkinson, Hazel Grove.

144 Jack Broomfield, Corsham.

145 Tony Butt, Gurnard,Isle of Wight.

146 Colin Knapp, Midanbury.

147 Brian Knapp, Hamble

148 Raymond Edwards, Eastleigh.

149 Richard Manly, West Coker, Yeovil.

150 Les Erridge, Southampton.

151 Paul Bassett, Dunfermline.

152 Keith Fray, Reading.

153 Brian Smith, Eastleigh.

154 John Caddy, Shirley.

155 M & M & J Pirrie, West End.

156 Ron Squires, Eastleigh.

157 Peter Hood, Sarisbury Green.

158 Steve Atkins, Winchester.

159 Saints Zulu Motorbike Club, Eastleigh.

160 John Lawrence, Portsmouth.

161 Christopher Leach, Basingstoke.

162 Peter Lacey, Shirley.

163 Robert Churcher, Titchfield Common

164 Ian Taylor, Swanmore.

165 Charlie Adams, Bitterne Park.

166 Aaron Dear, Alderbury.

167 Michael Dear, Dibden Purlieu.

168 Chris Payne, Funtley.

169 Tony Woadden, Branksome.

170 Howard Woadden, London.

171 Derek Powell, Rownhams.

172 Nick Wolfe, Andover.

173 Matthew Rudd, Cowes.

174 Mike Mansbridge, Sholing.

175 Peter Rendall, Chesterfield.

176 Michael Fenn, Basingstoke.

177 R J Finlay, Whiteley.

178 Joshua Ohajah, London.

179 Chris Domoney, Laindon.

180 Stephen Cheffy, Crawley.

181 Paul Cheffy, Hove

182 Dave Pickard, Southbourne.

183 Cliff Pickard, Andover.

184 Dennis Robinson, Salisbury.

185 G.R.Taylor, Salisbury.

186 Ross Taylor, Andover.

187 Trevor Newell, Highfield.

188 Malcolm Wing, Eastleigh.

189 Clive Hevicon, Lordswood.

190 Douglas Crossley, Bournemouth.

191 Ray Parker, Weymouth.

192 Robert Dodd, East Dean.

193 John Brinson, Bournemouth.

194 Leon Aquilina, Bitterne.

195 Michael Clark, Chiswick.

196 Keith Legg, Didcot.

197 Mike Lucas, Orkney Islands.

198 David John Gray, Salisbury.

199 D.W.Ashley, Bitterne.

200 David Stephens, Hamble.

201 Kevin Hill, Norwich.

202 Stuart Edwards, Lee on the Solent.

203 Mike Roberts, Peterborough.

204 Malc Sims, Chandlers Ford.

205 Rob Kiely, Bitterne.

206 Graham Hepburn, Chandlers Ford.

207 Martyn Biddiscombe, Chandlers Ford.

208 Richard Croxford, Brockenhurst.

209 Peter Hamerton, Crowborough.

210 Barry Goldsmith, Heathfield.

211 Brian Dear, Hedge End.

212 Mike Davage, Norwich.

213 Andrew Murray, Lordshill

214 Kevin Jones, Wadebridge

215 Glenne Wheeler, Fair Oak

HAGIOLOGY PUBLISHING

Formed in 1998, Hagiology Publishing is a collective of Saints fans committed to the collection and dissemination of accurate information on the history of Southampton FC.

Its first publication, in 1998, was **DELL DIAMOND,** the story of Ted Bates's first 60 seasons with the Saints (republished, in a commemorative paperback edition in 2004).

Its second publication, **MATCH of the MILLENNIUM**, was originally published in 2000, as the first venture within an agreement with Southampton FC and the *Southern Daily Echo* to produce a regular flow of books on aspects of Saints' history. It was generously promoted, at signing sessions, by Ted Bates and Matthew Le Tissier – as pictured, below, with the book's editors and several of the contributors.

Back row (left to right): Bob Brunskell, Norman Gannaway, Tom Kelly, Keith Trevis, Andy Mercer, Clay Aldworth, Gary Chalk.
Front Row: Dave Juson, Duncan Holley, David Bull, Chris Newman.

The next two publications were **FULL-TIME at THE DELL** (in 2001) and **IN THAT NUMBER** (2003).

The publication of those last three titles has pushed two others, each long since planned, down the list initially promised to the Club and to would-be readers:

SAINTS v POMPEY – a study of the rivalry

CONSTANT PAINE – a biography of Terry Paine.

Secretary
Duncan Holley
1 Park Lane
Otterbourne
Hants SO21 2HY
Tel: 023-80-266085
e-mail: duncanholley1@aol.com

www.hagiologists.com

Editor
David Bull
170 Westbury Road
Bristol
BS9 3AH
Tel: 0117 962 2042
e-mail: bull.hagiology@blueyonder.co.uk